# Controlling Hollywood

Controlling Hollywood
Censorship and Regulation in the Studio Era
Edited by Matthew Bernstein

The essays in this volume examine the way in which film regulation and censorship has brought into play social mores, religious tenets, business concerns,
political positions and conventions of representation during and just after the
classic studio era. Together they show how films inspired immediate anxiety
about their effect on cinema audiences and a high degree of uncertainty about
what was permissible. Beyond this, the volume illustrates how film censorship
and regulation mediate the larger debate between social values and film content.

Contributors include Garth S. Jowett, Shelley Stamp, Richard Maltby, Lea Jacobs,
Ruth Vasey, Clayton R. Koppes, Gregory D. Black, Matthew Bernstein, Jeff Smith,
Ellen Draper and Justin Wyatt.

Matthew Bernstein is Associate Professor of Film Studies at Emory University.
His publications include *Walter Wanger: Hollywood Independent* and *Visions of the East:
Orientalism in Film* (ed.).

*Edited and with an introduction by*
*Matthew Bernstein*

# Controlling Hollywood

## Censorship and Regulation in the Studio Era

THE
ATHLONE
PRESS
LONDON

First published in Great Britain 2000 by
THE ATHLONE PRESS
1 Park Drive, London NW11 7SG

This collection copyright © 1999 by Rutgers, The State University.
For copyrights to individual pieces, please see first page of each essay.

British Library Cataloguing in Publication Data
*A catalogue record for this book is available from the British Library*
ISBN 0 485 30092 3

Manufactured in the United States of America

*For my parents,*
*Elayne P. Bernstein and*
*Harold P. Bernstein,*
*who have taught me so much*

# Contents

Acknowledgments    ix

Introduction    1
*Matthew Bernstein*

"A Capacity for Evil": The 1915 Supreme Court
*Mutual* Decision    16
*Garth S. Jowett*

Moral Coercion, or The National Board of Censorship
Ponders the Vice Films    41
*Shelley Stamp*

*The King of Kings* and the Czar of All the Rushes:
The Propriety of the Christ Story    60
*Richard Maltby*

Industry Self-Regulation and the Problem
of Textual Determination    87
*Lea Jacobs*

Beyond Sex and Violence: "Industry Policy" and the
Regulation of Hollywood Movies, 1922–1939    102
*Ruth Vasey*

Blacks, Loyalty, and Motion Picture Propaganda
in World War II    130
*Clayton R. Koppes and Gregory D. Black*

A Tale of Three Cities: The Banning of *Scarlet Street*    157
*Matthew Bernstein*

"Controversy Has Probably Destroyed Forever the Context":
*The Miracle* and Movie Censorship in America in the 1950s    186
*Ellen Draper*

"A Good Business Proposition": Dalton Trumbo, *Spartacus,*
and the End of the Blacklist    206
*Jeff Smith*

The Stigma of X: Adult Cinema and the Institution
of the MPAA Ratings System                                    238
    *Justin Wyatt*

Annotated Bibliography                                        265

Contributors                                                  277

Index                                                         279

# Acknowledgments

This volume arose from my conviction that a number of worthwhile essays had been published in diverse academic journals on the history of American movie censorship and self-regulation and that an anthology of such works might prove useful to students, scholars, and interested readers.

I have several debts from assembling this volume. Annie Hall, administrative assistant in the Film Studies Program at Emory University, provided cheerful and efficient help in preparing the manuscript. Terry Geeskcn and Mary Corliss at the Museum of Modern Art/Film Stills Archive put up with my many visits; Ben Brewster and Maxine Fleckner-Ducey at the Wisconsin Center for Film and Theater Research, as well as Kristine Kreuger at the Margaret Herrick Library of the Academy of Motion Picture Arts and Sciences, provided last-minute aid. Permissions to reprint essays were facilitated by Professor David Culbert (*Historical Journal of Film, Radio and Television*); Pierre Steiner (Harwood Academic Publishers); Haley Harvey (Oxford University Press); Michael Regoli (Organization of American Historians); and especially Marci R. McMahon (University of Texas Press). William Randall Gue provided wonderful research assistance. A special thank you goes to Jason Mittell, Ph.D. student at the University of Wisconsin–Madison and an editor of *The Velvet Light Trap*, for recovering some crucial photos.

I thank the contributors to this volume for their timely and enthusiastic cooperation in preparing this book; Depth of Field editors Robert Lyons and Mirella and Charles Affron for supporting it. It has been once again a great pleasure to work with Marilyn Campbell, Managing Editor at Rutgers University Press, and Leslie Mitchner, Associate Director and Editor in Chief. Leslie's wisdom and enthusiasm for film is an unbeatable combination, which I especially appreciated when she helped me over quite a hurdle in the preparation of the book. Thanks as well to David and Maria denBoer of Nighthawk Design and Amy Hegeman for preparing for the book's production so carefully.

Natalie, Justin, and Adam Bernstein provided inspiration, refreshing respites, and constant affection; they are the source of so much joy and love in my life.

I dedicate this book to my parents, Elayne P. Bernstein and Harold P.

Bernstein, who were, by the way, firm yet open-minded about the movies I watched as I grew up. I remember many joyous moments with them inside, and even more outside, the theater. No words can express my profound admiration and my appreciation for them, their strength of character, their generosity of spirit, and the way they raised me. I love them dearly.

# Controlling Hollywood

# Introduction

We currently take for granted the fact that most films made in Hollywood today are created and shown without hindrance. It was not always so. Throughout the history of American movies, there have been countless, often furious struggles to control or influence what could be produced and what could be seen. The cinema has been the most frequent target of the censoring impulse in this century because partly film was the first visual and aural mass entertainment form of the twentieth century, and its power seemed overwhelming. Moreover, film was the most popular mass medium during its first fifty years.

This volume explores some of these many efforts at censorship and self-regulation, in the belief that Americans should neither forget nor dismiss the colorful and varied history of attempts to control the film industry simply because today other media (television, rap music, the internet) occupy what was film's hotly contested position. Movies still generate vigorous controversy from time to time as part of what has come to be called "the culture wars." Moreover, we know a great deal about those historic efforts concerning movies, which have many similarities—and enormous relevance—to current debate about those media. And, of course, we have much more to learn.

Scholars usually distinguish broadly between two kinds of control over movie content. One is external to the film industry. Historically, it took the official form of state and city censors (the film industry called this "local" or "political" censorship), who to some degree reflected a consensus of values and attitudes held by a dominant group in that locale. In cinema's earliest years, official censorship could involve theater licensing. But beginning with Chicago in 1907, it entailed a government body that assessed the moral qualities of particular films—the "prurient" sexuality of Jane Russell's character in *The Outlaw* (1942 and 1946), for example, or the unsettling "social equality among the races" in *Lost Boundaries* (1949).

Often such boards were created in response to public protests against the films, either nationally or locally. Be they women's committees of the teens and 1920s, the Catholic Legion of Decency from the 1930s to the 1960s, or diverse "cultural identity" groups of the 1980s, protest groups could and did bring varying degrees of pressure and persuasion to bear on the movie studios in an attempt to regulate their movie content.

Whatever their provenance, municipal—state or city—civil servants passed judgment on the suitability of movies for audiences. They could excise scenes, shots, or lines of dialogue; or they could ban films outright—such actions are what we typically mean by the term "censorship." The 1915 Supreme Court ruling that movies were not entitled to First Amendment protection provided a legal rationale for imposing prior-restraint on movie exhibition. Films thereby served as an excuse for the public exercise of cultural power, until, with the 1952 *Miracle* decision, the Supreme Court began to undermine the vaguely worded statutes that authorized local censorship.[1] Yet this power was never absolutely secure, nor was it always supported by those it purportedly protected.

A second type of effort at controlling movie content is frequently characterized as "self-regulation." This has taken various forms over the decades. There was the sympathetic advice to filmmakers given—but not enforced—by the National Board of Censorship in the teens. Then there was the more closely observed strictures about representing sex, crime, violence, the professions, and morality generated by Hollywood's trade organization, the Motion Picture Producers and Distributors of America, Inc. (MPPDA) in the 1920s. These guidelines were designed to fend off public criticism of Hollywood. They crystallized into the notorious, though often modified Production Code, drafted by Catholics and revised by Hollywood executives, from 1930 to 1966. Under this latter system, individuals at the MPPDA's Studio Relations Committee (SRC) and Production Code Administration (PCA) intervened in the writing of script drafts and the shooting and editing of finished films from the major Hollywood studios, indicating what might and what would not provoke local censorship against a particular movie and trying to shape films to avoid such consequences.

In fact, this was the primary rationale for Hollywood's self-regulation: the urgent necessity that movies not disturb the political and social status quo in American society or interrupt the flow of box office dollars with controversial material.[2] Even if controversy itself could sell a film successfully in the short run—as with *The Outlaw, Blockade* (1938), or foreign films like *The Miracle* (1950)—Hollywood, and the film industry in general, had an enormous stake in maintaining cultural prestige and approval over the long term. And in 1968, as changing values and mores pervaded America, Hollywood's self-regulation became self-classification with the ratings system, developed by the Motion Picture Producers Association (MPAA, successor in 1946 to the MPPDA), which still operates today under the auspices of the major Hollywood producer-distributors.

What makes the histories of both censorship and self-regulation so fascinating is the various ways in which they expose the fault lines of differing political ideologies, class and religious affiliations, and ethnicities in American culture. Wealthy and influential industrialists objected to Hollywood's portrayal of corrupt coal mining companies (as they did with Warner Bros.' *Black Fury* [1934]); Southern women resented David O. Selznick's insistence on depicting at length what should have been private—Melanie Wilkes's struggle to deliver her child in war-torn Atlanta in *Gone With the Wind* (1939); some African Americans condemned the unconscious racism of Disney's *The Song of the South* (1946), a reenactment of the Uncle Remus Br'er Rabbit stories.[3] Up through the late 1940s, everyone watched the movies faithfully, and many had a great deal to say about what they saw.

Film critics often assert that movie genres—westerns, musicals, melodramas, comedies—represent an aesthetic and social contract between audiences and filmmakers as to what kinds of entertainment films audiences wish to see. Genres thereby provide the most revealing link between films and society.[4] I would argue that an examination of movie censorship and self-regulation compels film students and scholars to trace with even greater clarity the dynamic relationships among Hollywood production, audience demand, political ideologies, psychical processes (such as pleasure and repression), and aesthetic traditions (the conventions of movie genres among them).

Perhaps that is why social historians, mass communications scholars, film historians, and film theorists are constantly drawn to exploring the topic. In fact, I would argue that current research into the regulation and censorship of movies is more voluminous and diverse in methodologies and source materials than ever before.

Although censorship studies have been published throughout the century, our current interest in the topic dates back to studies of the 1960s and 1970s. Ira Carmen's *Movies, Censorship and the Law* (1966) looks at Supreme Court cases in relation to the current workings of local censorship, two years before the advent of the ratings system. Richard Randall's *Censorship of the Movies* (1968) expands upon Carmen's work by considering informal as well as legal forms of censorship. Edward DeGrazia and Roger K. Newman's *Banned Films* (1982) similarly provides a survey of censorship history and summaries of 137 court cases involving local censorship of movies.[5] All three books focus largely on the highly visible instances of how state and city censors banned or cut particular films. This legalistic framework is invaluable because it stresses the serious considerations that resulted from the movies' constitutionally vulnerable status after the 1915 *Mutual* case. Such a model dramatically portrays a battle between filmmakers seeking free expression and responsible but often misguided and usually repressive civil servants.

A second wave of Hollywood histories, such as Robert Sklar's *Movie-Made America* (1975) and Garth S. Jowett's *The Movies: A Democratic Art* (1976), recast the history of struggles over movie content as reflections of popular social values and attitudes rather than as primarily legal issues.[6] Drawing on current historical methodologies, these authors see movies as a cultural battleground. On one side were established and generally conservative forces, whom Sklar labeled "cultural custodians," and characterized as generations-old Americans. On the other were the urban, modern sensibilities embodied in the film industry's (mostly Jewish immigrant) founders, whose companies internalized the concerns of cultural custodians in part by adhering to the MPPDA's Production Code. As synoptic social histories of American movies, Sklar's and Jowett's works are landmarks in the writing of American film history and they remain illuminating and highly significant, as virtually all subsequent research into the movies' social dimension has drawn upon or debated their findings.

These more recent studies of censorship and self-regulation have been enriched by drawing on assumptions, perspectives, and methodologies from American, cultural, and reception studies. The cultural studies framework in particular has emphasized that cultural power, such as that exercised by local censors or Hollywood's own regulators, is never secure and always under siege (as opposed to the fixed connotations of the legal framework). Cultural studies has encouraged researchers to consider the immediate historical context in which controversial films are viewed and the possibility that audiences often impose interpretations upon films that evade the terms of a publicity campaign, a newspaper critic's review, or a censorship board. This work further demonstrates that differing perspectives may struggle for a fair hearing or for some kind of dominance in public discourse such as that which surrounds a censorship controversy. As Richard Maltby once observed, the movie censor resembles the film critic by proposing, or anticipating, an audience's interpretation of a film;[7] that interpretation could in turn, be subject to debate, scrutiny, even ridicule.

Moreover, the lines of public debate do not always fall neatly into two camps: a recent essay by Francis G. Couvares, for example, demonstrates that in the 1920s, different religious groups did not simply oppose what they perceived as Hollywood immorality, but engaged in disputes among themselves about how best to address the Hollywood problem—government regulation, local censorship, putting pressure on the industry themselves, or outright suppression of offensive films.[8] This of course has always been the primary fascination and fundamental issue at stake in movie censorship—it inevitably entails the issue and nature of cultural authority, the power to enforce it, and the various rationales that accompany it.

While new studies of Hollywood's self-regulation and censorship have grown sensitive to the notion of competing voices at work in the shaping of a film, the workings of the MPPDA/MPAA have also been understood as a function of Hollywood's institutional history. This also entails studio workers' trade unions, technicians' and creative artists' guilds, the organization of filmmaking itself at the studios, and the assumptions these factions shared or disputed as they went about their work.[9] As Hollywood's trade group, the MPPDA struggled to earn federal and state government cooperation and support (for both its domestic and international markets), to issue favorable publicity for the industry, to answer disgruntled organizations and pressure groups, and perhaps even to enlist their support. These delicate relationships Hollywood established with external groups answer many questions about the informal functioning of film regulation.

Viewing the MPPDA as an institution also reminds us that Hollywood's self-regulation was an integral part of daily moviemaking. The Code and its enforcement served many functions for the industry, not the least of which was providing the studios with public proof that filmmakers were earnestly trying to create wholesome and harmless entertainment. The availability since the mid-1980s of the MPPDA's files has given scholars access to case histories of specific films, allowing them to construct a more nuanced portrayal of the SRC and PCA's arduous work with filmmakers to diminish what the MPPDA considered unnecessarily inflammatory but undoubtedly profitable elements.

Thus, the censorship, regulation, and self-regulation of films was a multifaceted phenomenon in the studio era, and they constitute topics that reward various forms of research and inquiry, especially at present, which I believe is a particularly rich moment for the writing of this history. The essays in this volume are my primary evidence for that claim, and I have organized them to reflect a chronology of American movie censorship and regulation.[10] While these essays do not constitute a comprehensive history of these phenomena, they examine important facets of censorship, regulation, and self-regulation while embodying significant trends, methods, and concerns that have informed film scholarship.

Garth S. Jowett's "'A Capacity for Evil'" examines the milestone 1915 *Mutual v. Industrial Commission of Ohio* Supreme Court case which rendered film the first mass medium vulnerable to prior censorship, a condition that lasted for over thirty-seven years. Most historians know that the Supreme Court ruled in this infamous case that the movies were "a business pure and simple," not capable of expressing ideas and therefore not entitled to First Amendment protection (this just months before D. W. Griffith's *The Birth of Nation* would prove otherwise). Yet Jowett's analysis looks even more closely at the case, and explains that the Court endorsed Ohio's vaguely phrased censorship statute as a means of ensuring flexibility for censors to handle films on a case-by-case basis; while this elasticity seemed desirable to the judges, it facilitated the highly a rbitrary practices of local censors throughout the country in the years to come.

Moreover, while his topic evokes the legalistic framework of previous studies, Jowett emphasizes the social dimensions of the ruling. He sees the *Mutual* case as the culmination of an eighteen-year effort by primarily Protestant cultural custodians to control the movies' "increasing popularity and socializing power," evident in the 1890s and the movies' later years. He concludes by exploring the different, intriguing reactions to the Supreme Court ruling among various interested civic and national groups.

One of the latter was the National Board of Censorship (NBC), a Progressive era reform organization that aided the fledgling film industry of the teens in fighting government censorship even before the *Mutual* case was decided. The NBC encouraged filmmakers to produce movies of moral uplift, yet it had no power to enforce its recommendations and relied instead on what chairman Frederic C. Howe imaginatively termed "moral coercion." Meanwhile, industry critics and moviegoers assumed, not unreasonably, that a group with "censorship" in its title was a censoring body, pure and simple.

Shelley Stamp explores the dilemmas facing the NBC in late 1913 with the release of two "white slavery" films, *Traffic in Souls* and *The Inside of the White Slave Traffic*. These movies tested the NBC's effectiveness and provoked nationwide debate over whether films with unprecedented sexual explicitness were edifying and appropriate movie content or prurient proof of the movies' 'capacity for evil.' Stamp demonstrates how the NBC deemed *Traffic in Souls* edifying because of its moralistic tone and conventionally melodramatic story line, while the group refused to judge *The Inside of the White Slave Traffic* at all, because of its more "naturalistic" depiction of its subject. She demonstrates the value of applying close analysis to censorship cases while she outlines the arbitrary, yet conventional thinking of the NBC, the film industry's greatest ally. Within three years of the white slavery films' appearance, the Board would abandon evaluating any such films; changing its name to the National Board of Review, and operating in the shadow of the 1915 *Mutual* case, it thereby acknowledged its circumscribed authority and status, and left the fate of controversial films to local censorship.

The American film industry's most significant response to local censorship (and its foreign markets) was the 1922 creation of the MPPDA, which advanced Hollywood's trade concerns and functioned as a multifaceted publicity office, responsibilities that have been overshadowed by the heavily publicized and often dramatic workings of its SRC and PCA. One strategy Will Hays undertook immediately to defuse criticism and local censorship of Hollywood was to enlist support for upstanding Hollywood movies from national civic, religious, and educational groups. Their good opinion, circulated to parishioners and members, could build up the box office and generally create the perception that Hollywood producers, while seeking sensational subjects, could be trained to make desirable films. Further, the industry offered to provide advice and funds for making instructional films to be used in churches as sermons.

Richard Maltby's essay examines how this dynamic of courting the churches worked uneasily—and unsuccessfully from Hollywood's point of view—in the making of Cecil B. deMille's 1927 Biblical epic, *The King of Kings.* The film benefited from the advice of several religious leaders as deMille strove to realize a nondenominational, inoffensive portrait of Christ. The director also chose to model his protagonist after a contemporary best-seller that depicted Christ as a virile 'prophet of modern business,' a strategy consonant with Protestantism's increasingly secularized doctrines. Unfortunately, offended Jewish groups felt the film portrayed Jews as Christ-killers, Protestant leaders grew impatient with their inability to have even greater say in Hollywood filmmaking, and a multi-voiced chorus of condemnation rained on the industry in the late 1920s. Maltby suggests that while things might have turned out differently, the box office disappointment of *The King of Kings* and the failure to create a mutually supportive relationship between Hollywood and Protestant and Jewish religious groups gradually led the MPPDA toward Catholic representatives and the 1930 Production Code.

The Code itself, written by a group of Catholic laypersons and priests in consultation with studio heads and industry leaders, was not Hollywood's first set of production guidelines but it lasted the longest and proved the most effective and infamous instance of content self-regulation. Lea Jacobs' essay represents a highly influential rethinking of the workings of the SRC and PCA. New Dealer Raymond Moley's landmark 1945 *The Hays Office* had portrayed the PCA as a censoring body (more effective than its predecessor through 1934, the SRC) which enforced the Production Code in a quasi-legal fashion, forbidding studio filmmakers to depict certain aspects of sexuality and violence and denying films seals of approval when necessary.

Studying MPPDA/MPAA personnel's memoirs and unpublished interviews as well as newly available MPPDA case files on early 1930s "fallen women" films, Jacobs describes an operating dynamic different from that of Moley's semilegal model. She situates MPPDA activity as self-regulation: SRC and PCA workers in fact negotiated with producers, screenwriters, and directors, enabling them to portray sensational material in a manner that would disarm potential objections from external censorship. MPPDA officers thus aided filmmakers in representing troublesome subjects; their work was "an integrated part of film production" in Hollywood, and the industry's self-regulation "did not simply reflect social pressures; it articulated a strategic response to them."

Given this conceptual framework, Jacobs recharacterizes the perceived split between "pre-Code" and post 1934 self-regulation, whereby the MPPDA is alleged to have become more forceful in regulating film content after the Legion of Decency boycott. Instead, Jacobs argues that self-regulation of content under Joseph Breen was more thorough after 1934, attending to set design, actors' performance, and general "tone." The result was varied but pervasive "instability of meaning" in PCA-influenced films—ambiguity about when, where, and how sexual transgressions occurred. The promiscuous nature of a heroine might be signaled to the audience not through direct dialogue but with scenes of them alone in the streets. In stressing the SRC and PCA's work on the fallen woman genre in particular—with films like *Baby Face* (1933) and *Camille* (1937)—Jacobs underlines the crucial interplay of generic conventions and MPPDA regulation, which produced extremely variable results. In short, Jacobs's essay decisively recasts our understanding of how the MPPDA interacted with filmmakers in Hollywood.

Ruth Vasey's essay extends our understanding of the MPPDA's impact on movie content by examining two usually neglected aspects of Hollywood's self-regulation: "industry policy" and international distribution. The SRC and the PCA were guided by the Production Code, but they took as much responsibility for topics and situations not explicitly addressed in the Code—the depiction of foreigners, foreign nations, racial or ethnic types, various professions, the nature of American politics, and the conduct of American business—as those the Code addressed. This "industry policy" contributed to the studio films's conventional implication that there were no corrupt industries or professions, just "bad apples," debased and depraved individuals. Criticizing certain professions, such as journalists, broadcasters, politicians, or social reformers, could have immediate negative consequences for the studios.

As Vasey shows, Hollywood's attempt not to offend *anyone* extended abroad. The MPPDA endeavored to secure government cooperation for location shooting and discouraged distributors from importing films offensive to important foreign nations. In film production, Joseph Breen, Colonel Ted Herron, and their associates encouraged filmmakers to avoid offending the nationalities of important foreign markets; for example, to make their movie villains Russian, and not German, since the Soviet Union represented a pittance in foreign income and the Germans were a significant source of revenue. Through such policies, the MPPDA ensured that the industry continued to earn 35 percent of its gross revenues from markets abroad, and that trade restrictions, bans, and other disruptions were minimal. In stressing the international dimensions of Hollywood's self-regulation efforts, whose substance often coincided with domestic concerns, Vasey enhances our knowledge of the MPPDA's work.

The representation of race and ethnicity was part of the MPPDA's industry policy, and the SRC and PCA frequently had occasion to advise filmmakers against staging scenes in which blacks and whites were treated as social equals, for fear of offending the Southern market. Breen and his associates even advised producers on how African Americans should be referred to in script dialogue: one can chart a progression from "darkies" (in the 1930s) to "Negroes" (in the 1940s and after) like a barometer of the industry's and the country's racial politics.

World War II was of course a watershed period in the representation of African Americans in Hollywood film, for the nation's conscience was slowly aroused as it recognized domestic racism while battling the

Nazis and the Japanese. During this period, the Hollywood studios found themselves further subjected to the directives of the Office of War Information, a federal agency created by President Roosevelt to consolidate wartime government propaganda. In their informative and comprehensive book *Hollywood Goes to War*, Clayton Koppes and Gregory D. Black demonstrated the significant influence the OWI had on the making of combat and home-front films. OWI accomplished what it did in spite of the studios' palpable resentment of such unprecedented intrusions from the federal government and of their anxious awareness that blatant propaganda was box office poison.[11]

Koppes and Black's essay here, written within the framework of social and political history, examines the particular challenge the OWI faced in convincing African Americans that World War II was not just a "white man's battle" and in persuading the studios to cooperate with their goals. The authors use OWI surveys and research to show both the nature of black alienation from the war effort—hating Nazis, for example, but sympathizing with Asians as people of color—and the OWI staff's perceptions of this challenge. As Koppes and Black vividly establish, African Americans were ambivalent about the war for many good reasons made known to the OWI: all of them were associated with domestic racism. The OWI chose to deploy propaganda to give blacks a sense of their stake in the war rather than to propose that the armed forces implement far-reaching changes in racial etiquette, and the OWI's primary goal was that national unity would overcome any other single consideration in the African American's mind.

This policy's impact on Hollywood filmmaking was disappointing as well, as OWI officials failed to comprehend the experience and perspectives of black Americans. The OWI advised the NAACP not to protest the blatantly pro-South *Tennessee Johnson* (1942), whose few cuts and reshootings preserved the film's Horatio Alger portrait of Andrew Johnson as a champion of absolute democracy and the film's ignorance of more accurate and innovative interpretations of the Reconstruction period. After the all-black musicals *Cabin in the Sky* (1943) and *Stormy Weather* (1943) offended African American leaders, and under political fire from a budget-cutting Congress, OWI became less ambitious, hoping to demonstrate the integration of blacks in American life through bit parts and ordinary scenes. The Office assessed films like *Casablanca* (1943), *The Ox-Bow Incident* (1943), and *Bataan* (1943) primarily by what image of black Americans they presented abroad. In drawing on OWI correspondence and film reviews, Koppes and Black provide a distinct picture of Hollywood's uneasy relationship with the federal government even during a period of closest cooperation, and how the racial politics of these films were interpreted at the time of their release.

My own essay uses archival materials and newspaper accounts to examine the strategies Universal Pictures deployed, informally and formally, to counter the bannings of *Scarlet Street,* a 1945 film noir, in three different locales: New York State, Milwaukee, and Atlanta. Reflecting some liberalization in the PCA, the film had been approved by the industry after minimal script changes, but the sleazy milieu of the story and the fact that the film's protagonist goes legally unpunished (though emotionally tortured) for committing a murder outraged civil servants and civic leaders in three regions of the country. I argue that one can view these bannings as evidence of Hollywood's shifting status at war's end from one of prestigious participant in the war effort and primary form of mass entertainment to that of soon-to-be denounced and dismantled industry in the late 1940s.

At the same time, I see these bannings from a cultural studies perspective, in that they demonstrate regional resistance to Hollywood filmmaking in the postwar era, as each locale's condemnation of *Scarlet Street* was overcome or modified in response to different strategies employed by the distributor: friendly negotiation in New York, a "wait and see" low-key approach in the lesser market of Milwaukee, and failed negotiations and a lawsuit in Atlanta. By stressing the "informal" negotiations undertaken to permit the film to be shown, I offer a counterpoint to more legally minded studies of censorship that would focus solely on notorious court cases. In surveying newspaper coverage of the event, particularly in New York and Atlanta, I find community sentiment highly ambivalent about the institution of censorship itself in the wake of the Allied victory over fascism. And in considering the hallmarks of the naturalistic *Scarlet Street,* I suggest that such works carried their moral ambiguity into the arena of public discourse, where different interpretations of the film competed for public assent.

Public discourse is also the focus of Ellen Draper's study of the landmark Supreme Court *Miracle* decision that granted motion pictures First Amendment protection as a form of speech, thereby reversing the Court's ruling in the 1915 *Mutual* case. Draper reminds us that in the *Miracle* case, the judges did not invalidate movie censorship entirely, but struck down only the criterion of "sacrilegious" as a nationwide standard (condemning the "flexibility" the 1915 Supreme Court had granted censors). Only subsequent cases would strike down other criteria for prior censorship, and these piecemeal rulings reflected "a deep disagreement about the proper role of film in society" among Americans. Cardinal Spellman had denounced *The Miracle* as the work of atheistic communism and a satanic perversion, yet other religious leaders and journalists begged to differ. The gradual erosion of the Production Code during the early 1950s meant that debates about the nature of film no longer had a clear starting point; participants in the *Miracle* controversy framed their comments around the appropriateness of censorship, notions of cinematic realism, and how foreign films had proven more worthy and thought-provoking than their Hollywood counterparts. Like Garth S. Jowett, Draper examines the cultural context of a major court case; and as in the *Scarlet Street* essay, Draper sifts through public discourse, the ways in which people discussed the movies and the assumptions supporting those discussions, to discern continuing ambivalence and uncertainty about the place of movies in American society.

The *Miracle* controversy unfolded amidst another, major self-regulatory strategy on Hollywood's part: the notorious Hollywood blacklist of the late 1940s and 1950s. Here, self-regulation was accomplished not through script revisions but through employment policies, specifically denying work to alleged and actual Communists in the industry. Yet, as Jeff Smith points out, most previous accounts of the blacklist neglect its demise, simply indicating that it ended with Hollywood Ten member Dalton Trumbo's onscreen credit for *Spartacus* (1960). In addition, as Smith perceptively notes, most blacklist histories cast blacklistees as heroic artists who struggle on principle against fascistic, anti-Communist conservatives in a clear-cut "morality play" that still inspires bitter outrage, evidenced in 1999 with the much-resented special Oscar awarded to director Elia Kazan, a "friendly" witness in the 1950s HUAC hearings.[12] Drawing on archival documents, Smith rethinks this historic phenomenon, and argues that the blacklist was overcome by cooperative, not combative, blacklistees.

Dalton Trumbo worked steadily in the black market, writing without complaint for producers who paid him a fraction of his former wages. This very fact proved the blacklist to be a public relations move that continued for economic rather than political reasons—it was a way of distracting government officials from even stronger regulation of movie content, much as the Production Code had functioned earlier to disguise the major studios' monopoly power over distribution and exhibition. Trumbo finally received onscreen credit for *Spartacus* after anti-Communist hysteria calmed down, after blacklistees won a series of Awards that embarrassed the Academy, and when the revelation of the black market left the industry with nothing to hide. Throughout this period, Trumbo's solicitous, conciliatory approach to his potential employers sped the process of the blacklist's demise. Much as Lea Jacobs's essay reframed our sense of the MPPDA's role in filmmaking, Smith's essay demonstrates the powerful hold and misleading views that result from understanding censorship in melodramatic terms; it also provides a detailed, enlightening look at how the black market operated.

A few years after the blacklist faded, the MPAA, under the leadership of Jack Valenti, disbanded self-regulation and the PCA in 1966. In 1968, the MPAA created the ratings system, which was administered by the MPAA's Code and Rating Administration (CARA), still with us today. Most censorship studies have examined the reign of the PCA. There is as yet no book-length history of the ratings system and the significance of this shift from self-regulation to self-classification on the part of the film business.

Justin Wyatt's essay considers the inauguration of the ratings system in the late 1960s and early 1970s, within the framework of the new "adult film" and Hollywood's recognition of new audience markets to exploit. Wyatt traces the adult film phenomenon to the effects of several landmark First Amendment Supreme Court cases, to the popular and increasingly frequent depictions of sex in foreign "art" films, and to the rise of soft- and hard-core pornographic films. As Wyatt describes, however, the MPAA's application of the new ratings system immediately appeared arbitrary, leaving the qualifications for an X versus R rating ambiguous or contradictory. This created uncertainty for producers, distributors, and exhibitors, amidst industry timidity and doubts about how Americans would respond to the adult films. These conditions eventually inspired the major studios to produce and distribute such daring, X-rated films as *Midnight Cowboy* and *Last Tango in Paris* in the early 1970s, thereby co-opting and eventually dominating the adult film market, which had begun as an independent, foreign (anything but Hollywood) phenomenon.

Wyatt's perspective is that of the industry analyst; rather than considering the ratings classifications primarily from the framework of social history and vocal protest, he considers how ratings functioned in the movie marketplace, as an aid to targeting audience factions and focusing advertising and publicity campaigns.[13] In so doing, he reminds us that censorship, self-regulation, and even self-classification have economic roots and consequences.

Moreover, Wyatt's research reminds us that the apparent arbitrariness of the ratings system dates back to, and was inherent in, its inception. Since the early 1970s, two incidents have forced the MPAA to modify the system: the outcry over Steven Spielberg's *Indiana Jones and the Temple of Doom* (1984), which inspired the PG-13 category, and the 1990 inauguration of NC-17, replacing X, for Philip Kaufman's *Henry and June*. The MPAA has even endured charges of racism in its application of NC-17.[14] It seems clear that the ratings system will continue to be dogged by the appearance of sometimes capricious judgments.

Each of these essays provides an exemplary examination of the ways in which movie censorship, regulation, and self-regulation brought into play social mores, religious tenets, business concerns, political positions, and representational conventions before, during, and just after the studio era. Together they demonstrate how the powerful medium of the movies inspired immediate concerns about their effect on audiences and uncertainty over what was permissible on the screen. From white slavery films through films noir to adult art films like *Last Tango in Paris*, movies have provoked multiple interpretations and concerned criticism.[15]

Hollywood's desire to stimulate but not to offend audiences and thereby preserve its extensive distribution networks and cash flow can be said to have affected directly what was shown on the screen. This was accomplished through the various negotiations and strategies for representation that arose from industry self-regulation and local censorship. Censorship and self-regulation thus provide the most substantial middle term between various social values and Hollywood film content—and these often unspoken values and ideologies become explicit when controversy erupts over censored and uncensored films.

Since the ratings classification era began, filmmakers have enjoyed more freedom than ever before to express controversial ideas or to violate prevailing canons of taste.[16] Yet movie content regulation has continued in new forms. As Charles Lyons has demonstrated, boycotts and protests against movies have continued, particularly in the 1980s culture wars.[17] Feminists, ethnic groups, gay/lesbian rights activists, and Christian fundamentalists all have found particular films of recent vintage offensive (*Dressed to Kill* [1980], *Year of the Dragon* [1985], *Basic Instinct* [1991], and *The Last Temptation of Christ* [1988]); in 1998, Arab Americans protested the depiction of Manhattan terrorists in Edward Zwick's *Siege*. While officially eschewing any program of censorship and claiming only to offer an alternative analysis of the movie in question, the group protests, sometimes at the theater entrance as well as in the media, have often affected a film's box office as well as audience members' interpretation of and reaction to it. It is important to recall as well that since the 1980s, these public criticisms of Hollywood films have occurred while conservative social forces have successfully diminished government support (most notably the National Endowment for the Arts) for the traditional arts.

The 1990s have seen new formations and targets in movie protests. The enormous outpouring of criticism and analysis of Oliver Stone's *JFK* (1991) can be seen as a turf war in which audiences are warned—by journalists, political historians, and various pundits—that filmmakers should not attempt to reenact American history or to dramatize minority interpretations of that history. In this case, the protesting group is not a religious, ethnic, or political association, but a group of related and highly public professions.[18]

Some protest activists have targeted businesses, not movies, such as the summer 1997 call by the Southern Baptist Convention for a boycott against an entire company, Disney. The SBC was provoked by Disney's tolerant attitude toward gay/lesbian movie and television content (*Priest* (1994), the sitcom *Ellen*) and its employment and theme park policies; the group resented what it called Disney's "Christian-bashing, family-bashing, pro-homosexual agenda."[19] The boycott was to extend to Disney's ABC and ESPN television networks, its theme parks, as well as its films and television shows. While this may account for a chilling atmosphere in Hollywood (evidenced, for example, by the postponed release of Adrian Lyne's 1997 *Lolita*), the SBC boycott has generally been regarded as a failure; a multiform entertainment conglomerate is too diffuse to be vulnerable to the intended effect (members of the SBC might be purchasing

Disney products without being aware of it).[20] Yet other constituencies might try refined versions of similar tactics in the future.

Our country's chronic amnesia often prevents us from recalling the past as we confront new problems from technologically based mass media—warning labels on contemporary music, the advent of television ratings, the promise of the television v-chip, and the need for internet regulation most prominent among them. 1998 will be remembered primarily as the year that virtually pornographic accounts of an American president's sexual misadventures were published by mainstream newspapers and became accessible via home computer. While the national and political dimensions of "Monicagate" are unique, this explicitness has provoked considerable dismay and generated many uneasy reflections about what restraints, if any, govern public discourse in contemporary American democracy and regulate the media by which that discourse is conveyed.[21] Such questions revive debates among reformers and protest groups over the movies.

I hope this volume will help to acquaint readers with this rich history, its political and social dynamics and the contours of the previous debates over the movies, especially as they are resurrected. Perhaps it will also stimulate new ways of thinking about and researching the varied efforts to control the movies.

## NOTES

I thank David B. Pratt for his suggestions for this essay.

1. As Francis G. Couvares has pointed out, the external censors could never fulfill their promises to protect vulnerable viewers, even when bolstered with constitutional rulings, because "as in all protection rackets, there was more in it for the protector than for those allegedly being protected." See Francis G. Couvares, "Introduction," *Movie Censorship and American Culture* (Washington, D.C.: Smithsonian Institution Press, 1996), 3.

2. Ruth Vasey makes this point forcefully in her *The World According to Hollywood, 1918–1939* (Madison: University of Wisconsin Press, 1997).

3. These examples arise from the Production Code Administration Archive, Margaret Herrick Library, Academy of Motion Picture Arts and Sciences, Los Angeles, California.

4. See, for example, Thomas Schatz, *Hollywood Genres: Formulas, Filmmaking, and the Studio System* (New York: Random House, 1981).

5. Ira Carmen, *Movies, Censorship and the Law* (Ann Arbor: University of Michigan Press, 1966); Richard S. Randall, *Censorship of the Movies* (Madison: University of Wisconsin Press, 1968); and Edward DeGrazia and Roger K. Newman, *Banned Films* (New York: R. R. Bowker, 1982).

6. Robert Sklar, *Movie-Made America* (New York: Random House, 1975; rev. 1994); Garth S. Jowett, *Film: The Democratic Art* (Boston: Little, Brown, 1976).

7. Richard Maltby, "'Baby Face,' or How Joe Breen Made Barbara Stanwyck Atone for Causing the Wall Street Crash," *Screen* 27, no. 2 (1986): 22.

8. Francis G. Couvares, "Introduction: Hollywood, Censorship, and American Culture," *American Quarterly* 44, no. 4 (1992): 511–17, discusses new trends in American Studies and the writing of censorship history. Couvares's own "Hollywood, Main Street, and the Church: Trying to Censor the Movies Before the Production Code" in the same issue discusses disagreements within Protestant groups and the changing alliances that led the MPPDA to

adapt the Production Code (585–87). Both essays were reprinted in Couvares, *Movie Censorship*, 1–15 and 129–58, respectively.

9. See, for example, *The Velvet Light Trap*, no. 23 ("Hollywood Institutions," 1989) and Janet Staiger, *The Studio System* (New Brunswick: Rutgers University Press, 1995).

10. This volume also includes three essays that literally pre- and postdate the studio era (usually defined as 1920 to 1960): those by Garth S. Jowett, Shelley Stamp, and Justin Wyatt. The first two pieces help to explain why censorship and self-regulation took the forms it did in the studio era, and Wyatt's provides a retrospective view in examining the ratings system that took hold in 1968.

11. Clayton R. Koppes and Gregory Black, *Hollywood Goes to War: How Politics, Profits and Propaganda Shaped World War II Movies* (New York: The Free Press, 1987; rpt. University of California Press, 1990).

12. Smith's characterization of blacklist histories bears similarities with what Clayton R. Koppes has called the "heroic" interpretation of PCA activities, whereby the MPPDA suppressed the artistry of creative talents. See Koppes's "Film Censorship: Beyond the Heroic Interpretation," *American Quarterly* 44, no. 4 (1992): 643–49.

13. For more background on the creation of the ratings system, see Richard Randall, "Censorship: From *The Miracle* to *Deep Throat*," in Tino Balio, ed., *The American Film Industry*, 2nd ed. (Madison: University of Wisconsin Press, 1985), 523–30; Garth Jowett, *Film: The Democratic Art* (Boston: Little, Brown, 1976), 419–21; and Jowett, "Moral Responsibility and Commercial Entertainment: Social Control in the United States Film Industry 1907–1968," *Historical Journal of Film, Radio and Television* 10, no. 1 (1990): 25–27.

14. See Bernard Weintraub, "Film Ratings Under Attack from More Than One Angle," *New York Times*, September 6, 1994, C13; and Christopher Stern, "Cheers, Jeers on Ratings Code Birthday," *Variety*, November 28, 1998, 7.

15. It is extremely valuable to examine self-regulation and censorship in relation to specific genres, as does Lea Jacobs in this volume; I look forward to more studies of romantic comedies, westerns, gangster films, and other popular genres as scholarship advances. See the Annotated Bibliography for examples of already published work. Similarly, I look forward to new studies of controversial film stars; Mae West has been the primary focus of such work thus far.

16. For a journalistic overview of censorship in American culture, see the articles under the heading, "Censorship in the Age of Anything Goes" in the *New York Times*, September 20, 1998, sec. 2: James Sterngold, "For Artistic Freedom, It's Not the Worst of Times," 1, 26; Warren Berger, "Where Have You Gone, Standards and Practices," 1, 31; and Michael Scammell, "Why Not Let the Show Go On, Then Rebut It?," 27.

17. Charles Lyons, *The New Censors: Movies and the Culture Wars* (Philadelphia: Temple University Press, 1997). This paragraph summarizes Lyons's study.

18. Thanks to Andrew McAllister for this last insight.

19. Quoted in Frank Rich, "The Baptist Pratfall," *New York Times*, November 22, 1997, A23.

20. Disney's earnings rose by 22 percent during the third quarter of 1997, the period just after the boycott was announced. "Disney Earnings Rose 22% in Quarter," *New York Times*, November 19, 1997, C12.

21. The unfortunate April 1999 shootings at Columbine High School have focused extraordinary attention on the depiction of violence in films, television shows, and computer and video games—a topic too frequently ignored in previous censorship/regulation efforts, that attended instead, and hypocritically, to sex and sexuality. President Clinton's unprecedented call for a study of the marketing of violence may well prove to have a chilling effect on this phenomenon, however temporary it may be, and in spite of Clinton's political motivations for initiating it. See John M. Broder, "Clinton Orders Study on Selling of Violence," *New York Times*, June 2, 1999, A18.

*Garth S. Jowett*

# "A Capacity for Evil": The 1915 Supreme Court *Mutual* Decision

*"Congress shall make no law . . . abridging the freedom of speech, or of the press."*
Amendment I, The Bill of Rights,
Constitution of the United States

*"Today the moving picture machine cannot be overlooked as an effective protagonist of democracy. For through it the drama, always a big factor in the lives of the people at the top, is now becoming a big fact in the lives of the people at the bottom."*
Joseph Medill Patterson, "Nichelodeons,"
Saturday Evening Post, November 23, 1907, 10

On February 23, 1915, the Supreme Court of the United States handed down a unanimous decision in *Mutual Film Corporation v. Industrial Commission of Ohio* which denied the motion picture the constitutional guarantees of freedom of speech and press.[1] Although not widely recognized as such at the time, this was a momentous decision that would affect the course of the motion picture industry in the United States for the next thirty-five years and have a profound effect on the nature of the content which this new medium of communication would be allowed to explore. From our historical vantage point, the *Mutual* decision can be seen as the culmination of an eighteen-year struggle, caused by the increasing popularity and socializing power of this new entertainment medium in conflict with the desires of those who wished to curb its influence and to make it more responsive to a variety of social and legal controls.

The motion picture controversy was much more than a fight between reformers and a morally suspect group of filmmakers. For the long-dominant Protestant segment, the new entertainment medium was, in

From *Historical Journal of Film, Radio and Television* 9, no. 1 (1989): 59–78. Reprinted by permission of the author and the journal's editor, Professor David Culbert.

reality, a dramatic and highly visible symbol of those social and political changes in turn-of-the-century America which they seemed powerless to prevent and which threatened to inexorably alter the face of the nation they had striven to build. For most of its history the United States had been a Protestant nation, but at the beginning of the twentieth century this was changing. As late as 1927 Andre Siegfried noted: "the civilization of the United States is essentially Protestant. Those who prefer other systems, such as Catholicism, for example, are considered bad Americans and are sure to be frowned upon by the purists. Protestantism is the only national religion, and to ignore that fact is to view the country from a false angle."[2]

The fact that America had essentially been created as a Protestant nation, despite the legal fiction of separation of church and state contained in the Constitution, had led to an ingrained belief that only through Protestantism could one be a true 'Christian' and an American. David Reimers, in his thoughtful essay on the subject, has pointed out that at the turn of the twentieth century, American Protestants accepted this contention, and often used the word 'Christian' as a synonym for 'Protestant,' and that, "Protestants also claimed that America was a Protestant nation in the sense that the political, moral, and social norms of American life were derived from Protestantism. Basically the churches were identifying Americanism with Protestantism."[3] It was firmly believed that America had achieved its high level of industrial and material civilization because of the inherent superiority of Protestantism and its underlying moral code, which stressed hard work and adherence to a simple, God-fearing, evangelic faith. It is against the background of this unerring belief in the positive role of Protestantism in American society that we must view the reaction to the introduction of the motion picture in the late 1890s. By the end of the nineteenth century, the security of Protestantism's position in American life was being threatened by a variety of powerful changes. The combined forces of industrialization, urbanization, and immigration represented a demographic, religious, and political threat to the dominance of the rural-based, Protestant hegemony. Leaders of the Protestant church indicated their concern about the growing influence of these forces, aiming most of their wrath at the place where the changes were most obvious—the city. The Reverend Josiah Strong, in his widely read book *Our Country: Its Possible Future and Its Present Crisis* (1885), attacked the city as the source of all the greatest evil in American society:

> The city has become a serious menace to our civilization. . . . Because our cities are so largely foreign, Romanism finds in them its chief strength. . . . The city, where the forces of evil are massed, and where the need of Christian influence is peculiarly great, is from one-third to one-fifth as well supplied with churches as the nation at large.[4]

It was also in the cities where the most visible aspects of the recreation revolution were taking place, and by 1907, the movie house was a common sight throughout working-class districts, and just beginning to emerge as a popular middle-class entertainment.[5]

The increasing number of non-Protestant immigrants during these years, as well as the large number of migrants from the rural areas, served to swell the cities with a working-class population that eagerly sought out new, inexpensive forms of entertainment as diversion from the tedium of their long working hours.[6] The emergence of dance halls, professional sports, dime museums, beer-gardens, bowling alleys, saloons, and even trolley rides was in response to the need for recreation by the new urbanites of every class. In particular, the institutionalization in the late nineteenth century of vaudeville, and its racier cousin burlesque, foreshadowed the emergence of the true 'democratic' theater, and the most widely attended of all the new entertainment forms—the movies. Each of these entertainments had its own particular role to play, but they often served as potent socializing agents for 'explaining' the American way of life to newcomers.[7] It was precisely this obvious but little understood ability to be both a diversion and a disseminator of information which aroused deep suspicion about all of these popular theatrical entertainment forms, but nowhere was this concern more concentrated, or more clearly articulated, than in the attack against the motion picture.

## Protestantism, Progressivism, and the Movies

By 1907, one journalist estimated that there were more than five hundred movie houses in New York, which had a daily attendance of more than two hundred thousand.[8] There were similar statistics in other urban centers, and the ubiquitous nickelodeon was already a familiar sight in smaller cities and towns across the nation.[9] The age of the nickelodeon was, in fact, short-lived as most theater operators, seeking to capture more of the middle-class trade, turned their attention to improving their operations and moving to larger theaters, which often featured a mixture of vaudeville and movies. We know that in New York City and Boston this did indeed succeed in creating a wider audience; however, it is difficult to generalize about the exact nature of the early motion picture audience across the country.[10]

What can be established with some certainty is the initial reaction to the growth of the movies as a social and cultural force as the medium soon became the largest commercial entertainment in the nation. Almost from its first appearance in penny arcades, and then later in projected form in storefront nickelodeons and larger theaters, the medium found itself under intense scrutiny from social workers, teachers, and members of the clergy, as well as those interested in the welfare of children or the general moral state of the public. These were the "Progressives"—the newly emerged professional middle class who would "form the bulwark of those men and women who dedicated themselves to replacing the decaying system of the nineteenth century."[11] It is ironic that while their training and urban orientation provided them with the insight to recognize that the old ways and old values could no longer meet the demands of the new urbanized society, they forged their urban ideals in the crucible of the traditional rural-based value system. While they were obsessed with the development of viable bureaucracies, they also indicated a concern for the individual, which tended to continue the domination of traditional village and "Protestant" values. The Progressives undoubtedly contributed to solving the problems created by the wrenching experience of urbanization and industrialization; however, they often did so with a Protestant-based perspective. While not all social reformers were motivated by religious fervor, the desire to create a "Christian," that is, "Protestant" nation was a deep concern for many, and this was evidenced by the emergence of such evangelical activities as the social gospel movement in the late nineteenth century, with its emphasis on individual renewal and revivalism, and a belief that the teachings of Jesus Christ could be applied to industrial and urban America.[12]

The Progressives placed a great deal of faith in 'science' and the use of rational, scientific reasoning as the answer to many of the social ills of the day. In particular, the emerging social sciences of psychology and sociology were lauded as a means of gaining greater understanding of the behavior of mankind as a collectivity, while economics and political science also gained academic and public acceptance. Educational theory also became more scientific in approach, and this resulted in a major reorientation of the American school system toward a pragmatic form of "learning by doing" which adapted the subject matter to the everyday world and the needs of the child. The school was now perceived as a lever of social change, and the educator as a social reformer.[13] Because of the difficulty in legislating against technology, the school also became the ideal place to give instruction on how to cope with these changes, and to instill the proper form of Christian morality at an early age. This ideological shift was of significance in the subsequent attitude toward the movies, because when it became obvious that these seemingly innocent diversions could also inform as well as entertain, educators took a vital interest in the issue of "the evils of the movies." The motion picture soon proved itself to be a potent competitor to the formal instruction of the classroom, and many a teacher was heard to complain about the unfair nature of the competition.

It is little wonder that, faced with the perspective of the destruction of the traditional American society they revered so much, Protestant leaders responded by attempting to legislate not only against change but also the carriers of change. Clearly the long fight for the prohibition of alcohol can be seen as an attempt to legislate a peculiarly Protestant form of morality (Catholics have never had any objection to the appropriate consumption of alcohol), intensified in the face of "un-American" cultures which increasingly consumed beer and wine in public places such as parks and restaurants with obvious enjoyment.[14]

In its response to the changes around it, the Protestant church demonstrated its awareness of the threat to its dominant status, and taking a firm legislative stand where this was possible, it succeeded in introducing a significant amount of moral legislation. Ultimately, this would have far-reaching implications for the motion picture industry, which became a prime target upon which to vent the frustrations brought about by "a loss of status."[15]

Why all this fuss about the motion picture? Surely there were other more pressing issues in society, and certainly there were more obvious vices which deserved the attention of the reformers and social workers. In fact, a great deal of attention and effort was devoted to combating prostitution, child labor, unsanitary housing conditions, alcoholism, tuberculosis, and a myriad of other social ills. Viewed from this wider perspective, the attack on the motion picture was only one of a series of reactions to the convulsive changes then shaking the roots of American society. However, there are several reasons why this particular issue is of historical significance. First, the intensity of the attack was so unexpected, in that initially the nickelodeons were considered to be a mere passing diversion for the immigrant working classes; however, once the medium gained in popularity and began to attract the patronage of the middle classes, it became more symbolic of the loss of control over the socialization of the child being experienced by the Protestant hegemony. As a form of communication the motion picture established direct contact with its audience, at least a third of whom were under the age of 16, thereby circumventing the traditional socializing role of home, church, and school in imparting information. As alarmed reports filtered back about children learning crime and sex techniques directly from the movies, this confirmed the fears that outside agencies were now replacing these bastions of Protestant America.[16]

Second, the movie houses were highly visible and permanent targets, easily identified, and unlike many other social ills, subject to direct pressure from authorities in the form of legislation and licensing, even though it took several years for specific legislation to be passed that dealt adequately with problems such as lighting, ventilation, fire regulation, and sanitary conditions.[17] The filmmakers were less subject to direct pressure because they were widely scattered throughout the nation in the early period, besides which, their product was distributed by regional (usually state-based) organizations, and these could be subjected to state regulations.

Third, there was a great deal of suspicion concerning the ethnic origins of some of the filmmakers, especially after the first decade of the industry. Robert Sklar has pointed out that "before 1910 the movies were as completely in the hands of respectable, established Anglo-Saxon Protestant Americans as they were ever to be."[18] However, after 1911, a new breed of immigrant, mostly Jewish entrepreneurs rose from their storefront theaters to become the heads of the giant film studios, which eventually controlled the industry. While the vestiges of Victorian decorum prevented outright articulation of anti-Semitic sentiments, the issue of "foreign" control of the motion picture industry was never far from the surface, and undoubtedly was an important motivation in the continued desire to control the medium. These concerns underscore the clash between the established Protestant power and the threat of new alien cultural influences in American society.

Finally, the motion picture represents a significant anomaly in American legal history. It has the distinction of being the only medium of communication ever subjected to systematic legal prior-restraint in the history of the United States. So great was the fear of the perceived power of the motion picture, and so persistent were the reformers in their zeal, that the motion picture industry was eventually denied the right of protection of "freedom of speech" guaranteed by the First Amendment to the U.S. Constitution. As such, the history of this legal decision stands as a monument to what can be accomplished by a group in the last throes of a "loss of status." Together with the creation of prohibition by the passing of the Eighteenth Amendment and the Volstead Act in 1919, the control of the motion picture represented a hollow triumph for the forces of Protestant conservatism faced with the immense changes in their "Christian" environment.

## The Introduction of Censorship

No sooner had the first peep show machines been introduced in 1894 than the specter of censorship loomed over the entertainment. The first recorded court case involving a movie was *People v. Doris* in 1897, in which the presiding New York judge ruled that a pantomime of a bride's wedding night was "an outrage upon public decency."[19] Throughout this early period of the motion picture industry's development there were official attempts to control the new entertainment by the imposition of various licensing laws, which were often the same laws used to control circuses and other forms of traveling sideshows and carnivals.[20] While these regulations were often nuisance laws as much as attempts to bring legitimate municipal order, they failed to control the content of films, and this led to continued pressure for a more systematic method of dealing with what many saw as an increasing social menace.

On November 4, 1907, after continued pressure from reformers and the press, the Chicago City Council passed a movie censorship ordinance to be effective November 19 of that year. The ordinance empowered the general superintendent of police to issue permits for the exhibition of motion pictures, with the right of appeal to the mayor, whose final decision was binding. Permits could be refused if in the superintendent's judgment a film was "immoral or obscene, or portrays depravity, criminality or lack of virtue of a class of citizens of any race, color, creed or religion and exposes them to contempt, derision or obloquy, or tends to produce a breach of the peace or riots, or purports to represent any hanging, lynching or burning of a human being."[21] This was the first movie censorship ordinance ever passed in the United States, and with occasional amendments, was in force until 1961. The violation of this provision led to a fine of not less than fifty dollars, nor more than one hundred dollars for each offense, but each day's showing was to constitute a separate violation. For practical reasons, the superintendent delegated his power to deputies, who levied a fee of three dollars for every one thousand feet of film inspected. The ordinance also contained the first age classification scheme ever used to control the attendance of patrons at movie houses, providing for a special permit for movies which could only be seen by those over 21 years of age.[22] This ordinance raised the ire of the moviemakers, the distributors, and especially the exhibitors, and was immediately tested in the courts. The resulting case, *Block v. Chicago* (1909), stands as a landmark because it was the first movie censorship case to be tried in the U.S. courts.[23] The superintendent refused to issue permits for the films *The James Boys* and *Night Riders* because they were deemed to be immoral. The exhibitor of these films argued before the Supreme Court of Illinois that the ordinance was discriminatory because it did not apply to the legitimate theater, that it constituted a delegation of legislative power to the superintendent of police, and that it deprived him of his property without due process. All of these arguments were swept aside because, according to the court, the purpose of the ordinance was to secure decency and morality in the motion picture business, "and that purpose falls within the police power," unless constitutional rights were transgressed. Further, the standards of 'immoral' and 'obscene' were quite adequate, since "the average person of healthy and wholesome mind" knew what these terms meant. The court specifically examined the films, as well as the constitutional questions, and noted that one of the films did depict the lives of the James brothers, which was a part of American history; however, movies that attempt to document such happenings "necessarily portray exhibitions of crime . . . [and] . . . can represent nothing but malicious mischief, arson and murder. They are both immoral, and their exhibition would necessarily be attended with evil effects on youthful spectators." The court forcefully pointed out that the issue relevant to the due process clause of the Fourteenth Amendment was not applicable, because the plaintiff could have no legitimate property rights in immoral or obscene commodities.[24]

This case also represents the first time that we can find a clear legal articulation that movies were potentially dangerous because they were considered to be a lower-class activity, and therefore needed to be carefully controlled. Chief Justice James H. Cartwright, speaking for the court, noted that the ordinance applied to the "five and ten cent theaters," which "on account of the low price of admission, are frequented and patronized by a large number of children, as well as by those of limited means who do not attend the productions of plays and dramas given in the regular theatres. The audiences include those classes whose age, education and situation in life specially entitle them to protection against an evil influence of obscene and immoral representations."[25] We can safely assume that all of *Block*'s constitutional arguments would probably prevail today, but in 1909 a different set of political, religious, and moral conditions determined the attitude toward the motion picture.

Another historically significant event took place in New York on December 24, 1908, when Mayor George B. McClellan issued an order to close down all of the movie houses in that city, following a clamorous public meeting the previous day that discussed the general conditions of movie theaters. Earlier, in June 1907, the mayor had received a report from his police commissioner, which recommended the cancellation of all licenses for nickelodeons and penny arcades. The issue then lay smoldering for eighteen months before the mayor decided to take action. The reasons for his drastic decision were not really clear, but it was claimed that he was influenced by a group of reformers, headed by Canon William Sheafe Chase of Christ Church, Brooklyn, who had charged at the public hearing that the exhibitors "had no moral scruples whatever. They are simply in the business for the money there is in it."[26] For the next twenty years Canon Chase would devote a large part of his life to the cause of cleaning up the movies, and he was a prominent leader in the drive to establish federal control over the content of the medium.

As a result of this action, the movie house owners obtained an injunction against the mayor's decision, which was granted by Justice Gaynor on Saturday, December 26. This was the last serious attempt to close down all the city's movie theaters, and it underscored the seriousness with which this issue was viewed by the parties involved. The main outcome of this New York incident was the establishment of the National Board of Censorship in March 1909, under the auspices of the People's Institute, a local civic organization that had previously conducted a lengthy investigation of the conditions of motion picture exhibition. The National Board of Censorship (an unfortunate choice of name, because it never really censored films) acted as an advisory board between the film producers and the general public, basing its power not on legal authority but rather on "moral coercion" of the film industry.[27]

John Collier, the executive secretary of the People's Institute, who had been one of the earliest social workers to recognize the importance of the motion picture as an integral part of the lives of the working class, became the architect of this attempt to make the motion picture industry more responsive and sensitive to its social and cultural obligations. Collier felt that if the motion picture was to exist, then it had to recognize the need to conform to prevailing moral norms. He also stressed that the exhibitors had to put pressure on the film manufacturers and demand better films. To demonstrate the good intentions of the industry, Collier proposed a form of censorship that would be enforced by the exhibitors, with control vested in the hands of civic bodies representing the public interest. It was essentially this model that was put into operation in March 1909; however, the plan to inspect films in the theaters was soon abandoned, and the more practical approach of reviewing films at their source—the manufacturer—was adopted. Thus films could be modified, if necessary, prior to their exhbition in the nation's theaters. After some hesitation all of the major film manufacturers, including the powerful Motion Picture Patents Company, agreed to have their films reviewed and certified by the National Board. The film manufacturers' willingness to voluntarily submit their product was based upon the knowledge that without a certificate of approval they ran the risk of having their films refused by the important Association of Exhibitors of New York, which commanded enormous audiences.

The Board was only partially successful in its attempt to quell the rising tide of criticism about the content of motion pictures. While it was able to censor about 85 percent of the films exhibited in the United States, it could not exert control over the exhibition of "special release" or wildcat productions which traveled the theatrical circuit. Having set itself up as the agency to mediate between movie content and public morality, the National Board became a ready target for the whole variety of complaints about the state of the motion picture industry. Also, because it depended upon the financial support of the motion picture industry in the form of licensing fees, it was always under suspicion for being a dupe of the filmmakers. The industry initially supported the Board, even though it was generally opposed to censorship of any sort on constitutional grounds, because it preferred to have to obtain just one form of approval rather than have to face a variety of censorship boards at all legislative levels, with widely differing standards. For this reason, some motion picture industry leaders flirted with the notion of a Federal Censorship Commission in 1914 and 1916, which they quickly backed away from when the National Board pointed out that even if federal censorship was instituted, few states would be willing to give up their power to Washington.[28] Recognizing that the word "censorship" was a misleading indication of its real function, it became the National Board of Review in 1916.

In the long run the National Board of Censorship (Review) not only failed to prevent the clamor for the reform of the movies, it also served to underscore for many convinced reformers that only officially legislated prior-restraint could bring about a morally responsible film industry. Staffed by well-meaning social reformers, the Board represented a compromise between complete freedom from legal censorship and the various forms of local, state, or possibly federal censorship by politically appointed commissions. There was no disagreement by the various camps of social reformers that the movies were in desperate need of controlling. The conflict was essentially between those who wished to see the establishment of viable self-regulatory mechanisms, which fell within the guidelines of the First Amendment guarantee of "free speech," and those who were unwilling and afraid to concede that the movies were indeed legitimate forms of "speech" or "free press."

## The Movies and the Supreme Court

The case of *Block v. Chicago* was based upon a local city ordinance, but by the time it was decided, several states were already considering the introduction of statewide movie censorship laws. Pennsylvania was the first to legislate official censorship of motion pictures in 1911, with Ohio following in 1913, Kansas in 1914, Maryland in 1916, and New York and Virginia in 1922. Operating under various provisions, these states set up censorship boards to review and license films that met vague and often arbitrary standards of morality and decency. It was a protest against state censorship which formed the basis of the landmark case in motion picture history considered by the U.S. Supreme Court in 1915.

The only way to make any sense of the decision in *Mutual Film Corporation v. Industrial Commission of Ohio* is to consider both the legal and social conditions that were prevailing upon the deliberations of the justices of the Supreme Court. The facts of the case were these: Ohio had passed in 1913 a statute that provided for the creation of a motion picture censorship board whose duty it was to examine, in advance, all film that was to be shown publicly for profit in any part of the state. Section 4 of the Act stated that "only such films as are in the judgement and discretion of the board of censors of a moral, educational or amusing and harmless character shall be passed and approved." Section 3 required a mandatory inspection fee from those submitting films to the censorship agency.[29]

The film industry was obviously concerned that state laws such as this would inflict serious financial damage to their business, and the large interstate film exchange conglomerate, Mutual Film Corporation, decided to challenge the constitutionality of the Ohio censorship law in court. Mutual shipped films into Ohio from their base in Detroit, and because movie house owners would not rent uncensored films for fear of prosecution, Mutual was forced to pay for the state inspection. The film distributor sought an injunction to restrain the enforcement of the law, claiming that the statute imposed an unfair burden on interstate commerce, that it was an invalid delegation of legislative powers to the board of censors because it failed to set up precise standards by which films were to be approved or rejected, and that it violated the free speech guarantees of the Ohio constitution and the First Amendment. The request for the injunction met with failure and the case was appealed to the Supreme Court.

In their appeal before the Supreme Court, the attorneys for Mutual assumed that the justices knew little about the workings of the film industry, and they therefore prepared an elaborate background paper describing the role of Mutual as a film distributor and the industry as a whole. As the Court pointed out, "The bill is quite voluminous."[30] In particular, Mutual tried to show that motion pictures were similar to the press, in that

> They depict dramatizations of standard novels, exhibiting many subjects of scientific interest, the properties of matter, the growth of the various forms of animal and plant life, and explorations and travels; also events of historical and current interest—the same events which are described in words and by photographs in newspapers, weekly periodicals, magazines and other publications, of which photographs are promptly secured a few days after the events which they depict happen; thus regularly furnishing and publishing news through the medium of motion pictures under the name of "Mutual Weekly." Nothing is depicted of a harmful or immoral character.[31]

The Mutual lawyers were obviously aiming directly at the heart of the issue, trying to demonstrate that by 1915, the movies had clearly become transmitters of information on a wide range of isues, and were therefore comparable to other news media.

The Supreme Court heard the case on January 6 and 7, and reported its findings on February 23, 1915. The unanimous Court, speaking through Justice McKenna, ignored the federal free speech claims and rejected the other complaints. Although the list of justices who heard the case included such legal luminaries as Oliver Wendell Holmes Jr. and Charles Evan Hughes, there was to be no freedom from prior-restraint for the motion picture at this time. A close analysis of the decision reveals the somewhat tortured reasoning of the justices to justify their decision. In rejecting the claim that the law placed an unfair burden on interstate commerce, Justice McKenna noted that "The censorship . . . is only of films intended for exhibition in Ohio, and we can immediately put aside the contention that it imposes a burden on interstate commerce." Once the films were in Ohio they were "mingled as much from their nature as they can be with other property of the State," and at this time they were subject to regulation by the state.[32]

In rejecting the delegation-of-power issue, the Court decided that the Ohio statute did not suffer from "arbitrary judgment, whim and caprice . . . resulting 'in unjust discrimination against some propagandist film,' while others might be approved without question." The justices felt that the law could be fairly enforced because, "its terms . . . get precision from the sense and experience of men and become certain and useful guides in reasoning and conduct."[33] The statute could not be specified with any greater clarity because the law relied upon the ascertainment of the facts of the individual case, based upon which the policies would be applied with this "sense and experience." The question of the precise definitions of such terms as "immoral" and "obscene" was to plague the film industry throughout its history, and even today, courts are forced to deal with the various interpretations arrived at by individual judges and juries.

It was the decision on the question of whether movies fell within the free speech guarantees of the Ohio state constitution that was to make *Mutual* such an historically significant case. Despite the evidence provided by the appellant, the justices were not prepared to accept the parallel between the motion picture and the press. First, the Court noted that under the statute films of a "moral, educational or amusing and harmless character shall be passed and approved," and therefore "however missionary of opinion films are or may become, however educational or entertaining, there is no impediment to their value or effect in the Ohio statute."[34] This reasoning, of course, did not deal with the constitutionality of prior-restraint, for no matter that films meeting these standards "would be passed" the real issue was why they needed to be examined and licensed before their public exhibition. The answer to this question is found in Justice McKenna's description of motion pictures for, despite their educational or entertainment value, motion pictures were to be treated differently because

> they may be used for evil, and against that possibility the statute was enacted. Their power of amusement and, it may be, education, the audiences they assemble, not of women alone nor of men alone, but together, not of adults only, but of children, make them the more insidious in corruption by a pretense of worthy purpose or if they should degenerate from worthy purpose. . . . They take their attraction from the general interest, however eager and wholesome it may be, in their subjects, but a prurient interest may be excited and appealed to. Besides, there are some things which should not have pictorial representation in public places and to all audiences. . . . We would have to shut our eyes to the facts of the world to regard the precaution unreasonable or the legislation to effect it a mere wanton interference with personal liberty.[35]

The Court considered Mutual's arguments that motion pictures were a "means of making or announcing publicly something that otherwise might have remained private or unknown," and therefore within the protection of the Ohio constitution; however, this argument was rejected, even though the justices conceded that motion pictures were "mediums of thought," but then so were many other things, such as "the theater, the circus and all other shows and spectacles." The Court held that "the argument is wrong or strained which extends the guarantees of free opinion and speech to the multitudinous shows which are advertised on the billboards of our cities and towns."[36] Further, there was a long history of legal precedent for extending police power over such forms of entertainment.

In trying to gauge what was on the minds of the justices as they considered what to do with this new medium of information, there is little doubt that they were unwilling to leave the general public unprotected from what they saw as a powerful, unregulated social force. It is here that we see the clear articulation of the problem that the motion picture symbolized. The telling phrase was Justice McKenna's declaration that

> It cannot be put out of view that the exhibition of moving pictures is a business pure and simple, originated and conducted for profit, like other spectacles, not to be regarded, nor intended to be regarded by the Ohio constitution, we think, as part of the press of the country or as organs of public opinion. They are mere representations of events, of ideas and sentiments published and known, vivid, useful and entertaining no doubt, but, as we have said, capable of evil, having power for it, the greater because of the attractiveness and manner of exhibition.[37]

Thus the movies were capable of disseminating ideas, but the fear of the Court was that they could be used for "evil" purposes by those seeking merely to make a profit, and that this danger was only increased by the enormous inherent attraction the medium held for the public, especially those classes who were more susceptible to outside influences. In the face of this further threat to the power of the traditional (i.e., "Christian/American") socializing agencies, the concerns of the Protestant hegemonists were perfectly echoed in the words of the Supreme Court.

The decision of the Supreme Court in the *Mutual* case can be faulted in three specific ways. First, the reasoning that the motion picture was to be excluded from First Amendment protection because it was "a business pure and simple, originated and conducted for profit," has been rightly condemned for being constitutionally unsound.[38] Newspapers and magazines had long been operated for private profit, and this had never led to their disqualification from protection. There was certainly no precedent in law for the blanket condemnation of a form of communication because it made money.

Second, the classification of the movies in the same category as circuses and other sideshow spectacles reflected the traditional judicial suspicion of the theater and the arts, expressed in the dichotomy between entertainment and ideas. The belief that because motion pictures were entertainment they therefore could not convey ideas was clearly false, for by 1915 they had amply demonstrated their ability to inform and even influence. Throughout history there had been a fear of the theater as a medium for conveying ideas, and both the English and American courts had long held the legitimate stage to be subject to arbitrary restraint. For many years plays were forbidden altogether in Massachusetts, and in 1915 the drama was not considered as a medium under the protection of the First Amendment. There was, however, no systematic legal censorship of plays in the United States at this time, although theaters themselves were licensed. The courts were clearly reluctant to extend the protection of the First Amendment to new and potentially dangerous forms of expression, and it was not until *Hannegan v. Esquire* in 1946 that the Supreme Court actually held that materials which were characteristically entertainment were protected free speech.[39]

The third criticism of the *Mutual* decision is in the characterization of the motion pictures as having a greater 'capacity for evil' than other forms of mass communication, and therefore subject to prior-restraint. As the *Yale Law Journal* pointed out: "Such a capacity has certainly affected the type and amount of community control, but has never meant that all expression within a medium will be restricted from the outset. It has meant only that when a particular act of expression is sought to be restrained, the community's need for protection against the evil must be weighed against the value of the expression."[40] The acceptance of this view of the motion picture was clearly the major motivation for the decision to allow the continuation of censorship, although, as Ira Carmen has noted, this finding "was unnecessary to establish the fact that the medium itself was not protected by the free speech clause of the Ohio Constitution."[41]

Once the Court had found that the motion picture was not speech, it was unnecessary to consider the claim of protection under the First Amendment; in any case, in 1915 it had not yet been settled as to whether the First Amendment was binding on the states. Only in 1925, in the case of *Gitlow v. New York* did the Supreme Court (including four of the justices who had decided the *Mutual* case) decide that the states must be mindful of the guarantees of free speech and free press set forth in the Constitution.[42] While this equally significant decision did not immediately remove state and local censorship of motion pictures, it did leave open the issue of when a state could properly censor speech, and ultimately provided one of the legal precedents upon which the downfall of censorship was based.

## The *Mutual* Decision: The Evaluation and the Effects

In his evaluation of the *Mutual* decision, one of the founders of the National Board of Censorship, John Collier, pointed out that the Court had

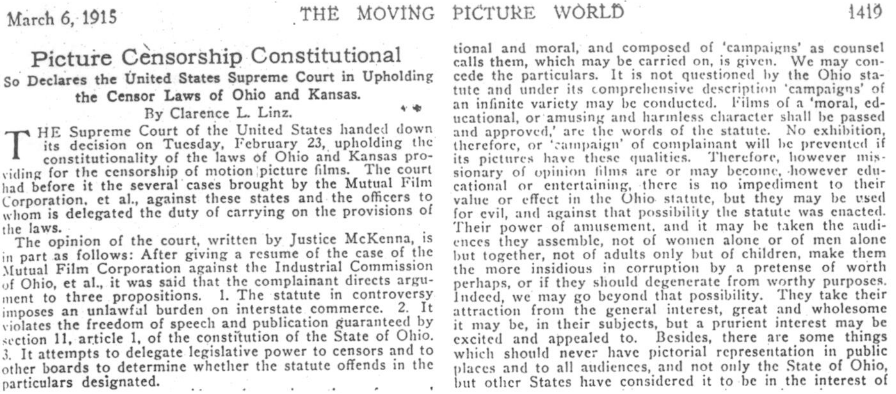

### Picture Censorship Constitutional

So Declares the United States Supreme Court in Upholding the Censor Laws of Ohio and Kansas.

By Clarence L. Linz.

THE Supreme Court of the United States handed down its decision on Tuesday, February 23, upholding the constitutionality of the laws of Ohio and Kansas providing for the censorship of motion picture films. The court had before it the several cases brought by the Mutual Film Corporation, et al., against these states and the officers to whom is delegated the duty of carrying on the provisions of the laws.

The opinion of the court, written by Justice McKenna, in part as follows: After giving a resume of the case of the Mutual Film Corporation against the Industrial Commission of Ohio, et al., it was said that the complainant directs argument to three propositions. I. The statute in controversy imposes an unlawful burden on interstate commerce. 2. It violates the freedom of speech and publication guaranteed by section 11, article 1, of the constitution of the State of Ohio. 3. It attempts to delegate legislative power to censors and to other boards to determine whether the statute offends in the particulars designated.

tional and moral, and composed of 'campaigns' as counsel calls them, which may be carried on, is given. We may concede the particulars. It is not questioned by the Ohio statute and under its comprehensive description 'campaigns' of an infinite variety may be conducted. Films of a 'moral, educational, or amusing and harmless character shall be passed and approved,' are the words of the statute. No exhibition, therefore, or 'campaign' of complainant will be prevented if its pictures have these qualities. Therefore, however missionary of opinion films are or may become, however educational or entertaining, there is no impediment to their value or effect in the Ohio statute, but they may be used for evil, and against that possibility the statute was enacted. Their power of amusement. and it may be taken the audiences they assemble, not of women alone or of men alone but together, not of adults only but of children, make them the more insidious in corruption by a pretense of worth perhaps, or if they should degenerate from worthy purposes. Indeed, we may go beyond that possibility. They take their attraction from the general interest, great and wholesome it may be, in their subjects, but a prurient interest may be excited and appealed to. Besides, there are some things which should never have pictorial representation in public places and to all audiences, and not only the State of Ohio, but other States have considered it to be in the interest of

Figure 1. The Moving Picture World *published this excerpt from the recent Supreme Court ruling in its* March 6, 1915 *issue.*

chosen to use a narrow interpretation of the Constitution to justify its decision, and the justices' use of legal precedent was faulty, for while playhouses were traditionally licensed, individual plays themselves were never licensed, until now. In a series of articles in late 1915 under the general title "The Lantern Bearers—A Series of Essays Exploring Some Thoroughfares of the People's Leisure" appearing in the social work journal, *The Survey*, he traced the history of legal restraint of expressions of opinion in the theater and the motion picture. While these well-researched and articulate essays can be seen as an attempt to intellectually justify the function of the National Board of Censorship as the ideal form of social control, Collier was also one of the few individuals at this time who was astute enough to recognize what the motion picture really symbolized for the reformers. He pointed out that "It is clear that the court was swayed by what it believed about public opinion and public necessity; that its grounds for decision were psychological, not primarily legal, and were the consequences of its lack of first-hand experience with motion pictures."[43]

Collier was also concerned that this decision would lead to legal censorship being applied to other forms of expression, particularly to the theater itself, and "it would involve no radical extension of the motion-picture decision to validate constitutionally a form of censorship of comic supplements and even of illustrations in general." Even political censorship, or the censorship of opinion which the Supreme Court seemed so confident could not take place under the Ohio statute, was possible, for "there are always reasons to spare for every censoring act, and the inner heart cannot be placed in evidence." Subsequent history has demonstrated that Collier had every reason to be apprehensive about the encroaching power of legally protected censors, for, in the years to come, many films were censored or attacked for their political or social ideas.[44] Collier was at his most perceptive about the *Mutual* decision when he suggested that it was the result of the "manifold influences" that were at work in extending the power of censorship, and that "They have concentrated on motion-pictures for the moment because these are ubiquitous, disturbingly potent, and new, and because their producers are as yet hopelessly unorganized to defend themselves. . . . A vastly extended censorship is the aim of many of those who have been in sympathy with this beginning."[45]

Nowhere can these "manifold influences" be better observed at work than in the two hearings held before the U.S. House of Representatives Committee on Education, on the Bills to Establish a Federal Motion Picture Commission in 1914, and again in 1916.[46] These two hearings, on essentially the same bill, but in different congressional sessions, neatly frame the period of the *Mutual* decision, and provide insight into and confirmation of the Protestant reformers' position.

In 1914, Congressman Dudley M. Hughes of Georgia was prevailed upon by the Reverend Wilbur Crafts, superintendent of the International Reform Bureau, to introduce a bill (H.R. 14805) which would have established a Federal Motion Picture Commission, composed of five commissioners appointed by the president to "license every film submitted to it and intended for entrance into interstate commerce, unless it finds that such a film is obscene, indecent, immoral, or depicts a bull fight or a prize fight, or is of such a character that its exhibition would tend to corrupt the morals of children or adults or incite to crime." The penalty for violating this act was "a fine of not more than $500, or imprisonment not more than one year, or both."[47] The Reverend Crafts, in his opening testimony in favor of this bill, went to great pains to establish the right of the federal government to censor films based upon the interstate nature of film commerce. He claimed that the National Board of Censorship ("the unofficial board of censors in New York") had failed to do an adequate job, so that "State and local boards have turned down a great many of the pictures which they have passed." He also suggested that he had firm evidence that "the moving-picture men desire one censorship that will take the place of the vexatious State and local censorships."[48] The real issue for Crafts was that motion picture theaters were teaching lessons in morality as well as entertaining, and so, he pointed out, it was only natural that movies should be supervised by a division of the Bureau of Education. He reasoned:

> The public would recognize the fact that the pictures to be presented would be of real educational force, and it would incline, in my opinion, a great many more of the thoughtful mothers to take their children to moving-picture shows. They would feel, if the business was under the board of education, that it was a safe place for them and their children to attend, and the moving-picture men would themselves gain dignity in the business. They would gain patronage from among the solid class of citizens which would more than offset any loss there might be from the riffraff

who might have attended a salacious picture that had been cut out. At any rate, they recognire that censorship of some sort' or licensing of pictures, which is the preferable way to do it' is a coming event.[49]

In the period just before the *Mutual* decision, Crafts and other reformers favoring this bill always went to some lengths to claim that they were advocating the "licensing" of films, and that this was different from censorship, because it merely utilized the federal authority to license interstate commerce. Technically, under this bill, a film produced and confined within the geographic boundaries of a state would not be subject to examination. Of course, as the industry always pointed out, the economic structure of film production and distribution was such that this meant that in practice all films would be censored by the federal commission.

The major speaker for the reformers was the Reverend William Sheafe Chase, rector of Christ Church, Bedford Avenue, Brooklyn; head of the Social Service Commission of the Diocese of Long Island; and also vice president of the New York Society for the Prevention of Crime, and very well known in Protestant reform circles. The Reverend Chase read into the record a series of debates he had precipitated in *Motion Picture Story Magazine* in 1914 with Frank L. Dyer, president of General Film Co., which neatly outlined the different views of censorship held by the industry and the advocates of legal control. Chase clearly subscribed to the notion that the motion picture was a potentially dangerous weapon, because "a bad motion picture does ten times as much harm among children as a bad book. An evil book injures only those that can read and have some power of imagination. But the evil motion picture carries its influence to the youngest and most ignorant." Further, "This form of amusement makes no demand of punctuality, or patience, or of intelligence. Those who can not understand the English language and those who can not read at all are attracted." In referring to the impending *Mutual* decision, he noted that even if the court found the Ohio statute to be unconstitutional, "it will not affect my contention, for the Ohio law is more sweeping in its provisions than any moderate and reasonable restriction . . . and is much more open to the charge of improperly restraining the freedom of the press."[50] However, just twenty months later, after the *Mutual* decision, which affirmed the state's right to legally censor films, Chase and others were only too eager to praise the Court's denial of First Amendment protection to the motion picture.[51]

Despite a unanimous Education Committee report in favor of establishing a Federal Motion Picture Commission, the first Hughes bill did not make it through Congress, so in 1916, the same bill was reintroduced, this time with the weight of the *Mutual* decision behind it. Dr. Crafts introduced the findings of the Supreme Court at the start of the January 1916 hearings with the statement that "The same principles are involved in the

Federal censorship proposed in this bill as in the Ohio . . . case, and the same constitutional objects were urged there as have been urged here; . . . the Supreme Court denies that there is any analogy between the press and miscellaneous pictures exhibited for amusement and financial profit."[52] In his testimony, Crafts offered a unique insight into how he perceived his achievements as a long-time advocate of social and movie reform, as well as providing a glimpse of his personal philosophies. In referring to another Supreme Court ruling,[53] which condoned the barring of prize fight films, specifically the Willard–Johnson heavyweight title fight, he explained his own role in this case:

> The initiatory work on this law was my first work in restraining motion-picture films. *I would be content if I had initiated only this one of the 16 acts of Congress introduced at my request,* and had no other definite civic accomplishment to my credit for my whole life. It would have been worth while to have lived if only to save the country from being flooded with pictures of a negro indicted for white slavery and a white man voluntarily standing on the same brutal level, which, but for that law, would have been shown all over the country as a brace of heroes.[54]

While Crafts could not be called an outright racist, he was reflecting the commonly held viewpoint that motion pictures could widely disseminate such antisocial information, which was so antithetical to the accepted values of middle-class Protestant America.

The same parade of reformers and industry witnesses appeared before the education committee, as in the 1914 hearings, but this time the industry was much more on the defensive, while the reformers exhibited a confidence resulting from the affirmation of their task provided by the *Mutual* decision. Given that decision, the reformers wondered why the committee even bothered to hold hearings, for, as Crafts told them, "I hope the committee will hold the other side down to using their time in the presentation of new matter that has not been outlawed by the Supreme Court."[55] Much to Crafts's and the Reverend Chase's consternation, the industry continued to insist that motion pictures were being unfairly singled out, and that censorship was unconstitutional, despite what the Supreme Court may have said.

The industry's position, as described by William Marston Seabury, the general counsel to the motion picture people, was in opposition to the bill and to censorship in general. Seabury, who would become one of the most articulate proponents of a 'free' use of motion pictures in society, came straight to the point: "We are opposed to what we call prepublication censorship. We say it is vicious, un-American, and unfair in every principle."[56] The industry claimed that *Mutual* only dealt with the censorship of a film within its borders by a state, and that this did not sanction federal censorship. Throughout these hearings the industry also produced a parade of witnesses who tried to make the case that movies were analogous to other forms of speech, while the reformers constantly cited *Mutual* as a refutation of this claim. Clearly, the Supreme Court's decision was now a major weapon in the reformers' arsenal against the motion picture industry.

Not all Protestant clergymen were fearful of the motion picture in the way that Crafts and Chase were, and those who worked in poorer working-class districts were more inclined to be sympathetic to the need for such diversions in the lives of their neighbors. In opposing the bill, the Reverend Cyrus Townsend Brady of Yonkers, the author of some sixty-five books, made this clear:

> it is a discriminating measure; it is a measure which discriminates against the poor man, for the moving play is the poor man's grand opera. It is the poor man's motor car, it is the poor man's trip to Europe; it is the poor man's golf club; it is his only recreation. . . . I know the lack of amusement, I know the monotony—the life of loneliness in these communities—and it can scarcely be imagined. . . . The Church is back of this desire for censorship. . . . And there is no more pernicious tendency in American institutions than the tendency of the church as an organization to come up and demand the passage of laws to do what the church ought to do itself. . . . If the church can not compete with the moving pictures, it is a sign that it is not using its influence in the right way. . . . We can not make men righteous by law.[57]

Brady's testimony before this committee elicited one of the few recorded instances of applause from segments of the audience, no doubt the representatives of the industry, and their friends, when he said, "if there is another thing besides the greatest amount of personal liberty consistent with the rights of man for which this country stands without regard for special privilege, it is disassociation of church and state."[58]

The reformers, however, saw it in a different light. They were not about to give up their privileges without a fight against those forces which they saw as a threat to their position as the moral arbiters of Americanism. In this regard they felt that they were representing the fundamental will of the majority of Americans. Reverend Chase made this quite clear when he said:

> Now, this Smith–Hughes law is progressive. It is not reactionary. New occasions make new duties. . . . We must have new laws to meet new conditions. . . . Here is a new condition with reference to the childhood of our country, a new danger that confronts them, and we come, representing the will of the whole people, and ask you to appoint a few good men to carry out the will of the whole people in order that the good of the whole people may be secured. . . . Who are going to be the people, if this bill is not enacted, who will educate the children of our lands? A few motion-picture manufacturers, whose principal motive is making money.[59]

These 1916 hearings represented a unique forum for airing the debate about the concept of separation of church and state in deciding who should take responsibility for shaping the moral direction of the United States. The Protestants were adamant that only they could provide the guidance needed to ensure the correct path, for, as Reverend Chase put it, "We have to prepare this country for the future. Preparedness is what we are talking about here today, and the preparedness of soul and spirit is of tremendous importance. The education of our children is of supreme importance in national preparedness. Have we not a right to insist that the morality of the theater-going public shall be raised to the standard of the general morality of the people?"[60] This was answered by John D. Bradley, president of the Washington (D.C.) Secular League, who claimed that the commission established by this bill would have as its main function "to censor not the food of the body, but the food of the mind, to say what shall and what shall not be given expression from the minds and to the minds by means of this great instrumentality for the expression and communication of thought—the motion picture." Attacking the reference to members of the education committee as "representatives of God" made by Reverend Chase the night before, Bradley called attention to the fact that, "the Constitution of this secular Republic knows neither gods nor devils; that it knows no source of political power but that of the people and recognizes no divine prerogative or representation in the representatives of the people."[61]

After six evenings of testimony, the committee on education voted 11 to 5 to send the bill forward; but it too died in Congress. Both in 1923 and in 1926 there were other serious attempts to establish a federal motion picture commission. In 1926 once again there were lengthy hearings held to discuss the issue. Reverend Chase had by this time been promoted to Canon Chase, but he was there, voicing the same concerns, leading the charge. However, by 1926 the film industry had become much more organized under the leadership of former Postmaster-General Will H. Hays, who had become president of the Motion Picture Producers and Distributors of America in 1922. Under Hays's direction the industry had managed to stave off several state censorship bills, most notably in crushing a censorship referendum in Massachusetts in 1922.[62] In fact, the high-pressure tactics used to defeat this referendum by the politically astute Hays, who had previously managed Warren G. Harding's election campaign, was the subject of much debate at these hearings.[63] It was no happy coincidence that Hays was a prominent member of the Presbyterian General Assembly at the time that he was selected to provide the film industry with a veneer of public respectability.[64]

At these 1926 hearings it was clear that the concerns about film content were now widening beyond the original Protestant reformer group to include a variety of social organizations, particularly women's clubs. The public relations efforts of the Hays Office (known as the "Open Door Policy") was also very evident in the number of civic and special interest groups represented who opposed the bill, including many citizens' "Better Films Committees" from all over the United States; the International Federation of Catholic Alumni; the National Catholic Welfare Conference; the American Federation of Labor; and the Women's Cooperative Alliance.[65] Speaking in favor of the bill were such groups as the Women's Christian Temperance Union; the Citizens League of Maryland for Better Motion Pictures; and the Department of Moral Welfare of the Presbyterian Church of the United States of America.[66] The official presentations on behalf of the film industry were all made by representatives from the Hays Office, who provided details about the cooperative efforts they were mounting to improve the relationship between the industry and the general public by providing a forum for public input through a series of conferences and representative committees.

But it was precisely the failure of the industry to appease the ardent reformers that had brought about the introduction of this bill in 1926. Despite the *Mutual* decision eleven years before, which had legally sanctioned the establishment of a substantial number of state and local censorship boards (especially in the largest states and cities), the Protestant reformers would only be satisfied with censorship at the federal level, much like they had achieved with prohibition and the passing of the Volstead Act in 1919. The comparison was even clearly articulated by Charles A. McMahon, representing the National Catholic Welfare Conference, when he told the committee that "Personally I can not help but think that these proposals represent the most pessimistic appraisal of the character and the moral fiber of the American people ever made, as well as the most reckless intrusion upon their rights and upon their personal liberties that has been submitted to Congress since the passage of the Volstead Act."[67] To which the sponsor of the bill, Representative Upshaw of Georgia, replied, "I will only ask you to remember that the Volstead Act was made mandatory by the eighteenth amendment . . . the law was passed, after generations of education and agitation by both branches of Congress . . . and we stand by it."[68]

It was, however, Canon Chase who summed up the frustration that the reformers felt about the motion picture industry, and why they had thought it necessary to fight for federal censorship since 1914:

> The producers have centralized their business and fortified it by engaging a political manipulator of wide experience and influence to whom it has entrusted czarlike power . . . [Will H. Hays]. To expect to meet this incorporated, highly financed, national evil by local or State laws or by the vague and academic process of education is puerile. . . . whenever any business is so great and so intricate in its control and influence over the life and morals of the people, that business should be regulated by the United States Government or it should be regulated by some power big enough to regulate it—big enough to control it.[69]

It was only an ironic accident of history that during the same period the film industry had become a major social influence in American life, the traditional power of the Protestant majority had declined. Despite repeated attempts to seize control of this ubiquitous and very tangible symbol of their increasing loss of status in American society, the best the Protestants could achieve was their victory in the *Mutual* decision. This was not an unimportant triumph, for it provided the legal platform to sustain film censorship for a period of more than thirty-seven years, between 1915 and 1952. However, the *Mutual* decision by itself was unable to bring about the desired result of making the content of motion pictures more responsive to the pure version of what Protestant Americanism stood for. Yet American movies did, on the whole, represent the basic American virtues; but these were no longer exclusively Protestant in origin or outlook. Also, while the motion picture was singled out for attention, there were other vast social and cultural forces at work in America at this time which contributed to undermining the Protestant hegemony.

The true measure of Protestant decline was made obvious in the early 1930s, when after decades of complacency, the Roman Catholic Church, angered and alarmed by the increasing "anti-Catholic" nature of the content of the new "talkies," which featured sophisticated and often suggestive dialogue, divorce, and birth control, decided to take up the cause of "cleaning up the movies." In three short years, through the efforts of the Catholic Legion of Decency, the power of the pulpit, and the reluctant backing of the Hays Office, the Catholic Church was able to achieve in 1933 a viable form of social control through the acceptance of the infamous Production Code.[70] The Protestants could debate control and introduce legislation, but the organized power to authorize morality and achieve effective control now lay with the Catholic Church.

## NOTES

This is the third revision and updating of a chapter that originally appeared in Ray B. Browne and Glenn I. Browne , eds., *Laws of Our Fathers: Popular Culture and the U.S. Constitution* (Bowling Green: Popular Press, 1986), 42–65, and subsequently in *The Historical Journal of Film, Radio and Television* 9, no. 1 (1989): 59–78. I would like to acknowledge the initial help of Allan Stegman, who, following a suggestion of mine, wrote a graduate essay on "The Mutual Film Corporation versus the Industrial Commission of Ohio: A Critical Review." Stegman's analysis of the case precipitated my own further research. The concept of the Protestant response is entirely my own.

1. *Mutual Film Corporation v. Ohio Industrial Commission,* 236 US 230 (1915) (hereafter cited as *Mutual*).

2. Andre Siegfried, *America Comes of Age* (New York: Harcourt, Brace & World, 1927), 33.

3. David Riemers, "Protestantism's Response to Social Change: 1890–1939," in Frederic Cople Jaher, ed., *The Age of Industrialism in America* (New York: The Free Press, 1968), 364–65.

4. Josiah Strong, "Perils of the City," in Anselm Strauss, ed., *The American City: A Sourcebook of Urban Imagery* (Chicago, Ill.: Aldine, 1968), 127–29.

5. For a detailed discussion of the history of the recreation revolution and the emergence of the nickelodeon, see Garth Jowett, *Film: The Democratic Art* (Boston: Little, Brown, 1976), 11–50; Russell Merritt, "Nickelodeon Theaters 1905–1914: Building an Audience for the Movies," in Tino Balio, ed., *The American Film Industry*, rev. ed. (Madison: University of Wisconsin Press, 1985), 83–102.

6. The history of urban amusements is dealt with in Foster Rhea Dulles, *America Learns to Play* (New York: Appleton-Century-Crofts, 1968), 211–29.

7. For the importance of vaudeville as a socializing agent, see Albert F. Mclean, *American Vaudeville as Ritual* (Lexington: University of Kentucky Press, 1965).

8. Barton W. Currie, "The Nickel Madness," *Harper's Weekly*, August 24, 1907, 1246–47.

9. For a discussion of motion picture exhibition in small towns, see Kathryn H. Fuller, *At the Picture Show: Small-town Audiences and the Creation of the Movie Fan Culture* (Washington, D.C.: Smithsonian Institution Press, 1996), and Greg A. Waller, *Main Street Amusements: Movies and Commercial Culture in a Southern City, 1896–1930* (Washington, D.C.: Smithsonian Institution Press, 1995); see also David O. Thomas, "From Page to Screen in Small Town America," *UFVA Journal* 32, no. 3 (1981): 3–13.

10. The history of nickelodeons and the difficulties in trying to analyze the compositions of audiences is dealt with in an elegant manner in Robert C. Allen, "Motion Picture Exhibition in Manhattan, 1906–1912: Beyond the Nickelodeon," in Gorham Kindem, ed., *The American Movie Industry* (Carbondale: Southern Illinois University Press, 1982), 12–24; and for Boston, see Merritt, "Nickelodeon Theaters, 1905–1914." Recent scholarship has questioned the traditional assumptions about the nature of the early film audience, and the social and cultural function of early movie houses. These issues are discussed at length in Ben Singer, "Manhattan Nickelodeons: New Data on Audiences and Exhibitors," *Cinema Journal* 34, no. 3 (1995): 5–35; and a very detailed further examination in Sumiko Higashi, Robert C. Allen, and Ben Singer, "Dialogue: Manhattan's Nickelodeons," *Cinema Journal* 35, no. 3 (1996): 72–128.

11. Robert H. Wiebe, *The Search for Order* (New York: Hill & Wang, 1967), 129. This book is an excellent introduction to the emergence of the Progressive movement.

12. See Charles Hopkins, *The Rise of the Social Gospel in American Protestantism, 1865–1915* (New Haven: Yale Unversity Press, 1940) and Henry May, *Protestant Churches and Industrial America* (New York: Harper & Row, 1949).

13. For information on the shift in educational ideology, see Lawrence A. Cremin, *The Transformation of the School* (New York: Random House, Vintage Books, 1964).

14. The Protestant role in prohibition is discussed in Joseph R. Gusfield, *Symbolic Crusade: Status Politics and the American Temperance Movement* (Urbana: University of Illinois Press, 1963); and Andrew Sinclair, *Era of Excess* (New York: Harper Colophon Books, 1962).

15. The results of the decline in status for groups is discussed in detail in Richard Hofstadter, *The Age of Reform* (New York: Vintage, 1960).

16. The issue of socialization and the reformist response is discussed at length in Jowett, *Film*, 74–107; and Robert Sklar, *Movie-Made America* (New York: Random House, 1975), 122–40.

17. It was not until 1913 that the New York City Council was able to pass a comprehensive law dealing with motion picture theaters. See Sonya Levien, "New York City's Motion Picture Law," *American City*, October 1913, 319–21.

18. Sklar, *Movie-Made American*, 33.

19. 14 App. Div. 117, 43 NYS 571 (1st Dept. 1897).

20. The history and legal issues of film censorship are discussed in the following books: Ira H. Carmen, *Movies, Censorship and the Law* (Ann Arbor: University of Michigan Press, 1966); Francis G. Couvares, ed., *Movie Censorship and American Culture* (Washington, D.C.: Smithsonian Institution Press, 1996); and Richard S. Randall, *Censorship of the Movies* (Madison: University of Wisconsin Press, 1968).

21. Quoted in *Block v. Chicago*, 239 Ill. 251, 87 NE 101 (1909).

22. Carmen, *Movies,* 186–89.

23. *Black v. Chicago.*

24. Carmen, *Movies,* 188; Randall, *Censorship,* 12.

25. Edward DeGrazia and Roger K. Newman, *Banned Films* (New York: R. R. Bowker, 1982), 178.

26. *New York Times,* December 24, 1908, 1. Singer, "Manhattan Nickelodeons," suggests that "The high percentage of Jewish exhibitors reaffirms the interpretation that Mayor McClellan's Christmas Eve, 1908, closing of every nickelodeon in New York City—one of the pivotal incidents of the nickelodeon era—was fueled in part by anti-Semitism. . . . One hardly need point out the symbolic resonance of the shut-down's timing on Christmas Eve, a day that above all others would have lent a sense of moral validity to the Christian activism against a Jewish business" (35, n. 50).

27. The best description of the history and function of this organization is found in Charles M. Feldman, *The National Board of Censorship (Review) of Motion Pictures, 1909–1922* (New York: Arno, 1975). The history of the motion picture industry's relationship with the National Board of Censors and the subsequent role of the National Association of the Motion Picture Industry (NAMPI) has been unjustly neglected. Nancy J. Rosenbloom, through an examination of original files and papers, has provided the first detailed assessment of the industry's anticensorship activities during this period. See Nancy J. Rosenbloom, "Between Reform and Regulation: The Struggle over Film Censorship in Progressive America, 1909–1922," *Film History* 1, no. 4 (1987): 307–25.

28. For details of the motion picture industry's attitude toward all levels of censorship, see Jowett, *Film,* 108–38.

29. Carmen, *Movies,* 11; Jowett, *Film,* 119–29; Randall, *Censorship,* 18.

30. *Mutual,* 231.

31. Ibid., 232.

32. Ibid., 241.

33. Ibid., 245–46.

34. Ibid., 241–42.

35. Ibid., 242.

36. Ibid., 244.

37. Ibid.

38. For a useful analysis of this case, see "Motion Pictures and the First Amendment," *Yale Law Journal* 60 (1951): 701–5.

39. *Hennegan v. Esquire,* 327 US 146 (1946).

40. "Motion Pictures," 703.

41. Carmen, *Movies,* 14.

42. Ibid. *Gitlow v. New York,* 268 US 652 (1925).

43. John Collier, "The Learned Judges and the Films," *The Survey,* September 14, 1918, 516.

44. See Carmen, *Movies;* DeGrazia and Newman, *Banned Films;* Morris Ernst and Pare Lorentz, *Censored: The Private Life of the Movie* (New York: Jonathan Cape and Harrison Smith, 1930); and Randall, *Censorship,* all outline this long history of film censorship for political and other social reasons.

45. Collier, "Learned Judges," 516. There is, of course, a wide range of potential "manifold influences" that could have affected the Supreme Court's decision in the *Mutual* case. In a forthcoming article in *Cinema Journal,* Lee Grieveson makes a very sound and interesting case for considering the moral and racial issues surrounding boxing films, especially those of the African American Jack Johnson, as a catalyst for this decision. Grieveson points out that in 1912 the interstate transportation of boxing films was banned, largely to prevent the exhibition of Johnson's victories over white opponents. Subsequent legal decisions leading up to the *Mutual* case further defined the concept of motion pictures as a commercial "commodity." Grieveson suggests that the Supreme Court's decision was as much motivated by the complex racial issues as it was by other concerns to protect the public morality.

(See Lee Grieveson, "Fighting Films: Race, Morality, and the Governing of Cinema, 1912–1915," *Cinema Journal*, forthcoming.)

46. These two hearings have been conveniently made available in reprint editions. They are *US House of Representatives; Committee on Education, Motion Picture Commission Hearing, 1914*; and *US House of Representatives; Committee on Education, Motion Picture Hearing, 1916* (New York: Arno, 1978). Hereafter they are cited as *Hearings, 1914* and *Hearings, 1916*.

47. *Hearings, 1914*, 3–4.

48. Ibid., 6.

49. Ibid., 21–22.

50. Ibid.

51. Chase insisted on having the full record of *Mutual* inserted into the record. See *Hearing, 1916*, 151.

52. Ibid., 8.

53. *Weber v. Freed*, 224 F355 (1915), which dealt with the banning of the film of the boxing match between Willard and Johnson. See DeGrazia and Newman, *Banned Films*, 185–86 for a complete description of this case.

54. *Hearing, 1916*, 8–9 (italics added).

55. Ibid., 12.

56. Ibid., 28. Seabury later wrote two important books, *The Public and the Motion Picture Industry* (New York: Macmillan, 1926); and *Motion Picture Problems: The Cinema and the League of Nations* (New York: Avondale, 1929).

57. *Hearing, 1916*, 119–21.

58. Ibid., 121.

59. Ibid., 155.

60. Ibid., 169–70.

61. Ibid., 209–11.

62. For details of this, see Jowett, *Film*, 167–69.

63. U.S. Congress, House of Representatives, Committee on Education, *Hearings, Proposed Federal Motion Picture Commission*, 69th Cong., 1st sess., 1926, 200–204.

64. For his important role in the National Presbyterian hierarchy, see Will H. Hays, *Memoirs of Will H. Hays* (New York: Doubleday, 1955), 559–68.

65. The public relations activities of the Hays Office was always a point of great contention during this period. For more details on this issue, see Herbert Shenton, *The Public Relations of the Motion Picture Industry*, for the Federal Council of Churches, 1931 (rpt., New York: Jerome S. Ozer, 1971).

66. At these hearings, Miss Maude M. Aldrich, National Director of Motion Pictures, Woman's Christian Temperance Union, read into the record a motion passed by the WCTU at the National Convention in 1925. It said, in part, "we work for Federal, State, and local regulation of motion pictures of such a nature that each may supplement the other and all may seek to preserve American ideals at home and guarantee a right interpretation of American life to the nations of the world." *Hearings, 1926*, 117.

67. Ibid., 240.

68. Ibid., 241.

69. Ibid., 139.

70. It has only been in recent years that important works on the Legion of Decency using primary sources have appeared. The best of these are the two volumes by Gregory D. Black, *Hollywood Censored: Morality Codes, Catholics and the Movies* (New York: Cambridge University Press, 1994), and *The Catholic Crusade Against the Movies, 1940–1975* (New York: Cambridge University Press, 1997). See also a few earlier sources which are still useful, Paul W. Facey, *The Legion of Decency: A Sociological Analysis of the Emergence and Development of a Pressure Group* (New York: Arno, 1974); and John M. Phelan, S.J., *The National Catholic Office for Motion Pictures: An Investigation of the Policy and Practice of Film Classification* (unpublished Ph.D. diss., New York University, 1968). See also Jowett, *Film*, 246–56.

# Moral Coercion, or The National Board of Censorship Ponders the Vice Films

When several sensational films on white slavery appeared in late 1913 and early 1914 they presented the fledgling National Board of Censorship of Motion Pictures with the biggest challenge of its early years. Vice films, which depicted virtuous young women brazenly abducted by organized prostitution rings, became the focus of intense debate about what ought to be shown on the nation's movie screens, who ought to be permitted to see such material, and which organizations ought to regulate motion picture content and exhibition standards just as cinema was becoming the nation's principal entertainment form. In the face of such controversial material the Board of Censorship found itself fighting for jurisdiction with local police enforcing obscenity laws, with vocal advocates of greater state and federal movie censorship, and with those who defended the cinema's ability to handle key social issues of the day, even such delicate matters as prostitution and vice. White slave films, which proffered risqué subject matter under the guise of upright instruction for the nation's young women, enraged cinema's critics while testing the Board's own inclination to endorse morally uplifting films.

The National Board of Censorship had been formed in 1909 as an industry self-regulatory body, specifically designed to ward off escalating calls for greater official film censorship and the resulting rise in state and municipal control over motion picture exhibition.[1] Eager to prove the industry was capable of monitoring its own output free from government intervention, New York exhibitors sought the help of the People's Institute, a respected Progressive organization that had been regularly reviewing the city's dramatic performances since 1907 and had released a favorable report on motion pictures in 1908. While many middle-class reformers and clergy remained suspicious of moviegoing in these years, the People's Institute acknowledged the value of commercial leisure in working people's lives and recognized cinema's cultural potential. The Institute agreed to form a Board of Censorship to which film companies would voluntarily submit their productions for review by one of the Board's censorship committees, staffed entirely by volunteers drawn from the Progressive community. Industry leaders and social activists both benefited from the association in what Michael Budd has called a "dance of interlegitimation":[2] if the Board of Censorship bolstered the industry's reputation, the People's Institute surely also reveled in the chance to sway the nation's viewing habits in the direction of uplift. Within months of its formation, the New York-based operation quickly became the *National* Board of Censorship, and by the early teens was previewing up to 85 percent of the country's film output. Its weekly bulletin was widely subscribed to by municipalities and civic groups around the nation eager for the Board's guidance.

However broad its intended reach, the Board of Censorship was not entirely successful in averting the rise of motion picture regulation during these years. In 1907 Chicago became the first municipality to practice censorship after the city passed an ordinance prohibiting the exhibition of "immoral or obscene" films and requiring exhibitors to obtain a police permit for each film shown. Several states followed suit, with Pennsylvania passing motion picture censorship legislation in 1911, followed by Ohio and Kansas in 1913. Unlike state and municipal censorship bodies, the National Board had no legal authority to enforce its rulings. Instead, the organization operated through what Chairman Frederic C. Howe called "moral coercion." Its mandate lay less in stifling or curtailing films than in shaping their treatment of delicate issues, seeking always "the gradual improvement of the quality of motion pictures."[3]

When the first white slave films appeared in the autumn of 1913, just four years into the Board's early tenure, they posed a significant challenge for the organization, since they combined sexual material, among the most explicit the Board had been asked to consider, with an avowed educational purpose. The complex manner in which the Board had elected to deal with depictions of prostitution and sexuality on screen only complicated matters further. Rather than ban these subjects outright, as many advocated, the Board permitted their treatment under limited circumstances that inscribed such portrayals within a didactic, moralizing framework. As Tom Gunning has stressed, "the Board was not only engaged in eliminating objectionable material from films, but in reinforcing a conception of film narrative as a form of moral discourse, a form that had a responsibility to present 'moral lessons.'"[4]

The National Board of Censorship reviewed the first of the "slavers," *Traffic in Souls,* in October 1913, nearly a month before it opened, fully aware that "a precedent would be created by any action taken" since the picture dealt "in a more deliberate and extensive way than any previous film with the so-called white slave traffic."[5] The film tells the story of several women trapped in white slavery in New York City, all victims of an elaborate vice ring whose operatives prowl the city's ports of entry and its entertainment sites looking for vulnerable young women. Two Swedish sisters arrive at Ellis Island alone, unable to speak English, and are led to a brothel by a man seeming to offer assistance; a "Country Girl" arrives at Penn Station looking for work, only to follow a stranger's directions right into the trafficker's lair; and a young sales clerk unwittingly accepts a "date" from a vice ring procurer, who drugs and kidnaps her at the earliest opportunity. Such tales stress the vulnerability of women in America's cities, particularly immigrants new to the country, rural women emigrating to urban centers for the first time, and young working women eagerly participating in a new commercial dating culture. In the end, the victims are rescued unharmed from the brothels where they are held captive through the combined efforts of the police force and the shop girl's family.

Volunteers on one of the Board's censorship committees screened the film, as was the normal procedure, but deferred judgment until a wider body of experts could be assembled to assess the picture's impact. Mindful of the delicacy of the subject, General Secretary William D. McGuire Jr. invited representatives of New York's most prominent social organizations to join the Board's General Committee for a second screening of the film. Members of the censorship committee had found that it would be "easy to rid [*Traffic in Souls*] of all elements which might be called suggestive," but for McGuire larger questions remained: "the propriety of the treatment of these darker social problems through the medium of the stage or motion pictures" and, more significantly, "whether it is rightly within the province of the National Board of Censorship to interfere with such public discussions through motion pictures."[6] In other words, faced with a film on one of the era's most contentious issues, McGuire quite openly (and remarkably) pondered the suitability of using motion pictures to address topics of such gravity, and the Board's own mandate in policing the nation's movie screens.

Several community and religious leaders accepted McGuire's invitation and a screening of *Traffic in Souls* was arranged at Universal headquarters in New York. Eager to promote the film's seriousness of purpose, rather than its racy subject matter, the studio circulated a pamphlet to those who attended the showing, stressing the film's educational objectives: "It is a picture that every girl, on reaching maturity, should be taken to see by her mother." Universal touted the film's links to depictions of the vice trade in more elevated art forms, like the novel *The House of Bondage*, which had been a best-seller in 1910, and the stage plays *The Lure* and *The Fight*, which had opened on Broadway that summer, while also being careful to point out that the film did not show "any of the offensive scenes which have made these plays notorious." Moreover, it was not the studio's intent "to pander to sensationalism, or the cravings of the

masses for a glimpse . . . of the so-called 'red-light' life. . . . There is nothing of a lascivious nature in the whole picture."[7]

Evidently the studio's promotion struck the right chord, for Francis Couvares has shown that those who attended the Universal screening
were chiefly concerned with whether the film's portrait of vice would
pose sufficient warning to vulnerable young women. One of the key debates
that day centered around whether the film ought to replace its alarmist
white slave abduction plot with a more nuanced consideration of the factors that led women into prostitution, echoing broader debates within the
reform movement between those who fanned the flames of white slave
panic and those who feared that tales of vice trafficking rings obscured
very real economic and social causes of prostitution.[8] In the end the Board
decided to approve *Traffic in Souls* with only minimal alterations, effectively endorsing its ersatz kidnapping and rescue plot. Upholding the film's
presentation of prostitution, as well as the viability of engaging motion
picture audiences in the anti-vice crusade, committee members issued a
public statement declaring their belief that "this subject [white slavery]
and this method of treatment were legitimate in motion pictures," dub-
bing *Traffic in Souls* "a high-grade picture capable of real moral and dramatic entertainment."[9]

*Traffic in Souls* likely passed the Board's inspection with relative
ease because its treatment of white slavery was already embedded within
the kind of unequivocal moral language that the Board sought, serving up
a melodramatic plot of punishment and redemption in place of an un-
sparing exposé of urban vice. In the end, the Board of Censorship only had
two chief objections to the film. First, it requested that "disorderly house"
sequences be trimmed to one brief "flash," presumably to limit opportunities for prurient viewing. Despite the instruction to restrict views of
brothel interiors, the film nonetheless contains several such scenes; most
notable are those involving Little Sister, the candy store clerk who becomes the focus of the narrative. Of all the women victimized by slave
traffickers in the film, it is only Little Sister who is enticed sexually, agree-
ing to accompany the vice ring's procurer to a café and a dance hall on a
supposed date. Whereas the film's other victims are only misled by their
innocence and their disorientation in urban space, Little Sister is held
somewhat accountable for her fate, since her willing participation in the
city's dating culture puts her at particular risk.

Little Sister's story is developed primarily through a contrast with
her elder sister, Mary: the younger daughter is shown to be rather careless
and perpetually late for work, while Mary is dedicated to the girls' invalid
father and exceedingly modest in her romantic relations, even refusing to
kiss her boyfriend in public view. Issues of desire and sexuality raised by
Little Sister's plight are therefore contained within Mary's rather asexual
romance and her traditional role within the family. Cross-cutting becomes
the central trope of this containment in scenes matching the younger

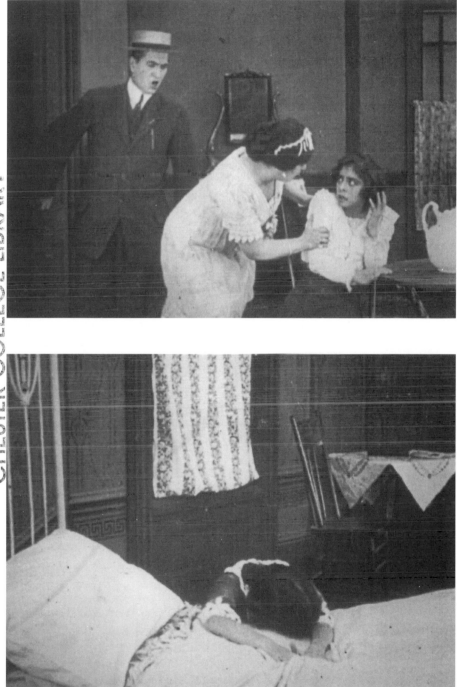

Figures 2 and 3. Images of Mary Barton praying for her Little Sister simultaneously censor and amplify sexual connotations of the brothel scenes in Traffic in Souls.

sister's enslavement with the elder sister's efforts to save her. Little Sister's limp and drugged body is dragged into the brothel, where she is hauled upstairs to a bedroom and her suit jacket is forcibly removed, while Mary remains at home in her own bedroom consumed with fear about her sister. Shots of Mary draped across her bed sobbing and praying for her sister's safety are intercut with these brothel scenes, simultaneously censoring and amplifying sexual connotations manifest in the brothel images, returning Little Sister's eroticized posture to that of piety and repositioning the bedroom in a domestic setting. Even as the film exhibits concerns about urban dating customs through the specter of white slavery, it aims to circumscribe female sexuality within the chaste figure of Mary Barton.[10]

In addition to its concerns about the film's brothel sequences, the Board of Censorship was also eager to eliminate suggestions that the film's vice ring leader, William Trubus, was also involved in Progressive social causes. The Board requested that all titles describing Trubus as an "eminent philanthropist and reformer" be revised so that he was characterized only as "the man higher up," a change Universal agreed to with apparent willingness, suggesting something of the Board's authority during these early years. A title that cited the Travellers' Vigilance Society was also eliminated to prevent any implication that the group had endorsed the film. These were changes clearly designed to protect the reform community by limiting its liability for the lessons learned in the film, and more important, by eliminating any suggestion that its members might be engaged in duplicitous activities. By insisting upon the change in Trubus's character, the Board was downplaying the *social* causes of prostitution in favor of dramas of individual vice and virtue.

Not so easily exorcised was the obvious visual resemblance between actor William Welsh (who played Trubus) and real-life vice crusader John D. Rockefeller Jr., a coincidence noted at the time.[11] Rockefeller headed New York's grand jury investigation into organized vice trafficking in 1910, then founded the Bureau of Social Hygiene, which sponsored a highly publicized 1913 report, *Commercialized Prostitution in New York City*, released just months before *Traffic in Souls* appeared. Much to his displeasure, Rockefeller's name was frequently linked to vice films eager to cloak their salacious narratives in the guise of scientific study. Advertisements for *Traffic in Souls* alleged the film was "based upon the Rockefeller white slaves report and upon the grand jury investigation undertaken by [New York] D.A. Whitman," while subsequent publicity for *The Inside of the White Slave Traffic* claimed that title was "based on Real existing facts gathered by U.S. Government Investigator Samuel H. London, the man that Rockefeller uses as an authority on White Slavery."[12] Alarmed by such claims, Rockefeller took deliberate steps to distance himself from motion picture treatments of the slave trade: "I and those associated with me in this work regard this method of exploiting vice as not only injudicious but positively harmful," he maintained.[13] However,

Figures 4 and 5. *Advertisements for the white slave films highlighted connections to legitimate antivice crusades.*

an obvious likeness between Trubus and the Standard Oil heir, one of the best-known vice crusaders of the era, a man whose name already appeared in much of the film's advance publicity, would undoubtedly have undercut Rockefeller's attempts to dissociate himself from the film, not to mention the Board of Censorship's efforts to curtail any implied indictment of the Progressive movement.

Scenes that link Trubus to a duplicitous circulation within upper-crust New York society, reform organizations, and the vice syndicate only underscore the film's pointed critique. Trubus is a wealthy and respected citizen who uses his ostensible position as head of the "International Purity and Reform League" to disguise his dealings in the slave trade. Under cover of his reform work, Trubus also runs the white slavery ring that preys upon the city's women, supervising a tangled network of pimps, procurers, madams, and go-betweens. Trubus manages his spurious reform organization from an office above the traffickers' headquarters, a position that allows him to listen in on their illicit transactions through a dictagraphic wire. Though his connection to the vice operation remains tangible, it is also obscured. A graphic match aligns a shot of Trubus sitting in his upstairs office with one showing his go-between identically positioned at a desk downstairs, illustrating the interconnectedness of each enterprise and mocking the sanctity of Trubus's assumed guise. Perhaps most pointedly, the sign on Trubus's door identifying his "International Purity and Reform League" is only visible in reverse from the office's interior, a clear visual pun on his double-dealing existence, posing as virtuous while acting precisely the opposite. Ironically, then, the euphemism assigned to Trubus in lieu of "reformer"—"the man higher up"—describes perfectly his covert relation to the vice ring from a position of assumed social and moral superiority. And while the Board of Censorship had been scrupulous in overseeing language used in the film's titles, it did not go so far as to request changes in the film's mise-en-scène, inadvertently creating a space for this kind of irony.

However clandestine his vice dealings, Trubus cannot prevent them from contaminating his placid home life. Emphasizing the tangible spread of corruption from public to private through prostitution and sexuality, *Traffic in Souls* stresses the physical contiguity among prostitutes, procurers, and slave traffickers, all of whom repeatedly shake hands and transfer money. After Trubus's henchman shakes hands with a madam in the downstairs office, Trubus repeats the gesture in the following shot when he shakes the hand of his daughter's upstanding fiancé, introducing lingering traces of moral contagion into his own household.

Why would *Traffic in Souls* skewer Rockefeller while at the same time appealing to his research in order to lend credibility to its own message? Janet Staiger, who also notes this connection, suggests that the characterization of Trubus offered audiences a chance to mock pious, wealthy do-gooders like Rockefeller, admittedly easy targets, while also hinting that these men controlled a capitalist sexual economy that trapped women much more effectively than the torrid vice rings they chased so publicly. Somewhat paradoxically, while Rockefeller's own grand jury report found little evidence of organized vice trafficking, only small-scale police corruption, *Traffic in Souls* painted the opposite picture: upstanding police officers fighting a prostitution cartel headed by the city's wealthy and

*Figure 6. Even though titles no longer refer to William Trubus as an "eminent philanthropist and reformer," his ties to Progressive causes cannot be disguised.*

powerful elite.[14] Yet while *Traffic in Souls* skirts the margins of social critique with its portrait of Trubus, in the end it dispenses with any complex consideration of prostitution and vice, instead favoring a bald narrative of capture and liberation. A story of individual vice and virtue allows wholesome, chaste women to prevail over those who sample the pleasures of urban recreation, and permits old-fashioned patriarchs to triumph over those who scheme against decency. Dramatic rescues from cruel kidnappers replace any call for broad social and economic reform. *Traffic in Souls* proved that treatments of even the most salacious material were permissible under Board guidelines, provided that lessons could be learned and solutions proposed.

The Board of Censorship's approval of *Traffic in Souls* clearly held currency in the film industry, where many feared that torrid white slave pictures "stirred up the imps of censorship," just as industry leaders were hoping to prove that they could regulate their own output without state or federal intervention.[15] Noting that *Traffic in Souls* "has been carefully reviewed by the censors" and that "several eliminations have been made," *Moving Picture World*'s review openly touted the Board's sanction: "Surely its friends, and among these are the members of the National Board of Censorship, are entitled to ask that the production be seen before it is condemned." Vice trafficking was "dealt with so reverently [in *Traffic in Souls*] that even the members of the National Board of Censorship could not find fault," the *Motion Picture News* boasted. *Motography*'s two-page review carried a headline announcing, "Censors Have Endorsed It."[16] Still, the publication suspected that by issuing the General Committee's endorsement of *Traffic in Souls* in a public statement, the Board was adopting an overly defensive posture: "the action of the Censor Board in issuing this advance explanation manifestly anticipates criticism from some source," *Motography* claimed, suggesting something of the Board's own reticence about its mandate.[17]

As *Motography* surmised, the Board's cautious handling of *Traffic in Souls* exposed a lingering uncertainty about the white slave films made all the more apparent in its subsequent treatment of *The Inside of the White Slave Traffic*, a much more explicit and alarming film released two weeks after its predecessor. Unlike *Traffic in Souls*, which framed a depiction of slave trafficking within a story line emphasizing punishment and redemption, *The Inside of the White Slave Traffic* promised a realistic depiction of prostitution, tantalizing viewers with an "inside" peek into the nation's vice wards and brothels, rather than lessons on how they might avoid falling prey to scurrilous vice ring operatives.

Reports that many of the film's sequences had been shot in several notorious red-light districts were touted conspicuously in ads and advance publicity, only fueling such voyeuristic curiosity. When members of the production crew were arrested while filming in El Paso, Texas, industry observers vouched that "they secured a film the likes of which, so report says, has never been approached before."[18] In New Orleans, local officials admonished the filmmakers for photographing only that city's worst districts, while ignoring its historic charm.[19]

By shooting on location around the country *The Inside of the White Slave Traffic* aimed to furnish "as near a photographic representation as possible of the great evil," according to producer Samuel H. London.[20] Surviving reels of the film contain a significant amount of urban location shooting, but few explicitly candid scenes of prostitution survive. Still, *Variety*'s critic identified at least three vice districts visible in the release print: West 27th Street and West 34th Street in New York, both part of the notorious Tenderloin, and Chicago's Armour Avenue, center of that city's vice district. "The setting is real, the girls actual, the 'sailors' apparently caught by the camera . . . under the broad glare of disillusioning mid-day," he concluded.[21] With the inclusion of such scenes, *Motion Picture News* surmised, *The Inside of the White Slave Traffic* is "probably the most authoritative" of the white slave films, since "it shows actual scenes in the underworld."[22] Industry commentators predicted from the outset that the film's documentary emphasis would cause problems with censorship organizations. Whereas *Traffic in Souls'* dramatic story line "omits the soul of a subject it aims to reveal" and was therefore likely to escape the wrath of most local and state censorship bodies, *Variety* argued, *The Inside of the White Slave Traffic* clearly risked the censors' knife by engaging "the utmost fidelity in picturing the evil."[23] Unlike more conservative censorship organizations, which prohibited the depiction of prostitution and "disorderly houses" on any grounds, the Board's ruling on *Traffic in Souls* proved it would be willing to pass depictions of "social evil," even including formerly unthinkable images of brothel interiors, provided such views were brief and couched within an explicit educational purpose. *The Inside of the White Slave Traffic* offered no such guarantees.

The Board of Censorship's General Committee reviewed *The Inside of the White Slave Traffic* during the second week of December when it opened, voting to approve the picture only if significant eliminations and additions were made. Producers were asked to "greatly reduce" scenes shot in the New Orleans vice district and to "shorten the disorderly house sequences, leaving these scenes only long enough to show the action taking place without dwelling unnecessarily on the scene." Images of negligee-clad women in the brothel would have to be cut entirely. By allowing only those views of vice districts and brothels that advanced the film's narrative, Board members were obviously concerned to curtail opportunities for prurient viewing of the film's much-touted documentary sequences.

The Board was also concerned to offset any potential salacious interest in sexual material with heavy-handed lessons about the downfall of those enmeshed in the slave trade. In addition to the requested cuts, producers were asked to include new scenes, precisely dictated by the Board, that would castigate vice trafficking. Before the Board would agree to pass *The Inside of the White Slave Traffic* producers would have to include "scenes showing the punishment of the trafficker" and "scenes showing the downfall and end of the girl," the contours of which were outlined in some detail: "These scenes should show the kind of catastrophe which usually overtakes a girl living this kind of a life, such as becoming a down and out hag, a victim of disease, a suicide, a specimen for the doctor's dissecting table, and filling a grave in Potter's Field (or something like this)."[24] According to the Board's logic, limited views of prostitution might be permitted if accompanied by clearly judgmental, fictional scenes.

Even had he agreed to make such substantial alterations to *The Inside of the White Slave Traffic,* producer Samuel H. London was not given a chance to revise the film before the Board changed its ruling. Fearful that London would exploit the Board's approval for publicity purposes, turning a "pass" into an open endorsement, and suspicious that the film had been submitted for its adjudication only "after being publicly and commercially exploited," the Board of Censorship voted to suspend judgment on *The Inside of the White Slave Traffic* five days after it had opened. Rather than passing or denouncing the film, the Board categorized it as a "special release," a designation that left censorship decisions up to local communities.[25] Officially, the Board took "no stand either for or against" *The*

*Inside of the White Slave Traffic.* Here again committee members registered their uncertainty about the Board's mandate. *Traffic in Souls* underscored their unease adjudicating films of sociological merit that fell strictly outside the entertainment spectrum. In the case of *The Inside of the White Slave Traffic,* Board members quickly replaced an initially decisive assessment of the film with an acknowledgment that they could not determine national standards on material of this nature, admitting they would have little control over whether their censorship recommendations were carried out or how their rulings might be manipulated for publicity purposes. It also seems safe to assume that dealing with London, who was new to the film trade, made the Board more nervous than they had been while negotiating with Universal on *Traffic in Souls,* even though the independent studio remained outside the powerful motion picture Trust that controlled the Board.

Although the Board of Censorship attempted to diminish its jurisdiction over *The Inside of the White Slave Traffic* by designating it a "special release," the Board was drawn further into the debate as the film continued to play in New York's motion picture houses, where it was receiving considerable scrutiny from police concerned that the film contravened that city's obscenity laws.[26] Prominent members of the Progressive reform movement who had endorsed the film spoke out on its behalf, declaring its message "good for the public" in the face of continued police intervention.[27] Complicating matters, no doubt, was the fact that Board Chairman Frederic C. Howe was among those whose endorsement graced the film's opening titles. One of the film's chief proponents became Fredrick Robinson, head of the Sociological Fund of the *Medical Review of Reviews.* He monitored raids on theaters where the film was shown and castigated police for suppressing the film, hoping the debate would "determine once and for all time whether the police may constitute themselves the judges and censors in our community."[28]

Likely motivated by the escalating tenor of police interest, Samuel London put considerable pressure on the Board of Censorship to revisit *The Inside of the White Slave Traffic,* furnishing written assurance that he would abide by its judgment and not exploit a favorable ruling in his advertising. Finally bowing to London's pressure, the Board agreed to reconsider the film two weeks into its run after theater managers showing the picture had already appeared twice before police magistrates in New York. The Board's General Committee convened at the Park Theater on Columbus Circle to view *The Inside of the White Slave Traffic* following a sensational weekend in which the venue had twice been closed by police raids, events that had been reported on the front pages of the city's dailies and which drew sellout crowds of curious viewers.

Although London had evidently added some new material to the film since the Board had first reviewed it, every member of the General Committee, with the exception of Howe, refused to pass *The Inside of the*

*White Slave Traffic,* citing its sensationalistic title, its portrayal of brothel interiors, and its failure to vitiate the slave trade. It was, they declared, wholly unsuitable for popular audiences. In a statement released to the press that evening, committee members complained that "the picture was distinctly an illustration of the white slave traffic, thinly veiled as an attempt to educate the public. The subject is not made unattractive, does not arouse repressive action, and tends to satisfy morbid curiosity. Instead of pointing to a moral, it points to an easy method of obtaining money by both men and women. This film is an illustration, rather than an education."[29] This last phrase defines most clearly what the Board objected to: not the representation of vice itself, but the failure to cloak such depictions within a readily digestible morality tale.

After finally receiving the Board of Censorship's condemnation, *The Inside of the White Slave Traffic* continued to play at several New York theaters, only confirming the Board's initial concern that it would have no power to enforce its rulings. Ultimately, it was the city's police force that closed down theaters showing the film on obscenity charges in late December. Not satisfied, London returned to the Board with a further revised print in early February 1914, evidently hoping that with Board approval he might successfully exhibit the film without further police interference. Viewed for a third time and "discussed at length," *The Inside of the White Slave Traffic* still failed to win the Board's sanction. Despite the incorporation of new scenes enacting the apprehension of slave ring operatives and the prostitute's grave in Potter's Field, additions specifically requested in the Board's first assessment of the film, committee members continued to cite the film's lack of sufficient moralizing; in their view the film remained "an illustrative rehearsal" of prostitution that was "not sufficiently dramatic to appeal to the imagination" nor sufficiently rigorous to be considered educational. They found the film's moral tenor "unconvincing," since little was done to persuade audiences that "the girl usually or inevitably lands [in Potter's Field]," and merely depicting the vice trafficker's arrest was hardly adequate, since "true drama would demand that the procurer should suffer both morally and physically."[30] By dutifully enacting the trafficker's capture and the victim's death London carried out the letter of the Board's requests, but not their spirit.

Not only did *The Inside of the White Slave Traffic* fail to engage in the heavy-handed sermonizing demanded by the censors; it also presented a much more complex view of the causes and consequences of prostitution than was typical of many white slave tracts. Wedded to the documentary footage that grounds the film's "inside" view of vice trafficking is a rather conventional narrative of slave trade procurers and innocent victims not unlike many of the genre. But whereas *Traffic in Souls* concentrates on scare mongering abduction plots, *The Inside of the White Slave Traffic* frames the "downfall" of its heroine within a much broader critique of American social and economic institutions, making it more difficult for the Board of Censorship to endorse the film. Where was the clear moralizing it had seen in *Traffic in Souls?* Where were the villains? Who was precisely to blame in this tale of deep-seated social problems?

In order to paint the permissive climate that allows prostitution to flourish in American cities, *The Inside of the White Slave Traffic* opens with a portrait of George Fischer, a pimp at the helm of a nationwide slave ring. George runs the most public of vice operations, conducting all manner of transactions in full view: he receives telephone calls and sets up appointments at a corner store; he and a prostitute meet a client on the sidewalk outside the shop; and another prostitute delivers George's take of the money to a local restaurant hangout. These early scenes establish how ubiquitous George's operation is, how it thrives on the tacit complicity of shopkeepers, landlords, and community residents who witness these transactions daily.

Within the corrupt environment it sketches, the film shows the easy means by which vice trade procurers lure young women into prostitution. Annie, a garment worker bored with her tedious job, is introduced as "The Innocent in Danger," whom George easily recruits for the slave trade in a swift series of episodes. She accepts his company on the pretext of a date, but when George takes her to an outdoor café, she suddenly feels drowsy—a sure sign to knowing audience members that the man has drugged her drink. Awakening in his bedroom the following morning, she glances back at the bed in horror. When she returns home to face her parents, Annie's irate father banishes her from their home. A titles warns, "Parents, beware the 'Out of my House' policy," for George has clearly counted on this outcome as the final element of his plan.

Whereas *Traffic in Souls* is quick to stage a rescue of its innocent victims, before they are actually forced into prostitution, *The Inside of the White Slave Traffic* tracks the slow "downfall" of its heroine, emphasizing less her physical incarceration—the key issue in *Traffic in Souls*—than her moral imprisonment: she cannot leave the profession because of restrictive expectations governing female sexuality. The film traces her descent into several different brothels across the country, where she is taken farther and farther from her family and the life she once knew. Plagued by fond memories of her parents and her former home life, Annie realizes a return to this world is no longer possible. Captive in the world of vice, Annie can neither be rescued nor returned to her family. Without much fanfare, the story ends bleakly when a title, likely proscribed by the Board of Censorship, proclaims, "And in the end, she was laid away, an outcast in Potter's Field." A final shot of anonymous, numbered graves ends the film.

Even more so than *Traffic in Souls*, *The Inside of the White Slave Traffic* emphasizes the vulnerability of its heroine. By charting her gradual introduction to prostitution through courtship, phony marriage, and promised annulment, it chronicles the stages of her deception much more forcefully than a brutal kidnapping. At the same time, these events also hint more broadly at a critique of women's role in society. Bored with demoralizing, low-paying factory work, young working-class women were largely dependent upon courtship and marriage for excitement and social advancement. Annie's odyssey implies that the dependency inherent in such arrangements rendered women vulnerable to abuse. And the film clearly demonstrates that without a family network to fall back upon, young women might quickly find themselves out on the streets, forced to rely on the marketability of their bodies.

Thus, *The Inside of the White Slave Traffic* attempts to present the broad social context of urban vice: an increasingly public leisure culture taking place in restaurants, in cafés, and on city sidewalks; changing patterns of work and recreation for young women, which placed them in potentially threatening situations; and families unwilling to confront the lives of their modern daughters. Hence, the film expands simplistic tales of white slave abductions by showing the tangled network of economic and social circumstances that permit vice operations to thrive in American cities, as well as the equally diverse circumstances that draw women into prostitution and effectively hold them captive there. What differentiates the abduction plot in *The Inside of the White Slave Traffic* from those presented in *Traffic in Souls*, then, is that emphasis shifts away from simple stories of kidnapping that center around the moral culpability of individuals like vice ring operatives, two faced reformers, and wanton shop girls; instead, *The Inside of the White Slave Traffic* furnishes a nuanced portrait of prostitution grounded in an awareness of the cultural and economic factors that support a sexual traffic in women. The film's incorporation of greater social critique and documentary footage mitigated against the elementary moralizing that the Board of Censorship hoped to see in pictures of this sort. It was no wonder, then, that the Board continually refused to pass the film, despite repeated requests from both the filmmaker and members of the Progressive community who supported its educational aims.

The furor over white slave films in late 1913 caused the Board to clarify its position on motion picture treatments of this delicate subject. Hoping to differentiate more clearly between those vice films with educational potential, and those which merely "stimulated an unwholesome and morbid curiosity,"[31] as one reformer put it, the Board of Censorship issued a "Special Bulletin on Social Evil" in February 1914, carefully delineating the limited circumstances under which it would permit depictions of the slave traffic.[32] Distinguishing between "indecent pictures," which simply exploited the phenomenon for the purposes of titillation (for which *The Inside of the White Slave Traffic* was a likely model), and "sex-problem photoplays," which might act as responsible agents of reform (a likely model being *Traffic in Souls*), the Board warned filmmakers that only the latter category would meet its approval.

Board Chairman Frederic Howe and Orrin G. Cocks, its newly appointed Advisory Secretary, both defended the organization's handling of the white slave films in articles published in Progressive journals later that year.[33] Acknowledging that the dialogue surrounding motion picture censorship "rises in volume when films which portray sex questions, the white slave traffic, or the social evil make their appearance," Howe admitted there was bound to be little accord between those who believed that vice films could serve a highly educational purpose by "letting in the light" on prostitution, and those who felt such screen treatments only tended to awaken "curiosity and the inclination to imitate."[34] Eager to clarify the circumstances under which the Board might permit depictions of the "social evil," Cocks emphasized the Board's interest in narratives that cloaked what he called "various forms of sex lapses" within easily digestible moral lessons. The Board would look unfavorably upon treatments of the white slave question which "arouse rather than minimize passion . . . which reveal easy ways of gratifying desire and of making money in the 'trade' or which simply . . . recite the dreary detail of the lives of 'prostitutes.'" On the other hand, Cocks maintained, "there is a place on the screen of the motion picture theater for presentations which unquestionably indicate the causes, the dangers and the effects of sexual misconduct." In the future the Board would sanction depictions which "arouse fear in the minds of both sexes, which develop a hatred on the part of the audience of this ancient evil, which stimulate efforts to rescue the prostitute, and which indicate sensible and workable methods of repression or suppression."[35]

By issuing its "Special Bulletin on Social Evil" and discussing permissible representations of prostitution in national magazines, the Board clearly also aimed to solidify its stance as the ultimate arbiter of motion picture content, a position that was rapidly eroding. Despite its attempt to exert nationwide influence over film exhibition standards, many state and municipal censorship bodies either banned vice films that the Board had passed, or allowed presentations of titles it had censured. Even with Board of Censorship approval, for instance, *Traffic in Souls* was banned by many local censorship boards, including those in Pittsburgh, New Orleans, and, most important, Chicago, which set standards for many smaller midwestern communities. San Francisco, on the other hand, chose to defy the Board's condemnation of *The Inside of the White Slave Traffic* when an exhibitor there drew "large throngs" to see the film.[36]

Whether the Board of Censorship could indeed speak for *national* standards while located in New York also appears to have been of significant concern. Evidently fearing that reports of sensational Broadway stage productions might impugn the Board's standards, Cocks confessed that "though located in New York . . . the National Board does not accept as a basis of criticism the standards of the New York stage or of its complicated liberal and abnormal life."[37] Instead, Cocks and Howe stressed the contributions made by the city's prominent social organizations to the Board's review committee, insisting that its members acted "on behalf of the general conscience and intelligence of the country" and always sought "the point of view of typical Americans."[38]

That the Board of Censorship had to defend its charge so publicly in the wake of the white slave film controversy suggests that in their handling of the films little was resolved. Following the widespread controversy that surrounded *Traffic in Souls* and *The Inside of the White Slave Traffic* in late 1913, the Board continued to review white slave films, condemning *The House of Bondage* in 1914 and *The Little Girl Next Door* in 1916, while approving 1915's *The Lure* and 1916's *Is Any Girl Safe?*, decisions that remained controversial. Finally in 1916 the Board issued a bulletin stating that it would no longer consider films on the vice trade, acknowledging that "a great deal of criticism has fallen" on white slave pictures from members of the public as well as those in the entertainment industry.

> In the face of this public repudiation of such pictures, the National Board, as an agent of public opinion, has taken the position that no picture hereafter will be passed by the National Board which is concerned wholly with the commercialized theme of "white slavery" or which is so advertised as to give the impression that it is a "white slave" picture.[39]

In the end, the arrival of sensational vice films in the autumn of 1913 presented the National Board of Censorship with an opportunity to define its mission in clear, unequivocal terms at a point when its stature was already beginning to erode just four years into its tenure. Instead, the Board's handling of these films only pointed to the difficulties governing motion picture exhibition at a time when state and municipal censorship bodies fought with more liberal reform organizations for dominion over the nation's primary entertainment form. The Board's admitted inability to exert its authority over exhibitors, police organizations, and local censors during what was undoubtedly the most heated debate of its short history provides an early indication of the hobbled posture it would be increasingly forced to adopt in the teens, when its mandate shifted increasingly toward preventing government censorship. By changing its name to the National Board of *Review* in 1916 the Board all but admitted defeat, turning its energies toward classifying films rather than regulating their content. The Board ultimately ceded censorship authority to the Motion Picture Producers and Distributors Association when it formed in 1922 under the direction of Will Hays, who immediately turned to the problem of policing Hollywood's output from within. The Board's hesitant posture on vice films would not be repeated by its ultimate successor, Hays' Production Code Administration, which would include an explicit prohibition against any depiction of white slavery on screen.[40]

NOTES

1. On the early years of the Board of Censorship, see Robert Fisher, "Film Censorship and Progressive Reform: The National Board of Censorship of Motion Pictures, 1909–1922," *Journal of Popular Film and Television* 4, no. 2 (1975): 143–56; Charles Matthew Feldman, *The National Board of Censorship (Review) of Motion Pictures, 1909–1922* (New York: Arno, 1977), 20–87; Kathleen D. McCarthy, "Nickel Vice and Virtue: Movie Censorship in Chicago, 1907–1915," *Journal of Popular Film* 5, no. 1 (1976): 37–55; Daniel Czitrom, "The Redemption of Leisure: The National Board of Censorship and the Rise of Motion Pictures in New York City, 1900–1920," *Studies in Visual Communication* 10, no. 4 (1984): 2–6; Nancy J. Rosenbloom, "Between Reform and Regulation: The Struggle over Film Censorship in Progressive America, 1909–1922," *Film History* 1, no. 4 (1987): 307–25; Rosenbloom, "Progressive Reform, Censorship and the Motion Picture Industry, 1909–1917," in Ronald Edsforth and Larry Bennett, eds., *Popular Culture and Political Change in Modern America* (Albany: State University of New York Press, 1991), 41–60; Rosenbloom, "In Defense of Moving Pictures: The People's Institute, The National Board of Censorship and the Problems of Leisure in Urban America," *American Studies* 33, no. 2 (1992): 41–61; Czitrom, "The Politics of Performance: From Theater Licensing to Movie Censorship in Turn-of-the-Century New York," *American Quarterly* 44, no. 4 (1992): 525–53. The actual influence that the National Board of Censorship exerted over motion picture content remains in dispute. See the exchange between Robert Sklar and Lary May: "Review of Books," *American Historical Review* 86 (1981): 945; and "Communications," *American Historical Review* 87 (1982): 913–15.

2. Michael Budd, "The National Board of Review and the Early Art Cinema: *The Cabinet of Dr. Caligari* as Affirmative Culture," *Cinema Journal* 26, no. 1 (1985): 5.

3. Frederic C. Howe, "What to Do with the Motion-Picture Show: Shall It Be Censored?" *The Outlook* 107 (June 20, 1914): 414. John Collier, the People's Institute's most vocal advocate of cinema, made a similar point in an interview printed just months before the vice films were released. See Frederick James Smith, "The Evolution of the Motion Picture, Part VIII. From the Standpoint of the Film Censor. An Interview with John Collier, General Secretary of the National Board of Censorship," *New York Dramatic Mirror*, August 6, 1913, 33.

4. Tom Gunning, "From the Opium Den to the Theatre of Morality: Moral Discourse and the Film Process in Early American Cinema," *Art and Text* (September–November 1988): 34.

5. A statement released by the Board is reprinted in "To Censor or Not," *Motography*, November 15, 1913, 339–40.

6. Box 107, Controversial Films Correspondence, National Board of Review of Motion Pictures Collection, Rare Books and Manuscripts Division, New York Public Library (hereafter NBRC).

7. Ibid. Even Frederic Howe was quoted in the pamphlet defending the stage production of *The Fight* earlier that year.

8. Francis G. Couvares, "The Good Censor: Race, Sex, and Censorship in the Early Cinema," *Yale Journal of Criticism* 7, no. 2 (1994): 243.

9. "To Censor or Not," 339.

10. For a more developed treatment of these issues, see Shelley Stamp Lindsey, "Wages and Sin: *Traffic in Souls* and the White Slavery Scare," *Persistence of Vision* 9 (1991): 90–102.

11. *Variety*, November 28, 1913, 12.

12. *The Toledo Blade*, December 13, 1913, n.p. (Billy Rose Theater Collection, New York Public Library for the Performing Arts); and *Variety*, December 12, 1913, 12.

13. *New York Dramatic Mirror*, December 17, 1913, 30; and *New York Clipper*, December 20, 1913, 15.

14. Janet Staiger, *Bad Women: Regulating Female Sexuality in Early American Cinema* (Minneapolis: University of Minnesota Press, 1995), 136–37. The print of *Traffic in Souls* housed at the National Film Archive in London ends with an image not found in American

versions of the film: the final shot shows a garbage can where a discarded newspaper's headline broadcasts details of Trubus's slave ring, underscoring the reformer's public disgrace. I
found no indication in Board of Censorship records that this shot was among those excised
at the Board's request, so I am unable to ascertain why it is missing from prints circulating
in the United States. The significance of this alternate finale is discussed in Ben Brewster,
"*Traffic in Souls:* An Experiment in Feature-Length Narrative Construction," *Cinema Journal* 31, no. 1 (1990): 37–56; and in Tom Gunning, "From the Kaleidoscope to the X-Ray:
Urban Spectatorship, Poe, Benjamin, and *Traffic in Souls* (1913)," *Wide Angle* 19, no. 4
(1997): 25–61.

15. *Moving Picture World*, February 7, 1914, 653.

16. *Moving Picture World*, November 22, 1913, 849; *Motion Picture News*, November
22, 1913, 34; and *Motography*, November 29, 1913, 397–98.

17. *Motography*, November 15, 1913, 339.

18. *New York Dramatic Mirror*, September 24, 1913, 31.

19. Ibid.

20. *Motion Picture News*, December 20, 1913, 31.

21. *Variety*, December 12, 1913, 12. Surviving reels of *The Inside of the White Slave
Traffic* are held at the Library of Congress.

22. *Motion Picture News*, December 20, 1913, 31.

23. *Variety*, December 12, 1913, 12.

24. Box 105, Controversial Films Correspondence, NBRC.

25. Ibid. The Board's own use of the "special release" category to describe *The Inside
of the White Slave Traffic* appears to contravene normal practice, where producers themselves would adopt the term in order to sidestep Board scrutiny. See Garth S. Jowett, "'A
Capacity for Evil': The 1915 Supreme Court Mutual Decision," *Historical Journal of Film,
Radio and Television* 9, no. 1 (1989): 65.

26. For a more detailed account of the policy scrutiny that *The Inside of the White Slave
Traffic* encountered in New York, see Shelley Stamp Lindsey, "'Oil Upon the Flames of Vice':
The Battle over White Slave Films in New York City," *Film History* 9, no. 4 (1997): 351–64.

27. *New York Tribune*, December 22, 1913, 1, 4; and *New York Tribune*, January 19,
1914, 9.

28. *New York World*, December 29, 1913, 3; and *New York Sun*, December 29, 1913, 9.

29. Box 105, Controversial Films Correspondence, NBRC.

30. Ibid.

31. *New York Herald*, December 22, 1913, 5.

32. Box 171, Subjects Papers, NBRC.

33. Howe, "What to Do," 412; and Orrin G. Cocks, "Applying Standards to Motion Picture Films," *The Survey* 32 (June 27, 1914): 338. See also John Collier, "Censorship and the
National Board," *The Survey* 35 (October 2, 1915): 9–14.

34. Howe, "What to Do," 412, 416.

35. Cocks, "Applying Standards," 338. Cocks is paraphrasing a newly revised pamphlet
on "The Policies and Standards of the National Board of Censorship of Motion Pictures," issued in May 1914. See Box 171, Subjects Papers, NBRC.

36. *Moving Picture World*, January 3, 1914, 53; *Variety*, February 6, 1914, 22; *Variety*,
February 13, 1914, 23; *Variety*, February 20, 1914, 25; *Variety*, February 27, 1914, 22; *Variety*, January 30, 1914, 24; and McCarthy, "Nickel Vice," 45.

37. Cocks, "Applying Standards," 338.

38. Howe, "What to Do," 415; and Cocks, "Applying Standards," 338.

39. "The Standards and Policies of the National Board of Censorship of Motion Pictures," October 1916, 18. Box 171, Subjects Papers, NBRC.

40. Eric Schaefer argues that the increased censorship pressure faced by many sex and
vice films in the late teens and early 1920s led directly to the subsequent development of
exploitation cinema. See his article, "Of Hygiene and Hollywood: Origins of the Exploitation
Film," *The Velvet Light Trap* 30 (1992): 34–47.

Richard Maltby

# The King of Kings and the Czar of All the Rushes: The Propriety of the Christ Story

*Let those who tell us to uplift our art invest money in the production of a history play of the life of Christ. They will find that this cannot be staged without incurring the wrath of a certain part of our people.*

D. W. Griffith, 1916[1]

1

In his autobiography, Father Daniel Lord, the Roman Catholic advisor on *The King of Kings* (DeMille, 1927), tells of an occasion on which he was watching, as he put it, "some retakes of the Resurrection," with the Protestant minister advising on the film, Reverend George Reid Andrews:

> As we walked from the set, blinded by the fierce lights that flooded the figure of Christ as the stone rolled away from the tomb, the minister said to me, "How consoling that must be to those who accept the Resurrection literally." I think I blinked, but not with the strain of the lights. "I take it literally," I answered with as little emphasis as possible. "You do?" he said very much surprised. "Indeed I do," I replied, and he changed the subject.[2]

Lord's anecdote captures an intention, implicit in any Hollywood product but particularly in one as expensive as *The King of Kings*, to please all the people all the time. Commercially, the film had to be a nonsectarian biography of Jesus. The advertised cost of its production was $2.3 million; according to Robert S. Birchard, the actual figure was closer to $1.3 million.[3] To commit such sums to a film version of the life of Christ, it was

From *Screen* 31, no. 2 (1990): 188–213. Reprinted by permission of the author and Oxford University Press.

*Figure 7. The climactic crucifixion scene in* The King of Kings *(1927). Courtesy of the Museum of Modern Art/Film Stills Archive.*

necessary to ensure that it was acceptable to, for instance, both "those who accept the Resurrection literally" and to those who do not.

In his "uncensored" biography of DeMille, Charles Higham relates an incident that captures the distance between the project's intention and its achievement; if this story is not true, it ought to be. After the *The King of Kings* had been released, DeMille received a telegram from John C. Flinn, supervising the distribution of the film for Pathé in New York, demanding that Barrett Kiesling be fired as head of publicity for the film. Kiesling had released a press statement saying that the film "had certainly done something to encourage the enmity of the leaders of the many denominational faiths." When confronted by DeMille, Kiesling was mortified and protested that the statement should have read "to encourage the comity of the leaders of the many denominational faiths." DeMille fired him anyway.[4]

The history of the cinematic apparatus must at times be written in terms of its relation to other ideological apparatuses and institutions. This essay has little concern for aesthetics, and only a restricted interest in the thematic discourse of *The King of Kings*, to the extent that it typifies aspects of Protestant belief in the 1920s. My principal preoccupation is with the institutional context in which the film was produced, and the ways in which its production attempted to serve an institutional project: to establish a close and mutually supportive relationship between the liberal Protestant churches and the motion picture industry through the Motion Picture Producers and Distributors of America, Inc. (MPPDA). That institutional project failed, with uncomfortable consequences for the industry.

As an organization, the MPPDA dealt in the public relations activity of ensuring that the "organized industry" came as close as possible to its rhetorical goal of "pleasing all the people all the time." But as an institutional strategy, this positive rhetorical objective became inverted, negative: to displease as few people as little and as seldom as possible.[5] The MPPDA dealt primarily with organizations rather than individuals; it was much more sensitive to organized complaint than it was to that of a dissatisfied individual. In the case of *The King of Kings*, organized interest groups were more numerous and more clearly defined than on most occasions, and the differences among them—denominational disagreements over doctrine—were more substantial and less easily resolved.

2

_____

Why would anyone spend $1.3 million filming the life of Christ in 1926? Disregarding any of DeMille's purely personal individual intentions in the project, about which there is little reliable evidence, there were a number of sound commercial reasons for the venture. There had been at least thirty-nine earlier versions of the Christ story, of which the most commercially notable was probably Kalem's *From the Manger to the Cross* of 1912.[6] Biblical epics, including DeMille's *Ten Commandments* and MGM's *Ben Hur*, had taken large grosses over the previous three production seasons. Perhaps as relevant as these considerations was the substantial interest on the part of American churches of all denominations in using the appeal of motion pictures to their own ends. One 1923 estimate suggested that as many as 15,000 church schools and clubs were showing motion pictures as part of their work.[7] By 1927 the MPPDA estimated that there were 27,000 schools, churches, and other institutions equipped with projection machines, and while this nontheatrical sector hardly represented a major market in revenue terms, the head of the MPPDA's Department of Public Relations noted that "distributing companies, while they may disclaim it, appear to be anxious to secure the slight additional revenue resulting from the practice of renting to churches, pictures which are more or less current."[8]

More important, perhaps, than the financial rewards for addressing the educational and religious markets were the institutional incentives in promoting the industry's public relations with groups often acutely sensitive to both the moral dangers of the screen and the extent to which it competed with them for the attention of the nation's youth. In a variety of ways, including through the production of "worthy" pictures intended to appeal to the network of local Better Films Committees it had established, the MPPDA encouraged its member companies to service these markets and cater to the interest groups they represented. In return, they gained the cautious endorsement of some, at least, among the clergy. In a published sermon on "The Attitude of the Christian Toward Motion Pictures," the Reverend C. L. Collins, of Florida, argued:

> If Christian people always absent themselves from the picture theatre, the management is left with none but the baser element of the community for his patronage and he must cater to them or go out of business. It seems to me, therefore, that the moral and Christian people hold the question of better or poorer pictures very largely in their own hands. . . . We can help create and foster a virile public sentiment that will demand good pictures and none other . . . we should boost and boost hard whenever a notably good screen production comes along. . . . if we want the motion picture business turned over to the devil, lock, stock, and barrel, let Christian people boycott it. But our boycott would not put the motion picture out of business. Such action on our part would simply compel all connected with the industry to make pictures to suit people of low morals or of no morals at all. Just as the Church, long ago, began to make use of the best in music for the glory of God, so would I have us make use of the best of the art of the motion picture for the glory of God and the good of man.[9]

A big-budget version of the Christ story seemed to be an ideal instrument of the MPPDA's strategy.

If DeMille was looking for further commercial inspiration for the project, it was most obviously available in the success of *The Man Nobody Knows: A Discovery of the Real Jesus* by Bruce Barton, which retold the story of Christ as "the story of the founder of modern business."[10] Published in 1925, it became the best-selling nonfiction book of 1926, selling 250,000 copies in eighteen months.[11] One of the leading figures in the advertising industry, and also an extremely successful journalist, Barton put Jesus in the company of Benjamin Franklin, Abraham Lincoln, and other American "success stories" in the Horatio Alger mode:

> You who read these pages have your own creed concerning him; I have mine. Let us forget all creed for the time being, and take the story just as the simple narratives give it. . . . Stripped of all dogma this is the grandest achievement story of all![12]

Barton was one of several "religious" consultants employed on the *The King of Kings*, and DeMille's thought followed Barton's quite closely: "I wanted simply to take the four Gospels and tell the story of Jesus of Nazareth, and He appeared to those around Him, a figure no less human than divine." But DeMille also acknowledged that the director of *Why*

*Figure 8.  H. B. Warner as deMille's Bruce Bartonized Christ in the Last Supper scene.* Courtesy of the Museum of Modern Art/Film Stills Archive.

*Change Your Wife?, Male and Female,* and *The Affairs of Anatol* might seem an odd choice for such a project:

> I knew there would be in the audience religious people fearful of how a
> subject dear and sacred to them would be treated, and people who were
> sceptics and had come to scoff, and people who were cynics and had come
> to witness DeMille's disaster. I decided to jolt them all out of their pre-
> conceptions with an opening scene that none of them would be expect-
> ing: a lavish party in the luxurious home of a woman of Magdala.[13]

If DeMille's theological sense was in accord with Barton's neo-
humanist Protestantism, his sense of religion as spectacle chimed more
closely with the religious pageants staged by Father Lord's Sodality movement, or perhaps even more closely with the "religious vaudeville" of
Aimee Semple McPherson, "the world's most pulchritudinous evangelist,"
as she was billed.[14]

> Over 5,000 people jammed the Angelus Temple [in Los Angeles] every
> evening for Aimee's service. . . . Orchestras and choruses thundered out
> a variety of secular as well as sacred music. Sermons were often ani-

mated. . . . In "Throw Out the Life Line!" a dozen nightgowned maidens, clinging to the rock of Ages amidst crashing thunder and flashing lightning, were pulled across the stage to safety by sailors of the Lord.[15]

> Once I saw her stage a memorable dramatization of the triumph of Good over Evil. On the stage was an illuminated scoreboard. As the lights dimmed in the auditorium, one could see the forces of Good advancing on the citadels of Evil, stalking up ravines, scaling mountains, jumping precipices. To the flash of godly gunfire and the blaze of holy artillery, the forces of General Evil began to retreat. Then a miniature blimp came floating over the scoreboard terrain. A soldier of Good fired a single shot, exploded the blimp, and an ugly grimacing Devil landed on the stage with a thud as the spotlight centered on an unfurled American flag.[16]

Carey McWilliams described her as suggesting "sex without being sexually attractive. . . . But wherever she moved or stirred, sex was present, at least in its public aspects, its gross implications; sex in headlines, sex emblazoned in marquee lights."[17] She disappeared in May 1926, presumed drowned, and reappeared a month later, claiming to have been kidnapped. The revelations that she had spent the intervening weeks in a "love nest" with a married radio operator filled the tabloid press from September 1926 to January 1927, during the production of *The King of Kings*, when it was rivaled in newsworthiness only by the Hall Mills trial, in which the wife of an Episcopalian minister was accused of the murder of her husband and his lover. Both were scandals to rival Hollywood's best.

In its combination of spectacle, sexual scandal, and religion, and in its version of the Magdalen, Aimee Semple McPherson's performative style was in the same register as Hollywood's; she was called, among other things, "the Mary Pickford of revivalism," and she gave her followers what Roderick Nash called

> the best of both worlds—a simple, hopeful, authoritarian faith and "whoopee" salted with just the right amount of sex. . . . They [her followers] thrived on news of Aimee's risqué personal life and at the same time joined her in deploring jazz age morality. Piety served as whitewash. Aimee put sex and spectacle in a safe container where people who did not quite dare to be modern could enjoy them. . . . She rose to popularity on the wings of public ambivalence.[18]

She identified her audience quite specifically. "I bring spiritual consolation to the middle class," she declared, "leaving those above to themselves and those below to the Salvation Army."[19] And her Four Square Gospel was, as she readily acknowledged, firmly fundamentalist.

McPherson, like evangelists from Dwight Moody to Billy Sunday before her, applied the techniques of mass culture to revivalism and borrowed, or perhaps parodied, the styles of Hollywood far more effectively than did the liberal Protestantism it was in opposition to. But if their style echoed DeMille, the inflexibility of fundamentalist doctrine made it inappropriate as the basis for a necessarily nonsectarian film version of the life of Christ to be marketed at an undifferentiated audience. The problem with which the film had to deal involved ensuring that the forces of organized American religion remained friendly to it, so that it could successfully combine the interests of religious sincerity and business.

3

The film's doctrinal starting point was the religious doctrine of American cultural hegemony: an interdenominational, broadly liberal Protestantism. This situation was most immediately dictated by the principal commercial inspiration behind the project, Barton's *The Man Nobody Knows*— the Book of the Film—and also because the institutional encouragement to make the film came from the "organized industry's" relations with organized liberal Protestantism. Beyond these considerations, for a project with Hollywood's conventional rhetorical goals there was an element of commercial inevitability in the choice of the least doctrinally specific or demanding version of Christianity.

    T. J. Jackson Lears argues that the crucial moral change in liberal Protestantism's adaptation to its crises of modernism was

> the beginning of a shift from a Protestant ethos of salvation through self-denial toward a therapeutic ethos stressing self-realization in this world— a world characterized by an almost obsessive concern with psychic and physical health defined in sweeping terms. . . . This was a pattern typical in the expression of therapeutic ideals: clouds of religiosity obscured a growing preoccupation with worldly well-being.[20]

By contrast to the fundamentalism of such as McPherson, liberal Protestantism had more intimate relations to negotiate with capitalism, as "business" seemed in the process of superseding Christianity as the nation's established religion. When John D. Rockefeller Jr. justified the scale of his contribution to the building of Reverend Harry Emerson Fosdick's monumental Riverside Church in New York, he did so by saying he did not want the business world to look down on the churches.[21]

    Fosdick, the most influential liberal Protestant moralist of the 1920s, argued that "religion and life have been drifting apart," and that as a result, "multitudes of people are living not bad but frittered lives—split, scattered, uncoordinated." For this, he blamed the "endless unreality and hypocrisy" of an excessively formalistic Christianity, and sought instead an "intelligently defensible" faith that "will furnish an inward spiritual dynamic for radiant and triumphant living" and "contribute to man's abundant life." As Lears suggests, along with other religious spokesmen of the period, Fosdick unwittingly contributed to the decline of liberal Protestant Christianity by transforming it "into a form of abundance therapy."[22] In the process it became thinner, more "weightless."[23] As a system of beliefs, it seemed to require relatively little attention from its followers. One of the institutional paradoxes of liberal Protestantism was that while the value of church property doubled between 1916 and 1926, there continued to be a steady decline in the vitality of religious belief. There was no decrease in church membership during the period, but there was a decrease in church attendance, since people saw less reason for visiting the church they belonged to. If most Protestants maintained their theoretical belief in Christian doctrines, the practices of their lives reflected the spreading secularization of American culture. In 1929 the Lynds reported that in Middletown

> Secular marriages are increasing, divorce is increasing, wives of both workers and business men would appear to stress loyalty to the church less than did their mothers in training their children, church attendance is apparently less regular than in 1890, Rotary which boasts that it includes all the leaders of the city will admit no minister, social activities are much less centered in the churches. . . . In theory, religious beliefs dominate all other activities in Middletown; actually, large regions of Middletown's life appear uncontrolled by them.[24]

Offering a therapeutic message of humanist and ecumenical values hardly different from the secular values of business as service, the churches found themselves in competition for moral leadership with their corporate sponsors. Economist Roger W. Babson described the church as "the greatest industry in the world today," while ministers were encouraged to develop their "salesmanship" and the practice of religion was widely located within a dominant business discourse.[25] The circumscribed role of Christianity in this culture was exactly caught in the ambiguous terminology of a St. Louis "Business Bible Class":

> Taking the Bible all the way through, there are plenty of passages which have a direct bearing upon business today, and if these passages are studied and applied they will be found to be practical business sense. They will make for success in business—looking at the question from the material side only—and they will certainly make business a better and cleaner thing for all of us who are in it.[26]

In the public imagination of Elbert H. Gary of U.S. Steel or Theodore Vail of AT&T, corporate business enterprise was coextensive with the public interest and assumed responsibility for the welfare of society. The material prosperity brought by business offered a social salvation less troubling or contentious than the Social Gospel. Enmeshed as they were in the material and ideological infrastructure of capitalism, it was hardly surprising that the Protestant churches should have been so affected by the business ethic of the 1920s. In search of relevance, many ministers adapted business values to their own organization and activities. There was preached in the land a gospel of efficiency, and ministers were urged to adapt to the times by such slogans as

> Early to bed, early to rise
> Preach the gospel and advertise.[27]

Clergymen endorsed business statesmen and spokesmen and offered them their pulpits and periodicals. Fosdick offered Owen D. Young of General Electric the pulpit of the Riverside Church to deliver an address on "What is Right in Business."[28] Business spokesmen like Barton responded by endorsing ministerial programs of efficiency and service, and the application of business ideas to church work. In the mid-1920s, one of the new major metropolitan churches, like Fosdick's or Reverend Christian F. Reisner's Broadway Temple in New York City—the first skyscraper church—might have a real estate value of $15 million and annual budgets of $500,000.[29] Such organizations, complete with meeting house, gymnasium, clinic, and kindergarten, began to resemble a business devoted to social service, and more and more frequently business expertise was called in to give managerial advice. Some of the larger churches had business managers; others hired efficiency experts to reorganize them. Divinity schools offered courses in business administration for pastors, who could also take out a subscription to the journal, *Church Management,* or buy advice books such as *How to Make the Church Go.*

> Achievement was no longer measured in spiritual terms but in the size and numbers of salaries, budgets, members, and church buildings . . . partly because church authorities thereby hoped to reach the unchurched and partly because these activities gave the church the appearance of being a dynamic and necessary force in society.[30]

As one of the critics of this behavior, the Presbyterian president of Union Theological Seminary Dr. Henry Sloane Coffin put it, some ministers of the large churches had "ceased to be shepherds and had become ranchers."[31]

Many of them also became part-time exhibitors, and one of them, Thomas F. Opie, proselytized that in motion pictures he had found "the solution [to] the perplexing problem of attendance upon the almost deserted second service." He insisted, however, that it was necessary both to use recent commercial films and to have projection standards "comparable to those of the best moving picture palaces." He suggested that feature-length films were most suitable, preceded by "a short service of singing, Bible reading and prayer, taking preferably only fifteen or twenty minutes":

A silver offering, taken after the 'sermon in pictures' should partially if not entirely cover the cost of rental and carriage. . . . Most of the Bible films that have come to our attention . . . have lacked sufficient dramatic action and freshness of content to make an equal appeal to such films, say as *The Fool, Pilgrim's Progress, The Servant in the House, The Man Who Played God, The New Disciple, The Ancient Mariner*. . . . The picture services are held only on alternate Sundays, so that persons not enthusiastic over this form of worship may not be entirely debarred from evening service and so that the church's prescribed worship shall not be abandoned.[32]

One church in Rockport, Massachusetts, reported that its Sunday evening congregation had increased from twelve to five hundred when it began using films in its services, and the tactic was particularly effective in those states and cities which still enforced Sunday blue laws closing places of amusement on the Sabbath.[33] Small, independent exhibitors frequently protested the major companies' servicing of what they regarded as unfair competition. Other protesters, who objected to a "general tendency to resort to popular lectures, moving pictures, Rotarian methods, church suppers, wild advertising . . . cartoonists, whistlers, comedians, enormous signs at the church porch, dwarfs, Indians, Negro Jubilee singers, freaks of all sorts, free ginger ale, services conducted exclusively by children, and a thousand other Chautauqua devices, in the hope of drawing a crowd," were met by arguments that the church could not afford to neglect modern business methods: "If cigarets, breakfast foods, life insurance, and motor-cars are susceptible of successful advertising campaigns, why not the greatest thing in the world—religion?"[34]

4

Bruce Barton's *The Man Nobody Knows* was a typical expression of this dominant discourse. Barton took his version of liberal Protestantism even further down the road to nondenominationalism. As a journalist, he had written laudatory articles on both Billy Sunday and Harry Emerson Fosdick: the fundamentalist–modernist divide concerned him less than their willingness to apply modern business techniques to their activity. Barton's own sense of what it was necessary to believe was minimal: his readers could accept or reject miracles "according to the make-up of our minds";[35] and he saw no need to regard Satan as any more than "an impersonalization [sic] of an inner experience. The temptation is more real without him, more akin to our own trials and doubts."[36] Throughout the book, Barton's emphasis was on the humanity of Jesus, not his divinity. Above all he sought to demonstrate the mutual relevance of corporate business and a secularized, liberal Protestant Christianity, whose conjoined ideals saw business as service and all business as "my Father's business":

> Great progress will be made in the world when we rid ourselves of the idea that there is a difference between *work* and *religious work*. . . . All work is worship; all useful service prayer. And whoever works whole-heartedly at any worthy calling is a co-worker with the almighty in the great enterprise which He has initiated but which He can never finish without the help of men.[37]

In seeking to adapt his Christianity to his business environment, Barton constructed a version of Jesus against which he was rebelling: a sentimental, sacrificial Jesus, a weakling, a killjoy, that he claimed to be the Sunday school image of his childhood:

> . . . a pale young man with flabby forearms and a sad expression. . . . Something for girls—sissified. Jesus was also "meek and lowly," a "man of sorrows and acquainted with grief." He went around for three years telling people not to do things.
>
> . . . A physical weakling! Where did they get that idea? Jesus pushed a plane and swung an adze; he was a successful carpenter; he slept outdoors and spent his days walking around his favorite lake. His muscles were so strong that when he drove the money-changers out, nobody dared to oppose him!
> . . . A kill-joy! He was the most popular dinner-guest in Jerusalem. A failure! He picked up twelve men from the bottom ranks of business and forged them into an organization that conquered the world.[38]

Barton saw the parables as ideal advertisements; his muscular, sun-tanned Jesus was a middle-class advertising executive, an industrial states-man, who

> personified personal magnetism and outdoor living . . . a master self-promoter who created "big stories" by healing the sick and provoking controversy. . . . This was not merely a businessman's Jesus, but a Jesus fashioned to meet widespread longings for "more abundant life" and a revitalized sense of selfhood. . . . Far from debasing Jesus into a busi-nessman, Barton sought to transform businessmen into ministers of Christ. . . . The new corporate system was not secular but divine; that was Barton's message. . . . Spiritualizing the corporate system, he provided a theology for a secular age.[39]

This vision was far from being Barton's alone. Ministers such as Fosdick centered their belief in a reconstructed, therapeutic version of the New Testament, exalted Jesus as a healthy personality, and made the prac-tical connections to business. In 1923 Charles F. Stockton and William W. Totheroh published *The Business Man of Syria*, an account of Jesus as the "world's most successful man of business," written for "downcast business men" and omitting the crucifixion and resurrection as merely personal experiences and therefore of minor interest.[40] Harold Bell Wright's 1927 novel *God and the Groceryman* features a group of businessmen under the direction of an industrialist correcting the mistakes that ministers and laymen have made and restoring an interdenominational unity to the churches of the town and harmony to the community.[41] In a manual called *Ford Products and their Sale*, Ford salesmen and dealers were offered this uplifting anecdote:

> One spokesman, who had attended a meeting of executives which had opened with "one of the most basic prayers" he had ever heard, asked if it were standard procedure in that company to begin its deliberations with prayer. "Why, yes," the head of the company replied, "and more than that, we never even have a directors' meeting but what there stands at one of the table a vacant chair, and never do any of us make a decision or cast a vote but what we first think of the man of long ago were He sitting there, and say to ourselves, 'What would He have done?' I don't know . . . just what such things have meant for us. We are not religious, but somehow or other we always seems to be going ahead." If the head of the company did not "know, . . . just what such things have meant" his interviewer did: "So far as I know that firm has never had a strike, labor trouble, financial trouble, or any of those business disturbing things."[42]

<hr>

5

<hr>

The Jesus of *The King of Kings* is a figure derived out of the sensibility of *The Man Nobody Knows*, and thus DeMille's involvement in the project becomes, unexpectedly, appropriate to Barton's consumer Christian ideal. Like its source, *The King of Kings* was both textually and institutionally an object in a process of negotiation and accommodation between two elements of a dominant ideology in flux: a declining liberal Protestantism in search of a renewed sense of demonstrable relevance and an emerging therapeutic culture of consumption that had already assumed economic dominance but was still in the process of engineering, testing, and fine-tuning its ideological superstructure. DeMille, as much as Barton, was an appropriate figure for such a project. Jack Moreland (William Boyd), the "two-fisted" clergyman hero of his 1925 film *The Road to Yesterday*, is a cinematic example of the minister as salesman, making "deals" with Ken Paulton (Joseph Schildkraut, who played Judas in *The King of Kings*) over his talking "to this Fellow I work for." At the film's climax religious belief is demonstrated to be literally therapeutic, when Ken's invalid arm is cured sufficiently for him to rescue his wife.

*Figure 9. Cecil B. DeMille among the apostles on the set of* The King of Kings. Courtesy of the Museum of Modern Art/Film Stills Archive.

The textual evidence of Barton's influence is clear. In his autobiography, DeMille observed:

> All my life I have wondered how many people have been turned away from Christianity by the effeminate, sanctimonious, machine-made Christ of second-rate so-called art, which used to be thought good enough for Sunday schools. This Man of Nazareth was a man, with a body hard enough to stand forty days of fasting and long journeys on foot and nights of sleepless prayer, a man with a mind sharp as a razor and balanced as a precision scale.[43]

His description of the "note of admiration in the proud official voice of Pilate when he said of Him: 'Behold the Man,'" is also borrowed in both its sentiment and its language from Barton—although Barton tends to write shorter sentences. Elsewhere, DeMille reports that

> It was H.B. Warner who suggested to me how the scene [in which Christ drives the money-changers out of the Temple] should have been played. He simply picked up a leather thong and wrapped one end of it around his hand, but with such authority that it was entirely believable when the money-changers fled in confusion from a Christ whose anger was the most terrible because so perfectly controlled.[44]

If so, Warner was remembering Barton's description of the scene quite closely:

> The young man had picked up a handful of cords from the pavement and half unconsciously now was braiding them into a whip, watching the whole scene silently. And suddenly, without a word of warning, he strode to the table where the fat money-changer sat, and hurled it violently across the court. . . . There was, in his eyes, a flaming moral purpose; and greed and oppression have always shriveled before such fire. But with the majesty of his glance there was something else which counted powerfully in his favor. As his right arm rose and fell, striking its blows with that little whip, the sleeve dropped back to reveal muscles hard as iron. No one who watched him in action had any doubt that he was fully capable of taking care of himself. No flabby priest or money-changer cared to try conclusions with that arm.[45]

But beyond these textual allusions, hardly surprising given Barton's employment on the project, the nondenominationalism of Barton's biography provided not only the most immediately fashionable account of Christianity but also the emptiest, the one least likely to contain anything offensive, however offensive religious conservatives might find its omissions. Lears observes that in rejecting the "weightlessness" of liberal Protestant sentimentality and "yearning for a more vigorous and manly religion, Barton produced a creed even more vacuous than its predecessor."[46] But that vacuousness provided close to the ideal basis for DeMille's project. It needed only a little refinement to remove any existing irritating dogmatic impurities. The Catholic advisor on the project, Father Daniel Lord, reported in November 1926 that he had succeeded in persuading DeMille to omit references to specifically Protestant text, in the Lord's Prayer, for instance. In his opinion, DeMille "is anxious to conciliate, to see to it that the picture offends no-one, and feels that it will fail of its purpose unless it achieves this."[47] A later report, after he had seen the final edited version, similarly endorsed the film. His only anxiety was over the opening Mary Magdalen scene (about which he reported DeMille had observed, "This one scene is C.B. DeMille, the rest is the Evangelists"),[48] which he said had now been cut from 2,000 to 500 feet:

> It is not at all certain that it will be used at all, but Mr. DeMille argues that a beautiful color sequence, with gorgeous costumes, a spirit of opposition to Christ, a building up of conflict, will catch the unbelieving spectator who comes to scoff. . . . There is absolutely nothing objectionable in it now that my cuts have been made except possibly Mary Magdalen's costume. But I have got him to eliminate all close-ups of her, to eliminate scenes where she moves about, and have left just a minimum necessary for the story. . . . There is really a great deal at stake. If this picture is approved and succeeds, it may be the beginning of a real awak-

ening of interest in religious pictures. If it is not approved, the producers
will have a handle to say that we urge constructive work and then fail to
help it when done. If it is not a success, it will probably end religious picture making for a long, long, time.[49]

The intended ecumenism of the project was probably most graphically demonstrated by the service with which DeMille inaugurated
shooting, "participated in by representatives of the Protestant, Catholic,
Jewish, Buddhist, and Moslem faiths."[50] But it was also present in Lord's
tale of the retakes of the Resurrection bringing comfort to those who accepted it literally, while the liberal Reverend Andrews was happy to
demonstrate his tolerance. In that thematic project, *The King of Kings* as
a text must be counted as close to a complete success in producing as anodyne a version of the Christ story, and one as free from doctrinal impurities, as possible. Presumably, that accounts for its durability as a
religious text for Sunday school use. Unfortunately, at the time of its release, it did not prove anodyne enough.

6

Under the leadership of Will H. Hays, president of the MPPDA, the film
industry sought the moral endorsement of a wide spectrum of organizations. By mid-1922, within six months of the founding of the MPPDA,
Hays had developed a strategy to contain the threat posed to the industry
by the lobbying power of nationally federated civic, religious, and educational organizations. The aim was to "make this important portion of
public opinion a friendly rather than a hostile critic of pictures," and the
strategy was the same one the MPPDA would consistently employ: to
provide previewing facilities for representatives of participating organizations, and financial assistance in distributing their lists and reviews of
recommended films.[51] This policy was essentially a containment exercise:
cooperating organizations gave publicity to the movies they approved, and
made private complaint through the MPPDA about those of which they
disapproved. Hays had a cogent explanation of how such a system would
produce greater benefits than public criticism. That explanation relied on
and contributed to the mythology of Hollywood as "alien." Audiences, he
argued, had to be educated to want "better movies," and producers in Hollywood had to be educated to recognize this demand. Repeatedly this was
couched in the language of the industry maturing, "growing up," and in
the process moving away from its initial "alien" influences in production
to come under the sway of those among whom, as Hays was inclined to
put it, there was "little difference of opinion between what is fundamentally right and what is fundamentally wrong." But the mythology of alien

Courtesy of the Museum of Modern Art/Film Stills Archive.

standards in Hollywood was necessary to Hays as an explanation for mistakes or slips. Hollywood and its producers had to remain the scapegoat villains of this scenario, always being represented as unable or unwilling, without some form of compulsion, to recognize that decency was in their own best interests.

The MPPDA sought to project Hays as a business statesman in the image of Gary, Vail, or Young. They constantly employed the rhetoric of business as service: for instance, Hays's role as a Presbyterian elder, and his organization of a $15 million pension fund for ministers of the Presbyterian Church was held up as an instance of Hays doing his "Father's business," and as part of the MPPDA's claim to cultural respectability on behalf of the motion picture industry.[52] Another aspect of that claim to respectability was in the MPPDA's stance as an innovative trade association, aggressively pursuing policies of industrial self-regulation not merely in issues of film content but in matters of arbitration and in its relations with the Federal Trade Commission, for instance. Hays actively sought to project the MPPDA as being at the forefront of corporate organizational development, and its public relations policy, in its scale and in its apparent openness, was one part of that overall project.

Ideally, the MPPDA looked to cooperate with large national organizations that had local branches operating under a centralized and hierarchical structure: the Catholic Church, in the shape of the National Catholic Welfare Conference, was an ideal example. The problem with the Protestant churches was that they were far less hierarchically organized, and overall, relations with the Protestant churches were perhaps the most problematic of all the MPPDA's external contacts. The Federal Council of Churches of Christ in America (FCCCA) was a loose umbrella organization for Protestant denominations founded in 1908. Its social policies were broadly liberal, to the extent that it frequently came under attack from business groups as well as conservative and fundamentalist clergy. Although the FCCCA did not include the Episcopal Church among its members, and often adopted social and, indeed, theological, policies to the left of a position that the MPPDA might comfortably endorse, it was effectively the only broad national Protestant body with which the MPPDA could deal. In 1922 it had commissioned a report broadly favorable to the industry. Although the report had been written before the MPPDA came into being, and therefore was not influenced by it, the association had made sure that the report was widely distributed. However, the majority of the industry's sternest and most vocal critics were members of the Protestant clergy—notably the Reverend Wilbur F. Crafts, superintendent of the International Reform Bureau, and Canon William Sheafe Chase, rector of one of the largest Episcopalian churches in Brooklyn and president of the New York Civic League. There was thus a constant and open public discussion of the Protestant churches' attitude to motion pictures, to an extent that was not nearly so true of either Catholic or Jewish groups, and the lack of a hierarchically organized Protestant body to which the MPPDA could address itself meant that its attempts at communication were always susceptible to disruption or distortion by disaffected members of the Protestant clergy.

The MPPDA pursued two kinds of positive policies toward church interests in regard to film content. One was a policy of endorsement and cooperation. In March 1923, it established a Committee on Religious Pictures, whose brief was "to inform the motion picture industry of the needs of the churches in this respect and to acquaint the churches with the problems involved in meeting this demand."[53] From early on in the exercise, much of this campaign was directed toward the project of educating the tastes of the audience. Hays's argument to his civic groups was that the producers would respond to audience demand, and that, therefore, if they could create a sufficient demand for screen adaptations of literary classics, inspirational biographical, and historical pictures—for example, *The Covered Wagon* (1923), D. W. Griffith's *America* (1924), *Old Ironsides* (1926)— the companies would produce them. This diverted onto the Committee an economic responsibility for the success of such pictures. *The King of Kings* project fell firmly into this category. Many of the letters sent out to civic groups during its roadshow exhibition contained this paragraph:

> The producers of the picture were led to make the picture by their faith that *the solid, substantial men and women of the world* would support their efforts. A large sum of money was invested in that faith because this picture, of course, had to be accurate as well as beautiful. And so, quite naturally as well as quite frankly, the motion picture industry is watching us to see how we respond to the picture. The sincerity of our demand for the best pictures will be judged largely by our actions in connection with *The King of Kings*. We've got to show them, therefore, that we are sincere. We've got to make *The King of Kings* worthwhile.[54]

The other aspect of MPPDA policy was to aid in the production of pictures specifically for church use, through the Religious Motion Picture Foundation, formed in October 1925 to produce and distribute "special religious motion pictures based on Biblical themes and on the historical facts of religion for use in the churches in connection with the sermons and religious services now prevailing," with George Reid Andrews, chairman of the Religious and Educational Committee of the FCCCA, as its general manager.[55] Early in the life of this organization, Andrews had the idea of making a film version of the life of Christ. Initially, the project involved raising production funds from church sources outside the industry, with the intention that profits would then accrue to the Foundation and to the Protestant churches. Andrews was, in effect, claiming proprietary rights over the life of Christ, or at least over a cinematic version of it. Moreover, he appears to have thought that Will Hays was in a position to give them to him. As president of the MPPDA, Hays worked like any other trade association leader—largely through persuasion and pressure. But the public, and in particular the concerned public, had been led to believe that Hays had extensive and autocratic powers to ban people or pictures from the screen, and that he was, as he was regularly described, "The Czar of All the Rushes." Neither Hays nor the MPPDA actively denied these claims, although they never endorsed them.[56] However, when Hays declared, as he frequently did, that the industry "stands at attention" to do the bidding of civic groups, many, like Andrews, took him at his word.[57] Certainly Andrews, a liberal, business-oriented Protestant minister, seems to have seen in a big-budget motion picture life of Christ the chance to do some of his "Father's business."

The plan to fund production from church sources was abandoned fairly early in the Foundation's life, and during 1925 and 1926 Andrews discussed the project with D. W. Griffith, Famous Players, and First National, who went as far as to invest about $20,000 in story rights to Giovanni Papini's recent international best-seller, *The Story of Christ* (1921; tr. 1923). He later claimed that these projects had been delayed at Hays's request until after the release of *Ben Hur* (1926). In early 1926 the FCCCA were the prime movers behind the establishment of the Church and Drama Association, intended to be an interdenominational body to promote "the worthy things in the stage and screen and to educate the public to the appreciation for the best that the drama has to offer."[58] It again had Andrews as its chairman. DeMille's production plans were announced to the press in June, although there seems to have been some uncertainty as to whether he was planning a life of Jesus or Judas. These announcements led Andrews to write to Hays,

> You know my interest in the subject these many months and the difficulties we have faced in getting the picture made. The last conversation I had with you on the subject you said to me that no picture dealing with the life of Jesus would be made by one of your companies without a full and satisfactory understanding and settlement with us; that you considered, so far as your companies were concerned, that we had preempted [sic] the field. . . . I am not asking for a monopoly of the subject but I am asking for what seems to me to be reasonable consideration in the matter.

Andrews understood "reasonable consideration" to mean that the other companies agree not to pursue their projects, and that he be employed as a consultant. Further, he wanted the FCCCA to have a power of final veto over the script, and he also demanded "that ten per cent of the gross receipts of the picture be paid into the treasury of our Church and Drama Association."[59] Hays was not in a position to do any such negotiating on DeMille's behalf, nor was it likely that any production company would agree to any project on such terms. However, the MPPDA did put Andrews in contact with DeMille, who employed him as one of three clerical religious advisers. He was involved in script preparation during July and August 1926; later the MPPDA claimed that he was the only adviser paid a salary.

Shooting on the film began in September 1926 and was completed on January 17, 1927. The period between then and the film's release probably represented the high point of collaboration between the MPPDA and the Protestant churches. The MPPDA's publicity on the film stressed its ecumenical nature, listing ministers who had visited the production, and noting that "From the beginning, ministers of all denominations have been consulted."[60] Andrews, however, was claiming the leading role in their publicity, timing a membership campaign for the Church and Drama Association to coincide with prepublicity for the release of *The King of Kings.*

The picture was premiered on the evening of Good Friday, April 15, 1927, at the Gaiety Theatre, New York, and collected a body of suitably reverential reviews, several of which commented on the awed silence with which the film was received by its first night audience.[61] In June

1927, Reverend S. Parkes Cadman, president of the FCCCA, wrote to Hays, endorsing

> the deeply reverent and religious character of the motion picture *The King of Kings* and the great service it will undoubtedly render to the cause of Christ and to all humanity. . . . The Committee regards the outcome as a notable demonstration of what may be accomplished when the religious and dramatic forces cooperate in a spirit of understanding and appreciation. . . . it wishes to encourage the production of pictures which inspire and instruct while they entertain.
>
> My associate, the Rev. George Reid Andrews, has informed me of your quiet but effective aid in securing this fine production.[62]

There are, however, clear indications that the film was not a box office success. Despite DeMille's claim that "probably more people have been told the story of Jesus of Nazareth through *The King of Kings* than through any other single work, except the Bible itself," it probably did little better than break even on its initial release. Robert Birchard suggests that the film grossed $2.6 million, a figure that would barely put it into profit, even assuming that these earnings occurred entirely during its roadshow and first general release.[63] Charles Higham claims that the Los Angeles premiere was a disaster, partly due to a 2.5 hour-long Prologue staged by Sid Grauman to mark the opening of his Chinese Theatre.[64] It was exhibited in a fifteen-reel version in four roadshow prints for the remainder of 1927, and there is some evidence to suggest that the various special showings of the film to women's clubs, religious groups, and schoolchildren were designed to raise publicity for the film's lagging box office.[65] It may be that the film's exhibition pattern was affected by competition from sound pictures or by a dispute between DeMille and Pathé; DeMille was unhappy about the merger of the two companies, and detached himself from the new company as quickly as he could. It may simply have been that the pessimistic predictions about its audience appeal turned out to be correct. At any rate, it seems unlikely that *The King of Kings* was a clear financial success, which puts in a somewhat different light the claim in DeMille's autobiography that both he and Jeremiah Millbank gave up their profits from the film to charity.[66] Institutionally as important as this was the fact that the prognostications made by both Andrews and Lord about the fate of future religious filmmaking should *The King of Kings* not be successful seem to have come about, and this is perhaps the clearest evidence of the film's lack of financial success. Only one film based on a Biblical story, Warners Bros.' *Noah's Ark* (1928), which was in production at the same time as *The King of Kings*, was released by a major company over the next eight years, until RKO's *The Last Days of Pompeii* in 1935. Had *The King of Kings* demonstrated the existence of a market, it would certainly have been imitated.

For the MPPDA, however, the institutional crisis over the film was only just beginning. There had been a Jewish adviser, Rabbi J. M. Alkow of California, on the project, but Lord, certainly, claims that he was not much in evidence. When it opened, the film received at least one favorable review from a Jewish source. Rabbi Alexander Lyons, editor of "The Supplement," commented:

> I regard *The King of Kings* as one of the most impressive pictures I have ever witnessed. It is reverent, instructive and inspiring. I commend it for Jew as well as for Christian. It should make the Jew most nobly and proudly Jewish, the Christian more emulous of the character of Jesus. I forecast a great success, spiritually and materially, for the enterprise.[67]

But in October, an increasing number of Jewish protests began to cause serious concern. When confronted with this criticism, DeMille was not conciliatory. On October 13, he wrote to Hays, saying that he had been told by a representative of B'Nai B'Rith that "the picture should never have been made at all but that, having been made, it should be corrected so as not to give the impression that the Jews had anything to do with the crucifixion of Jesus." He reported that he had reedited the sequence with Pilate, on which most objection had been concentrated. He had determined that it was necessary to leave in at least one title reading "crucify Him," and he had offered the representative the choice of having the line spoken by Caiaphas the High Priest or by ruffians in the crowd. Neither seemed to be acceptable, at which point DeMille's attitude hardened, and he informed the Rabbi he was negotiating with that:

> I felt they would greatly harm the Jewish race by bringing the matter to the point of an open fight. I further stated to him that I did not want to be forced to put in the title, "his blood be upon us, and upon our children's children," nor any of the other titles that appear in the Gospels that might in any way be harmful to the Jews. . . . You can see from all of the above that someone in the Jewish race is trying to start trouble. This trouble should be stopped immediately for the good of all, as it could very easily lead to a situation that might be very destructive. Those Jews who are raising these rather violent objections would crucify Christ a second time if they had an opportunity, as they are so ready to crucify what, for want of a better term, I shall call His second coming upon the screen.

He advised Hays to negotiate with Andrews to "see if certain prominent Jews with whom you may both be in contact cannot be made to see that an open attack upon the picture would turn many millions of friends against the Jews, and that a surreptitious attack would place us in the position of having to defend ourselves and the picture as best we could."[68]

The MPPDA's tone was much more conciliatory, and its intent was to reach agreement with a committee of B'Nai B'Rith on appropriate eliminations and changes, and make them quietly, without calling attention to what Carl Milliken, the MPPDA's secretary and overseer of its Public Relations Department, described as "this delicate matter." Despite the fact that the Anti-Defamation League were demanding that the film be withdrawn from circulation, and that the Rabbinical Assembly of America were calling for "all Christian bodies engaged in the effort of promoting goodwill between Jews and Christians, to use their efforts toward the withdrawal of the film," Milliken even hoped to use the occasion as an opportunity to establish a permanent liaison with the organization:

> You realize that in the instance at present under consideration no offense was intended and our observation is that nothing offensive is noted by the great majority of those who see the picture. Yet we recognize the fact that some members of your race including persons of high standing and broad culture while disapproving of the picture as a whole do in fact find certain incidents and titles especially offensive.[69]

This was a situation that might have been anticipated, since according to *Variety*, D. W. Griffith had encountered exactly the same problem with B'Nai B'Rith over the Christ story in *Intolerance* (1916). He was reported as having burned the negative of the scene and reshot the sequence, showing Roman soldiers carrying out the crucifixion.[70]

The attempt to keep the issue quiet failed in early December, when prominent Rabbi Stephen Wise publicly denounced the film while negotiations between the MPPDA and B'Nai B'Rith were still going on. An agreed list of changes and eliminations was, nevertheless, finally arrived at in late December. These involved the addition of an introductory title, substantial changes to the Pilate scene, the addition of titles attributing sole responsibility for the crucifixion to Caiaphas, and considerable toning down of details in the scourging and crucifixion scenes. All these changes were agreed to by John C. Flinn, and made immediately in the roadshow prints. Flinn also agreed that the film would not be distributed in "those areas (particularly Poland, Hungary, Czecho-Slovakia and Roumania) where race hatred might be engendered."[71] On December 23, Flinn wrote to DeMille that "The picture must be cut later to a proper length for motion picture theatre exhibition, and in reediting for that purpose [we] can take into account incorporating any of the suggestions herewith without great difficulty."[72] The recommended alterations are visible in the eleven-reel theatrical print most commonly seen by contemporary audiences. But the project had clearly been sullied by the accusations of anti-Semitism, a charge that was peculiarly difficult for the industry to deal with, attacked as it itself frequently was by anti-Semites.

Both the MPPDA and the FCCCA, through the Church and Drama Association, had made heavy investments in the picture. Its lack of success led to recriminations, particularly between the two principal negotiators, Milliken and Andrews. Throughout 1927 they discussed the relationship between the MPPDA and the Church and Drama Association, but their negotiations foundered on two issues. One was the Association's reviewing policy. The MPPDA wanted it to review films on a monthly basis, producing a list of recommended pictures in the same way that the National Catholic Welfare Council did, and circulating that information to ten thousand Protestant churches. Andrews' scheme involved recommending only one picture, together with one Broadway play, per month. Milliken argued that this would cast undeserved aspersions on the majority of the industry's product. Andrews repeatedly tried to use this industry demand as a bargaining counter with which to gain increased financial support for the Association, to a level that Milliken, wary of having the Association appear to be a creature of the MPPDA, felt was excessive. By March 1928, with the unexpected public relations failure of *The King of Kings*, their negotiations reached a stalemate, and the MPPDA began casting around for other ways to organize the Protestant churches. By September, the relationship with Andrews had turned into one of increasing hostility, with Andrews taking the attitude that

> You seem to feel that our only mission is to give publicity to the picture when produced. We have thought of ourselves as something much more than the publicity agents of the motion pictures. . . . We are much more concerned in the great moral principles involved in the production of pictures and it was our understanding that we were to have some influential part in determining the content of pictures before produced.[73]

It was this line of argument that Andrews succeeded in persuading some of the liberal Protestant press to take up in 1929. In particular, the Episcopalian journal, *The Churchman*, began a campaign against the MPPDA in June 1929 that combined a vigorous critique of the industry's business practices with a vitriolic personal attack against Hays and Milliken. Within a year this line of attack, against the industry's business methods and the MPPDA's techniques for recruiting the support of influential public opinion groups rather than against film content, had been adopted by much of the Protestant religious press, including the widely circulated liberal *Christian Century*. As a result of this attack the FCCCA commissioned an investigation into the public relations of the motion picture industry, which reported in 1931. The report indicted the MPPDA's methods of recruiting support by what looked suspiciously like payments to lobbyists. It concluded that "it may . . . be argued that the chief significance of the facts here disclosed is in calling attention to the vague and indefinite ethics of the business community."[74]

In the aftermath of the 1929 Crash, as the liberal Protestant churches had to redefine the position they had taken toward business in the 1920s, the motion picture industry provided them with an available, highly conspicuous target for criticism. Beginning with the disputes with Andrews over the Church and Drama Association, the elaborate system for controlling the expression of public opinion that Hays and the MPPDA had tried to construct during the 1920s unraveled between 1929 and 1933, and came apart piece by piece. The institutional failure of *The King of Kings* was an important part of that unraveling; the MPPDA did not regain the confidence of the FCCCA or of liberal Protestant opinion, and in the early 1930s it had to turn to other sources of support, most visibly to the Roman Catholic Church.[75] Had *The King of Kings* been successful in promoting an undifferentiated liberal Christianity to an undifferentiated mass audience, had it managed institutionally to "please all the people all the time," the events of the next seven years—at least as far as the history of Hollywood and censorship was concerned—might have looked very different.

## NOTES

This essay was first delivered at the VIII Mostra Internatiozionale del Nuovo Cinema Rassegna Internationzionale Retrospettiva, "Il Più Grande Spettacolo del Mondo: Cecil B. DeMille, la Paramount, la formatzione di Hollywood," in Ancona in December 1989. Much of the research presented here was undertaken during the academic year 1983–84, in which I held an American Studies Fellowship from the American Council of Learned Societies. Further research has been facilitated by awards from the British Academy and the University of Exeter. I am greatly indebted to the Motion Picture Association of America, and to its secretary, James Bouras, for permitting me to consult documents in the MPA Archive in New York; to Father William Barnaby Faherty, S.J., and Mrs. Nancy Merz of the Jesuit Missouri Province Archives, St. Louis, Missouri; and to Sam Gill, Archivist of the Margaret Herrick Library of the Academy of Motion Picture Arts and Sciences, Los Angeles. Many colleagues—among them Kristin Thompson, Janet Staiger, Tino Balio, Phil Rosen, Guiliana Muscio, Francis Couvares—have made invaluable contributions to the ideas under discussion in this essay; but my greatest practical and intellectual debt is to Ruth Vasey, for exploring the research material used here with me, for organizing and explaining it to me, and for correcting the worst of my mistakes.

1. Quoted in Henry Stephen Gordon, "The Story of David Wark Griffith," *Photoplay* 10 (1916), in Harry H. Geduld, ed., *Focus on D. W. Griffith* (Englewood Cliffs, N.J.: Prentice-Hall, 1971), 42.

2. Father Daniel A. Lord, S.J., *Played by Ear* (Chicago: Loyola University Press, 1956), 263.

3. Birchard, working from DeMille's records, quotes a production cost of approximately $1,265,283. Robert S. Birchard, *Cecil B. DeMille, Program Notes For a Three-Part Film Retrospective*, American Museum of the Moving Image, New York, January–August 1989. Quoted in Piero Spila and Vito Zagarrio, *Il Più Grande Spettacolo del Mondo: Cecil B. DeMille, la Paramount, la formatzione di Hollywood*. Mostra Internatiozionale del Nuovo Cinema Rassegna Internationzionale Retrospettiva (Rome: Di Giacomo Editore, 1989), 139.

4. Charles Higham, *Cecil B. DeMille* (New York: Dell, 1973), 134.

5. For other accounts of this process, see Lea Jacobs, "Industry Self-Regulation and the Problem of Textual Determination," *The Velvet Light Trap* 23 (1989): 4–15; and Richard Maltby, "'Baby Face,' or How Joe Breen Made Barbara Stanwyck Atone for Causing the Wall Street Cash," *Screen* 27, no. 2 (1986): 22–45.

6. Richard H. Campbell and Michael R. Pitts, *The Bible on Film: A Checklist, 1897–1930* (Metuchen, N.J.: Scarecrow, 1981).

7. The Church at Work," *Homiletic Review* 85 (1923): 205. Quoted in Rolf Lundén, *Business and Religion in the American 1920s* (Westport, Conn.: Greenwood, 1988), 74.

8. Jason Joy to Will Hays, July 14, 1926, Public Relations File, Motion Picture Association of America Archive, New York (hereafter MPAA).

9. Quoted by Lamar Trotti, "The Bible in Motion Pictures," typescript of article, 1925, Trotti, L—Special Articles File, MPAA.

10. Bruce Barton, "How it Came to Be Written," *The Man Nobody Knows: A Discovery of the Real Jesus* (Indianapolis: Bobbs-Merrill, 1924).

11. Roderick Nash, *The Nervous Generation: American Thought, 1917–1930* (Chicago: Rand-McNally, 1970), 148.

12. Barton, *The Man*, 9.

13. Donald Hayne, ed., *The Autobiography of Cecil B. DeMille* (London: W. H. Allen, 1960), 245, 252.

14. Nash, *Nervous Generation*, 150–52; Carey McWilliams, "Aimee Semple McPherson: 'Sunlight in My Soul,'" in Isabel Leighton, ed., *The Aspirin Age 1919–1941* (New York: Simon and Schuster, 1949), 55.

15. Nash, *Nervous Generation*, 150–52.

16. McWilliams, "Aimes Semple McPherson," 59–60.

17. Ibid., 51.

18. Nash, *Nervous Generation*, 152.

19. Ibid., 149–50.

20. T. J. Jackson Lears, "From Salvation to Self-Realization: Advertising and the Therapeutic Roots of the Consumer Culture, 1880–1930," in Richard Wightman Fox and T. J. Jackson Lears, eds., *The Culture of Consumption: Critical Essays in American History 1880–1980* (New York: Pantheon, 1983), 4, 13.

21. Robert Moats Miller, *American Protestantism and Social Issues 1919–1939* (Chapel Hill: University of North Carolina Press, 1961), 31.

22. Lears, "From Salvation to Self-Realization," 13–14.

23. Lears derives the idea of the decline of Christianity in the late nineteenth century producing a condition of "weightlessness" from Nietszche. T. J. Jackson Lears, *No Place of Grace: Antimodernism and the Transformation of American Culture, 1880–1920* (New York: Pantheon, 1981), 41.

24. Robert S. and Helen Merrell Lynd, *Middletown: A Study in Modern American Culture* (New York: Harcourt, Brace & World, 1929), 406.

25. Lundén, *Business*, 58, 65.

26. *The Christian Herald* 46 (1923): 265, quoted in ibid., 63.

27. Miller, *American Protestantism*, 22.

28. Lundén, *Business*, 36.

29. Ibid., 80; Miller, *American Protestantism*, 31.

30. Lundén, *Business*, 58, 70.

31. Miller, *American Protestantism*, 25.

32. Thomas F. Opie, "How We Use Motion Pictures: Some Suggestions for Parishes," *The Churchman* 139, no. 3 (1929): 15.

33. Lundén, *Business*, 74.

34. Herbert Parrish, "The Break-Up of Protestantism," *Atlantic Monthly* 139 (1927): 301, quoted in Lundén, *Business*, 58; "Selling Religion," *The Literary Digest* 70 (1921): 28–29, quoted in Lundén, *Business*, 76.

35. Barton, *The Man*, 65.

36. Ibid., 16.

37. Ibid., 179.

38. Ibid., "How it Came to Be Written."

39. Lears, "From Salvation to Self-Realization," 33–37. Other useful analyses of Barton

and *The Man Nobody Knows* are Leo P. Ribuffo, "Jesus Christ as Business Statesman: Bruce Barton and the Selling of Corporate Capitalism," *American Quarterly* 33 (1981): 206–31; and Warren Susman, "Culture Heroes: Ford, Barton, Ruth," in *Culture as History: The Transformation of American Society in the Twentieth Century* (New York: Pantheon, 1984), 122–49.

40. Lundén, *Business*, 103–4.

41. Ibid., 37.

42. Don C. Prentiss, *Ford Products and their Sale: A Manual for Ford Salesmen and Dealers in Six Books* (Deteroit, 1923), book 5, 581, quoted in Sigmund Diamond, *The Reputation of the American Businessman* (Cambridge Mass.: Harvard University Press, 1955), 138.

43. DeMille, *The Autobiography of Cecil B. DeMille*, ed. Donald Hayne (London: W. H. Allen, 1960). 253.

44. Ibid., 254.

45. Barton, *The Man*, 34, 37.

46. Lears, "From Salvation to Self-Realization," 31.

47. Report on Cecil B. DeMille's *The King of Kings*, submitted by Daniel A. Lord, S.J. to the Catholic National Welfare Council," n.d. (November 1926). From Folder, "DeMille, King of Kings," Daniel A. Lord, S.J. papers, Jesuit Missouri Province Archive, St. Louis.

48. Ibid.

49. Lord to Reverend John J. Burke, C.S., National Catholic Welfare Council, n.d. (March 1927). Folder, "DeMille, King of Kings," Lord papers.

50. DeMille, *The Autobiography of Cecil B. DeMille*, 256.

51. Will Hays to Albert Warner, September 5, 1992. 1922 Civil Committee File, MPAA.

52. Will H. Hays, *The Memoirs of Will H. Hays* (Garden City, N.Y.: Doubleday, 1955), 559–68.

53. Minutes, Executive Committee of the Committee on Public Relations, MPPDA, March 10, 1923. 1923 Civil Committee File, MPAA.

54. E.g., Mrs. Newton D. Chapman, Chairman, Committee on Better Filmes, National Society, Daughters of the American Revolution, to "Better Films Chairmen of DAR chapters in and Near Philadelphia," September 26, 1927. 1927, Production Distribution File, MPAA.

55. Lamar Trotti, "The Attitude of the Church toward Motion Pictures," typescript of article, no publication reference, 6. 1925 Trotti, L. Special Articles File, MPAA.

56. Hays lists a variety of terms by which he was identified, and suggests that the popularity of "Czar" was "due to the fact that a single column of type has room for only four of the largest size used." Hays, *Memoirs*, 329.

57. *The Public Relations of the Motion Picture Industry: A Report by the Department of Research and Education, Federal Council of the Churches of Christ in America* (New York, 1931), 147.

58. Press release to Protestant newspaper, March 23, 1926. 1926 Federal Council of Churches File, MPAA.

59. Andrews to Hays, June 14, 1926. 1932 File, MPAA.

60. *The Motion Picture* 3, no. 2 (1927): 6.

61. *The Motion Picture* 3, no. 3 (1927): 3; *The Motion Picture* 3, no. 4 (1927): 6.

62. S. Parkes Cadman to Will Hays, June 10, 1927. 1927 Production-Distribution File, MPAA.

63. DeMille, *The Autobiography of Cecil B. DeMille*, 258. Birchard, quoted in Spila and Zagarrio, *Il Più*, 139.

64. Higham, *Cecil B. DeMille*, 137–38.

65. Memoranda by Jason S. Joy, May 20, 21, 1927, and letter, Carl Milliken to Joy, August 20, 1927. *The King of Kings* File, Production Code Administration Archive, Margaret Herrick Library, Academy of Motion Picture Arts and Sciences, Los Angeles.

66. DeMille, *The Autobiography of Cecil B. DeMille*, 252.

67. *The Motion Picture*, 3, no. 4 (1927): 6.

68. DeMille to Hays, October 13, 1927. 1927 Production Distribution File, MPAA.

69. Milliken to Senator Alfred M. Cohen, president of B'Nai B'Rith, November 22, 1927. 1927 Production Distribution File, MPAA.

70. *Variety,* April 7, 1916.

71. Milliken to Hays, December 14, 1927. 1927 Production Distribution File, MPAA.

72. Flinn to DeMille, December 23, 1927. 1927 Production Districution File, MPAA.

73. Andrews to Milliken, October 4, 1928. 1928 Church and Drama Association File, MPAA.

74. *The Public Relations of the Motion Picture Industry,* 148.

75. For an account of the relationship between the MPPDA and the Catholic Church in the early 1930s, see Richard Maltby, "'Grief in the Limelight': Al Capone, Howard Hughes, the Hays Code and the Politics of the Unstable Text," in James Combs, ed., *Movies and Politics: The Dynamic Relationship* (New York: Garland, 1993), 133–82.

*Lea Jacobs*

# Industry Self-Regulation and the Problem of Textual Determination

As the film industry has become the object of detailed historical investigation, it has provided new ways of thinking about the problems of film analysis, and prompted a reconsideration of how we might utilize the analysis of texts as historical evidence. Using economic modes of analysis, historians such as Douglas Gomery and Janet Staiger have challenged accepted notions about the structure and operation of the studio system.[1] One justification for this kind of research is that it offers the possibility of understanding film in terms of the institutional constraints upon its production. The importance of the study of the industry, in this view, is that it supports and in part determines filmic conventions.[2] The investigation of industry self-regulation poses the question of textual determination in a particular insistent way. That is, an explanation of the rhetorical manifestations or "work" of censorship involves not only an examination of specific cases (for example, an empirical description of how censors revised certain films), but, more generally, a conception of the industry as the site of a discursive logic. In sketching out this logic I seek to provide an account of how the administration of censorship functioned at the level of representation, as a set of rules that governed the production of meaning. Further, I propose to consider the problems of theory and method that subtend this project. For while obviously, as a point of *fact*, the industry makes films, this does not clarify the explanatory status and utility of the *idea* of the industry in the analysis of films.

The discursive ramifications of censorship cannot be understood outside the social context that gave it direction and force. Self-regulation was a function of the interplay between the film industry and a loose coalition of reform groups and state regulatory agencies. Of these groups, the most frequently cited is the Catholic Legion of Decency, which proposed a boycott in 1934 and is often said to have forced the industry to adopt

From *The Velvet Light Trap*, no. 23 (1989): 4–15. Reprinted (revised) by permission of the author and University of Texas Press. All rights retained by the University of Texas Press.

stricter controls on production. However, Garth Jowett has shown that from the mid-1920s the industry was also confronted by a number of women's and Protestant groups that objected to films on moral grounds and sought reform through the creation of a federal censorship board.[3] And while the industry faced opposition from groups which posed the threat of federal regulation, it also had to contend with existing state regulatory agencies. The *Film Daily Yearbook* of 1933 lists state censorship boards in Florida, New York, Massachusetts, Kansas, Ohio, Pennsylvania, Virginia, and Maryland.[4]

The Motion Picture Producers and Distributors of America (MPPDA), the film industry trade association, served to mediate points of social conflict between the industry and various external regulatory agencies. I would emphasize that in doing so it served the industry's political and economic interests. The MPPDA was able to enact industry-wide policies of censorship only insofar as these benefited the film production companies by serving as a means of defense against external threats.[5] Thus, the MPPDA sought to institute censorship in order to stave off the passage of regulatory legislation (it also maintained a vigorous lobby for this purpose) and help producers avoid interference by state agencies in the distribution and exhibition of features.

While the MPPDA acted on behalf of its member companies, it must be noted that studio personnel resisted its efforts to regulate production. The MPPDA case files are a record of internecine squabbles: producers and directors engaged in prolonged debates with censors and, in the early 1930s, sometimes put films into production without giving the MPPDA the opportunity of review.[6] The conflict between individual producers and their trade association may be explained in terms of a distinction between the short-term economic interests of production firms and the long-term collective interests of the industry. One can safely assume that individual producers were motivated by short-term interests—the maximization of box office receipts for single features. And, in the perspective of the short term, no single film was likely to bring on the passage of regulatory legislation or provoke drastic action by reform groups. There were grounds for conflict then, insofar as individual firms did not need to respond to the threats which confronted the industry as a whole over time.

In economic terms, then, self-regulation may be seen as a function of the industry's attempt to protect its own long-term interests; an attempt to anticipate and circumvent the difficulties posed by state censorship and the groups that complained about the morality of films. However, this account of the social and economic forces that motivated regulation does not account for the forms it assumed—the steps that led from social pressures to alterations in texts. For this it is necessary to provide some account of MPPDA policy and procedure, of the implicit and explicit rules that governed the process of revising films.

*Figure 11. Clara Bow in* Call Her Savage *(Fox Film Corporation, 1932)*. Courtesy of the Wisconsin Center for Film and Theater Research.

Until the past decade, when the MPPDA's files became available to researchers, the most extensive description of the MPPDA's policy and procedure was Raymond Moley's *The Hays Office,* published in 1945.[7] As his arguments have been widely accepted and have retained their currency, they should be summarized in some detail. Moley focuses on the Production Code, a statement of industry policy proposed by the MPPDA and adopted by the industry in 1930.[8] Moley explains the function of the Code in terms of what may be considered a legal model of self-regulation. Like a law, the Code is thought to provide a series of prohibitions or constraints on production (it contains a list of topics to be avoided and a "Reasons" section justifying regulation as such). According to Moley, these prohibitions could not be "enforced" prior to 1934. The Studio Relations Committee, a division of the MPPDA, was charged with censoring films to ensure that the studios abided by the Code. And, by an agreement reached in 1930, the studios were not to release any feature that did not meet with the Studio Relations Committee's approval. However, when a disagreement would arise between the committee and a producer, an appeal would be made to a panel composed of other producers—the so-called Hollywood Jury. Since the jury usually decided in favor of its fellow producers, the recommendations of the Studio Relations Committee were easily ignored. The situation changed following the Catholic Legion of Decency campaign of 1933–34. Hays was able to negotiate concessions from producers which made it possible to enforce the Code. The Studio Relations Committee was reconstituted as the Production Code Administration under Joseph Breen and the Hollywood Jury was eliminated. Moley claims that as of 1934 the Production Code Administration had the power to bar a film from exhibition in any theater owned by or affiliated with any member company of the MPPDA. I would add that until 1948, Paramount, Warners, RKO, MGM, and Twentieth Century-Fox, all members of the MPPDA, owned 77 percent of the important first-run theaters in the United States.[9] Implicit in Moley's argument, then, is the notion that the Code could be enforced because in the final instance a producer could not get access to the major, first-run release outlets without the approval or "seal" of the Production Code Administration.

Moley's argument hinges upon the idea that censorship was backed up by the capacity to restrict the circulation of discourse. But I find it unlikely that the Code was simply "enforced" in the manner of a law through the exercise of the power of restraint. Such an argument runs counter to the evidence that has become available to us since the publication of Moley's book in 1947: the MPPDA case files; the memoirs of a Hollywood censor, *See No Evil*; and the unpublished oral history conducted with Geoffrey Shurlock, a member of the Production Code Administration.[10] Further, considered as a model, it seems to me that the quasi-legal conception of censorship does not do justice to the peculiarities, the *specificity* of the system of self-regulation.

Moley's account leads us to expect that the office responsible for censorship in the early 1930s, the Studio Relations Committee, was substantially powerless, unable to conduct successful negotiations with producers. However, my examination of case files from this period reveals that the committee was a vigorous organization. It employed at least five, possibly six men. Its director, Jason Joy, experienced at least moderate success in persuading producers to make changes in films. And, while one might surmise that the events of 1933–34 put the Production Code Administration in a better position vis-à-vis the studios than the Studio Relations Committee had been, there is no evidence that the Production Code Administration regularly blocked the exhibition of films produced by the major studios. In direct opposition to Moley's argument, Geoffrey Shurlock, who worked under Breen in the Production Code Administration, claims that censors could not refuse to pass a film (withhold a "seal"): "No, we never refused seals. We were in the business of granting seals. The whole purpose of our existence was to arrange pictures so that we could give seals. You had to give a seal."[11] Shurlock's remarks make sense if one considers the economics of industry self-regulation. While the MPPDA was charged with protecting the long-term interests of the industry, it would hardly be considered desirable to wreck profits in the short term by preventing the exhibition of a complete film.[12] Thus, it is not likely that this kind of regulatory measure was adopted as a matter of MPPDA routine.

I am not interested in exposing the "errors" in Moley's history but in demonstrating the difficulties inherent in conceptualizing MPPDA policy and procedures along quasi-legal lines. The powers of and limits on self-regulation differ markedly from those of state or civil censorship bodies. It is important to distinguish between the two if we are to account for the specificity of self-regulation as a process. State censors, who are more or less independent of the film companies with which they deal, are in a position to prevent exhibition. And short of banning a film, they can alter its editing by excising segments at will from a final print. In contrast, the censors for the MPPDA were rarely in a position to block exhibition. Further, they exercised most power while films were in the planning stages rather than in the review of completed features. This description of the Production Code Administration's operating procedure by Jack Vizzard, who worked under Breen, gives a sense of the importance of preproduction:

> "Huddle" was the heart of the Code operation. . . . It started at ten o'clock sharp, like assembly call. It was nothing more or less than a story conference, in which the staff members reported on the scripts they had read on the previous day. It was during the huddle that decisions were made and lines of strategy were drawn up as to how this problem would be met, or that riddle dealt with. After the huddle, the staff members scattered and went their separate ways, some to studios for knock-down-drag-out fights with producers, some to write letters on scripts they had covered, and some to plunge into yet another script. Keeping up with the endless flow of scripts that poured through the office was like trying to run up a hill of sand. While the main body of the work was done on the scripts before the productions reached the sound stages, the right was always reserved to see the picture also.[13]

Vizzard's reference to the daily meeting of the Production Code Administration as a "story conference" points to one of the basic differences between self-regulation and state censorship. Self-regulation was an integrated part of film production under the studio system. Industry censors were in a position to request revisions in scripts and, in consultation with writers, directors, and producers, to effect changes of narrative. I take this to be Shurlock's meaning when he says, "The whole purpose of our existence was to *arrange pictures* so that we could give seals" (italics mine). This is very different from a power of restraint—blocking exhibition, "cutting things out" of films. Censors participated in the decision-making process by which the studio hierarchy orchestrated and controlled production. And they achieved their ends, within this hierarchy, by means of more or less successful negotiations.

What remains unclear, however, is how the various social forces that confronted the industry influenced the process of negotiation concerning specific films. If one abandons the idea that the Production Code Administration simply "enforced" the code through the power to restrain exhibition, then it becomes necessary to propose an alternate explanation of how the social relations between the MPPDA and external groups and, in particular, how the Catholic Legion of Decency campaign of 1934 determined censorship. This is possible if we assume that censorship, as a defensive operation, operated at the level of the text and that it sought to modify films that posed some threat to the industry's political and economic interests. The process of self-regulation may then be described in terms of two distinct but related stages. The first stage, evaluation, consisted in a number of procedures for isolating films or elements within films likely to offend reform groups or provoke action by government regulatory agencies. In fact, the case files indicate that the MPPDA employed a number of procedures for directly anticipating how external agencies might react to films. It regularly collected data on material cut by state boards and reviewed letters of complaint from reform groups. Indeed, in one letter, Hays states that the head of the Studio Relations Committee is supposed to be an expert on the boards and be able to anticipate their responses. Further, his decision, in 1932, to hire the head of the New York state censor board in an important position within the Studio Relations Committee can be seen as an attempt to acquire expertise in dealing with state censors.[14]

The second stage of censorship consisted of negotiations between the MPPDA and film producers. The MPPDA's object in these negotiations was to find some way of forestalling the anticipated complaints and minimizing the cuts that would be required by the state censorship boards. However, as a rule, producers did not want their films altered. They sought to retain potentially offensive elements, presumably in an effort to maximize their profits. Thus this stage of censorship, what Vizzard refers to as "knock-down-drag-out fight with producers," may be characterized as an attempt to compromise between the aims of the MPPDA, seeking to eliminate potentially offensive material, and the aims of producers, who sought to preserve this material.

It should be noted that this model of the process of regulation does not posit a direct relationship between the demands of external agencies and the form assumed by censorship in any given case. In particular, I would depart from the claim, advanced by historians such as Garth Jowett and Robert Sklar, that after 1934 censorship reflected the values and beliefs espoused by the Catholic Legion of Decency.[15] To be sure, after 1934, the MPPDA was particularly moved to respond to the Legion, but, in terms of the model proposed here, regulation did not entail the simple assimilation of the demands of this or any other pressure group. This is for two reasons. First, in any given case the MPPDA employed devices for antici-

*Figure 12. Joseph Breen (seated), head of the Production Code Administration from 1934 to 1954 with Geoffrey Shurlock, his assistant and successor (to 1966). Courtesy of the Academy of Motion Picture Arts and Sciences.*

pating or projecting what would offend external agencies. Theoretically it could be, and in fact it sometimes was, wrong in this anticipation. Even after 1934 the MPPDA released films that offended the Catholic Legion of Decency and were given a "Condemned" rating.[16] Second, even if the MPPDA perfectly anticipated the demands of external agencies, censorship proper consisted of a series of compromises between it and producers. The utopian, impossible ideal of self-regulation was to forestall criticism while at the same time allowing the producer maximal use of his original material. In practice there was continual tension, a kind of push–pull, between conflicting aims or tendencies. Thus censorship as an institutional process did not simply reflect social pressures; it articulated a strategic response to them. And this strategy was worked out on a case-by-case basis before films went into production.

The usefulness of strategy as a concept and a metaphor for censorship is that it explains the logic of determination in terms of tendencies—a dynamic interplay of aims and interests—rather than having to posit a cause (i.e., the Catholic Legion of Decency) which unilaterally produces an effect (i.e., the enforcement of the Code). The model allows for, indeed leads us to expect, a certain variation from film to film since there would be some latitude in defining problems and arriving at compromises. Yet it is possible to account for periodization in these terms. As a matter of routine, censors and producers would work out compromises that permitted some representation of material defined as potentially offensive. Certain compromises would thus become institutionalized, repeated with slight variation, from film to film. These *routines* were altered following the events of 1933 and 1934. In the face of burgeoning public criticism of the industry, censors were in a position to negotiate relatively more extensive revisions of films and scripts. Joseph Breen, in particular, refined the definition of what was acceptable under the Code. So, producers needed to devise and employ a new set of representational strategies in order to justify or defend what censors deemed potentially offensive. Thus, when I claim that censorship was "stronger" after 1934 I employ the word in a theoretical sense; there was a more far-reaching transformation of offensive material.

In illustrating how the process of self-regulation operated throughout the 1930s I have drawn examples from a specific genre, the fallen woman cycle, sometimes called the "kept woman story" or the "sex picture" by industry censors. The idea of genre necessarily enters into the model of determination proposed here. The fallen woman cycle was singled out as a type of story for women about deviant female sexuality. Much of the conflict between film producers and the MPPDA over these films resulted from the attempt by producers to maintain time-worn melodramatic conventions such as the heroine's sexual/moral fall through adultery. Thus to some extent the process of self-regulation was governed by the existence of previous texts, which exerted their own pressures on the production process. This also seems to hold true for other genres, such as the gangster film, which both producers and censors recognized as a type posing its own particular problems.

Frequently, the process of negotiation between industry censors and producers was resolved through the use of indirect modes of representation. Consider, for example, the entry on adultery in the Production Code. "Adultery and illicit sex, sometimes necessary plot material, must not be explicitly treated or justified or presented attractively." The code allowed for adultery, then, provided it was not condoned and, moreover, not made explicit. Offensive ideas could survive at the price of an insta-

*Figure 13. "The image of the heroine alone on the streets is used to imply the possibility of prostitution": Ruth Chatterton accosted by a stranger in* Female *(Warner Bros., 1933).*

bility of meaning. In practice, however, the compromise of an indirect mode of representation met with resistance from the studios, which generally sought to *reduce* ambiguity wherever possible. Thus, there was constant negotiation about how explicit films could be and by what means (through the image, sound, language) offensive ideas could find representation.

The process of negotiation is most evident at two levels: in the treatment of dialogue and the construction of blatantly offensive scenes or sequences (although the correspondence indicates that these debates were often linked to more general discussions concerning the overall trajectory and content of the story). Words such as "prostitute" and "kept woman" were routinely eliminated, not only because the expressions were considered offensive in themselves but also because they marked the heroine's status too bluntly. While it was possible to make a film about a kept woman, it was not considered advisable to call attention to this in dialogue. Thus, relatively more oblique means of indicating her status became a point of negotiation and eventual compromise. For example, in the case of *The Easiest Way* (MGM, 1931), the studio asked the Studio Relations Committee if the phrase "immoral woman" was acceptable. Further, prior to 1934, problems of language were frequently bypassed

*Figure 14. Before the elided rape scene in* The Story of Temple Drake *(Paramount, 1933).* Courtesy of the Wisconsin Center for Film and Theater Research.

through the use of music or visuals, which were not as closely scrutinized either by the Studio Relations Committee or the state boards. For example, in numerous films of the period, among them *Baby Face* (Warner Bros., 1933), *Call Her Savage* (Twentieth Century-Fox, 1932), *Faithless* (Paramount, 1932), *Pick Up* (Paramount, 1933), and *Female* (Warner Bros., 1933) the image of the heroine alone on the streets is used to imply the possibility of prostitution.

In contrast with these problems of language, the negotiations concerning specific scenes revolved around the *visual* depiction of material defined as offensive. Most obviously, the sex act could not be shown along with a number of related actions—seductions and, frequently, money changing hands. Prior to 1934, the studio would generally resort to a rather calculated use of ellipsis in such cases. Paramount's *The Story of Temple*

*Drake* (1933), an adaptation of William Faulkner's *Sanctuary*, provides a particular neat example. The novel describes a rape in which the impotent Popeye employs a corn cob. Censors would have preferred that this incident be written out of the screenplay entirely, but the studio found a way to retain at least a portion of the original plot. A plot device is contrived so that, at the moment of the rape, the lights suddenly go out. While the spectator's vision is blocked, a woman's scream is heard. The film then cuts to another scene. The ellipsis clearly serves to circumvent cuts by the state boards—the rape has already been removed, in the sense that it is not made visually explicit. While the Studio Relations Committee agreed upon this method of filming the rape, negotiations between industry censors and producers concerned how far the film could approach Faulkner's version, even by suggestion. James Wingate, an industry censor, reports on the negotiations: "The rest of our suggestions were concerned principally with the details whose elimination might help prevent those who are acquainted with the book from reading into the picture elements which the studio has already taken pains to remove."[17] Specifically, there was a question about whether or not to include a shot of a corn cob before the blackout. This example indicates, then, something of the continual interplay between industry censors, who strove to eliminate certain offensive ideas through ellipsis, and the studio, which generally strove to find some way of suggesting what could not be directly filmed.

The change in self-regulatory policy after 1934 is rather subtle, for there were many points of continuity between the two administrations. But under Joseph Breen the Production Code Administration virtually eliminated one of the basic characteristics of the films of the early 1930s—the play upon indirect means of representation to suggest what could not be explicitly shown. Thus, considering the representation of the sex act, Breen writes in a letter to Hays that it may be suggested but "must not be openly and explicitly established by detailed dialogue or action, particularly not immediately preceding or immediately following the actual transgression."[18] His prose is somewhat confusing here, but Breen seems to assume a case in which the sex act is elided. He refers to what is possible in the scenes that surround the "actual" transgression. These scenes cannot allude to the action that has been omitted. Thus, for example, the rape in *The Story of Temple Drake*, in which the scene prior to the ellipsis clearly shows the man advancing upon the woman, would not have been permitted under the redefinition of policy. In general, after 1934, ellipsis, in and of itself, is no longer seen as an adequate means of defense, and industry censors begin to initiate discussion concerning how it operated within a given sequence to suggest certain ideas or actions.

An examination of fallen woman films made after 1934 indicates that they do figure adultery, seduction, and other forms of illicit sexuality. But the instability of meaning which was a consequence of MPPDA policy in the early 1930s becomes much more pronounced in this period.

Often, it remains possible to interpret scenes or sequences in sexual terms, but this interpretation is not confirmed and is sometimes explicitly denied through action or dialogue. For example, in *Camille* (MGM, 1937), Marguerite goes to the country with her lover, Armand. The scene of the couple's arrival at the farmhouse in which Armand carries her over the threshold suggests that they spend the night together. However, in the next scene (the next morning), she is shown alone in her bedroom while it is announced that he has taken up a separate residence at an inn. Hence, the film sets up an interpretation in one scene that it denies in a later one.

The Production Code Administration also seems to have been more careful than the Studio Relations Committee in monitoring the nonverbal aspects of the scene. Prior to 1934, ideas that were occluded at the level of dialogue or action could be emphasized at other levels of significance. After 1934, censors devote relatively more attention to set design, performance, and what Breen calls "tone." Breen reports to Hays that the increase in office staff enabled the Production Code Administration to undertake the review of costumes and set construction.[19] He further notes the importance of atmosphere in the evaluation of films: "Low tone alone may render a whole production unacceptable. The location of scenes and the conduct, the demeanor, the attitude of the players enter very much into the question of the flavor of the appeal of the right or wrong presented."[20] An example of the change in routine occurs in the case of *Private Number* [Twentieth Century-Fox, 1936). The heroine's fall is precipitated by a man who takes her to what the script calls a "gambling house," where she is subsequently arrested on a morals charge. Nowhere is the house referred to as a house of prostitution. The point of contention between Breen and Darryl Zanuck, the producer, was the degree to which the script, and by extension the film, could indirectly suggest the nature of the heroine's liaison. Breen objected: "The house is operated by Grandma Gammon, a lady suggestive of an elderly madam. There is the trim colored maid who looks through a peephole before opening the door, Cokely's winking at the maid, the drinking of champaign in a private parlour and the painting of a voluptuous lady in a harem. All tend, in our judgement, to give this house the color and flavor of a house of ill fame."[21] Thus, even though, through the ruse of the gambling establishment, the script avoided mention of the word "prostitution," Breen moved to block the representation of this idea at the level of performance and decor.

After 1934, then, the treatment of potentially offensive material shifted in the direction of greater ambiguity. While seduction, adultery, and illicit sexuality were not forbidden as topics, it became much more difficult to call attention to such ideas even through the nonverbal aspects of the scene. As a result, in many cases, such as that of *Camille*, it is difficult for the spectator to pinpoint with certainty when or how the heroine's sexual transgression occur. In its treatment of detail, censorship thus becomes more subtle and pervasive.

*Figure 15. Robert Taylor with Greta Garbo in* Camille *(MGM, 1936): "it is difficult for the spectator to pinpoint with certainty when or how the heroine's transgressions occur."* Courtesy of the Wisconsin Center for Film and Theater Research.

While these examples do not provide an exhaustive catalog of the effects of self-regulation, they do suggest a way of conceptualizing the industry as a site of textual determination. The industry may be described in terms of an array of forces that are already in place and in conflict prior to the production of any given film. These conflicts are mobilized in the course of production and can give rise to various possible textual manifestations. Thus, instability of meaning, an effect of the process of negotiation and compromise between the MPPDA and producers, was more or less pronounced across the 1930s, and functioned at any one of several levels: through dialogue, costume and set design, montage. The power of censorship as an instrument of social control derives from the flexibility and infinite variability of this process. Pressure was constantly and "invisibly" exerted throughout the production process. And the power of censorship, especially after 1934, extended to the most delicate filiations of the text.

## NOTES

1. J. Douglas Gomery, "The Coming of Sound to the American Cinema: A History of the Transformation of an Industry" (Ph.D. diss., University of Wisconsin–Madison, 1975); Janet Staiger, "The Hollywood Mode of Production: The Construction of Divided Labor in the Film Industry" (Ph.D. diss., University of Wisconsin–Madison, 1981).

2. David Bordwell has initiated a debate on the place of historical study in textual

analysis. See "Textual Analysis, Etc.," *Enclitic* 5–6, nos. 2–1 (1981–82); Lawrence Crawford takes issue with Bordwell and Bordwell replies in "Textual Analysis," *Enclitic* 7, no. 1 (1983). See also David Bordwell, Janet Staiger, and Kristin Thompson, *The Classical Hollywood Cinema: Film Style and Mode of Production to 1960* (London: Routledge and Kegan Paul, 1985).

3. Garth Jowett, *Film: The Democratic Art* (Boston: Little, Brown, 1976), 170–71. See also Herbert Shenton, *The Public Relations of the Motion Picture Industry* (New York: Federal Council of Churches of Christ in America, 1931; rpt. Jerome S. Ozer, 1971), 106–11.

4. The boards' sphere of influence actually extended beyond their states, as Ira Carmen notes in *Movies, Censorship and the Law* (Ann Arbor: University of Michigan Press, 1967), 129: "The movie industry divides the nation into multi-state geographical areas for purposes of distribution so that each of these sectors is serviced by one exchange center. If deletions are ordered by a state censorship board the distributor . . . will simply alter the particular movie as ordered and send it along to the exhibitors within the total exchange area in its expurgated condition. Thus, before the demise of the Ohio law, West Virginia and Kentucky saw movies that had been censored in Ohio while Massachusetts' requirement carried over into Rhode Island, Vermont and New Hampshire."

5. Will Hays discusses his relationship to the industry in the late 1920s; see his *Memoirs* (New York: Doubleday, 1955), 343.

6. Jason Joy, of the Studio Relations Committee, complains about producers sneaking films past the MPPDA review board in a letter to Joseph Breen, December 15, 1931, *Possessed*, Production Code Administration Archive, Special Collections, Academy of Motion Picture Arts and Sciences Library, Beverly Hills, California (hereafter "PCA Archive").

7. *The Hays Office* (New York: Bobbs-Merrill, 1945), 77–82.

8. The text of the Code may be found in Jowett, *Film*, 468–72. Moley provides a different, and somewhat longer, version.

9. Moley, in what amounts to a celebration of Hays and the wonders of industry self-regulation, does not emphasize the majors' oligopolistic control of the first-run exhibition outlets. For a discussion of the significance of theater ownership, see Mae Huettig, "The Motion Picture Industry Today," in Tino Balio, ed., *The American Film Industry* (Madison: University of Wisconsin Press, 1976).

10. See James M. Wall, "Oral History with Geoffrey Shurlock," Louis B. Mayer Library, American Film Institute, Los Angeles, California (AFI, 1975), 209, and Jack Vizzard, *See No Evil: Life inside a Hollywood Censor* (New York: Simon and Schuster, Pocket Book Edition, 1971). The case files of the MPPDA have recently become available for research in Special Collections, Academy of Motion Picture Arts and Sciences Library, Beverly Hills, California.

11. Wall, "Oral History," 254–300.

12. Although Breen did prevent the rerelease of some early 1930s features by the major studios in the latter part of the decade, I have run across only one case in which a film was entirely closed out of major first-run release. The MPPDA sought to block the exhibition of the 1929 version of *White Cargo*. However, the film was produced in Britain by an independent, J. B. Williams, who was not a member of the Association. Significantly, the 1942 version, made by Twentieth Century-Fox, was released with MPPDA approval.

13. Vizzard, *See No Evil*, 63. Shurlock also mentions the importance of reviewing scripts prior to production in Wall, "Oral History," 126: "As usual in those days they had to take it [problematic material] out of the script before anything lurid could be even conceived. It was our policy to question everything, to be sure we had a basis to raise questions later on; we didn't want him [the producer?] asking us afterward: 'Why didn't you tell me at the script level?'"

14. Hays writes that the Studio Relations Committee personnel "ought to be able to gauge . . . the possible censorship reaction to any picture which they have seen and worked on." Letter to Jason Joy, November 18, 1933, *A Man's Castle*, PCA Archive. Also, a memo discussing possible replacements for Jason Joy notes that Joy's strengths lie in his knowledge of "previous reactions of censor boards . . . [and] facility in suggesting variations of treatment

to overcome code or censor worries." Memo to Hays from C. E. M. [Carl Millikan], June 25, 1932, Hays Collection, Indiana State Library, Indianapolis.

15. Discussing the MPPDA's pledge to "enforce" the Code in 1934, Sklar writes: "The movie producers already possessed a code of moral standards, the Production Code of 1930, which went about as far as it could toward expressing the Catholic bishops' viewpoint without converting the movies from entertainment to popular theology." *Movie-Made America* (New York: Random House, 1975), 173. And Garth Jowett writes: "By 1935 the motion picture industry was essentially under the control of a Catholic hegemony." *Film*, 256. For more recent accounts that make the same assumptions about the relationship between the Catholic Legion of Decency and industry self-regulation, see Gregory Black, *Hollywood Censored: Morality Codes, Catholics and the Movies* (Cambridge: Cambridge University Press, 1994); Frank Walsh, *Sin and Censorship: The Catholic Church and the Motion Picture Industry* (New Haven, Conn.: Yale University Press, 1996); and Gregory Black, *The Catholic Crusade Against the Movies, 1940–1970* (Cambridge: Cambridge University Press, 1997).

16. The Legion printed ratings of current releases and circulated these among its members. "C" (condemned) films were "considered to be those which, because of theme or treatment, have been described by the Holy Father as 'positively bad.'" "Explanation of Film Classifications," National Catholic Office for Motion Pictures, Library of Performing Arts, New York Public Library, New York. Shurlock discusses the case of Lubitsch's *Two-Faced Woman*, which was condemned by the Legion; see Wall, "Oral History," 249–50. A listing of films classified by the Legion shows a somewhat larger number of films given a "B" (objectionable in part, for all) rather than an outright "C" rating. Examples are *Kitty Foyle*, *Forever Amber*, *The Gay Sisters*, and *Dance, Girl, Dance*. See the fascinating "Motion Pictures Classified by the National Legion of Decency, February 1936–November 1948," Library of Performing Arts, New York Public Library.

17. James Wingate, letter to Adolph Zukor, n.d., *The Story of Temple Drake*, PCA Archive.

18. Joseph Breen, *Annual Report*, dated March 15, 1936, and covering the year 1935, in the files of the MPPA, Los Angeles.

19. *Annual Report*, February 15, 1935, in the files of the MPPA, Los Angeles.

20. *Annual Report*, March 15, 1936, in the files of the MPPA, Los Angeles.

21. Letter to Darryl Zanuck, n.d., *Private Number*, PCA Archive.

*Ruth Vasey*

# Beyond Sex and Violence: "Industry Policy" and the Regulation of Hollywood Movies, 1922-1939

Much of the attention given to the effects of self-regulation in the motion picture industry has concentrated on the Production Code and its consequences in terms of the treatment of sex and crime. Yet the regulation of Hollywood's output was actually far more broadly based than a reading of the Code would suggest. The Code was formulated in 1930 to meet specific public relations demands, especially ones that arose in connection with the introduction of sound. In practice, however, the regulatory policies of the Studio Relations Committee (SRC) and the Production Code Administration (PCA) were determined by a wider set of parameters, relating to both domestic and international issues, which were in existence well before the start of the sound period. The Production Code itself, with its particular emphasis on morality and obedience to the law, constituted only the most conspicuous subsection of industry regulation. Rather than being seen as an autonomous process, the PCA's role in guiding the representational practices of the studios can be more fully understood within the wider context of "industry policy"—a set of constraints that gradually took shape throughout the 1920s and 1930s in response to factors originating outside the industry itself.

## Domestic Concerns

The basic orientation of the PCA was determined as early as 1922, at the time when Hays established a "Committee on Public Relations" within the newly formed MPPDA. Faced with the task of improving the image of

From *Quarterly Review of Film and Video* 15, no. 4 (1995): 65–85. Reprinted by permission of the author and Harwood Academic Publishers/Gordon and Breach.

the industry prevalent among concerned and sometimes hostile sections of the bourgeoisie, Hays set about recruiting influential organizations in support of the screen by actively involving them in consultations about motion picture standards. The sixty groups that agreed to participate included such organizations as the Daughters of the American Revolution, the Boy Scouts, the General Federation of Women's Clubs, the National Congress of Mother and Parent-Teachers Associations, the YMCA, the American Federation of Labor, the Associated Advertising Clubs of the World, the Dairymen's League Cooperative Association, and the U.S. Chamber of Commerce.[1]

Catholic organizations were among the most active in maintaining contact with the industry, and by invoking their large and powerful constituencies they were able to exert considerable influence. For example, when Charles McMahon of the National Catholic Welfare Council took exception to the Vitagraph picture *Between Friends* in 1924, he was able to have the film withdrawn from circulation for additional cutting.[2] Rita McGoldrick of the International Federation of Catholic Alumnae claimed in 1926 that her organization had been able to effect changes in objectionable sequences with little resistance from the producers.[3] The practical definition of "objectionable" content embraced a number of overlapping concerns, including the treatment of Irish ethnicity and the Catholic Church itself, as well as the treatment of sex and violence. Negotiation over these issues created a precedent for Catholic involvement in the drafting of the Production Code in 1930 and for the much more public negotiations between the industry and the Catholic establishment surrounding the reorganization of the PCA under Breen in 1934. As the broadly based membership of the Committee on Public Relations suggests, however, the opportunity to negotiate over movie content was not restricted to organizations with moral or religious agendas; and in practice, the industry was willing to listen to representations from any disgruntled section of the audience that constituted itself into a lobby, whether or not that group was technically represented on the Committee. For example, in 1924 the National Billiard Association caused *Manhattan* (Famous Players-Lasky for Paramount Pictures, 1924) to be modified with cuts and retakes in response to protests on behalf of its "four million" members.[4]

In 1925 this openness to negotiation was formalized by the reconstitution of the Committee as a Department of Public Relations within the MPPDA with the Committee's former secretary, Jason Joy, as its head. Advertised as the "Open Door," it was supposed to act as a direct channel of communication between motion picture producers and the public.[5] In 1927 this department transferred to Hollywood and began its next incarnation as the Studio Relations Committee under the direction of Jason Joy and, from 1932, James Wingate. Its structure and essential function—which involved detailed negotiations with studio personnel over sensitive,

offensive, or libelous details of representation—was virtually unchanged
when it was renamed as the Production Code Administration under the
direction of Joe Breen in 1934.

The origin of these agencies in public relations initiatives illuminates their operational basis more clearly than does the aura of censori-
ousness and conventional morality with which they have subsequently
been associated. Their reason for existence was to avert trouble. Most obviously, they collated the excisions made by state and foreign censorship
boards, and warned producers about the likelihood of their products being
banned or heavily cut—"mutilated"—if their representations strayed across
certain consensual boundaries. The Production Code itself was based upon
a list of guidelines (the "Don'ts and Be Carefuls" of 1927) that were derived
from an analysis of eliminations made by censor boards over a period of
several years.[6] Beyond the immediate threat of censorship, however, the
possibility of legal action or bad publicity from commercial, political, or
even individual sources remained a matter of concern. Just as the specific
manner of the Code's administration depended upon a progressive case-
book approach in which the lessons learned from past misjudgments
guided present policy, experience also guided decisions about matters that
were formally outside the Code's jurisdiction. From 1930 such matters
were classified as questions of "industry policy" in deliberate distinction
to those matters that could be handled "under the Code."

Corporate Hollywood was particularly sensitive to pressures arising from other institutions of corporate capitalism. The advertising power
of the movies was widely recognized, and their ability to stimulate consumer demand gave them a privileged standing within the institutions
of capitalist enterprise as fashion leaders and trendsetters.[7] Abroad, Hollywood was considered to be the flagship of American trade.[8] On the other
hand, most businesses reasonably assumed that, just as strategic product
placement in motion pictures could increase profits, negative exposure
could damage their goods' chances in the marketplace. Consequently,
companies tended to be very touchy about the ways in which their products were deployed on the screen. For example, an otherwise innocuous
short comedy called *Furnace Troubles* (Fox, 1929) caused a storm of
protest from anthracite mine owners who resented its implied slight on
the efficiency of coal-fired heating. The movie's plot revolved around the
trouble a householder experienced with his smoky anthracite-burning
furnace, which constantly demanded his attention while he was trying to
play a game of cards. The operators of the minefields of northeastern Pennsylvania saw this as "propaganda circulated without disclosure of the interested parties on behalf of oil heating," and organized a local boycott
of Fox pictures.[9] The situation was only resolved after two officials from
the MPPDA personally visited the coalfields to apologize, and the movie
was withdrawn from circulation.

"Pulling" a film like *Furnace Troubles* was clearly inconvenient and expensive, but it was also a logical move in cases where mitigation of offense had to be negotiated around products that were already in the public domain. As the mechanics of content regulation became increasingly routine in the late 1920s and early 1930s, such hazards were more frequently identified before they were committed to film. During the production of Universal's *Imitation of Life* in 1935, Maurice McKenzie of the PCA was alert to at least one public relations problem other than the obviously contentious issue of race relations. He warned the studio that a proposed sequence involving a rail crash at the town of Camden could prove dangerous: "Have you considered the fact that Camden is served by only the Pennsylvania railroad and that a reference to a disastrous wreck at Camden might be resented by the Pennsylvania railroad?"[10]

The Warner Bros. property *Oil for the Lamps of China,* also made in 1935, was more fundamentally problematic in its representation of big business. It was based upon a book describing the experiences of a Standard Oil Company employee in China and his exploitation by the company. Although the studio changed the name of the company to The American Oil Company and inserted a foreword in the script that was complimentary to the oil business, Breen was still uncertain about the advisability of the project, and warned the studio to "take serious counsel before actually putting this picture into production in order to escape any possible serious criticism from some of the oil companies, if not actual litigation."[11] When Warner Bros. proceeded with the production, they worked out details of the script in close consultation with Standard Oil.[12]

Strikes and industrial unrest were also viewed by the agencies of self-regulation as problematic. During the making of Warner Bros.' *Black Fury* (1934), one of a brief cycle of films featuring industrial conflict, production supervisor Robert Lord remarked that the PCA seemed to be "extremely touchy" about the subject of capital and labor.[13] The movie involved a strike in the coal-mining industry. After consultation with Breen, the studio inserted some lines indicating that "conditions of the coal industry have vastly improved and are getting better all the time." As Breen explained, "The point here is to get in a line or two that may establish the fact that the miners have little to complain against."[14] Columbia's strike subject, *Mills of the Gods* (1934), was turned into a "family melodrama."[15] A third strike script, called *Call to Arms,* was slated for production in the same year, but the project seems to have been abandoned.[16]

By 1938 it was standard practice to decenter any material reflecting upon a particular industry in favor of an overarching love story, to the extent that Arthur Houghton of the PCA expressed surprise that the British Chamber of Shipping should object to a David Selznick project on the sinking of the *Titanic.* As he commented to Hays,

> I am positive that they are unable to see a picture as we see it, probably running for six and a half reels of love story and the incidents in people's

lives and the last reel and a half being devoted to the tragedy at sea and their reactions to it. Also the possible building up at the finish of the fact that the benefits and improvements resulting from the TITANIC disaster are the very things that stand out as making sea travel on all ships so perfectly safe today.[17]

Nevertheless, the movie (which was to have been directed by Alfred Hitchcock) was not made, illustrating the fact that the influence of industry policy was apparent not only in what eventually reached the screen, but also in what did not.[18]

The application of industry policy became more firmly set across the course of the 1930s. In 1938 the PCA took stock of the 19,000 letters of advice that it had issued since the reorganization of its office under Breen in 1934, and recorded some "general statements of policy" concerning the handling of issues that were not covered under the Code. "Professions" were treated according the following rubric:

> All of the professions should be presented fairly in motion pictures.
>
> There should be no dialogue or scenes indicating that all, or a majority of the members of any professional group, are unethical, immoral, given to criminal activities, and the like.
>
> Where a given member of any profession is to be a heavy or unsympathetic character, this should be off-set by showing upright members of the same profession condemning the unethical acts or conduct of the heavy or unsympathetic character.
>
> Where a member of any profession is guilty of criminal conduct, there should be proper legal punishment for such criminal conduct—such punishment to be shown or indicated clearly.[19]

This policy evolved from the general need to protect the industry from the disapprobation of any professional body that was apt to form itself into a lobby, from clergymen to circus workers.[20] Social workers and charity workers were among those handled with kid gloves: they came from the same stable as the "reformers," women's clubs and philanthropic organizations who were apt to lobby against motion pictures, and whom the industry was, therefore, particularly anxious to befriend. Social workers also worked with "delinquents," and, if provoked, were in a good position to accuse the motion picture industry of corrupting the nation's youth—a charge that was particularly dangerous to its public relations, and which the industry devoutly wished to avoid. In 1929, as a result of protests arising from *The Godless Girl* (deMille Productions for Pathé, 1929), the American Association of Social Workers was invited to advise the SRC on "all stories that directly or indirectly deal with some aspect of social work."[21] Joy expressed concern about a proposed characterization of a heartless social worker in *Street Scene* (MGM) in 1931,

> [T]he fight will not come from the social workers themselves, but from
> the bankers, lawyers, businessmen et al.—the very backbone of our coun-
> try who are not only interested in social work per se, but are responsible
> in every large city for the development and continuance of the commu-
> nity chest and other philanthropic functions.[22]

In this case the SRC's protests were unsuccessful, as Sam Goldwyn and the
author, Elmer Rice, insisted upon sticking to their original script, much to
Joy's dismay. By the late 1930s, however, when the mechanisms of self-
regulation had become more consistent, the "meddlesome and tyrannical"
social worker had largely dropped out of Hollywood's repertoire.

The SRC and the PCA also encouraged producers to afford particularly careful treatment to opinion-formers such as newspaper publishers
and broadcasters. Radio and the press posed a potential threat to the motion picture industry not only because they could give bad publicity to
individual projects but also because they could turn the tide of opinion
against the industry as a whole. William Randolph Hearst was a declared
proponent of federal government censorship, and was inclined to make his
opinions known in the editorial pages of his newspapers.[23] As a result the
relationship between movies and press was strained enough without producers throwing aspersions at press "barons" and reporters on the screen.
In 1930, Jason Joy expressed concern about the "rough, uncouth and unscrupulous" characterization of newspapermen in *The Front Page* (Caddo
Productions for United Artists, 1931).[24] At the suggestion of an SRC official, the film's director, Lewis Milestone, held discussions with Hearst as
part of the process of determining a treatment that would not bring about
reprisals from the press.[25]

In 1931, despite the fact that an MPPDA reviewer thought the property to be "exceedingly dangerous," Warner Bros. decided to film the newspaper story *Five Star Final*.[26] The story concerned the salacious muckraking
tactics of the "Evening Gazette," a fictional New York tabloid. The SRC advised the studio to deflect media criticism by drawing a strong distinction
between tabloids and the responsible press:

> We believe that you should make every effort to make it unmistakably
> clear that a tabloid is a paper quite separate and distinct from the usual
> paper. To do this we believe that it should be shown that the real news-
> papers of the city are unanimous in condemning the Gazette for its tac-
> tics. . . . This could be done be showing inserts of articles in the other
> papers.[27]

Unfortunately newspaper proprietors largely failed to make the distinction, and the movie was severely criticized.[28] In Boston, the mayor banned
the showing of the film "upon the urgent insistence of the editors of the
local Hearst papers."[29] Jason Joy tried to explain the need for diplomatic

handling to Darryl Zanuck, producer of *The Strange Love of Molly Lou-vain* (Warner Bros., 1932):

> As you know, the industry has been severely criticised of late by impor-tant newspaper editors and publishers for what they believe to be unfair description of newspapermen. It will take very little more to tip over the cart and have some of the strongest newspapers in the country on our necks, calling for further regulation.[30]

Advice to studios to revise derogatory characterizations of newspapermen as drunken or corrupt appeared throughout the 1930s, most conspicuously in 1937, which saw a mild flurry of newspaper subjects.[31] Breen might have liked the studios to have dropped the subject altogether, but in this case, because of the immediate bankability of newspaper properties, the PCA's influence was felt in the amelioration of negative stereotypes rather than in their abandonment. *Mr Smith Goes to Washington* (Columbia, 1939) was the subject of intense negotiation, but still managed to cause offense, both to the press and to the United States Congress.[32] In *His Girl Friday* (Columbia, 1940), a remake of *The Front Page,* the introduction of a semicomic love triangle deemphasized the theme of unscrupulous jour-nalism that had been perceived as dangerous in the original.

*Two Against the World* (Warner Bros., 1936) provides an example of a movie in which the PCA inserted "compensating" elements to bal-ance a negative characterization, in this case of a radio broadcaster.[33] The story is essentially a remake of *Five Star Final,* and involves a broadcaster who attracts the prurient interest of his listeners by hounding a woman who had been exonerated in a murder case twenty years previously. The investigation disrupts her life, causes her husband to lose his job, and throws her daughter's wedding plans into doubt. Eventually she poisons herself, and her husband shoots himself. Breen told Jack Warner that he was "gravely concerned, as a matter of policy," about the movie's impu-tations about the broadcasting industry's ethics.[34] Hays himself took an interest in the project, and asked Breen to make sure that the treatment of the broadcasting chains was "absolutely corrected":

> From what I gather of the story, it is one which will invite reprisals from the radio people—and properly so—if we present them in such a sordid and unfair light. It must be shown that there is no attack on or inferen-tial criticism of the major broadcasting chains. . . . The name of the broad-casting chain should not be anything like United Broadcasting System (UBS) or Universal Broadcasting System, or some similar name which will carry the impression that it is a nationwide broadcasting service.[35]

Breen conferred with the movie's production supervisor, Bryan Foy, "with the object of discussing the objections and finding some means of avoid-ing or eliminating them." As in *Five Star Final,* they adopted the strategy of differentiating between responsible and irresponsible elements in the industry, but this time they proceeded with less subtlety. The result was that between them they devised a new sequence to be inserted into the script:

> A scene will be played in the offices of an association of broadcasting chains and broadcasting stations. In the group will be a number of men, presumably representing the big broadcasting chains and Dr McGuire [a priest], whom we will meet earlier in the picture.
>
> The chain representing the broadcasting stations will thank Dr McGuire for bringing to their attention the reprehensible practices indulged in by the UBC and will put themselves on record, representing the legitimate radio stations and the national broadcasting chains, as not only opposed to such reprehensible tactics and wanting no part in them, but stating that they, themselves, will endeavour to bring the whole nasty business to the attention of the Federal Communications Commission in an attempt to have the license for the UBC stations revoked.
>
> The point involved here is to separate the sheep from the goats—definitely to indicate that the better type, the more legitimate, broadcasting stations do not sanction any such reprehensible practices as we know the UBC to have indulged in; to condemn these practices and to lend every possible aid to prevent such practices recurring.[36]

The sequence was scripted as follows:

> (A full shot in a council room. On the door are carved letters Association of Broadcasters. Five men, comprising the board of directors of the Broadcasters' Association, are seated in tall-backed leather chairs about an oval council table. Elderly businessmen who have about them that air of dignity and erudition becoming to a group of Supreme Court judges, they are listening with sympathetic attention to Dr McGuire, who is standing. Jim Carstairs [the husband of the wronged woman, played by Henry O' Neill] is seated alongside the doctor.)
>
> Dr McGuire (with righteous anger): Of all the deliberately vicious things for one man to do to another, I tell you gentlemen there has never been anything to parallel it. This man Reynolds has not the slightest shred of common decency.
>
> (Cut to close shot, board chairman, kindly and grey. Near him sits a board member. Both are listening to the almost impassioned doctor, expressions of wholehearted interest on their faces.)
>
> Dr McGuire's voice, continuing: He is using his broadcasting station for nothing more than personal gain, denying Mr Carstairs and his wife their inalienable right to live in peace and happiness.

*Figure 16. This scene of broadcasting heads was inserted into* Two against the World *(1936) at the insistence of the PCA to demonstrate that not all broadcasters were venal, scandal-hunting wolves and to avoid protests against Hollywood by influential mass media leaders.*

(At this point, the chairman and the board member look at one another. They are deeply impressed. Cut to full shot, council room, favoring Dr McGuire and Jim Carstairs.)

Dr McGuire, continuing: Mrs Carstairs paid her debt to society long ago for the murder of the man who had been her husband when a jury exonerated her. Reynolds and UBC must not be allowed to persecute her any longer. It's—it's *inhuman!* (then quietly) That, gentlemen is my own personal appeal to you who represent all the big national broadcasting companies.

(As he sits down there is a pause—then the board chairman rises.)

Board chairman: Dr McGuire, we have been watching Reynolds for some time. He and his kind constitute a real threat to honest broadcasting. They are known as bootleg broadcasters and operate just inside the law. We now have sufficient evidence to lay the case before the Federal Communication Commission. There can be no doubt as to the outcome—Reynolds' license will be revoked and he will be driven out of the business. As chairman of this board, I want you to know you have done us an invaluable service.

(All rise and we hear ad libs of "We've been waiting for this chance!" and "Now we've got him." The board chairman exits from the scene toward Dr McGuire and Jim Carstairs.)[37]

A version of this sequence was included in the finished film.[38]

The Code banned miscegenation in movies, but industry policy had more to say about the treatment of race relations on the screen. Southern states objected to social mingling of blacks and whites, and in order to preserve their trade such scenes were consistently altered during production. Joy's advice to Paramount concerning the script of *Morocco* (1930) was typical:

> The dressing of the cafe scene in which you have blacks sitting with whites etc etc, wealth being the only distinction, would be modified so that the blacks and whites are not seen together. In this connection Madame Cesare ought to be a French lady rather than a Moor.[39]

In the event there is some ethnic diversity, but Madame Cesare does appear to be French. In *I Am a Fugitive from a Chain Gang* (Warner Bros., 1932) the script originally depicted a prison housing a majority of blacks. Following advice from the SRC that "the preponderance of blacks makes the section unmistakably Southern," and therefore an indictment of Southern penal practices, the proportion of blacks to whites was reversed.[40]

Technically, warnings issued relative to matters of industry policy and probable official censorship action were merely cautionary, whereas pronouncements relative to the Code were binding. In practice, however, the distinction was often lost. The industry's "formula" for approving books and plays for picturization was an aspect of industry policy that predated the Code by three years, and was partly, but not wholly, subsumed by it in 1930,[41] leading to a certain blurring of administrative boundaries; and a resolution adopted by the MPPDA in 1935 concerning the handling of crime in motion pictures, and another adopted in 1937 concerning the depiction of drinking and drunkenness, seemed to fall between the stools of Code and industry policy jurisdiction. In any case, in terms of the *mechanisms* of self-regulation, the SRC and PCA routinely negotiated the treatment of corporate and "professional" matters alongside sexual, criminal, and "gruesome" subjects. However, because they were not central to contemporary public discourses about the potentially harmful effects of the screen, industry policy matters were handled with less fanfare than those that concerned morals or the law. The industry's main public relations problem in the 1920s and 1930s was the widespread conviction that children would be "coached" in sophisticated, violent, or antisocial behavior through their attendance at motion pictures;[42] the specific form of the Production Code itself, with its well-publicized strictures about "detailed" sexual and criminal representations, was largely designed to appease these anxieties. On the other hand, there was no particular public relations advantage to be gained by advertising the industry's accommodating attitude toward big business, the political process, or isolated lobby groups; indeed, it was important that the cooperative stance of the major producers should not be seen as impeding the "freedom of the screen," particularly when the industry was anxious to convince the Justice Department that it was not in breach of federal antimonopoly statutes.[43] Consequently, the areas of industry regulation that were designed to respond to pressure from limited (if powerful) constituencies were subject to little publicity, even though they constituted a significant proportion of the work of the SRC and the PCA.

## International Concerns

The industry's cautious approach to its treatment of subject matter was not confined to its domestic market. Between the World Wars, foreign revenues consistently accounted for about 35 percent of Hollywood's gross income, and the major companies had learned by the mid-1920s that trade negotiations could not be divorced from the issue of motion picture content. Just as the American industry had to persuade its domestic audiences that its products were neither morally nor economically damaging, its domination of the markets of the world depended, at least in part, upon its ability to convince foreign censors and trade representatives that its output was culturally inoffensive and ideologically neutral.[44] The argument could not be made exclusively at the negotiating table; it had to be made in the movies themselves. Well before the formulation of the Production Code, the MPPDA instituted procedures for scrutinizing Hollywood's products for potential causes of adverse foreign reaction, and began negotiating with producers over appropriate strategies for the treatment of motion picture subjects with international implications. Indeed, the business transacted at the inaugural board meeting of the MPPDA on April 13, 1922, included a resolution to "do everything possible to prevent the production of any new motion picture films which present the Mexican character in a derogatory or objectionable manner,"[45] which was designed to overcome a boycott of Hollywood films by the Mexican government.

More usually, contact between American producers and foreign governments in the early 1920s took place in the context of specific projects filmed abroad. The cultivation of official favor was important in these instances not only because it expedited practical matters surrounding production but also because it helped to counter foreign resistance to the American product by promoting benign and cooperative trade relations. The MPPDA initially offered its assistance not through its public relations wing nor even through its Foreign Department, but through the

Office of the President, with Will Hays himself being involved in making top-level contacts. In 1923 he personally enlisted the help of the Italian ambassador in the Rome-based production of *The Eternal City*, produced by Samuel Goldwyn for First National:

> I called up Prince Caetani, the Ambassador to the United States from Italy, and I told him we wanted to make this picture correctly. I asked him if he was interested. He came to New York the next day and we spent the afternoon together. Three times he visited me. He appointed a represen-tative, and for three weeks, this representative sat with the producer, the scenario writer and the director developing the scenario for *The Eternal City*. A member company went to Italy to make the picture. We employed a foreign princess that they picked out at a high salary and we made a picture that pleased Italy, pleased Mussolini himself; and we told the story of Italy as Italy would have it told, that all other nations might un-derstand it.[46]

In Goldwyn's version of the Hall Caine story the hero became a lieutenant of Mussolini, and the violent revolutionary ending of the book was re-placed with a peaceful one. Shots of Mussolini and King Victor Emanuel were introduced "as if cajoled by Goldwyn himself into making guest appearances."[47] The publicity for the picture emphasized the fact that it was filmed "at Rome, Italy, and New York, with the Co-operation of the Italian Government."[48] Similarly, in 1924 Famous Players-Lasky produced the comedy *Madame Sans-Gene*, starring Gloria Swanson, with a number of scenes being shot in and around Versailles. Through the good offices of Hays and the State Department they secured the cooperation of the French Embassy in Washington, and endeavored to make the production pleasing to the French.

Hiring Versailles was all very well for a foreign-produced super-production, but offense to overseas markets stemmed mainly from insen-sitivity and bad judgment in pictures routinely made in Hollywood.[49] Where high-level protests from diplomatic missions were involved, these cases, too, were usually handled by Hays. For example, in 1926 MGM's desire to rerelease their 1921 hit *The Four Horsemen of the Apocalypse* led to discussions between Hays and the German ambassador and "at least a dozen" conferences between Hays and the acting consul general.[50] At the end of World War I the industry had turned out *The Claws of the Hun* (Thomas H. Ince Corp. for Paramount Pictures, Players-Lasky, 1918) and *The Hun Within* (F-4 Picture Corp. for Paramount-Artcraft, 1918), but in 1926 Germany was a significant source of foreign revenue, providing just over 5 percent of foreign income. Moreover, in the previous year Germany had implemented the first of many European experiments in combating America's dominance in their home markets. Known as the Kontingent, the German initiative required, in substance, that only as many films could be imported as were produced in Germany. Since the terms of the

Kontingent could be reviewed at any time, the German market required particularly sensitive and diplomatic handling. MGM not only agreed to numerous eliminations in *Four Horsemen*'s U.S. rerelease negative, but also constructed a separate version—a precaution that was not unusual in the silent period. (The flexibility of the silent medium meant that foreign accommodations could be carried out as much in distribution as in production; a movie could withstand considerable modification before it became totally incoherent.) In the new version the content of the original was "rearranged" so that "it is still a good picture but so altered in regard to the German elements in it that it is so pleasing to Germany that the German representatives want it shown in Germany."[51] Chaplin's *Shoulder Arms* (Chaplin Pictures for First National, 1917) was another film that, when reissued by First National in 1927, had to be brought into line with the MPPDA's standards of diplomacy: a sequence showing Chaplin single-handedly capturing the kaiser, the crown prince, and General Hindenberg was entirely eliminated.

New productions were also handled with caution, as can be seen from the example of *The Woman Disputed* (1928), produced and distributed by United Artists. The original play by Denison Clift, set before and during World War I, had the French heroine submitting to the lustful advances of a German officer in order to secure the freedom of her five companions, one of whom was an important French agent disguised as a priest. When her fiancé, an American soldier, learned of the reasons behind her sacrifice the show ended happily.[52] The play was reviewed as a matter of course by Jerome Beatty, a member of the New York staff, in October 1926. He reported that the material was unsuitable for motion pictures for three reasons: the heroine was an ex-prostitute, one character was a spy disguised as a priest, and the villain was a German of the "typical Hun" variety: "It would offend the Germans, the Catholic Church and all the women's clubs. I don't think there is any way to patch it up so that it could be made into a picture that would get by."[53] Nevertheless, although the German consul general warned Hays that such a production "might easily spoil all your and our efforts to bring about peace and cooperation on the field of film production and film presentation,"[54] Joe Schenck announced plans for a movie adaptation. His formula for maintaining international good will was simple:

> The girl will be an Austrian girl, the hero an Austrian and the villain a Russian. It will be laid at the time when the Russian army marched into Austria and there will be nothing in the picture that either Austria or Germany could have any objection to.[55]

The film was finally released in this version in 1928.

While the modifications to the plot of *The Woman Disputed* were doubtless a comfort to Germany, they betrayed scant regard for the feelings of the Russians. The reason why this was of little concern to either

*Figure 17. In* The Woman Disputed *(1928), Norma Talmadge played the (originally French) Austrian girl, who agrees reluctantly to sleep with a villainous, lustful (originally German) Russian officer (Arnold Kent) to save her compatriots. Their nationalities were changed to avoid offending the Germans.* Courtesy of the Museum of Modern Art/Film Stills Archive.

Schenck or Hays was that in the mid-1920s, Russia, unlike the capitalist nations of Europe, welcomed American films and erected no barriers to their importation. Apparently unperturbed by the U.S. Department of Commerce's claim that Hollywood movies were the "silent salesmen" of American capitalism, the Soviets were engaged in rebuilding their own industry with profits generated by exhibition of mainly imported films.[56] Since the state had monopolistic control of the business, the Soviets did not have to reconcile the conflicting demands of producer and exhibitor lobbies, and their trading position was non-negotiable and free of contingent arrangements. As a result, they did not wield any bargaining power about the nature of the product they received, and could be vilified by Hollywood producers with impunity.[57] In any case, the Russian market was never a lucrative one for the Americans. In 1925, when exports to that country were at their highest level (comprising 241 features, or 59 percent of the total exhibited in the Soviet Union) the total value of the films was only $10,500.[58] The Soviets did not recognize international copyright conventions, and, although Hollywood distributors took the precaution of sending them positive prints rather than negatives, unauthorized duping reduced the value of the market.[59]

When the SRC moved from New York to Hollywood in 1927, it began to assume responsibility for alerting producers to potential causes of trouble abroad. At first, foreign concerns constituted a particularly conspicuous area of the Committee's regulatory activities, as they were handled in a comparatively ad hoc way. However, since foreign censors often objected to the same kind of material that caused problems in the United States—typically criminal, moral, and sexual matters—the integration of foreign and domestic matters was a logical step toward greater bureaucratic efficiency. By 1930 the process of content regulation within the SRC had become relatively streamlined. Jason Joy and his staff kept production files on individual films, and on "each foreign country with which we usually have trouble,"[60] assisted by member companies' reports and information supplied by the MPPDA's Foreign Department.[61]

Colonel Frederick ("Ted") Herron, the Foreign Department head, gradually assumed responsibility for articulating the interests of the foreign market. From the late 1920s he was in daily contact with foreign trade and diplomatic representatives, and conducted much of the diplomatic negotiation that had previously been conducted by the Office of the President, although Hays occasionally stepped back in when particularly sensitive matters were involved. Herron kept an eye on material acquired for production and alerted Joy to potential foreign hazards, often contacting producers himself from his New York office when he detected dangerous materal. The convergence of his work at the Foreign Department with the activities of the SRC is exemplified by his contact with producers over French sensitivities in 1928.

Early that year the French had proposed aggressive quota legislation (similar to the Kontingent), with the intention of limiting American access to their market. Hays visited Paris in March, and managed to have much of the sting removed from the measures by threatening to boycott the market. In reaching agreement on compromise measures he specifically offered as a bargaining chip the assurance that the American industry would make no films derogatory to the French.[62] It was thus essential that appropriate tact be demonstrated in the treatment of French themes. An especially sensitive point was Hollywood's representation of the French Foreign Legion. *Beau Geste* (Paramount) had been a great box office success in 1926, and producers saw considerable mileage left in the Legion's romance and exoticism. From their point of view the Sahara was a mythical landscape of the heart, like the American West. Unfortunately, the French were wont to interpret Foreign Legion movies more literally, and saw *Beau Geste* as an insulting slight upon their methods of colonial administration. Herron had difficulty communicating their sensitivity to producers. As he commented in exasperation upon the release of *Plastered in Paris* (Fox, 1928), a Foreign Legion spoof starring the comedian Sammy Cohen, "The French Foreign Legion is one thing that you cannot burlesque under any circumstances, any more than you can burlesque the English Royal Guard. We have nothing in this country that corresponds to those outfits which are old and have traditions that they consider sacred."[63]

*Figure 18. On "exotic" location to shoot Universal's* Foreign Legion *(1928). Universal had to make cuts and change a villain from French to Russian (again) to receive tepid French approval, after* Beau Geste *had earned French animosity.* Courtesy of the Museum of Modern Art/Film Stills Archive.

*Beau Geste* had been the subject of diplomatic protests, and French officials had attempted to stop its exhibition in many centers around the world. Its Paramount sequel, *Beau Sabreur* (1928), seems to have been developed with this experience in mind, since there is no record that it caused any trouble. In March 1928, however, Universal brought out *The Foreign Legion*, containing scenes of brutality just as bad as those which had caused the uproar over *Beau Geste*. The imitation of a proven money-spinner by a rival studio followed the usual logic of production cycles, but from the point of view of foreign relations it was a show of exceptionally poor timing. Upon viewing it, Herron wrote urgently to N. L. Manheim, Universal's export manager:

> I don't think it is necessary to tell you that if this film is issued with this material in it that you will not only hurt your own company in France, but will hurt the whole American industry throughout the world as a result of the agitation which will follow this. At the present time, the French are in the midst of passing a decree which gives them the privilege to do just about anything they want with the films. They can prohibit a company from doing business in their country if they feel so inclined. I feel so strongly on this film that I hate to even show it to the

French Ambassador in its present condition. However, before releasing it in any condition, I would suggest that it should be sent to Washington and shown to the French Embassy, because just as soon as this is released in any form at all we are going to have a bad reaction in the French newspapers.[64]

The picture was shown to representatives of the MPPDA and the U.S. Department of Commerce in Paris,[65] and they advised against its release in case it jeopardized their negotiations with the French government. Robert Cochrane of Universal cabled Hays that he would reedit the film in any manner requested, even shooting new scenes if necessary, but would not consider permanently shelving a negative worth a quarter of a million dollars.[66] Finally the changes were made, apparently to everyone's satisfaction, although the French commercial attaché could not be persuaded to put his approval in writing. Herron was particularly pleased, as he wrote to Joy in May:

> Someone is certainly to be congratulated in Universal on having done a beautiful piece of work in cleaning up a very bad picture. When I say bad, I mean, of course, from the French standpoint. The work in this picture is cleverly done, and I believe they have eliminated all the points that were so strenuously objected to by the French attachés, and smoothed the edges off so that they still have a story and a film just as good as the original one which will not cause a frightful kick back.[67]

One of the changes in the new version was the renaming of the villain Arnaud, a Foreign Legion officer, as Markhoff, demonstrating again the representational price paid by the Russians for failing to impose conditions on their American purchases. The Russification of the villain was being adopted as a more or less routine practice in the interests of avoiding offense to other Europeans, although sometimes plots had to be considerably contorted in order to accommodate their presence. For example, Herron's suggestion of a Russian locale seems to have been a less than perfect choice for Universal's proposed production *Grease Paint* (1928):

> This may or may not cause objection from the Austrians. They are very sensitive people and one never knows what they are going to object to. . . . In Austria we are under a contingent system already. If possible, I would suggest that this locale be switched to Russia where there is not a chance of a protest. I realize, of course, that the Viennese waltz and the atmosphere may make this impossible, but it is better to lean backwards in a proposition of this sort than to go ahead and take a chance on stirring up bad publicity.[68]

In this case the difficulties presented by introducing a Viennese waltz to a Russian locale were insurmountable, for the movie was never made.

A scenario typical of those that met an early death at the hands of the SRC was Universal's property, *I Take This Woman*. The company submitted the synopsis for review in June 1928, declaring with a hint of hollow confidence that "It is a war story, involving Austria and Italy, and while we do not see any possible objections that might arise in any part of it, still we would appreciate it if you would give us your opinion."[69] The story involved a beautiful Austrian girl who came under threat from various brutal Austrians and Italians. Joy wrote to Hays that he was "naturally a little worried because of the international angle," and suggested that Herron might take it up with the Italian consul;[70] however, upon reading it Herron decided that it would be "inadvisable to even present the script to the Italian Ambassador in present form."[71] Joy proposed that he hold a conference with Universal about the matter, but the idea was carried no further.

The American fate of the English picture *Dawn* (British and Dominion Film Company, distributed in the United States by Columbia, 1928), depicting the wartime heroism and execution of Nurse Edith Cavell, demonstrated that caution was exercised in distribution and exhibition as much as in production. The German embassy contacted both the MPPDA and the Department of State when they heard that the picture was in production, and attempted to gain assurances that it would not be imported into the United States.[72] There were no grounds for any official exclusion, but Herron assured William Castle, the assistant secretary of state, that there would be no trouble:

> Confidentially, the members of this organization have all agreed not to touch this film. . . . Our motion picture companies have too much money invested in Germany and returns from the German market are too valuable for them to take a chance in stirring up ill feeling against them by taking on anything of this sort.[73]

Although Herron judged the finished film to be completely harmless the boycott stood and the movie received only limited distribution by nonmember companies.

In some cases strong representation of national groups within the United States blurred the line between domestic and foreign public relations issues. The Italian ambassador was apt to protest to the industry at the behest of both Italian Americans and the Italian government. The Irish represented a powerful combination of interests, the least influential of which was the Irish state. When the MGM picture *The Callahans and the Murphys* (1927) was forced out of circulation on the grounds that it was "a gross insult, deliberate or otherwise, to the ancient faith and culture of the Irish people,"[74] "Irish" was interpreted as a synonym for "Catholic," and the main agent behind the wave of protest was the National Catholic Welfare Conference.[75]

The studios took a financial gamble when they ignored the advice of Joy and Herron. In the case of *The Gallant Gringo* (1928), MGM worked with Herron on a treatment that was (unlike the original) inoffensive to Mexico and the countries of South America. When the picture was released, however, it contained all the dangerous sequences that the company had agreed to eliminate. The result was that it had to be withheld from circulation and modified at considerable expense to the studio.[76] Other movies were put into release only to be stopped or abridged by censor boards. Such cases demonstrated the value of Joy's advice not just in terms of "good will," but also in terms of dollars and cents. In 1928, when the majority of films produced by the "organized industry" were made without reference to the SRC, they suffered, by Joy's count, 2,839 eliminations at the hands of censor boards:

> It is roughly estimated that the loss in production costs of the scenes eliminated, amounts to $3,540,000, to say nothing of the probably greater amount which has failed to reach the companies because of "total rejections" and pictures so badly censored as to cause them to "flop." This does not take into consideration the 1,927 titles which have been eliminated or changed. This indicates, of course, that we have hardly started, but it also indicates that with its proper development it may be possible to save our companies a vast amount of money and worry, providing we are able promptly and positively to give them the information they require, and assuming they will act upon the information, once received.[77]

An inevitable result of the work of the SRC was the narrowing of the field of representation normally attempted by filmmakers. After losing money on the script of *I Take This Woman*, Universal was unlikely to buy another story with equally contentious European elements. Joy or Herron only had to request the substitution of a Russian for an Austrian so many times before scenario writers beat them to it; and even the Foreign Legion was hardly worth the bother when the same stories could be told with impunity on the Western frontier. To this extent, self-regulation can be seen as equivalent to a kind of generic pressure that channeled aspects of representation into certain safe, well-defined, and well-worn paths.

Simply switching the action from one place to another was not always an adequate strategy to render a movie unobjectionable. As Hays remarked to the SRC in 1933, "I note the change of locale of *Tampico* to Northern Africa and while that will no doubt avoid the Mexican angle we must watch that it does not inject, in lieu thereof, a French angle."[78] Some nations, notably the Chinese and certain Latin American countries, increased their leverage over Hollywood in the 1930s by instituting diplomatic agreements with some of their trading partners, according to which they mutually agreed to ban movies that either party found offensive.[79] When Warner Bros. decided to produce a third remake of Porter Browne's *The Bad Man* in 1937 they decided to avoid trouble with the Mexican government by moving the location to China, only to run into considerable difficulty with the Chinese consulate both during the film's preparation and at the time of its release as *West of Shanghai*.[80]

One solution was for the studios to avoid the overt representation of any existing political entities, just as they routinely avoided references to actual corporations, as well as the "explicit" treatment of sexual and violent scenes. The "mythical kingdom" was a favorite device to fictionalize foreign locales, as in the Marx Brothers' invention of Freedonia (*Duck Soup*, Paramount, 1933). However, many "mythical" settings inevitably suggested actual locations by the choice of landscape, dress, customs, or accent. For example, in trying to remove *The Command to Love* (Universal, 1930) from the dangerous territories of France and Spain the company considered placing it in "a mythical kingdom or Russia or some kingdom where it will do no harm,"[81] to which Herron suggested Belgra and Slavia "because of their similarity to Belgrade and Yugoslavia."[82] *The Merry Widow* (MGM, 1932) is set in the fairytale kingdom of Marshovia, which is nevertheless identified as lying on the border between Hungary and Romania. The country's self-consciously fictional status is comically underlined in the opening shot of the film, in which it can only be discerned in an "establishing shot" of a map of Europe with the aid of a magnifying glass. In *Only Angels Have Wings* (Columbia, 1939), the country of Barranca is literally a banana republic, a "port of call for the South American banana boats." While containing the full range of stereotypes that were guaranteed to irritate South American diplomats—quaint but filthy streets, musical peasants, sultry and exotically dressed women—it avoided direct protest through the nominally fictional nature of the locale.

In such cases it was essential that the movie offered no evidence to definitely tie it to any actual location, leaving audiences responsible for drawing their own conclusions. The importance of this is demonstrated by the example of the Pathé picture *Her Man* (Pathé Exchange, 1930), in which the process of fictionalizing the location malfunctioned. *Her Man* was a variation of the "Frankie and Johnny" story, about a prostitute whose life is ruled by her pimp. The story was updated for the movie, and in order to avoid American censorship problems Pathé decided to place it in Cuba.[83] The details pointing to the identity of the location were routinely removed, and by the time the movie was reviewed by the SRC's James Fisher he was able to pronounce it to be reasonably censor-proof:

> The police who figure at points during the picture are the only definite characterizations which hint at the Spanish background. There should be no objection on this score however since the setting is never definitely placed. The rest of the characters are all Americans, or else unlabelled.[84]

This pedantic emphasis upon the literal details of representation in *Her Man* was typical of the modus operandi of the SRC's reviewers (in the case of *Dracula* [Universal, 1932] Fisher recorded that "Dracula is not really a human being so he cannot cause any trouble"),[85] as well as of the censors

*Figure 19. A café scene from* Her Man *(Pathé Exchange, 1930). The Studio Relations Committee insisted that the film have no definite clues about its Cuban location. Unlike this studio set, location footage of Morro Castle in the film, reproduced in posters, outraged the Cuban embassy and created problems for the MPPDA.* Courtesy of the Museum of Modern Art/Film Stills Archive.

and government officials whom they sought to satisfy. In the case of *Her Man*, however, he was guilty of an apparently trivial oversight that resulted in a minor diplomatic incident: he failed to recognize a stock shot of Morro Castle, a Cuban landmark, that figured prominently in one scene of the movie. Unfortunately for the studio, this picturesque scene was then picked up by its publicity men, who emblazoned it on posters along with the claim that the movie was set in the "scarlet streets of the wickedest pleasure-mad city of the Universe."[86] Understandably, the Cuban embassy immediately issued protests, which were then carried extensively in the Latin American press. Ted Herron of the MPPDA's foreign department complained to the SRC that under the circumstances the picture was left "no alibi," and that the bad publicity would give the rest of Latin America the chance to "take a shot at us."[87]

T. S. Dellahanty, the vice president and general manager of Pathé, was contrite. He told Herron that he had ordered the offending shot to be removed from all prints, including, at large expense, those already in circulation.[88] Dellahanty insisted that there had never been the remotest intention to imply that the action took place in Cuba:

> There was no intention of laying the story in Havana, as we preferred the mythical island locale and you will note, of course, that no reference to Havana or Cuba was made in any way in the dialogue used in the picture.[89]

Herron himself, as the one left to bear the brunt of diplomatic reaction in circumstances like these, was unconvinced that mythical kingdoms provided the representational safety zone that the producers desired. Commenting in 1932 on *The Pink Chemise* (unidentified) and *The Dictator* (Famous Players-Lasky for Paramount, 1922), both of which had offended Latin America—especially through the representation of American marines overthrowing local revolutionists—he claimed that "although they were placed in mythical kingdoms . . . there was no question of the customs and background used."[90] A script for *Soldier of Fortune* (Universal), which contained the same elements, was rejected outright in 1936 on the basis that "it would doubtless prove offensive to Latin American countries generally."[91]

The Production Code itself stipulated that "the history, institutions, prominent people and citizenry of other nations shall be represented fairly." The SRC at first interpreted this rather legalistically, introducing compensating scenes and characters to "balance" pictures, in the same manner as was adopted to offset protests about representation of various professions. During the production of *East is West* (Universal, 1930), Joy noted that "for every Chinese 'heavy' the writer is going to develop a Chinese hero."[92] To alleviate the Italian reaction to *Scarface* (Caddo Productions for United Artists, 1932) a scene was inserted depicting an upright Italian American character condemning the activities of the gangster protagonist. Nevertheless, neither picture managed to avoid condemnation as culturally offensive. Fisher's comment that the characters in *Her Man* were "all Americans, or else unlabelled" is significant: it was an ironic effect of the global distribution of Hollywood's product that, for safety's sake, villainy became largely restricted to either "American" (Caucasian) characters or those whose ethnic origins were sufficiently semantically confused to avoid causing specific instances of offense.[93]

The general effect of industry regulation was to encourage the elision or effacement of sensitive subjects; if the cinema of the 1930s was erotic, it was because it was suggestive, allowing the spectator a relatively free rein to impose his or her desires upon the partially completed or displaced images on the screen.[94] As Jason Joy commented, "two pictures may contain sequences identical in substance, but the one may be handled more adroitly than the other and escape the censors, while the other will be mutilated."[95] Such "adroit" handling generally took an oblique form, and its application to foreign issues marks their thorough integration into the regulatory procedures that the SRC applied to salacious, criminal, or corporate subjects for domestic consumption.

During the 1930s the SRC and the PCA applied their regulatory procedures to the vast majority of the major companies' output, establishing parameters within which cinematic "reality" could be elaborated. A survey of Hollywood titles between the World Wars might suggest that the profile of the industry's source acquisition, with its dependence upon popular literature and plays, determined its social, moral, and political outlook. In fact, source acquisition was a relatively poor indicator of the Hollywood's priorities; its cinematic worldview is revealed much more clearly by its *treatment* of subjects. For example, one major studio (Warner Bros.) derived only 5 percent of its properties from foreign sources,[96] while 100 percent of its products were subject to scrutiny for potential foreign offense. The result of such uniform treatment according to a broad range of industry policies (including the Production Code) was the creation of a broadly self-consistent, if oddly delimited, cinematic realm: stars could change movies, but the peculiar collection of moral, political, and physical assumptions governing their existence remained broadly similar. Treatments of sexuality were displaced into the amorphously erotic, while foreign nations became "mythical kingdoms," and the America of the screen was an ethnically undifferentiated nation served by oddly benevolent corporate, professional, and political institutions. To this extent Hollywood's cinematic universe, like its foreign locations (and like "Hollywood" itself), also achieved coherence as a kind of mythical kingdom. The social and personal effects of the biweekly visitation to that kingdom by a substantial proportion of the earth's population in the 1930s have yet to be calculated.

## NOTES

1. The total list of groups represented on the Committee comprised the following: Academy of Political Science, Actor's Equity Association, American City Bureau, American

Civic Association, American Federation of Labor, American Home Economics Association, American Legion\*, American Library Association, American Museum of Natural History, American Sunday School Union, Associated Advertising Clubs of the World, Boy Scouts, Boys Club Federation, Camp Fire Girls, Chamber of Commerce of United States\*, Chautauqua Institution, Child Health Organization of America, Child Welfare League of America, Colonial Dames of America, Commonwealth Club of California, Community Service, Cooper Union for the Advancement of Science and Art, Council for Jewish Women\*, Dairymen's League Cooperative Association, Daughters of the American Revolution, Federal Council of Churches of Christ in America, General Federation of Women's Clubs, Girl Scouts\*, Girls' Friendly Society in America, International Federation of Catholic Alumnae, Jewish Welfare Board, National Association of Civic Secretaries, National Catholic Welfare Council, National Child Labor Committee, National Civic Federation, National Community Center Association, National Council of Catholic Men, National Council of Catholic Women, National Health Council, National Congress of Mothers and Parent-Teachers Associations\*, National Education Association, National Safety Council, National Security League, National Society for Prevention of Blindness, National Tuberculosis Association\*, New York Child Welfare Committee\*, New York City Federation of Women's Clubs, Russell Sage Foundation, Safety Institute of America, Salvation Army, Sons of the American Revolution, United Society of Christian Endeavor, War Department, Woodcraft League of America, Women's Trade Union League, YMCA\*, Young Men's Hebrew Association, YWCA\*, Young Women's Hebrew Association. (*Note:* \* indicates two representatives.) Mrs. Frank H. Percells, Mrs. Charles S. Whitman, and Mrs. Charles Bull were on the Committee without institutional affiliation. Memo, "Committee on Public Relations," June 1922, Civic Committee file, Reel 1, MPPDA archive, Motion Picture Association, New York (hereafter MPPDA Archive).

2. A. E. Smith (Vitagraph), letter to Charles McMahon, September 25, 1924, *Between Friends* file, Reel 1, MPPDA Archive.

3. *Federal Motion Picture Commission*, U.S. 69th Cong., 1st sess., H.R. 4094 and H.R. 6233. (Washington, D.C.: U.S. Government Printing Office, 1926), 33.

4. J. J. O'Neill, memo to Courtland Smith, January 14, 1925, Protests File, November 1924, Reel 1, MPPDA Archive. O'Neill suggested specific cuts and alterations and added "At the same time, however, it might be well to let our directors know that there have been a couple of kicks about Pool Room pictures and to suggest that the directors lay off them." The only organization given short shrift was the American Association for the Advancement of Atheism, which complained about the prejudicial treatment of atheism in *The Godless Girl* (deMille, 1928). See Hays, Letter to Charles Smith (President, American Association for the Advancement of Atheism, Inc.), November 2, 1927, Protests file (1927), MPPDA Archive.

5. Motion Picture Producers and Distributors of America, Inc., *The "Open Door"* (New York: MPPDA, 1924).

6. For a discussion of the Studio Relations Committee's policy and procedures, see Lea Jacobs, *The Wages of Sin: Censorship and the Fallen Women Film, 1928–1942* (Madison: University of Wisconsin Press, 1991), esp. ch. 5.

7. See Charles Eckert, "The Carol Lombard in Macy's Window," *Quarterly Review of Film Studies* 3, no. 1 (1978): 1–21.

8. In 1926, Congress appropriated $26,000 for the formation of a Motion Picture Section within the Specialties Division of the Department of Commerce, based partly on the premise that motion pictures established a widespread demand for American goods in foreign countries. See *Hearing Before Subcommittees of House Committee on Appropriations*, U.S. 69th Cong., 1st sess. (Washington, D.C.: U.S. Government Printing Office, 1926), 302–4. In Europe, Hollywood's advertising power was a major source of concern about the international predominance of American movies. See, for example, *Minutes of Evidence to the Committee on Cinematography Films* (London: HMSO, 1936).

9. Janice Pierce (Anthracite Operators Conference), letter to Will Hays, August 8, 1929, Fox file, Reel 7, MPPDA Archive.

10. Maurice McKenzie, letter to Breen, April 3, 1934, *Imitation of Life* file, Production

Code Administration Archive, Margaret Herrick Library, Academy of Motion Picture Arts and Sciences, Los Angeles (hereafter PCA Archive).

11. Joe Breen, letter to Jack Warner, January 21, 1935, *Oil for the Lamps of China*, Warner Bros. Archive, Special Collections, University of Southern California–Los Angeles (hereafter Warner Bros. Archive).

12. The film was nevertheless banned in China. See John Harley, *World-Wide Influences of the Cinema* (Los Angeles: University of Southern California Press, 1940), 113.

13. Robert Lord, letter to Hal Wallis, May 2, 1934, *Black Fury* file, Warner Bros. Archive.

14. Breen, letter to Jack Warner, September 12, 1934, *Black Fury* file, Warner Bros. Archive.

15. Clive Hirschhorn, *The Columbia Story* (London: Pyramid, 1989), 53.

16. Breen, report to Hays, September 14, 1934, *The Gay Divorce* file, PCA Archive.

17. Arthur Houghton, letter to Hays, September 2, 1938, Prod Code file, Reel 12, MPPDA Archive.

18. Fifteen years later, Fox was able to make *Titanic*—a melodrama that conforms in every respect to Houghton's formula.

19. "Characterizations of Newspaper Editors, Reporters and Publishers in Motion Pictures," Reel 12, MPPDA Archive. Although the document is not dated, the survey extends to April 1, 1938.

20. In relation to a proposed circus fire in *Auction in Souls* (Tiffany, 1933), Maurice McKenzie of the MPPDA advised Joy's successor, James Wingate, that "the circus people have a most effective organization composed of substantial people who get at work immediately, the minute they think any wrong has been done to them." Letter, McKenzie to Wingate, February 18, 1933, *Auction in Souls* file, PCA Archive.

21. Arthur DeBra (MPPDA), letter to Jane Hoey, Welfare Council of New York City, July 10, 1929, Pathé—Godless Girl file, Reel 7, MPPDA Archive.

22. Memo, Jason Joy to Hays, April 1931, *Street Scene* file, PCA Archive.

23. See, for example, "Protect the Movie with National, Uniform Censorship" in both the *Los Angeles Times*, February 6, 1929 and the *Washington D.C. Herald*, February 13, 1929.

24. Letter, Joy to Howard Hughes, December 10, 1930, *The Front Page* file, PCA Archive.

25. Lamar Trotti, report to Hays, December 12, 1930; Joy, resume, December 16, 1930, *The Front Page* file, PCA Archive.

26. The MPPDA kept a close watch upon current plays, seeking to be forewarned about any particularly controversial material. Regular reviewers were James Fisher and, as in this case, Lamar Trotti.

27. Joy, letter to Hal Wallis, April 6, 1931, *Five Star Final* file, PCA Archive.

28. Letter, Breen to Jack Warner, February 18, 1936, *Two Against the World* file, PCA Archive.

29. Joe Breen, letter to Joy, November 5, 1931, *Five Star Final* file, PCA Archive.

30. Joy to Darryl Zanuck, December 1931, *The Strange Love of Molly Louvain* file, PCA Archive.

31. In 1937, studios were cautioned about their characterizations of newspapermen in *Love is Free* (Fox), *Behind the Headlines* (RKO), *There Goes My Girl* (RKO), *Back in Circulation* (Warner Bros.), *Exclusive* (Paramount), *Atlantic Flight* (Monogram), *Women Men Marry* (MGM), and *Nothing Sacred* (Selznick).

32. See Charles Wolfe, "*Mr. Smith Goes to Washington:* Democratic Forums and Representational Forms," in Peter Lehman, ed., *Close Viewings: An Anthology of New Film Criticism* (Tallahassee: Florida State University Press, 1990), 300–332.

33. For a discussion of the relationship between the movies and the broadcasting industry, see Michele Hilmes, *Hollywood and Broadcasting: From Radio to Cable* (Urbana: University of Illinois Press, 1990).

34. Letter, Breen to Jack Warner, February 18, 1936, *Two Against the World* file, PCA Archive.

35. Letter, Hays to Breen, February 27, 1936, *Two Against the World* file, PCA Archive.

36. Letter, Breen to Warner, March 26, 1936, *Two Against the World* file, PCA Archive.

37. Script extract included in *Two Against the World* file, PCA Archive.

38. A discussion of a comparable "compensating" scene in *Baby Face* (Warner Bros., 1933) can be found in Richard Maltby, "'Baby Face,' or How Joe Breen Made Barbara Stanwyck Atone for the Wall Street Crash," *Screen* 27, no. 2 (1986): 22–45.

39. Joy, memo to B. P. Schulberg, April 15, 1930, *Morocco* file, PCA Archive.

40. Trotti, Joy, Wilson, and Fisher, letter to Darryl Zanuck, July 26, 1932, *I Am a Fugitive from a Chain Gang* file, PCA Archive. The script was originally called *I Am a Fugitive from a Georgia Chain Gang.*

41. An executive document dated October 31, 1930, provided that

> When a member company is interested in a book or play which contains elements which should be avoided, but which book or play might possibly be produced under the Code . . . the judgement of the Association and its recommendations shall be obtained by submission of the question to the Association as to whether or not such questionable book or play should be:
>
> a. Made at all
>
> b. Made under the Authors' League Agreement
>
> c. Made in compliance with the Production Code.

The question of the suitability of such book or play "shall be a matter of discussion between the President of the Association and any member company so interested." See "Memorandum Commenting Upon Document Entitled Code, Extra-Code and Industry Regulation in Motion Pictures: A Study of the Effect of the Production Code and its Administration upon the Type and Content of American Motion Pictures, and Certain Other Basic Industry Policies and Their Current Application," June 22, 1938, Industry file, Reel 12, MPPDA Archive, 4. See also Richard Maltby, "'To Prevent the Prevalent Type of Book': Censorship and Adaptation in Hollywood, 1924–1934," *American Quarterly* 44 (1992): 554–83; reprinted in Francis G. Couvares, ed., *Movie Censorship and American Culture* (Washington, D.C.: Smithsonian Institution Press, 1996), 97–128.

42. Fears about the movies' effects upon children culminated in 1933 in the publication of the Payne Fund Studies, a series of sociological and psychological inquiries into the effects of motion pictures on youth. Conducted under the auspices of the Motion Picture Research Bureau, an organization advocating federal regulation of the industry, the studies arguably constituted the single most influential factor in the decision to publicly restructure and strengthen the office of the PCA in 1934.

43. See Richard Maltby, "The Production Code and the Hays Office," in Tino Balio, ed., *Grand Design: Hollywood as a Modern Business Enterprise, 1930–1939* (New York: Scribner's 1993), 37–72.

44. See my "The International Language Problem: European Reactions to Hollywood's Conversion to Sound," in David W. Ellwood and Robert Kroes, eds., *Hollywood in Europe: Experiences of a Cultural Hegemony* (Amsterdam: VU University Press, 1994), 68–93.

45. Cited in "Memorandum Commenting Upon Document Entitled Code, Extra-Code and Industry Regulation in Motion Pictures," June 22, 1938, Industry file, Reel 12, MPPDA Archive, 2.

46. Hays, "Foreign Relations and Anti-Censorship Activity of the MPPDA," transcript of speech (context unrecorded), April 21, 1927, MPPDA file, Reel 3, MPPDA Archive.

47. Alvin H. Marill, *Samuel Goldwyn Presents* (New York: A. S. Barnes, 1976), 35.

48. Poster reproduced in ibid., 37.

49. Director Roland V. Lee claimed these problems were largely due to ignorance on the part of production personnel: "we have not the slightest idea what happens to our pictures [abroad]." Stenographic record, "Production Economy Meeting Between Producers and

Directors," Conference of Academy of Motion Picture Arts and Sciences, July 14, 1927, 40–41, AMPAS file, Reel 3, MPPDA Archive.

50. See Hays, letter to Joe Schenck, December 21, 1926, Titles file, Reel 5, MPPDA Archive.

51. Hays, letter to Joe Schenck, December 21, 1926, Titles file, Reel 5, MPPDA Archive.

52. Ronald Bergan, *The United Artists Story* (London: Octopus Books, 1986), 34.

53. Jerome Beatty, "Daily Report," October 2, 1926, Titles file, Reel 5, MPPDA Archive.

54. Dr. G. Heuser (Acting German Consul General), letter to Hays, December 20, 1926, Titles file, Reel 5, MPPDA Archive.

55. Joe Schenck, letter to Hays, December 29, 1926, Titles file, Reel 5, MPPDA Archive.

56. See Vance Kepley Jr. and Betty Kepley, "Foreign Films on Soviet Screens, 1922–1931," *Quarterly Review of Film Studies* 4 (1979): 429–42.

57. The consistent characterization of Russians as villains did not concern the industry because it did not affect profits, and was disregarded by the State Department because the United States did not recognize the government of the Soviet Union. It is difficult to estimate the extent to which this stereotyping may have informed later political and diplomatic developments, but it is reasonable to assume that its legacy was felt during the Cold War. See Michael Paul Rogin, *Ronald Reagan, the Movie and Other Episodes in Political Demonology* (Los Angeles: University of California Press, 1987).

58. "The Outlook Abroad for 1928," *The Film Daily Year Book,* '201928, 977.

59. Sam Morris of Warner Bros. suspected that unlicensed duplicates were being made of American films that entered Russia in the 1930s, and advised Jack Warner not to send any films there for preview. Sam Morris, letter to Jack Warner, May 12, 1936, JLW correspondence, Box 59, Folder 8, Warner Bros. Archive.

60. John V. Wilson, memo to Carl Milliken, November 23, 1928, California Office file, Reel 4, MPPDA Archive.

61. Reports from the Motion Picture Section of the Commerce Department, in the form of *Commerce Reports, Trade Information Bulletins,* and a newsletter called *Motion Pictures Abroad,* were collated at the offices of the SRC and forwarded to member companies.

62. Kristin Thompson, *Exporting Entertainment: America in the World Film Market 1907–1934* (London: BFI, 1985), 119–20.

63. Frederick Herron, review, September 14, 1928, *Plastered in Paris* file, PCA Archive.

64. Herron, letter to N. L. Manheim, March 1928, Censor—Fgn file, Reel 4, MPPDA Archive.

65. These were Edward G. Lowry, who was appointed as the MPPDA's European representative in 1925, and George R. Canty, who was a special trade commissioner appointed to investigate motion picture conditions in Europe. (An MPPDA office was also established in Paris in March 1928, and Harold L. Smith, a vice consul at the American Consulate in Paris, was appointed as a Parisian representative.)

66. Robert Cochrane, letter to Hays, March 29, 1928, Censor—Fgn file, Reel 4, MPPDA Archive.

67. Frederick Herron, letter to Joy, May 16, 1928, Censor—Fgn file, Reel 4, MPPDA Archive.

68. Herron, memo, 1928, Censor—FGN file, Reel 4, MPPDA Archive.

69. E. J. Montagne, letter to Fred Beetson, June 21, 1928, *I Take This Woman* file, PCA Archive.

70. Joy, letter to Hays, June 22, 1928, *I Take This Woman* file, PCA Archive.

71. Hays, telegram to Joy, June 26, 1928, *I Take This Woman* file, PCA Archive.

72. For German diplomatic pressure exerted on the movie's exhibitors in England, see James C. Robertson, *The British Board of Film Censors: Film Censorship in Britain, 1896–1950* (London: Croom Helm, 1985), 42–44.

73. Herron, letter to William N. Castle Jr. (Assistant Secretary of State), March 26, 1928, Fgn Rel. file, Reel 5, MPPDA Archive.

74. Charles McMahon, press release through National Catholic Welfare Conference News Service, July 25, 1927, *The Callahans and the Murphys* file, PCA Archive.

75. See Francis R. Walsh, "'The Callahans and the Murphys' (MGM, 1927): A Case Study of Irish Catholic and Catholic Church Censorship," *Historical Journal of Film, Radio and Television* 10, no. 1 (1990): 33–45; also Francis G. Couvares, "Hollywood, Main Street and the Church: Trying to Censor the Movies Before the Production Code," *American Quarterly* 44 (1992): 584–616, reprinted in Couvares, *Movie Censorship*, 129–58.

76. Joy, memo to Hays, January 18, 1928, Dept. of Pub. and Ind. Rel. file, Reel 4, MPPDA Archive.

77. Ibid.

78. Hays, letter to Wingate, February 14, 1933, *She Had to Say Yes* file, PCA Archive.

79. See Ruth Vasey, "Foreign Parts: Hollywood's Global Distribution and the Representation of Ethnicity," *American Quarterly* 44 (1992): 617–42, reprinted in Couvares, *Movie Censorship*, 212–36.

80. See Ruth Vasey, *The World According to Hollywood, 1918–1939* (Madison: University of Wisconsin Press, 1997), 175–9.

81. Hays, memo, July 23, 1929, *The Boudoir Diplomat* file, PCA Archive.

82. Joy, memo, November 25, 1929, *The Boudoir Diplomat* file, PCA Archive.

83. "F.S.," report, April 10, 1930, *Her Man* file, PCA Archive.

84. James Fisher, report, August 26, 1930, *Her Man* file, PCA Archive.

85. Fisher, review, January 14, 1931, *Dracula* file, PCA Archive.

86. Herron, letter to Wilson, October 17, 1930, *Her Man* file, PCA Archive.

87. Herron, letter to Wilson, October 17, 1930, *Her Man* file, PCA Archive. To the extent that advertising constituted the principal site of offense, *Her Man* was a relatively unusual case among films that excited foreign protests. By contrast, objections to sexual themes often owed more to the advertising posters than to the movies themselves.

88. This undertaking notwithstanding, when a print of the movie from William Everson's collection was screened at the National Film Theatre, London, on July 21, 1990, it still contained the offending scene. For a discussion of the difficulties inherent in tracing the provenance of prints, see Richard Maltby, "Grief in the Limelight: Al Capone, Howard Hughes, the Hays Code and the Politics of the Unstable Text," James Combs, ed., *Movies and Politics* (New York: Garland, 1993), 133–82.

89. Letter, T. S. Dellahanty to Herron, October 29, 1930, *Her Man* file, PCA Archive.

90. Herron, letter to Wilson, April 19, 1932, *The Cuban Love Song* file, PCA Archive.

91. "Memorandum Commenting Upon Document Entitled Code, Extra-Code and Industry Regulation in Motion Pictures," June 22, 1938, Industry file, Reel 12, MPPDA Archive, 10.

92. Joy, resume, June 19, 1930, *East is West* file, PCA Archive.

93. See Vasey, "Foreign Parts."

94. See Jacobs.

95. "Resume of Dinner-Meeting of the Studio Relations Committee," Dept. of Pub. and Ind. Rel., Reel 4, May 17, 1928, MPPDA Archive.

96. Robert Gustafson, "The Buying of Ideas: Source Acquisition at Warner Bros. 1930–1949" (Ph.D. diss., University of Michigan, 1983), 81.

*Clayton R. Koppes*
*Gregory D. Black*

# Blacks, Loyalty, and Motion Picture Propaganda in World War II

White America fought World War II as a remarkably unified country. In black America, however, a strong current of apathy, and sometimes barely muted opposition to the Allies, was evident. For blacks the war brought into sharp relief their duality in American society. Franklin D. Roosevelt identified Allied war aims with democracy's Four Freedoms. But Walter White, executive secretary of the National Association for the Advancement of Colored People (NAACP), pointed out that blacks had to "fight for the right to fight" for democracy. Horace Cayton, a Chicago sociologist and black leader, posed the issue starkly in December 1941: "Am I a Negro first and then a policeman or soldier second, or should I forget in any emergency situation the fact that . . . my first loyalty is to my race?" Millions of blacks had to ask themselves that question during World War II.[1]

That potential fissure in the drive for mass mobilization alarmed wartime policy makers. As the agency charged with interpreting war aims to the public and arousing mass support for the war, the Office of War Information (OWI) played a crucial, if little known, role in trying to mobilize black support and in interpreting American race relations to an international audience. This essay analyzes the racial aspects of OWI's propaganda campaign, in particular its longest-lived and most significant effort—its liaison with Hollywood motion picture studios. Although black leaders and OWI policy makers hoped to work together to improve Hollywood's portrayal of people of color, the objectives of black leaders and those of the propagandists proved to be incompatible.[2]

The Office of War Information came into being on June 13, 1942, when Roosevelt consolidated several propaganda agencies, some of which had been in operation since 1939. Heading OWI was Elmer Davis, a pop-

From *The Journal of American History* 73, no. 2 (1986): 383–406. Reprinted by permission of the authors and the Organization of American Historians.

ular, interventionist radio commentator for the Columbia Broadcasting System (CBS) but a fledgling bureaucrat. The Agency, staffed by New Dealers and liberal Republicans, had a liberal, internationalist tone. Among its key executives were Robert Sherwood, three-time Pulitzer Prize playwright turned Roosevelt speechwriter, who was an assistant director; Archibald MacLeish, poet, playwright, and librarian of Congress, who was also assistant director until he left in late 1942; Milton S. Eisenhower, a top civil servant, who served as associate director until 1943; and Gardner Cowles Jr., founder of *Look* magazine and a key backer of Republican presidential nominee Wendell Willkie in 1940, who oversaw OWI's Domestic Branch until mid-1943, when he was succeeded by E. Palmer Hoyt, publisher of the *Portland Oregonian*. Two key figures for OWI's liaison with Hollywood were Lowell Mellett and Nelson Poynter. Mellett, former editor of the *Washington Daily News* and director of the Office of Government Reports from 1939 to 1942, headed OWI's Bureau of Motion Pictures in 1942–43; his deputy, Poynter, a journalist, ran the bureau's Hollywood office. Within OWI's liberal tent, however, the agency was riven with turf fights and quarrels over tactics, such as how much of the short, pungent imagery of the advertising world ought to be incorporated into American propaganda.[3]

Realizing how controversial and politically charged its activities were, OWI portrayed itself as simply an innocuous information agency. Elmer Davis averred that its only strategy was "to tell the truth." Archibald MacLeish believed that OWI ought simply to give the people "the facts" and let them make up their own minds. But within the agency officials discussed their role as propagandists. OWI was not a clone of Nazi or Soviet propaganda agencies, and it tried to avoid the crude caricatures of "the Hun" and the blatant atrocity stories disseminated by the Committee on Public Information (Creel Committee). OWI's approach was subtler, but Davis and MacLeish did not suppose that their job called for neutral reporting. The purpose of a propaganda agency is not to encourage quiet contemplation but to arouse people to belief and action. OWI devoted most of its efforts, not to "the facts," but to their interpretive contexts—in short, to provide a favorable field for the reception of carefully selected material.[4]

The efforts to enlist black support began with prewar interventionist groups. In June 1940 William Allen White's Committee to Defend America by Aiding the Allies urged the NAACP to join its activities. The Committee argued that fascism threatened blacks and that they had more opportunity in America that anywhere in the world. Thurgood Marshall, the NAACP's legal counsel, discounted the request. "It is the same type of propaganda that was used in the last war," Marshall said. He noted that the argument that "we must have national unity regardless of whether or not we have democracy at home" was directly "in conflict with our position." Blacks were wiser and warier for their experience in World War I.

Hoping to secure minimal improvements, they had followed W. E. B. Du Bois's call to "close ranks" and enlisted in Woodrow Wilson's crusade for democracy. Their hopes were dashed by their humiliating treatment in the armed forces and trampled in the ensuing race riots. Two decades later their suffering seemed tragically unrequired, and blacks vowed not to be used again. The pervasive structural and individual racism "curdled the morale" of blacks, wrote Alain Locke, the Howard University philosopher and social critic, in 1942.[5]

Polls taken by OWI's Bureau of Intelligence produced "formidable evidence of the degree to which racial grievances have kept Negroes from an all-out participation in the war effort." In one survey the agency's interviews asked Harlem blacks whether it was "more important right now to beat Germany and Japan or to make democracy work at home." Fifty percent of black respondents agreed that defeating the Axis ought to take priority, but fully 38 percent believed it more important to make democracy work at home. (Eleven percent were undecided.) Race, not class, was the distinguishing element. A poll of poor whites revealed that an overwhelming 90 percent gave priority to winning the war while only 5 percent chose home-front democracy.[6]

The endemic racism of Nazi doctrine made blacks shudder; by contrast the perception of the Japanese as fellow "people of color" stimulated strong positive identifications from blacks. Asked whether a Nazi victory would improve their lot, a mere 1 percent of black respondents told OWI's black interviewers that it would. Sixty-three percent believed they would be worse off. (Embitterment ran deep enough, however, that 22 percent of blacks thought their treatment would not change.) Harlem leader Adam Clayton Powell Jr. cleverly used American racism to explain Nazism: "Despite our apathy toward the war, it is not because we don't recognize the monster Hitler. . . . We recognized him immediately, because he is like minor Hitlers here. . . . The Gestapo is like the Ku Klux Klan here."[7]

The Japanese, on the other hand, were the beneficiaries of a strong current of transnational racial identification, or what OWI labeled "pan-colored feeling." A significant percentage of blacks identified themselves as "brothers of the colored Asiatics who are assailing the white man's civilization," OWI concluded. A survey carried out in early 1942 by the Office of Facts and Figures, a predecessor of OWI, asked blacks whether they would be better off under Japanese rule. Eighteen percent said the Japanese would treat them better; these blacks believed "the Japanese are also colored and, therefore, would not discriminate." Thirty-one percent said treatment would be "the same." In short, nearly one-half of the respondents believed they would be at least as well off under Japanese rule. Only 28 percent believed they would be worse off. The "don't know" category fell to 23 percent. Better-educated blacks were "more kindly disposed to Japanese rule than the less educated," probably because better-educated blacks felt the sting of blocked mobility more acutely. The contrast between the responses of blacks and those of lower-class whites was significant. Only 5 percent of lower-class white respondents believed blacks would be treated better by the Japanese, while 16 percent believed treatment would be the same; a hefty 52 percent believed the Japanese treatment would be worse.[8]

Telling impressionistic examples reinforced OWI's concern. A widely circulated story concerned an old sharecropper who, after receiving his ration of cornmeal and fatback from the plantation owner, said: "By the way, Captain, I hear the Japs done declare war on you white folks!" Black children at play showed "a pronounced inclination" to pretend they were Japanese soldiers; "they are fond of imagining that they are in a position to avenge themselves against white oppressors," said OWI. Adults often expressed satisfaction with Allied reverses. When the Japanese sank HMS *Repulse* and HMS *Prince of Wales,* Horace Cayton happened to encounter in the halls of the War Department two black messengers who sang out to each other: "We just got the 'Repulse' and the 'Prince of Wales.' Good hunting, eh?" For a black soldier, forced to ride in the Jim Crow section while on leave, the bitterness welled up: "The Japanese are our friends—they gonna look out for us. I ain't fixin' to fight no Japanese. These Japanese fighting for me. I'm gonna fight myself some crackers."[9]

Despite such graphically expressed sentiments, few blacks yearned for an Allied defeat. OWI thought blacks wanted white society "changed, not conquered." A. Philip Randolph, president of the Brotherhood of Sleeping Car Porters and spearhead of the March on Washington Movement in 1941, concurred. He found no blacks who wanted the Allies to lose, but he cautioned that many blacks "before the war ends, want to see the stuffing knocked out of white supremacy and of empire over subject peoples." America's alliance with European imperial powers created further problems for the identification of the Allied cause with democracy. Gandhi warned Roosevelt that the Atlantic Charter rang hollow so long as India remained subject and American blacks lived as second-class citizens. The cause of Indian independence in particular excited American blacks, who saw it as a struggle of fellow people of color against white domination. Transnational racial ties thus created an added dilemma for OWI propagandists.[10]

The theme of "changed, not conquered" found expression in the "Double V" campaign. Popularized by the influential black newspaper *Pittsburgh Courier,* the Double V stood for victory at home as well as abroad. The Double V went beyond the call during World War I to "close ranks," and it generated heated debate. Many whites interpreted the slogan as a declaration of conditional loyalty: "two victories or none." However radical the slogan may have sounded to the Roosevelt administration, it was in reality an attempt by moderate black leaders to channel the anger of the black masses into safer bounds. The black elite, fearing both the explosive potential of mass protest and their own loss of control, attempted to relieve hostility by directing it to democratic aspirations simultaneously with arousing support for the war effort. The Double V was not conditional but concurrent with the war effort.[11]

The agenda for victory at home was lengthy and remained mostly unaddressed at war's end. In civilian society blacks gave top priority to improved job opportunities; they observed minimal improvement, thanks in part to the Fair Employment Practices Committee, which the March on Washington Movement had wrung from a reluctant Roosevelt. Political rights seemed far away when even so basic a step as an antilynching bill died in the Senate. Polls showed that 92 percent of the public favored continued racial segregation. Blacks who volunteered for civilian-defense duty found their applications filed under "Negro and dead." Discrimination pervaded the armed forces. Organized in segregated units, blacks had to press hard to see combat, and although black units such as the Tuskegee airmen often distinguished themselves, the navy relegated them to little more than menial duty. Black soldiers had to bear such gratuitous humiliations as the segregation of black plasma and even the refusal of service in restaurants where German prisoners of war dined. Many blacks sensed an emotional bond with Japanese Americans—fellow people of color— who were interned as potentially disloyal because of their race. These indicators of indelible racism demonstrated the necessity of serious efforts to move toward racial justice, but at the same time underscored the formidable political obstacles to speedy advances.[12]

Many OWI officials believed strongly that racial discrimination was antithetical to democracy. "Any form of racial discrimination or religious intolerance, special privileges of any citizen are manifestations of Fascism, and should be exposed as such," the agency insisted in 1942. Taken at face value that remarkable dictum, imbued with the left liberalism of the 1930s, would have subjected the United States to heavy criticism. OWI evaded the dilemma by arguing that although American minorities had "not entered utopia," progress toward racial equality was possible only in a democracy, whose individualist creed contrasted with fascism's racist foundations. America might have racists but America was not racist. The propagandists read blacks' progress since 1933—perhaps too optimistically—as evidence of the evolutionary possibilities of American liberal democracy.[13]

But how to convince blacks that the war really was their fight? Reflecting contemporary social science theory, OWI analysts believed that "the prime determinant of morale within a nation at war is the identification of the individual with the community." Nothing would evoke that identification so well as concrete measures to make blacks full members of the community. Early in the war OWI officials sketched a program that would have been a down payment on "a more equalitarian society." They emphasized jobs and better treatment for servicemen, the two areas of most immediate concern to blacks, according to the agency's surveys. OWI proposed that the government set an example by hiring more black employees, appointing blacks to key positions such as membership on the board of the Manpower Administration, and energizing the Fair Employment Practices Committee. In the armed forces mixed volunteer units could be established, or separate units of white and black soldiers could constitute part of a larger combat force. Black servicemen on leave "should be guaranteed, by whatever means may be necessary, the respect due to any man" wearing the uniform. Finally, the government ought to take stands of "unqualified firmness in test cases" of black rights, in contrast to its pitiful weakness when integration of the Sojourner Truth housing project in Detroit was attempted in 1942. This program, at best a modest start toward racial justice, proved too ambitious for wartime.[14]

Instead, OWI consciously substituted propaganda for black rights. The agency adopted what Deputy Director George A. Barnes described as "in effect a direct and powerful Negro propaganda effort as distinct from a crusade for Negro rights." To blacks the propagandists stressed the ideal of unity. They cooperated with "the less extravagant" leaders, said Philleo Nash, an anthropologist who served as OWI's chief troubleshooter on racial matters. Equally strong was OWI's desire to alleviate tensions, or as Nash said, "keep the lid on," for racial tensions were already building dangerously in 1942. The agency hoped to "lower hostility on the part of whites and reduce militance on the part of blacks." Such an approach sounded evenhanded unless one remembered that blacks' rather mild "militance" was directed to the white hostility that kept them from enjoying those rights for which other Americans said they fought. OWI set out to "discreetly promote" recognition of minorities' achievements by "the dominant groups." That goal was worthwhile, to be sure, but unless coupled with pressure for black rights, it was more a holding action than a program for change. Nash conceded as much when he described OWI's goal as to "keep us out of trouble, keep pressure groups off our necks." OWI's approach was broadly compatible with the Roosevelt administration's stance toward wartime racial issues—a mixture of honeyed words and star-spangled symbolism, impassioned warnings of the fascist menace, subtle threats if cooperation were not forthcoming, and occasional concessions granted tardily and grudgingly.[15]

OWI employed what social theorist Robert Merton termed "sacred and sentimental" symbols—beliefs and opinions grounded in emotion as is characteristic of patriotic and religious feelings. Such techniques were useful because they seemed to bring favorable responses from large numbers of people. So long as that was the goal, Merton said, "the choice of techniques of persuasion will be governed by a narrowly technical and amoral criterion." That mode of operation was dangerously manipulative, he warned, because it encouraged "the use of whatsoever techniques work." Merton did not contend that all appeals to sentiment are manipulative.

But he offered a distinction that is useful in interpreting OWI's activities: "Mass persuasion is not manipulative when it provides access to the pertinent facts; it is manipulative when the appeal to sentiment is used to the exclusion of pertinent information." By employing the sacred and sentimental symbols of unity, OWI tried to manipulate opinion through denying or obscuring pertinent realities about American race relations.[16]

The challenge, as interpreted by Gardner Cowles Jr., was that "unless the Negro is made to *feel* he is part of America we cannot expect him to be a good American." OWI seized the theme of unity. Nash suggested the metaphor of "Uncle Sam's family"—diverse but equal members of the family who shared a common stake in an Allied victory. For the most part OWI tried to minimize racial consciousness. Instead of thinking of oneself as a member of a particular race, one ought to identify oneself as an American—race was incidental. OWI encouraged moviemakers to stud their cinematic combat units with symbols of America's ethnic and geographical diversity; the Boston Irish, the Brooklyn Jew, and the Kansas farm boy mixed happily. The movie's battle groups were racially integrated before the armed services were. "Uncle Sam's family" exuded prosperity. Its middle-class values were the utopia of the present; its scrubbed Main Street, leavened by a dose of New Deal social programs, the reincarnation of the presumed social cohesion and traditional values of the small town. The war was a "people's war, not a national, class or race war," OWI emphasized in a manual for the motion picture industry in 1942. Everyone would have a share of a "world New Deal"—an American cornucopia imbued with the liberalism of Henry A. Wallace's "Century of the Common Man."[17]

OWI's first attempt to appeal directly to blacks proved disastrous and ensured that the agency would stick to its theme of racial consciousness submerged in a broader American unity. In mid-1942 OWI published 2.5 million copies of the pamphlet *Negroes and the War.* The introduction, written by Chandler Owen, implied a "fight or else" threat to blacks. In contrast to fascism, America represented progress and hope. The pictorial essay depicted black progress in America, especially since 1933. The pamphlet pleased no one. Southern politicians charged that OWI was producing subversive materials; Republicans decried the New Deal "electioneering." Blacks discounted the pamphlet's message, for it ignored the issue of most direct concern to them—how and when conditions were going to improve. One black warned Elmer Davis: "Any program which attempts to improve Negro morale within the framework of the status quo without attempting to eliminate traditional methods of treating Negro citizens will be palliative, wasteful, and ineffective." Or as a black reader told an OWI interviewer: "just a bunch of baloney." Its attempt too cautious for blacks, too extreme for racists, OWI abandoned such overt pamphleteering.[18]

OWI's most significant effort to deal with the racial issue took place in its behind-the-scenes campaign to get Hollywood studios to improve their handling of racial issues on the screen. OWI ascribed great power to the movies. Davis said the "motion picture could be the most powerful instrument of propaganda in the world, whether it tries to be or not." Hollywood stood at the peak of its power. The "dream factory" ground out more than five hundred feature pictures per year. The box office recorded more than eighty million admissions per week during the war—equal to two-thirds of the U.S. population—and uncounted millions abroad imbibed impressions of America from Hollywood movies. These masses, many believed, were particularly susceptible to the power of visual images projected in a darkened room. Davis believed that "the easiest way to inject a propaganda idea into most people's minds is to let it go in through the medium of an entertainment picture when they do not realize that they are being propagandized." The movies seemed to afford an ideal field for OWI's messages. Such notions were based on a crude stimulus-response assumption that drastically simplified the complex process by which people are influenced. But Lenin—himself a master propagandist—had labeled film "the most important art," and people as diverse as Josef Goebbels, Pope Pius XI, and every Hollywood press agent concurred. The success of 1930s documentaries and Nazi propaganda films bolstered the argument that the cinema ought to serve democracy.[19]

To mobilize the movies for psychological warfare, OWI set up a branch of its Bureau of Motion Pictures in Hollywood. The liberal-left staff of the bureau found the liberal and leftist members of the film community—chiefly writers and some directors—willing to cooperate. The producers and studio heads, however, were suspicious of anything that smacked of propaganda or government interference with their hoary code of "pure entertainment." "If you want to send a message call Western Union," went Samuel Goldwyn's famous dictum. Political themes were especially dangerous. Studio executives' perceptions of the box office, augmented by the rigid production code imposed by the Hays Office in 1934 in league with the Roman Catholic Legion of Decency, cut the motion picture industry off from most potentially controversial social and political subjects. Hollywood eschewed explicitly antifascist pictures until 1939, when most of its markets in fascist countries had dried up. Those few movies that acknowledged problems in American society or politics usually affirmed the status quo by discrediting radicalism and stressing the efficacy of heroic individual action.[20]

"Pure entertainment," coupled with censorship boards in the southern states, relegated blacks to demeaning stereotypes. The studios exhibited a morbid fear of having their pictures cut or banned altogether in the South. Although that regional market was small, studios striving for the maximum market willingly molded their black characters to the tastes of the most racist part of the country. Hollywood, said screenwriter

Dalton Trumbo, made "tarts of the Negro's daughters, crap shooters of his sons, obsequious Uncle Toms of his fathers, superstitious and grotesque crones of his mothers, strutting peacocks of his successful men, psalm-singing mounte banks of his priests, and Barnum and Bailey side-shows of his religion." In the Shirley Temple vehicle *The Little Colonel* (1935), Hattie McDaniel, the archetypical mammy, said she didn't want to be free. Such docile folk had the good sense to turn away from the sinister abolitionists and carpetbaggers. Although several white women were executed as witches in colonial Salem, the film *Maid of Salem* (1933) showed only the black woman Tituba meeting such a fate. Exceptions might be noted. A black doctor, played by Clarence Brooks, helped Ronald Colman to fight the plague in John Ford's *Arrowsmith* (1931). A giant black helped hero Paul Muni to escape in Mervyn LeRoy's *I Am a Fugitive from a Chain Gang* (1932). Both pictures were made before the heavy hand of the Hays Office squelched most social comment films. At times, too, black performers, such as Clarence Muse, Bill Robinson, Louise Beaver, Hattie McDaniel, Butterfly McQueen, and the enigmatic Paul Robeson, transcended their roles by sheer force of personality. Yet they remained trapped. Civil rights organizations often protested their taking such roles, no matter how boldly they might play them. Hattie McDaniel and other established black performers feared that efforts to change blacks' roles threatened their livelihood.[21]

By the time of World War II, many blacks were no longer willing to temporize. Lena Horne, a harbinger of the new era of black performers, said that all they wanted was that "the Negro be portrayed as a normal person." An informal alliance of blacks (led by the NAACP), white liberals in the film community, and OWI began to form in 1942. Wendell Willkie played a uniquely influential role as both chairman of the board of Twentieth Century-Fox and special counsel to the NAACP. More liberal on racial issues than Roosevelt, Willkie gave a fiery speech to studio executives in early 1942 in which he pointed out the offensiveness of racial stereotypes and their danger to the war effort. Willkie and Walter White circulated among the tables at the annual Academy of Motion Picture Arts and Sciences awards dinner, visited studio commissaries, and met privately with motion picture industry leaders in their campaign to have Hollywood depict "the Negro as a normal human being and integral part of human life and activity." Many industry officials pledged to cooperate. OWI occupied a crucial position. Most studios gave extensive circulation to the agency's "Government Information Manual for the Motion Picture Industry," which explained how to present OWI's interpretation of the war. Every studio except Paramount Pictures submitted all scripts to the agency for review. Poynter and other officials of the Bureau of Motion Pictures had several standing appointments with the studios each week and carried on extensive negotiations over the scripts. OWI did not have formal censorship powers, but it gained enough influence with the Office of Censorship, which granted export licenses for movies, that by mid-1943 the propagandists' recommendations were almost always followed. Moreover, as Allied troops liberated Axis-held areas, OWI exhibited in those areas movies it approved of and held the proceeds in trust for Hollywood. To be sure, studios could make any pictures they wanted to for domestic exhibition. But as the *Motion Picture Herald*, ever zealous to protect the industry's bottom line, observed, no one would make a picture "known in advance to be doomed to domestic exhibition exclusively." Thus OWI's influence potentially could greatly assist blacks. White confidently told his constituency in 1942 that "some extraordinarily fine things are in prospect in the moving picture word . . . a new concept of the Negro." His optimism was premature.[22]

A key test case occurred in the summer of 1942 over a Metro-Goldwyn-Mayer (MGM) property entitled "The Man on America's Conscience." Although one might believe that man to be the American black, MGM thought the man who needed redress was none other than President Andrew Johnson. Released in December 1942 with the less emotionally charged title *Tennessee Johnson*, the film was a typical Hollywood "biopic." Though it was not an artistic or commercial success, the controversy surrounding its production makes it a key film for understanding blacks and wartime propaganda. Historian Thomas Cripps cites *Tennessee Johnson* as a "turning point" in Hollywood's depiction of blacks and a harbinger of the postwar alliance between blacks and white liberals.[23] OWI managed to get MGM to tone down some of the material that was most offensive to blacks—the first time Hollywood made significant changes in response to black protests. The controversy also exposed, however, the divergent aims of OWI and the NAACP. OWI tried to divert blacks' concerns into support for the war effort, and blacks were disappointed and offended.

The original script perpetuated the Hollywood tradition of sympathy for the southern point of view. Slavery evaporated. Andrew Johnson became the embodiment of Abraham Lincoln's generosity, and the former slave owners returned in glory to their plantations and to the Union. MGM daubed a thick layer of personal conflict over that backdrop. John L. Balderston, scriptwriter for the 1931 classic *Frankenstein*, turned his considerable talents with monsters to the character of Thaddeus Stevens. The Pennsylvania champion of the freedmen emerged as a crippled, demonic figure. He cajoled the helpless Johnson into drunkenness and even consorted at cards with John Wilkes Booth.[24]

Word of this impending travesty was leaked to the *Daily Worker*, whose report alarmed both OWI and the NAACP. Lowell Mellett asked MGM for the script and passed it on to Walter White. The black leader was appalled. The script glorified the president who opposed the vote for blacks, supported the notorious black codes that regimented black behavior, fought Stevens's program for the freedmen's economic advancement, and did little to curb violence against blacks. White perceived a direct

*Figure 20. Lionel Barrymore does a vivid character turn as Reconstructionist Thaddeus Stevens in MGM's Ten-nessee Johnson (1943), who became less ruthless and vindictive against the South as a result of OWI influ-ence.* Courtesy of the Museum of Modern Art/Film Stills Archive.

line from the failure of Reconstruction to the "evils which curse the South today." He cited Du Bois's *Black Reconstruction in America* (1935) and similar scholarly works. The picture would do "enormous injury to morale," he warned.[25]

The Bureau of Motion Pictures was seriously concerned about the film. Mellett told MGM that no one ought to do anything that was "apt to cause disunity or even bad feeling." He asked the studio to change the picture enough to avert trouble; if that were not possible, MGM would, he hoped, withhold the picture until the country emerged from the present crisis. That was strong medicine—or so it seemed. MGM protested bitterly, demanding whether "a minority in the country shall dictate what shall or shall not be on the screen through the Mellett office." Only war secrets ought to be considered suppressible, the studio contended. The argument was reasonable in the abstract, but it lacked credibility when coming from an industry that willingly kowtowed to the Legion of Decency and the southern censors and that blue-penciled material likely to be offensive to a variety of economic pressure groups. (Consider two examples from the Legion available: The script of MGM's version of Robert Sherwood's antiwar, antifascist play, *Idiot's Delight*—drastically altered to avoid offense to Benito Mussolini—was hand carried to Rome in 1938 for approval. When the National Coal Association protested, Warner Bros.' coal-mining saga, *Black Fury* (1934), was changed to shift the blame for labor unrest from mine operators to union radicals.)[26]

The purported alliance between blacks and white liberals did not produce a victory for blacks, however. The OWI staff wanted to improve the portrayal of blacks in the movies, but the war came first. As for the MGM picture, Nelson Poynter told a disappointed Walter White that it would be "a mistake to make a major issue of this film." Poynter explained: "We want to encourage the studios to make films with real guts, films that can cause complaint from pro Fascist minorities; therefore, I think we have to . . . register our complaints and be willing to lose a battle and win a war." The black minority could be sacrificed for OWI's larger, war-propaganda goal.[27]

OWI was also limited by its inadequate understanding of the black perspective. Even among supporters of black rights in the 1930s, awareness of black history and culture was minimal. Many historians still subscribed to the William Dunning school, which sharply criticized Reconstruction as a vindictive imposition on the white South, and to the James Randall and Avery Craven view of the Civil War, which saw the conflict as a tragic, avoidable mistake. Dorothy Jones, OWI's most perceptive social critic, concluded that the script of *Tennessee Johnson* reflected contemporary historical interpretations. Frank M. Garver, a Civil War historian at the University of Southern California, told her that historians almost uniformly viewed Andrew Johnson favorably. Thaddeus Stevens, on the other hand, was considered a "half-crazy fanatic" who was obsessed with punishing the South and who did not "'give a snap for the Constitution.'" "The Negroes had much finer friends in this period than Thaddeus Stevens," Jones reported. OWI concluded that Stevens was "a hero of the left-wingers rather than of the Negro people." Noting the origins of the controversy in the *Daily Worker*, Bureau of Motion Pictures staffers interpreted the issue as part of the Communist Party's campaign for black support. Nelson Poynter decided that it was not Stevens's championing of black rights but his desire to expropriate southern landholders that excited the Communists. As he quoted scriptwriter Balderston, "Stevens was for chasing the Kulaks off their land and this is very appealing to the Communists."[28]

When the NAACP tried to cash the pledges made by the movie industry and OWI, it found that, unlike other minorities such as the Legion of Decency and the southern box office, it could not "dictate" content. OWI had found scholarly backing for the portrayals in the film, and the communist issue had helped to discredit black protests. Moreover, the propagandists dared go no further. To have taken Walter White's position seriously would have meant exposing institutional violence against blacks and denial of their rights in order to maintain the privileged position of other groups in society. Yet those were the hallmarks of fascism, according to OWI. Instead, the propagandists mixed a selective reading of the past with hope for the future. OWI was, if anything, more chary of social problem pictures than were the studios. Poynter said he would oppose making a picture such as *The Grapes of Wrath* in wartime, even though it dealt with a widely known problem and even though Hollywood's treatment of it in 1940 drew the teeth of most of John Steinbeck's social criticism. OWI approved when the Office of Censorship banned the export of films that showed labor or class conflict in the United States since 1917.[29]

MGM reluctantly agreed to reshoot parts of the nearly finished film—an expensive operation—to soften the conflict. Thaddeus Stevens's personal villainy was reduced. The picture tried to focus on issues of principle, albeit with the embattled president clearly representing superior virtue. But the changes did not cut very deep. *Tennessee Johnson* was yet another variation on a favorite Hollywood theme—the success story. In the opening scenes the shackles are struck from the feet of Andrew Johnson, a runaway apprentice, and he begins his rapid climb from small-town tailor to political grandee. His dutiful wife represents his better nature. "A white man without property is a mudsill," he says. "We were all mudsills once," she responds. Gradually they achieve a political accord. In a final sequence they embrace on the world *equal.* Now the avatar of the common people, Johnson devotes his career to fighting those who complain he is "rousin' up the white trash and makin' levelin' speeches." As president he seeks to apply an ostensibly evenhanded idea of equality. When he grants amnesty to white southerners, he declares: "Here at this desk where Lincoln freed the slaves, I now free their masters." Shrewdly wary of Stevens, he fends off the proposal to give blacks "forty acres and a mule"—a notion made to seem purely vindictive. Played by Lionel Barrymore, Stevens, who "was originally conceived to look like the shaggy one of the Three Stooges, was slicked up a little," said *PM*'s film critic John T. McManus. The picture contains just four blacks, all of them docile servants in Washington, D.C. In one scene two blacks carry Stevens, riding a litter like Cleopatra, onto the floor of Congress. All of two lines hint of slavery. The finished product anticipated a frequent tactic when Hollywood faced OWI's racial strictures: writing out. If the portrayal of blacks was offensive, it was easier to eliminate them than to change them.[30]

OWI was greatly relieved when it saw the release print. Instead of

*Figure 21. Lena Horne as Sweet Georgia Brown and Eddie "Rochester" Anderson as a guy named Joe in MGM's all-black* Cabin in the Sky *(1942), which passed through OWI offices untouched in spite of agency liberals' complaint that the film was condescending and regressive minstrelsy. Courtesy of the Museum of Modern Art/Film Stills Archive.*

a threat to national unity, *Tennessee Johnson* had become, in Mellett's words, "a forceful dramatic exposition of the development of democratic government in this country." The film stressed the importance of achieving change through the ballot box rather than by violence. This was, of course, an ironic message for American blacks, who were systematically excluded from voting by violence. But ballots, not bullets, fit OWI's emphasis on democracy. *Tennessee Johnson* was also an allegory of "the little man in our society"—the very embodiment of the log-cabin-to-White-House myth that OWI wanted to beam to the world. The picture meshed neatly with OWI's stress on unity, but only by distorting and minimizing the central issues of race.[31]

Few shared OWI's upbeat assessment of the picture. Blacks and some leftist supporters were appalled. A star-studded cast, including Ben Hecht, Zero Mostel, Harold Clurman, Lee Strasberg, Canada Lee, Vincent Price, and Dorothy Gish, signed a public protest and asked OWI to "do everything in its power to have it scrapped." The black sociologist E. Franklin Frazier denounced it as a travesty and suggested that "perhaps white

America needs this form of hypocrisy to survive." The patient Walter White began to question the alliance with Hollywood liberals and OWI.[32]

White's fears were reinforced by the appearance of two all-black musicals in early 1943—*Cabin in the Sky* and *Stormy Weather. Cabin in the Sky* was an exaggerated fantasy that featured many leading black entertainers. Marc Connelly had withdrawn from participation in the film early on because of the burlesque he feared would develop. The Bureau of Motion Pictures' script review said blacks were presented as "simple, ignorant, superstitious folk, incapable of anything but the most menial labor" and worried the film would be "resented by Negroes" and would stimulate "already existing prejudices." But OWI's Washington headquarters dismissed its Hollywood reviewers' concerns and found nothing offensive to anyone in the picture. Liberal reviewers were disturbed when they watched *Cabin in the Sky.* James Agee was disappointed that the actors' outstanding artistic talents were sacrificed for roles as "picturesque, Sambo-style entertainers." Manny Farber praised the way in which Lena Horne, Eddie (Rochester) Anderson, and Louis Armstrong rose above the script's "religio-comic treatments." But he denounced their offerings as "well turned decorations on something which is a stale insult."[33]

*Stormy Weather,* a Twentieth Century-Fox release, dramatized the life of Bill "Bo Jangles" Robinson and featured Lena Horne and a host of other black entertainers. The picture had a turbulent production history. Musical supervisor William Grant Still, a distinguished black composer trained at the Oberlin College Conservatory, encountered repeated difficulties with the management at Twentieth Century-Fox. Still charged that producer Alfred Newman threw out his arrangements because they were "not authentic" and refused to hire the black musicians Still wanted. The composer noted sardonically: "The usual excuse in Hollywood [is] if it's Negro music it has to be crude to be authentic." The alternate musicians, he said, could barely sight-read, "clowned for the audition," and made a "pitiful" impression. An OWI review called attention to the implied segregation in the film but concluded that the film could not "possibly give offense to any group."[34]

Walter White found *Stormy Weather* dismaying. He objected to the "vulgar things" Lena Horne was called on to do, which producers would "not think of having a white actress do." Hollywood thought that where sex was concerned blacks were "primitive barbarians who never stop short of extremes." Latter-day audiences, fed on movies and television soap operas that routinely flaunt sexuality, find few extremes and little vulgarity in *Stormy Weather.* In the context of World War II, however, White's concern was understandable. He had high hopes that Lena Horne, a family friend, could break through the pervasive stereotypes and assume genuine dramatic roles. She became the first black actress signed to a long-term Hollywood contract and managed to avoid the maid or jungle roles that she and White had feared might be forced on her. "But they didn't make me anything else, either," she recalled. "I became a butterfly pinned to a column singing away in Movieland."[35]

*Stormy Weather* and *Cabin in the Sky* gave black entertainers a showcase for their talents. At the same time, however, they reinforced the reality of segregation. On the surface such films were a "whitewash," said Manny Farber, but they were "really a stab in the back." Although blacks might win occasional positive roles in wartime movies, Hollywood would truly merit respect, said Farber, only when "it brings out a movie where the central figures are Negroes living in a white majority." An OWI analysis of blacks in films released in late 1942 and early 1943 concluded bluntly that "in general, Negroes are presented as basically different from other people, as taking no relevant part in the life of the nation, as offering nothing, contributing nothing, expecting nothing." Blacks appeared in 23 percent of the films released during the period and were shown as "clearly inferior" in 82 percent of them. By early 1943 White concluded that his alliance with OWI and Hollywood liberals, which had seemed promising just a year earlier, was yielding few results. He decided to find a way to make available to the studios "authentic and unpurchased and unpurchasable advice and guidance on treatment of the Negro in the films." White's dream was a special NAACP office in Hollywood that would work with the moviemakers. Despite strenuous efforts, however, the office did not materialize.[36]

In the spring of 1943, OWI largely abandoned its efforts to change the portrayal of blacks. The agency was under sharp attack in Congress, in part because its stand on race relations, however mild, excited the ire of southern racists and the conservative coalition. Congress cut the budget of the Domestic Branch to less than 10 percent of its former size, effectively ending its operations. OWI's liaison with Hollywood continued until the end of the war. Although Nelson Poynter left with the demise of the Domestic Branch, his staff continued to operate under former journalist Ulric Bell, the representation of the Overseas Branch in the movie capital. OWI's movie reviewers jettisoned their remaining concern for domestic black opinion and instead focused on how the portrayal of blacks would affect the image of America abroad. By May 1943 George A. Barnes limited his cinematic recommendations to having occasionally a "Negro speak intelligently" and a "sprinkling of average looking Negro people" in crowd scenes or bank-teller lines. OWI thus hoped to incorporate the "sacred and sentimental symbols" of ordinary life to imply an essentially false impression to the rest of the world: that blacks were full participants in American life.[37]

Hollywood for the duration continued to treat blacks as a people essentially apart. Optimists might point to occasional successes, nonetheless. Two of the strongest portrayals of blacks occurred in *Casablanca* (Warner Bros., 1943) and *The Ox-Bow Incident* (Twentieth Century-Fox, 1943). Arguably the best known picture from the war period, *Casablanca*

*Figure 22. Humphrey Bogart as Rick and Dooley Wilson as his sidekick/bandleader Sam in* Casablanca *(1943): "though still in the cinematic ghetto of the entertainer," Sam "assumes a relatively equal role by wartime standards. OWI applauded."* Courtesy of the Museum of Modern Art/Film Stills Archive.

was notable for Humphrey Bogart's musical sidekick, Sam, played by Dooley Wilson. The black pianist, though still in the cinematic ghetto of the entertainer, assumes a relatively equal role by wartime standards. OWI applauded. But apprehensions over war-related issues submerged the positive racial features. OWI reviewers, including the prominent Hollywood writer Robert Riskin, disliked what they interpreted as Bogart's cynicism. They wanted him to announce his conversion to the Allied cause with a ringing peroration for democracy. The consequences for the tone of one of

*Figure 23. Kenneth Spencer in MGM's* Bataan *(1943), an example of a black character "almost equal" to his white fellow soldiers.* Courtesy of the Museum of Modern Art/Film Stills Archive.

the best films of the period would have been disastrous. OWI's Overseas Branch ruled the film unacceptable for export to the liberated areas of North Africa. *The Ox-Bow Incident* was a hit with the propagandists on all counts. Leigh Whipper played an affirmative role as one of a handful of men who held out against the lynching of an innocent man—a courageous action vindicated when justice in the end prevailed. Citing the "excellent characterization of a Negro" and the triumph of the judicial process, OWI ruled the picture suitable for export.[38]

Blacks escaped the old movie caricatures almost completely in some combat pictures. In *Crash Dive* (Twentieth Century-Fox, 1943) and *Sahara* (Columbia Pictures, 1943), a black played a heroic combat role in each, although *Crash Dive* followed the navy's policy of limiting blacks to menial tasks early in the war. Perhaps the greatest departure was *Bataan* (MGM, 1943), in which Kenneth Spencer added a black face to the baker's dozen of ethnically diverse GIs. Spencer is almost equal: He participates in discussions of strategy, although he speaks up only once, and then to voice his faith in the United States, not to argue tactics. He dies as heroically as the others in the face of the overwhelmingly superior

Japanese force. Yet even Spencer is not free of the stereotypes. As historian Daniel Leab observes, "he spends a good part of his onscreen time humming 'St. Louis Blues,'" and when he sets an explosive charge, he follows the instructions of his white partner, who pushes the plunger. Ironically, in this case Hollywood's ability to create a mythical world gave blacks a better deal than did real life, for there were no integrated army units at the time. The symbolism of *Bataan* conveyed a world that was still an aspiration, not a reality.[39]

Another movie that is often cited for a strong black character is *Lifeboat*, an atypical Alfred Hitchcock film of 1944. Eight survivors of a torpedoed liner, including a capitalist, a communist stoker, a woman correspondent, and a black crewman, Joe, band together for their common survival in a storm-tossed lifeboat. The symbolism is almost painfully obvious: Ideological differences are put aside, and the battered survivors proceed democratically to determine their fate in a hostile environment. Joe, well played by Canada Lee, is important in the evolution of movie blacks chiefly because he appears at all. He remains inferior. He logs less time on camera than do the others; he is treated patronizingly; his original nickname was Charcoal; and he is an adept, if reformed, pickpocket. The picture makes one unabashedly positive gesture—Joe is offered a vote on whether the Nazi submarine captain ought to be thrown overboard (Decision affirmative.) But the token is immediately undercut when Joe seems shocked at that benevolence and, perhaps suggesting that he cannot really exercise such judgment, abstains from voting. The picture was controversial, for some viewers thought the strongest character was the Nazi. *Lifeboat* was too ambiguous for OWI, which banned its export to liberated areas. Like combat films, *Lifeboat* partially escapes racial stereotypes by showing people understandably forging a unified front in the teeth of extraordinary, life-threatening conditions. In more normal circumstances blacks were not so fortunate.[40]

When the armed forces were on parade instead of at war, Hollywood resuscitated one of the most demeaning show business stereotypes—the minstrel show. Warner Bros., often considered the most liberal studio, offered a patriotic salute in 1943 with *This Is the Army*, a musical revue starring Ronald Reagan as the stage manager. Enormously popular, the picture grossed more than $5 million in its first year. The fragile plot concerned the transcontinental romance of Reagan and his girlfriend, which culminated in their military wedding outside the stage door in a Washington alley. Looking on was Reagan's beaming father, played by another actor-to-turn-politician, George Murphy. The picture, a restaging of Irving Berlin's World War I revue, *Yip, Yip, Yaphank*, with some new but outdated numbers by Berlin, seemed caught in a time warp. The movie's racial themes were virtually a throwback to the painful era of the first war. In their main sequence the zoot-suited black soldiers, made up as for a minstrel show, strut through a stereotypical Harlem set with "Dixie's" beauty shop and the "Orchid Club" gin mill. To a moderate bounce tempo, they sing "That's What the Well-Dressed Man in Harlem Will Wear":

> There's a change in fashion that shows in the Lenox Avenue clothes,
> Mr. Dude has disappeared with his flashy tie.
> You'll see in the Harlem Esquire
> What the well-dressed man will desire
> When he's struttin' down the street with his sweetie pie.
> Suntan shade of cream or an olive drab color scheme
> That's What the Well-Dressed Man in Harlem Will Wear.
> Dressed up in O.D.s with a tin hat for overseas
> That's What the Well-Dressed Man in Harlem Will Wear.
> Top hat, white tie and tails no more—
> They've been put away 'til after the war—
> If you want to know take a look at Brown Bomber Joe.
> That's What the Well-Dressed Man in Harlem Will Wear.

One man mimics playing a cello while a woman wearing an absurd costume with a garter above the knee and a big flower on a hat performs a crudely suggestive dance. Since this is an all-male revue, the soldiers dress in drag when women are needed. White GIs don the garb of Little Bo Peep and southern belles; black soldiers are done up as whores and tramps. The blacks break into the inevitable tap dance and, displaying a stereotypical sense of rhythm, dance circles around the white hoofers—figuratively, of course, for *This Is the Army* is as segregated as the real army of democracy.[41]

*Since You Went Away*, the 1944 film that David O. Selznick intended to sum up the home front, inadvertently provided a fitting epitaph for the struggle over the depiction of blacks. The picture paid tribute to women war workers, with the main character, Mrs. Hilton, taking a welding job—by now another cinematic cliché—while her husband was in the armed forces. Hattie McDaniel appeared once again as the stereotypical family cook, Fidelia. As James Agee wrote sardonically, she "satisfied all that anyone could possibly desire for a Negro in . . . restive times." Though she has to leave the household to get another job when Mrs. Hilton can no longer afford her, she returns after hours "to get in her day's measure of malapropisms, comic relief, mother wit, and free labor." The Selznick organization blanketed the black press with news releases proclaiming that the picture, in attempting to show the contributions of "all" citizens, would highlight "the colored Americans," who had not received enough attention. These handouts were cynical or perhaps merely insensitive, but neither interpretation offered much consolation for a minority group that had fought loyally for a democracy in which it had to fight for the right to fight.[42]

The struggle for a fairer depiction of blacks ended in frustration. A Columbia University study in 1945 found that of one hundred black

*Figure 24. Hattie McDaniel as Fidelia and Shirley Temple as the family's younger daughter in David O. Selznick's hymn to home-front resourcefulness,* Since You Went Away *(1944). Selznick's company promoted McDaniel's role heavily in the black press.* Courtesy of the Museum of Modern Art/Film Stills Archive.

appearances in wartime films, seventy-five perpetuated old stereotypes, thirteen were neutral, and only twelve were positive. Films had changed little since OWI's study in early 1943. Moreover, some evidence suggested that blacks were simply being "written out" of the movies. As the controversy over *Tennessee Johnson* indicated, it was easier to eliminate blacks than to create positive images. Membership in the black actors' union declined by 50 percent during the war.[43]

The relative ineffectiveness of attempts to improve the image of blacks is thrown into sharp relief when it is contrasted with the sensitivity OWI induced Hollywood to display toward Asians. Lowell Mellett persuaded Samuel Goldwyn not to rerelease *The Real Glory* in 1942. Depicting the Filipino struggle against the occupying U.S. troops at the turn of the century, the film would have been highly embarrassing during World War II. The head of the Bureau of Motion Pictures also got MGM to drop its planned *Kim*, whose glorification of British imperialism was sure to arouse widespread protest.[44]

The Chinese were the chief beneficiaries. Hollywood's stock China was a poverty-ridden land of marauding warlords, bowing Confucian scholars, and giggling peasants who spoke in riddles. That could not satisfy a propaganda agency intent on creating a powerful and modern—if mythical—China that could act as one of Roosevelt's four world policemen. MGM writers spent nearly two years drafting and redrafting a script based on Pearl S. Buck's *Dragon Seed* (1942). In early drafts the illiterate, backward peasants called a plane "an enormous flying bird," and one announced: "I come with big news in my mouth." Appalled, OWI reviewers passed the scripts to T. K. Chang, the Chinese consul in Los Angeles. When Chang talked, OWI and Hollywood listened. Vastly brighter than when MGM first conceived them, *Dragon Seed*'s peasants, though still beset by some Hollywood conventions, came to a realization of their part in the people's war of OWI. When Twentieth Century-Fox submitted its screenplay of A. J. Cronin's *Keys of the Kingdom* (1941), OWI induced the studio to change the peasants' squalid huts into "neat, little brick places with a considerable feeling of civilization about them." In other pictures OWI persuaded the studios to change their depiction of a divided China for that of a unified people intent on fighting the Japanese. For the propagandists such pictures demonstrated that "we are all bound together by a unity which transcends differences in customs and language." Sacred and sentimental symbols tried to blend East and West in an antifascist unity.[45]

OWI tried to soften verbal racial identification of the Japanese. The agency feared that racial slurs would stimulate hatred for the entire Japanese people, not just their government; it also worried that highlighting racial differences between Americans and Japanese would feed blacks' identification with Tokyo. The propagandists cautioned against the torrent of racial epithets in early wartime movies, such as the frequent references to "Nips," "slant-eyed," "yellow" "monkey," and "beasts" in *So Proudly We Hail* (Paramount, 1943). The agency succeeded in eliminating racial epithets from many pictures—for example, "East Ocean dwarfs" and "pygmies" from *Dragon Seed.* Even so august a figure as General Henry H. "Hap" Arnold, army air force chief of staff, bowed to OWI and cut his reference to "little yellow men" in *Bombardier* (RKO, 1943). But the propagandists went no further. The cinematic Japanese remained monolithically diabolical. Hollywood could conceive an occasional "good German" but never a "good Jap."[46]

OWI's intervention in racial themes had some beneficial results. Hollywood had a higher awareness of racial issues than before the war, and that was sometimes reflected in its products. Blacks occasionally stepped out of their stereotypical roles, although usually only in extraordinary circumstances. They sometimes assumed normal societal roles, although usually nothing more than crowd scenes or bank-teller lines, and then fleetingly. Those evanescent achievements had to be measured against the perhaps greater shortcomings. Some of the most demeaning stereotypes persisted—incredibly enough, even the minstrel show.

At war's end Hollywood was still a long way from the "new concept of the Negro" that Walter White had optimistically announced in 1942. White tried to interest various studios in making an epic that would trace black history from Africa to modern America, using a chief's family as its vehicle. Other people of color had had their day on the screen; Irving Thalberg's *The Good Earth* (MGM, 1937) was a classic, if cliché-ridden, panorama of Chinese life. Some producers found White's idea promising, but none would touch it.[47] Nor did OWI dare to propose such a film, for in dealing realistically with black history it would challenge the propagandists' vision of a united, democratic America. Instead, OWI used the "sacred and sentimental" symbols of unity and equality to imply that blacks were full participants in American life while they remained in fact a people apart. Had OWI cooperated fully with even the moderate black leadership, its racial message would have been strikingly different. The propagandists' vision was more benign than was the manipulation practiced by southern censors, and it held out the hope of eventual change. But until the Four Freedoms become a reality for American blacks, their loyalty would be the subject of manipulation by their self-proclaimed allies.

## NOTES

1. Walter White, *A Rising Wind* (Garden City, 1945), 145; Walter White, "The Right to Fight for Democracy," *Survey Graphic* 31 (1942): 472; Horace Cayton, "Negro Morale," *Opportunity* 19 (1941): 371.

2. This essay's interpretation of the portrayal of blacks is based on the (relatively few) motion pictures in which blacks or racial issues played a key part, especially the early test case of *Tennessee Johnson* (Metro-Goldwyn-Mayer, 1942), and on contemporary surveys of the usually minor roles of blacks in Hollywood movies generally. The essay represents a reconsideration of the authors' positive assessment of the influence of the Office of War Information (OWI) on the industry's portrayal of blacks. See Clayton R. Koppes and Gregory D. Black, "What to Show the World: The Office of War Information and Hollywood, 1942–1945," *Journal of American History* 64 (1977): 94, 104. The most complete study of OWI, which does not, however, address racial themes, is Allan M. Winkler, *The Politics of Propaganda: The Office of War Information, 1942–1945* (New Haven, 1978). David Lloyd Jones examines the OWI's worldview but not its activities to influence particular media. David Lloyd Jones, "The U.S. Office of War Information and American Public Opinion during World War II, 1939–1945" (Ph.D. diss., State University of New York, Binghamton, 1976).

3. Winkler, *Politics of Propaganda*, 8–37; Koppes and Black, "What to Show the World," 87–89. OWI was a not altogether happy amalgamation of the following agencies: Office of Government Reports, Office of Facts and Figures, Office of the Coordinator of Information, Office of Civilian Defense, and Division of Information in the Office of Emergency Management. As coordinator of Inter-American Affairs, Nelson A. Rockefeller logically ought to have been part of OWI, but Franklin D. Roosevelt yielded to the demands of Rockefeller and Undersecretary of State Sumner Welles, a personal favorite. Among the talents on OWI's roster were actor-director John Houseman, novelist Leo Rosten, journalists Alan Cranston and Robert Riskin, financier James P. Warburg, and academics Arthur Schlesinger Jr., Henry Pringle, Owen Lattimore, Ruth Benedit, John K. Fairbank, and Dick Bode.

4. For a favorable assessment of Elmer Davis and Archibald MacLeish, see Winkler, *Politics of Propaganda*, 12–13, 18–19.

5. Thurgood Marshall to Walter White, June 24, 1940, Box II A209, National Association for the Advancement of Colored People (NAACP) files (Manuscript Division, Library of Congress); Alain Locke, "The Unfinished Business of Democracy," *Survey Graphic* 31 (1942): 457; Kenneth B. Clark, "Morale of the Negro on the Home Front: World Wars I and II," *Journal of Negro Education* 12 (1943): 426; Theodore Kornweibel Jr., "Apathy and Dissent: Black America's Negative Responses to World War I," *South Atlantic Quarterly* 80 (1981), 322–38.

6. Office of Facts and Figures, Bureau of Intelligence, "Negroes in a Democracy at War," Box 22, Phileo Nash Papers (harry S. Truman Library, Independence, Mo.).

7. Ibid.

8. Ibid. These results were obtained by black interviewers. When white interviewers posed the question, 8 percent of black respondents said they would be better off; 30 percent, the same; 29 percent, worse; and 33 percent, don't know. The survey report concluded: "The intimation of a preference for Japanese victory being tantamount to a treasonable utterance, Negroes apparently were reluctant to voice such a view to white strangers." Ibid.

9. Ibid.; Horace Cayton, "Fighting for White Folks?" *Nation*, September 26, 1942, 267–70; Virginius Dabney, "Nearer and Nearer the Precipice," *Atlantic* 171 (1943): 99; Horace Roscoe Cayton, *Long Old Road* (New York, 1965), 276.

10. Office of Facts and Figures, Bureau of Intelligence, "Negroes in a Democracy at War"; A. Philip Randolph, "Why Should We March?" *Survey Graphic* (1942): 488. On transnational racial identification, see particularly Christopher Thorne, *Allies of a Kind: The United States, Britain, and the War against Japan, 1941–45* (New York, 1978), esp. 6–9. Pearl S. Buck observed in 1942: "The main barrier between the East and the West today is that the white man is not yet willing to give up his superiority and the colored man is no longer willing to endure his inferiority." Locke, "Unfinished Business," 456. Will Alexander, who headed the race relations unit of the Julius Rosenwald Fund, worried that to make the Pacific "a race war will leave us with a very serious problem on our hands when it is all over." Morton Sosna, *In Search of the Silent South: Southern Liberals and the Race Issue* (New York, 1977), 105–6. As the war drew to a close. Walter White reported from a tour of service units in the Far East in 1945: "Many of the men I have talked to believe that their fight for democracy will begin when they reach San Francisco on their way home." Christopher Thorne, *The Issue of War: States, Societies, and the Far Eastern Conflict of 1941–1945* (New York, 1985), 275.

11. Lee Finkle, "The Conservative Aims of Militant Rhetoric: Black Protest during World War II," *Journal of American History* 60 (1973): 692–93. However conservative the objectives of the black press, the Roosevelt administration toyed with prosecuting the journalistic advocates of "Double V." Gilbert Ware, *William Hastie: Grace under Pressure* (New York, 1984), 120–21. Reports of black newspapers' being banned at military posts were common, and black soldiers often said that the papers that reached them abroad were cut up like Swiss cheese. A thorough study of administration pressure on the black press, through threatened prosecution, actual censorship, and the like might prove revealing about the latitude the press was able to exercise during the war. As it was, vocal expression of preference for a Japanese victory could result in prosecution. In 1942 the Justice Department filed sedition charges against eighty blacks, among them Robert Jordan, who told Harlem blacks that the Japanese "wanted to help you and give you back your culture." He dreamed of "an Africa ruled by 20,000,000 American Negroes under the benevolent protection of Japan, after the Rising Sun Empire had conquered all Asia and overridden the United States." Richard Polenberg, *War and Society: The United States, 1941–1945* (Philadelphia, 1972), 101.

12. Neil A. Wynn, *The Afro-American and the Second World War* (New York, 1976); Richard M. Dalfiume, *Desegregation of the U.S. Armed Forces: Fighting on Two Fronts, 1939–1953* (Columbia, Mo., 1969); Ware, *William Hastie*, 95–141; Harvard Sitkoff, "Racial Militancy and Interracial Violence in the Second World War," *Journal of American History* 58 (1971): 661–81; John Morton Blum, *V Was for Victory: Politics and American Culture during World War II* (New York, 1976), 190–91; Lester Granger, "The American Negro Views Peace in the Pacific," *Far Eastern Survey*, April 29, 1945, 239.

13. "Government Information manual for the Motion-Picture Industry," prepared by OWI Bureau of Motion Pictures Hollywood Office, Summer 1942, Box 15, Office of War Information (OWI) files, RG 208 (National Archives).

14. Philleo Nash, "A Minorities Program for OWI, Domestic Branch," n.d. [ca. August 1942], Box 18, Nash Papers.

15. George A. Barnes to Ulric Bell, May 17, 1943, Box 3509, OWI files; "OWI Recommendations for Negroes," 1943, ibid.; Nash, "Minorities Program for OWI." Race relations provide perhaps the best example of what John Morton Blum has termed Roosevelt's "necessitarian" approach to the war—he would do whatever was necessary to win the war; all else was secondary. Blum, *V Was for Victory*, 8. It is not necessarily foreordained, however, what policy makers may perceive as necessary. Harry S. Truman chose a wartime situation, for instance, to desegregate the armed forces. During World War II the armed forces significantly relaxed their time-honored strictures against homosexuals—a minority that represented a taboo perhaps even stronger than race. Lesbians and gay men found World War II the freest period they had heretofore experienced and the least repressive until the 1970s. The Women's Army Corps (WAC) instructed officers to approach the lesbian issue with "fairness and tolerance" and to refrain from "hearsay, witchhunting, and speculation." "They are actually the same as you and I," a WAC training manual said of lesbians, "except that they participate in sexual gratification with members of their own sex." Race seemingly posed a more daunting—or at least more visible—threat. See John D'Emilio, *Sexual Politics, Sexual Communities: The Making of Homosexual Minority in the United States, 1940–1970* (Chicago, 1983), 28.

16. Robert K. Merton with Marjorie Fiske and Alberta Curtis, *Mass Persuasion: The Social Psychology of a War Bond Drive* (New York, 1946), 185–86.

17. Gardner Cowles Jr. to Committee on War Information Policy, August 12, 1942, Box 15, OWI files; "Government Information Manual for the Motion-Picture Industry," Summer 1942, April 29, 1943, January 1944; Philleo Nash to Jonathan Worth Daniels, August 7, 1943, Box 29, Nash Papers.

18. "Negroes and the War," n.d., Box 22, Nash Papers; Jones, "U.S. Office of War Information," 358–61; U.S. Congress, Senate, Hearings, Subcommittee of the Committee on Appropriations, *National War Agencies Appropriation Bill for 1944*, 78th Cong., 1st sess., June 23–26, 28, 29, 1943, 197–98, 246.

19. Elmer Davis, press conference, December 23, 1942, Box 1442, OWI files; Davis to Byron Price, January 27, 1943, Box 3, ibid., Mira Liehm and Antonin J. Liehm, *The Most Important Art: Eastern European Film after 1945* (Berkeley, 1977), 1.

20. The conclusion about Hollywood's political stance between 1934 and 1941 is based on the authors' analysis of politically related movies in the files of the Production Code Administration Records (Margaret Herrick Library, Academy of Motion Picture Arts and Sciences, Beverly Hills, Calif.). See also Leo Calvin Rosten, *Hollywood: The Movie Colony, the Movie Makers* (New York, 1941), 30–39, 133–62.

21. Dalton Trumbo, "Minorities and the Screen," in *Writers' Congress: The Proceedings of the Conference Held in October 1943 under the Sponsorship of the Hollywood Writers' Mobilization and the University of California* Berkeley, 1944), 497. On blacks and Hollywood, see Thomas Cripps, *Slow Fade to Black: The Negro in American Film, 1900–1942* (New York, 1977); Daniel J. Leab, *From Sambo to Superspade: The Black Experience in Motion Pictures* (Boston, 1975); and Donald Bogle, *Toms, Coons, Mulattoes, Mammies, and Bucks: An Interpretive History of Blacks in American Films* (New York, 1973). For the controversy over blacks' continuing to play such roles, see *Baltimore Afro-American*, January 9, 16, 23, 1943.

22. Thomas Cripps, "Movies, Race, and World War II: *Tennessee Johnson* as an Anticipation of the Strategies of the Civil Rights Movement," *Prologue* 14 (1982): 54, 60; Walter Francis White, *A Man Called White: The Autobiography of Walter White* (New York, 1948), 199–203; Leab, *From Sambo to Superspade*, 129–30; *Motion Picture Herald*, August 14, 1943.

23. Cripps, "Movies, 49, 54.

24. Ibid. To his credit John L. Balderston advocated playing the story straight without those absurd leaps of poetic license. "But a writer out here is a factory worker," he lamented. John L. Balderston to Lowell Mellett, September 17, 1942, Box 1431, OWI files. The image of Thaddeus Stevens was close to that propounded in D. W. Griffith's notoriously racist *The Birth of a Nation* (1915).

25. Mellett to Maurice Revnes, August 18, 1942, Box 1433E, OWI files; White to Mellett, August 17, 1942, ibid.; Louis B. Mayer to White, August 19, 1942, Box 3510, ibid.

26. Mellett to Revnes, August 18, 1942, Box 1433E, ibid.; *Idiot's Delight*, Production Code Administration Records; *Black Fury*, ibid.

27. Nelson Poynter to White, August 28, 1942, Box 3510, OWI files.

28. Dorothy Jones to Poynter, August 6, 1942, Box 3510, ibid.; Mellett, August 6, 1942, ibid.

29. Poynter to Mellett, September 24, 1942, Box 3515, ibid.

30. *PM*, January 13, 1943. Truman was fascinated by Andrew Johnson's presidency, and after he left the White House he asked Metro-Goldwyn-Mayer (MGM) for a print of *Tennessee Johnson*, which is now deposited at the Truman Library. The parallels Truman must have seen are suggestive: from apprentice and failed haberdasherer to a compromise choice for vice president late in a great war; succession to the presidency on the death of a towering figure and with little preparation for the monumental task ahead; an attempt to carry out his predecessor's policies as he interpreted them; villification (including actual impeachment in Johnson's case and threatened impeachment in Truman's); and eventual vindication at the bar of history. Although Hollywood has not made a "Missouri Truman" as an analogue to *Tennessee Johnson*, the man from Independence won a quicker apotheosis than Johnson with the stage and television show *Give 'Em Hell, Harry* (1975).

31. Mellett to Mayer, November 25, 1942, Box 3510, OWI files; Marjorie Thorson, feature review, *Tennessee Johnson*, December 1, 1942, ibid.

32. "Actors Cues" press release, December 7, 1942, ibid. Thomas Cripps implies that protests about the picture were limited to leftists, whether white or black. But in fact the moderate black leadership, including Walter White and William H. Hastie, were also dismayed at the result. Cripps, "Movies, 66–67; White to Howard Dietz, November 27, 1942, Box II A285, NAACP files; White to Edwin R. Embree, February 13, 1943, ibid.

33. Feature review, *Cabin in the Sky*, January 14, 1943, Box 3525, OWI files; Bell to Watterson Rothacker, February 11, 1943, ibid.; Ferdinand Kuhn to Bell, February 17, 1943, ibid.; *Baltimore Afro-American*, April 3, 1943; James Agee, *Agee on Film* (Boston 1958), 95; Manny Farber, "The Great White Way," *New Republic*, July 5, 1943, 20; *Time*, April 12, 1943, 96.

34. Feature review, *Stormy Weather*, May 5, 1943, Box 3518, OWI files; Warren Pierce to Jason Joy, January 6, 1943, ibid.; Arnold Pecker to Irving Mass, January 10, 1945, ibid.; William Grant Still to White, January 25, 1945, Box II A285, NAACP files.

35. White to Embree; Lena Horne and Richard Schickel, *Lena* (Garden City, 1965), 135. White's response to the picture reflected his perception that for political reasons it was important to show blacks as respectable, "normal" people; he may also have read his personal standards of behavior into the situation. This was an understandable position in the 1940s, but one that perhaps did not fully credit the subtlety of viewers' responses. The films were popular among black audiences and helped catapult Lena Horne to fame, especially among younger blacks. See Horne and Schickel, *Lena*, 172. When an earlier version of this essay was presented at an academic conference, a participant who had seen the picture as a teenager in North Carolina recalled: "I didn't know all that stuff was going on—I just wanted to look like Lena Horne." Another participant recalled that the film had given him his first realization that "black is beautiful." Annual Meeting, Great Lakes American Studies Association, Kent State University, Kent, Ohio, October 13, 1984.

36. White to Embree; Farber, "Great White Way," 20.

37. Barnes to Bell; Dorothy Jones interview by Clayton R. Koppes, December 6, 1974 (in Clayton R. Koppes's possession).

38. Feature review, *Casablanca,* October 26, 1943, Box 3515, OWI files; Robert Riskin to Bell, January 8, 1943, Box 3510, ibid.; feature review, *The Oxbow Incident,* December 19, 1943, Box 3526, ibid.; Barnes to Bell.

39. Feature review, *Bataan,* April 1, 1943, Box 3525, OWI files; Leab, *From Sambo to Superspade,* 125–26; Cripps, "Movies," 67.

40. Feature review, *Lifeboat,* July 27, 1943, Box 3518, OWI files; Pierce to Jason Joy, September 14, 1943, ibid.; Pierce to Eugene O'Neil, August 2, 1943, ibid.

41. *This Is the Army,* Warner Bros. production files (Special Collections, Doheny Library, University of Southern California, Los Angeles). The "Well-Dressed Man" lyrics evoked little protest but another Irving Berlin tune did: "Dressed up to Kill/Dressed up to Kill/Dressed up for Victory/Oh we don't like Killing/But we won't stop Killing/'Til the world is free." Various church groups protested that such lyrics could stir up hatred of Jews, blacks, and Japanese in America, and were inimical to a nation that wished to establish the Four Freedoms. Jack Warner implored Berlin to change the lyrics to "dressed up to win" because "when mass church organizations start after you, you don't have a leg to stand on." Harles F. Ross Jr. of the Methodist Commission on World Peace to Warner Bros., July 21, 1943, ibid.; Jack L. Warner to Irving Berlin and Hal Wallis, July 2, 1943, ibid. Some might argue that the notion of "killing 'til the world is free" fit rather well with the doctrine of unconditional surrender. Although the image of blacks aroused no comment in the Office of Censorship, the men in drag did. The censors banned export to Latin America of any film with female impersonation. Even kudos from OWI and the Department of the Army did not save *This Is the Army* from this ruling. Wallis to Warner, January 4, 1943, ibid.

42. Leab, *From Sambo to Superspade,* 119–20; Agee, *Agee on Film,* 108.

43. Writers' War Board, *How Writers Perpetuate Stereotypes: A Digest of Data* (New York, 1945).

44. Manuel Luis Quezon to Mellett, August 17, 1942, Box 1433B, OWI files; Mellett to Samuel Goldwyn, August 20, 1942, ibid.; Goldwyn to Mellett, August 22, 1942, ibid.; script review, "Kim," August 4, 1942, Box 1438, ibid.

45. Script reviews, "Dragon Seed," September 10, 1942, August 9, 1943, Box 3525, ibid.; T. K. Chang to Robert T. M. Vogel, August 20, 1943, ibid.; Dorothy Jones and Eleanor Berneis to Bell, August 20, 1943, ibid.; feature review, *Dragon Seed,* May 24, 1944, ibid.; script review, "Keys of the Kingdom," January 19, 1944, Box 3518, ibid.; Sailer to William Cunningham, April 19, 1944, ibid.; Cunningham to Sailer, April 13, 1944, ibid.; Gregory D. Black, "Keys of the Kingdom: Entertainment and Propaganda," *South Atlantic Quarterly* 75 (1976): 437–46.

46. "Government Information Manual for the Motion-Picture Industry," Summer 1942, April 29, 1943; script review, "So Proudly We Hail," November 19, 1942, Box 3511, ibid.; feature review, *Bombardier,* May 8, 1943, Box 3522, ibid.

47. White to Virginius Dabney, April 8, 1940, Box II 281, NAACP files.

*Matthew Bernstein*

# A Tale of Three Cities:
# The Banning of *Scarlet Street*

In *Scarlet Street* (Universal, 1945), a bourgeois bank bookkeeper/amateur painter named Christopher Cross (Edward G. Robinson) initiates an extramarital relationship with a prostitute, Kitty (Joan Bennett), kills her when he discovers her infidelity, and watches her lover/pimp Johnny (Dan Duryea) die for the crime. Cross is never brought to trial and the film ends as he wanders the streets, tortured by his obsession with Kitty. The film is a dense, well-structured film noir and has been analyzed and interpreted numerous times. Some of the earliest interpretations came from censors in three different cities.

On January 4, 1946, the New York State Censor Board banned *Scarlet Street* entirely, relying on the statute that gave it power to censor films that were "obscene, indecent, immoral, inhuman, sacrilegious," or whose exhibition "would tend to corrupt morals or incite to crime."[1] As if in a chain reaction, one week later, the Motion Picture Commission for the city of Milwaukee also banned the film as part of a new policy encouraged by police for "'stricter regulation of undesirable films.'"[2] On February 3, Christina Smith, the city censor of Atlanta, argued that because of "the sordid life it portrayed, the treatment of illicit love, the failure of the characters to receive orthodox punishment from the police, and because the picture would tend to weaken a respect for the law," *Scarlet Street* was "licentious, profane, obscure and contrary to the good order of the community."[3]

Since the late 1980s, primary research in newly available archives has invigorated the study of the Hollywood studio system's methods of self-censorship.[4] In contrast, the history of local censorship has remained indebted primarily to decades-old legalistic studies such as Ira Carmen's *Movies, Censorship and the Law*, Edward DeGrazia and Roger Newman's *Banned Films*, and, to a large extent, Richard Randall's *The Censorship of the Movies*.[5] All of these works are invaluable resources,[6] but none of

From *Cinema Journal* 35, no. 1 (1995): 27–52. Reprinted (revised) by permission of the author and University of Texas Press.

*Figure 25. The "prostitute" Kitty (Joan Bennett) and the bank cashier Christopher Cross (Edward G. Robinson): two-thirds of the immoral triangle in* Scarlet Street *(1945). Courtesy of the Museum of Modern Art/Film Stills Archive.*

them exhausts the subject, particularly when one recognizes that local censorship involves more than court cases. One component typically neglected is the strategies distributors used to challenge censorship *informally* prior to court cases, especially in the days before the landmark 1952 *Miracle* decision. In addition, these works neglect questions of local discourse (press coverage and debate among residents) about contested films, focusing their attention on the film producers and their antagonists, the cultural custodians.

New research in cultural studies—working within a framework influenced by Gramscian models of political hegemony and positing the potential of audience members to devise alternate meanings and uses of the texts they consume—has offered new ways of thinking about local censorship. Recent studies on the discourse surrounding specific texts or the political workings of censorship bodies break down the usual oppositions between competing cultural institutions (producers and reformers) in order to emphasize instead the fragmentation and struggles within each broadly defined group.[7]

This essay will examine the *Scarlet Street* disputes from a perspective informed by the concerns of cultural studies. Why this particular case? For one thing, we now have access to archival materials for an inside look at what resources a Hollywood studio, in this case Universal, mobilized to combat censorship; these materials complement our knowledge from newspapers and Hollywood's trade press of the negotiating and rhetorical strategies brought to bear on local bannings. In the case of *Scarlet Street*, the fact that the same film was banned in three different regions and markets of varying significance happily affords us a view of how differently a distributor would handle diverse situations involving the same film at a given historical moment.

Second, this historical moment is of interest in itself. Though the disputes surrounding the premiere of *Scarlet Street* in early 1946 have never been examined in detail, they were tied to urgent issues in postwar American society and culture. Since the debate also brought into question the legitimacy of the state and city film boards themselves, we can see in the playing out of the *Scarlet Street* controversies an effort by censors to retain whatever social authority they held. In cultural studies terms, censors offered a conservative resistance to Hollywood's hegemony as a purveyor of (on this occasion, possibly subversive) mainstream popular culture; but the censors' own hegemony within local communities was itself under siege. More generally, in the mid-1940s Hollywood's sense of its audience was abruptly contradicted by local moral and aesthetic standards, for which in turn there was no broad consensus.

The banning of any film in toto by a local censor board had always been highly unusual. The *New York Times* called its state's action against *Scarlet Street* "one of the most drastic actions ever taken . . . against a film produced by a major Hollywood studio"; similarly, this was Atlanta's first banning since the Mae West Paramount vehicle, *She Done Him Wrong* (1933).[8] Most typically, in the wake of the notorious 1915 Supreme Court ruling (*Mutual Film Corp. v. Industrial Commission of Ohio*)— that movies were "a business pure and simple" and that they were not entitled to First Amendment protection—movie distributors negotiated with state and city censors only for deletions of scenes whose potential offense the Production Code Administration and film producers had failed to anticipate.[9]

Total barring of *Scarlet Street* in New York meant that Universal would lose income from the biggest single movie market in the country; as Randall pointed out, not being able to open in Manhattan would also diminish a film's bookings and rental rates around the country.[10] The Atlanta and Milwaukee bannings were less important financially, but still significant in terms of defining the film's regional markets (the Southeast and Upper Midwest, respectively). Universal chose to contest the censors' action because the studio had participated in the financing of the film for over $1 million and studio executives felt *Scarlet Street* was the most prestigious and profitable release in the studio's recent history.[11]

Immediately after the three bannings, Universal's first step was to mobilize industry support and reconnoiter its opponents through informal channels. Studio publicity director John J. O'Connor urged his good friend Monsignor McClafferty, the head of the national Catholic Legion of Decency, to defend the film. Although the Legion awarded *Scarlet Street* a "B" rating ("objectionable in part"), McClafferty ultimately came forth with a statement to the effect that the film offered a "moral lesson."[12] Meanwhile, in New York, representatives of the Johnston Office (the Motion Picture Producers and Distributors of America, Inc. or MPPDA) immediately conferred with Dr. Irwin Conroe, acting head of the censor board. In the south, Paramount head Y. Frank Freeman urged his friend Atlanta Mayor William B. Hartsfield to take the distributor's side. In March, Freeman would also make a Paramount affiliated theater available in nearby Marietta, so that Atlanta critics could view *Scarlet Street* without too much inconvenience and, Universal hoped, advise their readers about the film's moral tone.[13] Freeman's gesture confirmed that the fate of *Scarlet Street* was, as one Universal executive put it, "an industry matter."[14]

These initial, unofficial forays encouraged Universal executives to think that the bannings were the height of capricious and parvenu censorship. In New York, Irwin Conroe informed the MPPDA that the state board consisted of newly appointed members; as one studio official put it, "we are the first ones to come up against the new board in their interpretation of their job" (Conroe himself had taken his position only in March 1945).[15] To these neophytes, *Scarlet Street* appeared to be a perfectly censorable film; presumably their inexperience also prevented them from suggesting deletions. In Milwaukee, Universal was told, an insurance salesman with "mayoral ambitions" led the city Film Commission and had engineered that action.[16]

Similarly, in mid-February, an Atlanta attorney would inform Universal that the Georgia legislature was considering the creation of a state censor position, and that city censor Christina Smith, who had assumed her Atlanta post just a year earlier, wanted the job. He concluded that "in order to get the notoriety sufficient to obtain this [state censor] position she must, of necessity, stir up a lot of ill feeling to show that she is the guardian angel of all our morals."[17] In short, the inside information Universal gleaned seemed to confirm what was often the case: that since no official criteria existed for censoring films or indeed for even qualifying censors, *Scarlet Street* was the plaything of ambitious politicians and ignorant citizens. But, of course, things were not as simple as all that. The social context of the immediate postwar period gave bulk—if not substance—to the censors' actions.

We usually think of 1946 as Hollywood's banner year: weekly theater attendance peaked at 90 million paying customers, profit margins at most of the major studios climbed to greater heights, and, as major stars returned from overseas service, Hollywood's palpable contribution to mobilization, home-front morale, and military training created its strongest measure of social prestige in the eyes of the federal government and audiences around the country. According to this view, 1947—with its box office decline at home, burdensome taxation in foreign markets, the looming *Paramount* case, and the infamous HUAC hearings—abruptly undercut each of these achievements.

Yet closer examination reveals that 1946 was no picnic. As countless social historians have pointed out, the postwar period was informed by a general sense of crisis. Americans pondered the moral and practical ramifications of the nuclear age, the incredible revelations of Nazi war crimes, and the communist menace whose dimensions were just emerging. On the home front, equally troubling issues had arisen: strikes for better wages were long past due and erupted around the country, while returning veterans and women in the workforce complicated traditional notions of how the nuclear family functioned.[18] And at the beginning of 1946, there was considerable controversy about the role movies had played in aggravating the social ills perceived in American society, particularly in relation to the family.

Film historian Richard Maltby has written of the intensive scrutiny American movies received at the hands of social scientists in the mid- to late 1940s;[19] but less imposing bodies of opinion were also examining Hollywood films during this period. Sociologists and journalists argued that the ranks of juvenile delinquents were swollen by latch-key kids, children whose mothers had entered the workforce during the war and who had not returned to their homes promptly when the war concluded. When a run of 1945 gangster films, most notably Monogram's *Dillinger*, was blamed for several violent incidents involving juvenile delinquents in Chicago and Milwaukee (where teenagers claimed the Monogram film was their inspiration), critics had only to connect the dots. Conservative columnist Hedda Hopper (a vehement member of the Motion Picture Alliance for the Preservation of American Ideals) epitomized the renewed fears about the movies, linking *Scarlet Street* to *Dillinger:* "With our juvenile delinquency soaring," she told her readers, "I agree with the censors. We shouldn't show the young how to get away with crime."[20]

*Dillinger* and *Scarlet Street* were just the beginning. In the postwar era, the Production Code Administration (headed by Joseph I. Breen), which had succeeded the MPPDA's Studio Relations Committee in 1934 to enforce a Catholic-influenced Production Code to anticipate the objections of local censors, was out of kilter with the sentiments of some of the leadership of Christian America.[21] After New York's action against *Scarlet Street*, the Breen Office promised to enforce the Production Code more forcefully.[22] But films already completed and approved were running the gauntlet.

In March 1946, with the popular *The Bells of St. Mary's* ringing in its ears, the Protestant Motion Picture Council announced plans "to rally national support for worthwhile films and suggest and encourage productions of feature films with high moral values."[23] The Legion of Decency announced in April that its "b" ratings for films "objectionable in part" had increased 100 percent over the number from the previous year; the dubious honor was granted to such films as MGM's *Saratoga Trunk*, Selznick–RKO's *Spellbound*, Cowan–United Artists' *The Story of G.I. Joe*, and Bogeaus–United Artists' *Diary of a Chambermaid*. The Legion announced its intentions, in *Variety's* colorful words, to "force" a "cleanup" of Hollywood films.[24] While *Boxoffice* magazine suggested there was no increase in *local* censorship action, the industry was not comforted: the *Hollywood Reporter* in mid-March of 1946 hysterically described the national groups' outcry as the "worst since 1922" when the Fatty Arbuckle case and other Hollywood scandals partly inspired the formation of the MPPDA.[25] A more apt analogy would have been to the Legion's campaign to boycott movies in the spring of 1934, shortly before the Hays Office officially created the Production Code Administration. The same concern with vulnerable adolescent audiences seemed to be motivating the same kinds of actions.

So while Universal executives might blame ambitious or incompetent individuals in particular cities for the *Scarlet Street* bannings, they also had to acknowledge that the temper of local response to their films had grown feisty. The challenge was to get the film into the theaters, and a few remedies were available: the rousing of local support, informal negotiation with censoring officials, formal appeal mechanisms, or, if necessary, a legal suit.[26] The differing dynamics of censorship and market in New York, Milwaukee, and Atlanta compelled Universal to try each of these tactics.

New York State, where the film industry based its distribution and corporate headquarters, proved the most cooperative. Universal was prepared to appeal to the state Board of Regents, which oversaw the censors, but Dr. Conroe had already indicated his regrets about the banning to MPPDA head Eric Johnston. Conroe had also agreed to meet with Universal representatives in private meetings.[27] To advance its views personally, Universal (and the semi-independent company Diana Productions, which had co-produced *Scarlet Street*) dispatched the film's executive producer, Walter Wanger, to discuss the censors' action in person.

Wanger was an apt choice for this mission: he was an articulate, college-educated, widely published, and even more widely-quoted semi-independent producer whose films included such critical successes as John Ford's *Stagecoach* (1939) and *The Long Voyage Home* (1940), Alfred Hitchcock's *Foreign Correspondent* (1940), and Lang's earlier *You Only Live*

*Once* (1937). On many occasions in the late 1930s, Wanger had publicly condemned industry, local, national, and foreign censorship, which several of his films (*Gabriel Over the White House* [1933], *The President Vanishes* [1934], and most dramatically, *Blockade* [1938]) had faced. His reputation nationwide had peaked during World War II, when he served as an industry spokesperson from his position as president of the Academy of Motion Picture Arts and Sciences.[28] Best of all, he was in his element when controversy arose.

With *Scarlet Street* editor Arthur Hilton in tow, Wanger flew to New York on January 22. He conferred with Universal's distribution executives in their Manhattan offices, where they had gathered clippings of favorable reviews of the film from all over the country. Thus armed, Wanger and Hilton met on the 23rd with Conroe. Wanger's handwritten notes for the meeting indicate that he impressed upon Conroe several points: his personal record as a producer and industry leader; the difficult position in which the ban had placed Diana Productions in terms of repaying bank loans that had financed part of the film's more than $1 million cost; Fritz Lang's record as an artistic director; the matter of what we now call spin control—the need to neutralize the aspersions cast on the film by publicity and press coverage of the banning; the fact that the Breen Office had passed the film the New York censors had rejected; the fact that critics around the country had praised the film, acknowledging that it was sordid, rather than glamorous in the usual Hollywood fashion; and that Conroe, as an educator, had a responsibility to allow the free exchange of ideas in the postwar era.

Since Conroe had already privately distanced himself from the board's action, Wanger's patrician mien and comprehensive spiel was icing on the cake. The question now became how Conroe would disentangle the censor board from this mess with dignity. The negotiations that ensued between Wanger and Conroe were remarkable: as Conroe suggested nominal cuts that would make the film acceptable, Wanger conferred with Hilton, who advised Wanger of the cuts' potential effects on story and visual continuity, and whether alternate shot angles of a scene were available.[29]

Typically, if a local censor found an industry-approved film offensive, the censor approached the film in a manner that paralleled that of James Wingate at the MPPDA's Studio Relations Committee from 1930 to 1934: she or he dictated the deletion of isolated dialogue lines or parts of scenes (since, of course, there was no opportunity to reshoot or rework the film); this created ellipses and discontinuities in the film that could still signal, however ambiguously, that illicit or criminal activity had taken place offscreen.[30] The film's distributor had no legal grounds to argue.

But while discussing *Scarlet Street* in New York with Irwin Conroe, Arthur Hilton and Walter Wanger refused several of Conroe's suggestions. For example, Kitty's roommate tells her at one point, "You never could get to work on time." Conroe found this too suggestive, and Hilton acknowledged that it could be eliminated without damaging the flow of the film. But, Hilton pointed out, the line had been inserted into the script at the request of the Breen Office as a means of countering other suggestions in the film of Kitty's prostitution; it existed to combat potential local censorship (which was the Breen Office's primary job). Conroe withdrew his objection.

In a more extreme case, Hilton advised against a cut in the name of narrative structure. Conroe proposed cutting the sequence in which Kitty's recording of "Melancholy Baby" gets stuck (she is too comfortable, lying on the sofa, to get up and fix it). Hilton argued that if cut, the scene would have to be reshot, for it was "essential": "we need to establish the damaged record which is so important for the end of the picture when Chris surprises Kitty with her lover Johnny." The stuck record was hardly "essential" to story coherence, even if it revealed how lazy "Lazy Legs" was; it did, however, establish a motif for a parallel with the later scene. Yet Conroe agreed to let the scene stand. His stance in this instance was not unlike that of Wingate's successor at the MPPDA, Joseph Breen: in negotiating some of the deletions with Wanger, Conroe kept in mind the overall form and shape of *Scarlet Street*.[31]

Hilton and Wanger finally agreed to cut one line of dialogue—"Where's the bedroom?" (Johnny's first question when he and Kitty inspect a new apartment)—and the repeated stabbings of Kitty by Chris Cross (instead of seven, there remained only one). Answering Wanger's concerns about publicity, Conroe made a public statement that basically affirmed Universal and Wanger's claim that the artistry of the film—sordid, morbid, and naturalistic—had been misunderstood: "It is unfortunate," Conroe told the press, "that the publicity given to this motion picture following the original order for its rejection in New York State has caused it to be removed from the class of artistic achievement and placed in an entirely different category."[32] He went so far as to remark that it "deals with an important sociological problem."

Conroe's pronouncements carried little weight with the New York critics, however, who recognized that the cuts were merely "face-saving" devices for the censor board. The reviewers had been skeptical of the board's actions to begin with: Bosley Crowther characterized the banning as a "bewildering action," called the censorship system a "medieval state of affairs," and eventually argued for the imposition of federal standards, something the film industry certainly did not want.[33] After the banning was rescinded, Archer Winsten complained in the *Post* that the censors operated too secretly and that they effectively inhibited future films.[34] John T. MacManus, of the liberal *PM* magazine, noted how the state censor board had passed *Captain Marvel* and *Doctor Maniac* serials without rancor, while documentaries such as *The Fight for Life* and comedies like Warner Bros.' *Yes, My Darling Daughter* had faced cuts or worse:

In short, murder, robbery, arson, prurience, cupidity, planetary imperialism . . . and abysmal stupidity have been okay all along with the New York State "censors," but childbirth and some sex manifestations have invariably fallen afoul of the educational law in the eyes of its administrators.[35]

Director Lang had asked a Pittsburgh journalist, "Iss [sic] it immoral to stab a woman four times—moral to stab her only once?"[36] One *New York Sun* columnist agreed, going so far as to compose a poem on the occasion, which concluded:

So give the picture to the kids
  For children's matinees!
They will not mind a missing stroke
  Wherein the killer slays;
Proclaim it in the super lights
  And show through super star,
THAT SEVEN STROKES TO TAKE A LIFE
  ARE SIX STROKES OVER PAR.[37]

*Scarlet Street* premiered on February 20 in the super lights of Loew's Criterion theater near Times Square.

Eleven days before Wanger and Hilton arrived in New York to talk with Conroe, the Milwaukee Film Commission announced its ban on the film. Members who voted for it cited the rise in juvenile delinquency and a local gang's admiration for *Dillinger*.[38] In direct contrast to their decision in New York, Universal distribution and publicity executives elected to respect the Milwaukee action, even after the Commission banned the "New York" version from Milwaukee showings in February.

The studio's plan here was "not to press our legal position until such time as we have laid the groundwork for public opinion."[39] The Universal executives were also concerned that should they try to challenge the Milwaukee ruling, their actions might prejudice the outcome of the more important Atlanta controversy.[40] By late February, they appealed to "the citizens of Milwaukee" with a full-page ad urging them to "express their dissatisfaction" with the board's action, as residents of the city that was "the cradle of the mid-western liberal tradition."[41] Universal's strategy paid off. By waiting until the censors calmed down, and until the Atlanta banning was resolved, Universal was able to see *Scarlet Street* premiere (with the New York deletions) in Milwaukee in October 1946, ten months after its initial release. Clearly, Milwaukee was not a market worth negotiating for in person.

Atlanta was, however. When Christina Smith issued the Atlanta ban ten days after the New York situation was resolved, it seemed clear what Universal needed to do. But Atlanta officials and community opinion were less conciliatory than in New York. Unlike the New York board,

*Figure 26. "Lazy Legs" Kitty with her boyfriend/pimp Johnny (Dan Duryea). Among the Atlanta censor's supports was a Baptist pastor who denounced* Scarlet Street's *"gross irreverence toward womanhood."* Courtesy of the Museum of Modern Art/Film Stills Archive.

Christina Smith had acted alone.[42] More significantly, unlike Dr. Conroe, Smith admitted no error of judgment.

Christina Smith and her supporters justified their vigilance, like their counterparts in New York and Milwaukee, on local concern about rising juvenile delinquency.[43] By the end of the year, Atlanta would be hit by a rash of incidents in which teenagers vandalized upper-middle-class homes, smashing "objets d'art" and furniture and smearing eggs and ketchup into carpets; another cycle of misdemeanors involved releasing the parking brakes on twenty-eight cars, which rolled and crashed. Perhaps the most shocking aspect of these events was that the perpetrators were not "poor, black, nor hungry [sic]," but "the sons and daughters of well-to-do Northsiders."[44] Then too, just days before Christina Smith banned *Scarlet Street*, Georgia's state legislature marked a new, more flexible phase in marital relations by passing a statute permitting couples to obtain divorces without the ordeal and expense of a jury trial.[45] No wonder Smith found allies who shared her sense that *Scarlet Street* could undermine the morals of the community.

Several clergymen and church elders (Presbyterian, Methodist, and Baptist) were among Smith's strongest supporters. The strongest was Dr. Louis Newton, a conservative and highly influential Baptist pastor who served on the Fulton County Library board which oversaw Smith. Newton told the *Atlanta Journal*, after seeing the film for the second time:

From the opening scene, with its episode of drinking and the remark of the boss, "I have a woman waiting for me," the picture moves on, scene after scene, glorifying drunkenness, crime, infidelity, gross irreverence toward womanhood, obscenity, vulgarity, and a tangled web of lies and deception which lead at last to the sordid murdering of the supposed heroine.[46]

He told the *Atlanta Constitution,*

To argue that 'Scarlet Street' will do good in combating juvenile delinquency is tantamount, it occurs to me, to claim that the city of Atlanta, through its public libraries, is rendering a moral ministry in providing free copies of [Lillian Smith's novel] "Strange Fruit" as the ideal solution of the problem of sex immorality.[47]

Christina Smith also had supporters in the business community. Aubrey Milam, a "prominent businessman" and chairman of the library board, acknowledged that the film was "superbly performed" and "artistic," but he also called it "the most sordid thing I have ever seen on the screen. . . . It is the story of a man and woman who have an illicit romance, and I don't think that is good entertainment."[48] Milam told the press he wouldn't "give a dime" for the studio's chances of reversing the censor's action.[49]

The rise of juvenile delinquency and the dispute with Hollywood were both jolts to the "Atlanta Spirit," a term that described this landlocked state capital's enormous hometown boosterism that dated back to the Reconstruction era. The city's very history was bound up with business—it was founded as a train depot—and Atlanta welcomed commerce as its lifeblood. The city was certainly susceptible to the glamor and charms of Hollywood, especially after it hosted the world premiere of *Gone With the Wind* in December 1939: in early 1946, the *Atlanta Journal* was happy to place Academy Award results on the front page or report on Lana Turner's tours in foreign countries, and local exhibitors advertised Twentieth Century-Fox's innocuous comedy *Colonel Effingham's Raid* (also starring Joan Bennett) by trumpeting the fact that the film was "produced by Atlanta's own Lamar Trotti."[50] But the city could be highly skeptical of arrogant outsiders who tried to intimidate them. Nothing illustrates this dynamic at work so much as the city press's response to Wanger's claims about *Scarlet Street.*

Initially the local press, the *Atlanta Constitution* and the more conservative *Atlanta Journal,* must have provided Universal and Wanger with some encouragement about the outcome of the latter's negotiating efforts. One article in the *Constitution* announcing Smith's banning had the subtitle, "Shall We Drop Office of Censor?" Without having seen *Scarlet Street, Constitution* editor Ralph McGill, the nationally prominent progressive journalist, was "inclined to doubt . . . that [*Scarlet Street*] is

any worse than some of the other films which have shown in local theaters from to time, it having run without objection in cities far more strait-
laced than this."[51] He further articulated the city's self-consciousness
about its prominence on the national scene, noting the danger of becoming like Boston, where publishers and producers eagerly got their works
banned for greater publicity. The following day, an associate editor at the
*Constitution*, recalling the controversial *Traffic in Souls* (1913), complained that "censorship is regimenting us all, as to what we shall see
and hear, more than it did in the old days."[52]

These signals, along with Wanger's handy success in New York,
only emboldened him, and Universal, to take a peremptory and condescending attitude toward the Atlanta situation. Wanger may well have
imagined that if he could personally impress New York's Conroe, he would
be that much more effective in Atlanta. Speaking by phone to a local reporter, Wanger informed him that

> Your Atlanta censor has misinterpreted the entire theme of the picture.
> It is not an invitation to sin, but a warning against sin. . . .
>
> I have no doubt that when I meet with the entire membership of
> the Atlanta censorship board and present my case as I presented it before
> the board of New York State, that 'Scarlet Street' will be approved in
> Atlanta.[53]

These comments were printed in a front-page article in the *Atlanta Journal*, accompanied by a large photo of Wanger and Bennett in Hollywood.
Before the piece concluded, Wanger further invoked his personal prestige:
he claimed he would never allow his wife Joan Bennett, whom he dearly
loved, to appear in an immoral film.[54]

Unfortunately, Wanger's comments, especially the last, met with
considerable skepticism, even in the Atlanta papers, which had been cautiously critical of Smith's action. Now, the *Atlanta Constitution* published
an editorial entitled "Walter (The Woman I Love) Wanger Hams It Up":

> From out of the west, Producer Walter Wanger is winging his way to
> defend "the woman I love" and the picture into which he has sunk two
> million dollars. In a melodramatic, cross-country interview, Brother
> Wanger—who is the current husband of Joan Bennett, the picture's star—
> has declared his intention of coming to Atlanta and denying publicly,
> quite publicly, the implication that "Lazy Legs," the part the woman he
> loves has in the picture, is wicked or licentious.
>
> Producer Wanger should stick to producing. And leave the acting to
> his wife.[55]

Such sentiments informed the paper's subsequent coverage. The
very next day, as Wanger arrived with Universal's Eastern publicity manager Al Horwits, the *Constitution*, countering all previously published
sentiments, carried an opinion column suggesting that Atlanta should

support Smith (a former *Journal* reporter). Acknowledging Hollywood's role in bolstering public morale and the contribution of movie stars who had performed for the armed forces during the war, columnist Morgan Blake nonetheless maintained that Smith and Milam should be listened to. They were "in no sense fanatics. They are fair minded, have good judgment and are very lenient."[56] The day after that, an article in the same paper characterized Wanger (inaccurately) as a "multi-millionaire" producer who had arrived "with typical flash and fanfare" in "a specially chartered plane" to defend his "lurid" film (which of course the reporter had not yet seen).[57]

Neither Wanger's reputation nor his echoes of Hollywood war time prestige carried weight with the Atlanta community. In fact, the more personal and high-toned Wanger tried to get, the more dubious the journalists became. With perceptive skepticism, they recognized that Wanger was desperately anxious to recoup the investment on the film. His presence and actions stirred up deep-seated expressions of mistrust and dislike of Hollywood glamour and profligate ways. Christina Smith understood that "Instead of regretting the publicity on the [banning], [Wanger] and Mr. Horowitz [sic] have sought publicity and have done all they can to create and continue the publicity."[58] And one article exaggerated to *Constitution* readers that Universal would lose $500,000 in income and Wanger personally would miss $50,000, if the ban was upheld.[59]

Upon his arrival in Atlanta on February 11, Wanger held a breakfast press conference in his hotel room. Here, sensing the disbelief his earlier claims had met in the Atlanta community, Wanger changed the emphasis of his rhetoric from the issue of personal prestige to the prerogative of authorial intent. He told the *Atlanta Journal*, "I am sure the last thing Miss Smith wants to do is make this picture attractive to an audience that will read into it implications that conflict with the concepts of the author, director and artists."[60] Echoing Conroe's statements to the press, Wanger argued that Smith's ban effectively removed "a sincere picture from the classification of artistic triumph to the classification of sensationalism," and that this reclassification was more detrimental to the film than the loss of box office which the ban entailed. Smith had interpreted immorality where none existed. She didn't know a work of art when she saw one.

Late in the afternoon of Tuesday, February 12, Wanger elaborated on this line of argument when the other six members of the library board convened with Wanger for a screening of the film (four of them had not seen it before). By profession they were a diverse group: Dr. Newton, Mayor Hartsfield, county officials, and other "prominent Atlantans" who practiced law, worked in advertising and banking, or had positions in city government. Wanger made his case to the board, arguing that *Scarlet Street* was a work of art and that "Art is the truth, and the truth never should be censored. Its function is to hold the mirror up to life. It never glamourizes;

it never glorifies and it never debases." Wanger invoked as examples the unblinking realism of Italian Neorealism on the one hand and the "mature" subjects of British and French quality films on the other. *Scarlet Street*, as a comparable "clinical study," was an "experiment" that "should be encouraged" for the improvement of Hollywood filmmaking.[61] Having heard his sentiments, the board watched the film.

Significantly, for the ensuing debate led by Smith and her supporters, the board made Wanger leave the room. After a two-hour, "heated" discussion during which one of the board members offered to resign, four members (including Mayor Hartsfield) voted to rescind the ban, and three members (including Smith) voted to uphold it. At this point, the chairman of the board, Milam, who was supposed to vote only in case of a tie, cast his vote to uphold the ban, thus deadlocking the body. The next day, the Associate City Attorney J. M. B. Bloodworth determined that the deadlock sustained rather than overruled Smith's judgment. The ban would stand, and Wanger and Horwits returned home, shaking their heads over the protocols Milam had enforced and Bloodworth's findings.[62]

Unlike in New York, Universal was now compelled to undertake legal action. It had already contacted an Atlanta law firm for advice on Atlanta's statutes. Both counsel and client were convinced that they could mount a challenge on technical grounds and bring a writ of injunction against the ban. But Universal and the attorneys would have to do it alone. Mayor Hartsfield, a publicity-wise man who appreciated the contribution of the film industry to the city's economy (Atlanta was a major distribution exchange city for the Southeast), refused to repudiate Smith's actions. In a "hectic" session, Hartsfield failed to convince Aubrey Milam to reverse his views on the film, and told an industry representative that "no one in Atlanta will support us."[63] He knew whereof he spoke. The newspapers had already expressed outrage at Wanger's attempt to take the high road in contesting Smith's actions. Jimmy Fidler, a national radio show host based in Atlanta, also criticized Wanger on the air.[64]

Yet, as the city awaited the court hearings, resident opinion, as represented in letters to the editor in the two local papers, was evenly divided on the subject. Supporters (whom Smith privately complained were underrepresented in the papers)[65] reiterated Smith's concerns, stressing the realism of the film and its unquestioned impact on immature audiences. Dissenters advanced their criticism on various grounds. Some questioned the causal connections between art and real-life conduct: one writer asked if *Crime and Punishment* had ever been proven to cause criminal behavior, while another dismissed the delinquent behavior issue as "a pretty lame excuse for parents of these holy terrors to cover up their own mistakes and negligence." Other writers paid less attention to the film itself than to the democratic values upheld in the last war: following Universal district manager Henry Graham's outburst that Smith's action "smacks of Hitlerism for one group of people to tell 500,000 people what

# A Statement about the
# motion picture "Scarlet Street"

There has been much printed and much said about the banning of the motion picture "Scarlet Street" by the unwarranted action of the Atlanta Censor.

It is to be regretted that the banning has added a sensationalism to the character of this picture in Atlanta, especially since "Scarlet Street" reflects a serious dramatic theme and presents its thesis with a dignity and propriety commensurate with the importance of the subject matter.

The people of Atlanta should know that *Scarlet Street* was produced by persons of excellent and established reputation and is being distributed by Universal, a company which has to its credit thirty-five years of business prestige.

No one connected with either the production of *Scarlet Street* or its distribution to theatres of the world can benefit by any sensationalism nor does any one of these persons have any desire to capitalize upon sensationalism.

Universal Film Exchanges, Inc. has inserted this advertisement in the spirit of fair play and with the hope that the facts will speak for themselves.

## The people of Atlanta should know:

(1) *Scarlet Street* has been exhibited in approximately 200 representative cities throughout the country and has been seen by approximately five million persons.

(2) Has met the censorship requirements of those states that have censorship boards including the states of Ohio, Pennsylvania, Maryland, New York, Florida, Kansas, Massachusetts.

(3) Has been exhibited in a cross section of the country in cities which have local censorship boards such as Memphis, Boston, Providence, Kansas City, Mo., Washington, D. C., Chicago, San Francisco, Seattle.

In addition to Memphis, these other Southern cities have seen *Scarlet Street:* Greenville, Hattiesburg, Meridian, Gulfport, in Mississippi; Miami, Pensacola, St. Petersburg, in Florida; Richmond, Norfolk, Petersburg, in Virginia; Mobile, in Alabama; Alexandria, in Louisiana; Charleston, S. C.; Jackson, Tennessee, Ft. Smith, Little Rock, in Arkansas; San Antonio, Houston, Wichita Falls, Dallas, Abilene, Amarillo, Ft. Worth, Galveston, Austin, El Paso, in Texas.

These engagements were typified by record breaking attendance resulting from the natural appeal of the picture and without any unusual uproar occasioned by action such as the type of publicity resulting from the ban in Atlanta.

It is fair to state that every type of motion picture patron has seen *Scarlet Street* in every type of community, whether it be small town or large city. The press in these cities has been enthusiastic in its critical comment and endorsement of *Scarlet Street.* We think the people of Atlanta should read some of these comments.

*The New York Times, through Bosley Crowther, says:*
"'Scarlet Street' is a painfully moral picture, and in the light of modern candor, rather tame."

*The New York World-Telegram, through Alton Cook, says:*
"'Scarlet Street' is for adults, and it will leave them full of enthusiasm for what a good movie can do to an audience. This is the good kind of melodrama, baffling, breathtaking and evil. All the way through, this is such a good picture, you wonder why the censors dared monkey."

*The Boston Traveler says:*
"From where we sat we could see nothing to incite immorality in the sordid happenings of this splendidly produced photoplay."

*The New York Post, through Archer Winsten, says:*
"What's certain is that a lot of people are going to see 'Scarlet Street' and nobody will be morally impaired by the experience. Not if 'the wages of sin is death' still rates as a moral saying."

*The Spokane Spokesman-Review, through Margaret Bean, says:*
"'Scarlet Street' shouts a sermon!"

*The Washington Times-Herald, through Betty Hynes, says:*
"Certainly this picture unreels a segment of life a lot of people would rather believe does not exist, but it is there just the same and all the more dangerous when it is covered up and ignored. And the story treatment is in the classic tradition that rewards evil with death and suffering. . . . In other words, 'Scarlet Street' is a thoroughly moral film drama."

*The Memphis Commercial Appeal, through Mike McGee, says:*
"We found the shock content of 'Scarlet Street' practically nil."

*The New York Herald Tribune, through Howard Barnes, says:*
"It is rather absurd that 'Scarlet Street' had to go over the censorship hurdles recently. It is as moral as a Jeremiad. It makes its physical and spiritually melo-dramatic points with sense and considerable artistry."

*The Hartford Times, through John Crocket, says:*
"'Scarlet Street' is an excellent movie which substitutes for the Victorian finger-waving 'crime does not pay' ending, one of dramatic, literary and life-like realism with its many extreme subtleties. It will no doubt be voted one of the year's best."

*The Chicago Herald-American, through Ann Marsters, says:*
"If you think Robinson pays for his crime in conventional manner with the law catching up to him, you are quite wrong. And herein lies the most unusual part of the picture. It has the most intelligent ending we have ever seen in this type of melodrama."

*The Cincinnati Times Star, through Groverman Blake, says:*
"'Scarlet Street' is a potent melodrama in which sin, astonishingly outspoken and rampant for the films, receives one of the most severe and violent set-backs I can recall it ever having suffered on the screen."

*The Cincinnati Enquirer, through E. B. Radcliffe, says:*
"This picture adds another raw slice of life to the screen's swiftly growing library of realism."

*The Boston Globe says:*
"'Scarlet Street' does not make evil in any way attractive. It is sordid, cruel and mean."

*The Detroit News, through Al Weitschat, says:*
"'Scarlet Street' is a sordid tale, but done with a realism which has consistent, straight-from-the shoulder fascination."

*The Detroit Times, through Charles Gentry, says:*
"It's an expert drama, based on a darn good story."

*The Galveston Tribune says:*
"'Scarlet Street' is an outstanding cinema event in every respect."

WHY can cities in the South, West, East and North see "Scarlet Street" and Atlanta cannot have this privilege?

This is what happened when we sought a permit to exhibit the picture:

(1) *A single censor rejected the picture.*

(2) *On review of this arbitrary decision by the entire board, four members cast votes which approved of the picture's exhibition and three members voted to sustain the censor. Thereupon, the chairman insisted upon casting a ballot to sustain the censor, thus creating a tie vote.*

(3) *The City Attorney's office ruled that the tie vote was insufficient to grant a permit to show the picture.*

There are no finer men in the City of Atlanta than the four members of the Board of Censors who voted for the picture's exhibiton.

We believe that "Scarlet Street" is an artistic picture worthy of any screen in the City of Atlanta and we also believe that its banning is wholly unwarranted and improperly ordered.

We submit that the promiscuous comments and opinions expressed by persons who have not seen the picture are presumptuous. Without viewing the picture it cannot be judged.

Actually, the basic question is whether the people of Atlanta are entitled to see this picture and to form their own conclusions in regard to the quality of "Scarlet Street."

The sharp divison of the Censor Board is the best evidence that "Scarlet Street," in the opinion of representative persons, has merit.

The entire incident is unfair to the producers of the motion picture, its distributor and to the citizens of Atlanta.

We regret that our only recourse is to present the facts to the courts of the State of Georgia.

This we propose to do promptly.

Universal Film Exchanges, Inc.

*Figure 27. While awaiting its day in court, Universal Pictures appealed to Progressive opinion in the divided Atlanta community by publishing this full-page defense of* Scarlet Street *in the* Atlanta Constitution *on February 24, 1946.* Copyright © 1999 by Universal City Studios, Inc. Courtesy of Universal Studios Publishing Rights, a Division of Universal Studios Licensing, Inc. All rights reserved.

they can see on the screen of a theatre," several writers went further than Universal dared, and concurred that censorship was unbecoming in America.[66] One Methodist minister agreed, noting that "'Scarlet Street' cannot reach the indecencies of prostitutes of our city," and urging the city to "Give the public a break and let them see for themselves."[67] As this letter suggests, even religious leaders in Atlanta were not of one opinion; the city was, on balance, notably progressive about the issue.

Universal contributed to the discussion with full-page ads in the *Journal* and the *Constitution* that picked up many of the points Wanger had made successfully in New York—the ad quoted from critics around the country about *Scarlet Street*'s artistry and moral tone, indicated where the film had played in the south and around the country, affirmed that it was the product of a major studio and not some exploitation firm, and described the absurdities of the library board's review process.[68]

The reporters' pronouncements on the film would only aggravate Smith more. After the film opened in Marietta, open-minded columnists reverted to defending it: Ralph McGill thought *Scarlet Street* was "the most moral picture I ever saw," suggesting it would discourage men over forty from committing adultery. In this light he found Smith's banning arrogant and offensive.[69] Wright Bryan of the *Journal*, comparing Bennett's role with Bette Davis's in *Of Human Bondage*, agreed that it was a highly moral, if sordid, film:

> I didn't enjoy it. I wouldn't want to see it again. I felt I needed a bath when it ended. I wouldn't recommend it to anyone seeking a pleasant evening. But I admired the intelligence and the dramatic impact with which it told a story. And I don't think there is any danger of its corrupting the morals of anyone, young or old.[70]

Bryan concluded that Atlantans should be allowed to decide what they want to see. The most effective censor, he pointed out, was the paying customer. In short, as the *Scarlet Street* case came to court, there was no consensus among Atlantans about the issue.

In pleading its case before Judge Almand of Fulton County, Universal repeated the arguments advanced informally through publicity, the full-page ad, and to the censor board. Wanger's affidavit for the case, for example, asserted that Diana Productions, Inc. had been formed expressly to produce "realistic" films. Joseph Breen's affidavit compared Cross's punishment by conscience to the punishment meted out to Cain by God in the Bible. The distributor also called as witnesses over forty industrialists, financiers, educators, and other prominent citizens of Atlanta, all of whom had seen the film and could attest to *Scarlet Street*'s high quality and moral tone. These older arguments were included in a varied barrage of claims against the banning—most notably, but incidentally and briefly, that the city of Atlanta had prevented Universal from exercising its right of free speech under the First and Fourteenth Amendments. The city attorney countered with only six witnesses supporting the banning, Christina Smith among them.[71]

Universal got its way, finally, on the basis of none of these arguments. Instead, Universal persuaded Judge Almand to rescind the ban on technical grounds. On April 13, Almand agreed that Atlanta's censorship ordinance was too vaguely phrased to allow a single censor to act on the city's behalf; the entire board would have to make such rulings. He also agreed that the city censor was empowered only to order deletions rather than to ban films completely. Judge Almand gave Christina Smith ten days to mount a case to censor *Scarlet Street* on moral grounds as obscene. When she failed to meet the deadline, Almand granted Universal the right to book the film in mid-April.[72] The film opened on May 1 at the downtown Paramount; the manager reported that most of his patrons "appeared to enjoy" the film and voiced no objections to it.[73]

But Atlanta's city attorney chose to appeal the case. The following September, when it was heard, the Georgia Supreme Court reversed Almand's ruling on a procedural flaw in Universal's attorney's case. Smith's banning was reinstated. Fortunately for Universal, by September *Scarlet Street* had only one subsequent-run theater booking unfulfilled in the lucrative Atlanta market. Universal's attorney reasoned that the case "is at an end and . . . we accomplished the result desired for this picture." The Atlanta city ordinance empowering a city censor would not be permanently invalidated until 1962.[74]

For all the strong feelings they stirred up at the time, the *Scarlet Street* controversies have remained an undeservedly obscure chapter in the history of local film censorship. Perhaps Universal's argumentative tactics are partly responsible for this neglect. Universal embarked on a typical Hollywood-style solution to social difficulties, typical in that it characterizes many of the industry's so-called message movies: the institutions of censorship remained unquestioned, while the particular persons involved were characterized as guilty of abusing their power by misunderstanding an innovative film.

Yet, I would argue that Universal's responses to the bannings in Atlanta, New York, and Milwaukee are more typical of Hollywood's dealings with local censors than, say, Howard Hughes's obstinate bravado with *The Outlaw* (1942, 1946). They illustrate how producers and distributors could quietly (in New York and Milwaukee) or quite baldly (in Atlanta) attempt to rig local public opinion to their way of thinking. In fact, Universal's argumentative logic and diverse practical maneuvers offer us a paradigm of studio responses to local censorship in the postwar period, prior to the benefit of First Amendment protection and at a time when Hollywood sought to redefine its stature in American society.

In fact, the most notable feature about Universal's actions to combat censorship in the three cities was that the company did not raise the issue of free speech until the case went to court; and then they did so only in passing. (It would take an independent distributor of a "realistic" European film [Roberto Rossellini's *The Miracle*] to make that case before the Supreme Court, just five years later.) But Universal certainly had all the encouragement it needed to make the First Amendment the centerpiece of its argument.

The *Scarlet Street* bannings occurred at a turning point in the general assessment of film's communicative sophistication. Hollywood's effective wartime campaigns and instruction proved decisively, if anyone needed persuading, that contrary to the *Mutual* ruling, movies were in fact a medium of ideas. A New York attorney wrote the *New York Times* in January 1946 that the Supreme Court was sure to reverse the *Mutual* ruling when it next considered the issue of censorship; indeed, Justice William O. Douglas acknowledged that movies could communicate ideas in his comments on the *Paramount* case in 1948.[75] The postwar moment also encouraged journalists and concerned citizens, unlike Universal's lawyers, to juxtapose the successful victory over fascist nations with the undemocratic implications of local censorship; here were more profound grounds for suggesting that such boards should be abolished altogether.

More to the point, Elmer Rice of the American Civil Liberties Union offered to represent Universal in pursuit of a First Amendment hearing before the Supreme Court, and *Scarlet Street* director Fritz Lang was all for it: "Since we are known as two stinking liberals," he wrote Wanger, "I think we finally should do something to earn the title without the 'stinking.'"[76]

But, as Randall has pointed out, studios never challenged censors on the principle of free artistic expression alone.[77] Universal did not pursue the First Amendment line of argument, because it would prove too lengthy and costly—it would ultimately have required a Supreme Court hearing. The studio wanted the cash. Besides the time and financial expense, Universal was discouraged from challenging the constitutionality of the censors by the protests of the national religious groups over many other Hollywood films that arose as the Atlanta case went to court. There was too much outcry across the country for one distributor to settle the First Amendment question with one suit. Instead, by insisting on the abstract virtues of artistic realism, Universal's public rhetoric invoked First Amendment principles *implicitly*, pitching the debate at the level of interpretation rather than at that of constitutional issues, a battle between two institutions—Hollywood and local censors—intent on reconfirming their legitimacy as cultural arbiters.

If Universal's actions provide a menu of possible studio reactions to local censorship, we can in turn see in New York's, Milwaukee's and Atlanta's contrariness a paradigm of local response. Conroe's quick capitulation to Universal—becoming in effect an extension of the studio's publicity arm—and Smith's obstinate resistance to the studio were two opposed reactions that signaled local differences in the nation's sensibilities and its estimates of Hollywood's stature in the postwar period.

But when resistance occurred, even Smith's and Conroe's views had to vie with commercial and progressive interests that transcended class boundaries and gender, as evidenced in the divided public opinion published in the Atlanta and New York newspapers. Yet a third element was general skepticism, such as that of Ralph McGill, about both Hollywood *and* censorship. Like Conroe, McGill reminds us that local communities, like the studios themselves, were well aware of how their conduct would play on the national stage, and that the studios could find unlikely but articulate supporters in unexpected places.[78] The Atlanta and New York situations further remind us that there was division *within* a community about a film's tone and meaning, about what constituted immorality, and even about the validity of censorship itself.[79]

What made these opposing interpretations (even within censoring boards) especially vehement was the fact that *Scarlet Street* was an ambiguous, contradictory text within the framework censors and Universal adopted to discuss it; different elements of the film could be easily recruited to competing interpretations that stressed its moral (Chris is punished by a higher law) or immoral (Chris is never arrested and tried) ethos. As one perceptive reader of the *Atlanta Journal* put it, "If a certain picture producer has to go all the way to New York to convince the censors there that there was a definite moral to his picture, perhaps the moral isn't too clear."[80] Reviewing the censorship flaps in early 1946, screenwriter Dudley Nichols agreed, confessing to Wanger, "Actually, the fault is mine. I skated on ice as thin as possible in working out the script and believed that if the Hays Office approved we would be in the clear."[81] But no one who participated in the *Scarlet Street* controversies would publicly acknowledge the the idea that the film could have various valid meanings for different viewers.

The varied interpretations of *Scarlet Street* have persisted over the decades since the bannings. What strikes contemporary academic critics about *Scarlet Street* is that it raises the specter of a woman of independent spirit and sexuality who tempts a middle-class, middle-aged man into despair. E. Ann Kaplan, for example, has drawn an analogy between Chris Cross's emasculation and the experience of the returning veteran: the film's plot includes "the 'other man' in the background; the demand that he [Chris] be a full-fledged provider; the assertive, confident woman, able to take care of herself, yet feeling that she has earned the right to be taken care of."[82]

Such interpretations only partially account for the affront many traditional viewers felt upon seeing the film in early 1946. During the *Scarlet Street* debate in all three cities, Kitty's threatening sexuality was emphasized only in Milwaukee. In New York and Atlanta, it was incorporated under the more general issue of crime without punishment; the character of Chris seems to have been foremost in those censors' minds.

In May 1946, Smith explained that she objected to the film on several grounds: it was dangerous to lead an entire audience to rejoice in "an execution of an individual for a crime he did not commit"; then there were the class implications in Chris's boss J. J. Hogarth's December–May relationship with a young woman: that the rich escape punishment for illicit behavior. Most particularly, "The crimes depicted in this film picture, specifically theft, fraud, blackmail, embezzlement, illicit love and murder are presented in such a manner as to create sympathy for at least one of the characters." This sympathy, she felt, was "a dangerously misplaced emotion."[83] That there was any humor, irony, or distancing in Lang's satiric treatment of Johnny and Kitty, and of Cross's emasculated, middle-class bookkeeper did not occur to Smith; and the fact that Chris got what he deserved by the end of the film was not satisfying in any moral sense. Apparently, Smith had never considered Fritz Lang's question to the Pittsburgh journalist: "How could any one possibly want to copy any of ze sings zese [sic] characters do?"[84]

Studios like Universal could exploit this uncertainty, having it both ways. With Conroe's seal of approval, Universal's advertising in the *New York Times* titillated potential viewers by showing Joan Bennett in a prostitute pose, standing (alone or with Duryea, who says "Hello, Lazy Legs") under a street lamp.[85] (By contrast, after the court case, ads in the Atlanta papers featured a simple black square with star names, the film title, theater name, and the word "Now!") Publicly, Wanger articulated the studio's claims that the film was "a sincere artistic triumph" and that the sensationalism existed only in Smith's eyes; privately, he would claim two years later that its $3 million gross was based only on its sensationalism, which appealed only to large-city audiences.[86] Three years after affirming *Scarlet Street*'s realism and moral probity in his affidavit, Joseph Breen commented, "When these people [i.e., producers, directors, screenwriters] talk about realism they usually talk about filth."[87]

The ethical ambiguity surrounding *Scarlet Street*—it was sordid, but was it immoral?—transcends this particular film. It extends to all works of naturalistic fiction—literary, theatrical and cinematic—from the late nineteenth century and continues to the present day.[88] In the postwar period, Hollywood studios grew more adept at creating naturalistic, gritty, noiresque dramas and at distinguishing different audience appeals (particularly the family film from the adult film). These distinctions were codified with the adoption of the ratings system in 1968.[89] But even today, with the fragmentation of the movie audience well-established, Hollywood, as well as other entertainment industries, confronts the impulse to censorship (demonstrated, for example, with the ratings disputes over *Henry and June* and *Henry: Portrait of a Serial Killer* in 1990). These issues remain unresolved, a fact that further suggests the value of close examinations of Hollywood's typical, if less sensational, censorship battles in the past.

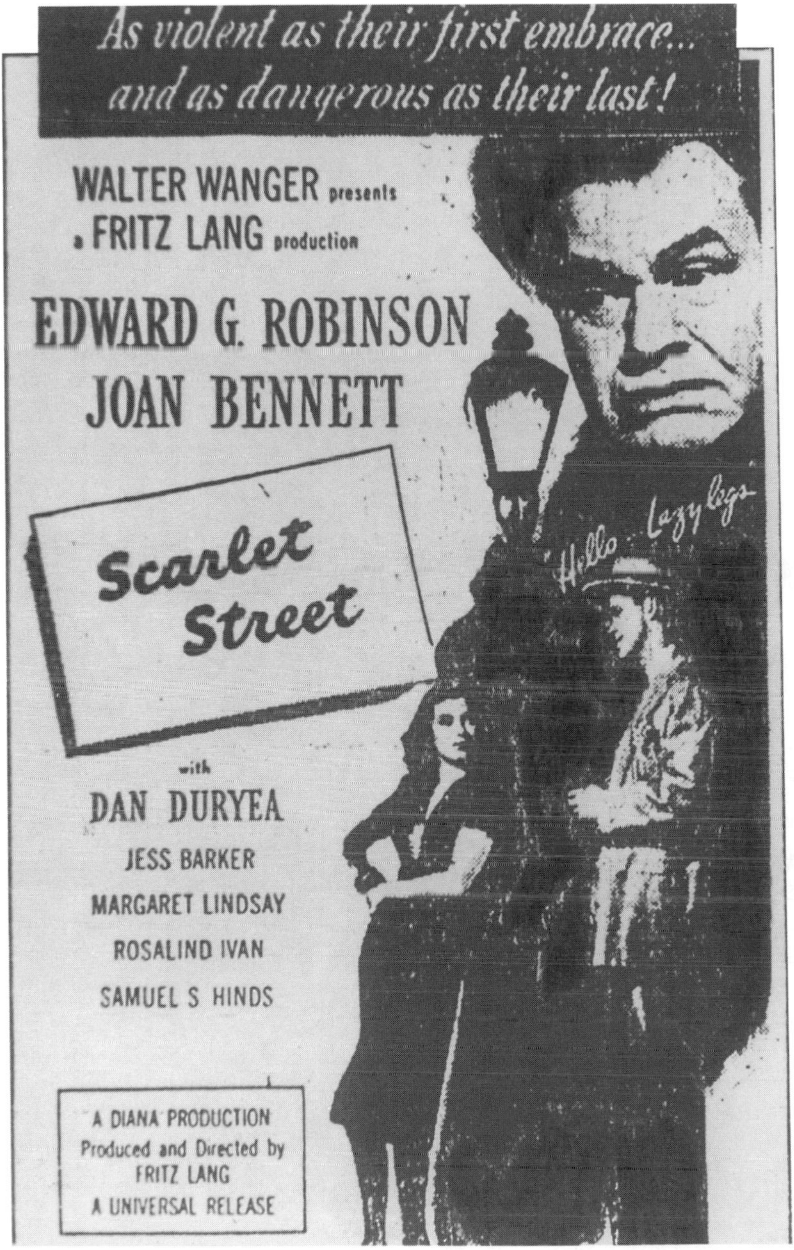

Figure 28. *Having quickly gained the approval of New York's state censor, Universal and a local exhibitor chose a titillating image to advertise the Manhattan premiere of* Scarlet Street *in the* New York Times. *The street-walker motif and "Lazy Legs" copy had unmistakable implications.* Copyright © 1999 by Universal City Studios, Inc. Courtesy of Universal Studios Publishing Rights, a Division of Universal Studios Licensing, Inc. All rights reserved.

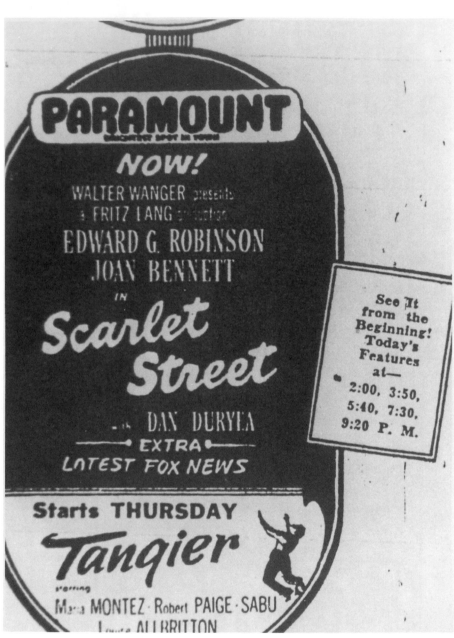

*Figure 29. After* Scarlet Street *opened in Atlanta, newspaper advertising simply listed the title with the word "Now" (as here on April 30, 1946), an allusive reminder of the film's banning. The streetlamp, "Lazy Legs" motif so prominent in New York ads appeared in Atlanta advertising only once.* Copyright © 1999 by Universal City Studios, Inc. Courtesy of Universal Studios Publishing Rights, a Division of Universal Studios Licensing, Inc. All rights reserved.

NOTES

I thank Stephanie Guest for permission to publish correspondence from the Walter F. Wanger Collection, Wisconsin Center for Film and Theater Research, State Historical Society, Madison, Wisconsin; and David Pratt for his feedback on this essay.

1. "Film Censors Ban 'Scarlet Street,'" *New York Times*, January 5, 1946, 16. This article noted that the film had been passed by censor boards in Ohio, Maryland, and Pennsylvania.

2. "Censors' Ban Put on 'Scarlet Street,'" *Milwaukee Journal*, January 12, 1946, 3. The quoted remarks are from Lester J. Bradshaw, executive secretary of the Commission.

3. Christina Smith is quoted in "Atlanta Bans 'Scarlet,'" *Variety*, February 6, 1946, 3. *Variety* had a field day with such headlines seven years after *Gone With the Wind*.

4. See Richard Maltby, "'Baby Face,' or How Joe Breen Made Barbara Stanwyck Atone for Causing the Wall Street Crash," *Screen* 27, no. 2 (1986): 22–45; Leonard J. Leff and Jerold Simmons, *The Dame in the Kimono: Hollywood, Censorship, and the Production Code from the 1920s to the 1960s* (New York: Grove Weidenfeld, 1990); Lea Jacobs, *The Wages of Sin* (Madison: University of Wisconsin Press, 1991); and Ruth Vasey, *The World According to Hollywood, 1918–1939* (Madison: University of Wisconsin Press, 1997).

5. Ira Carmen, *Movies, Censorship and the Law* (Ann Arbor: University of Michigan Press, 1966); Richard S. Randall, *Censorship of the Movies* (Madison: University of Wisconsin Press, 1970); and Edward DeGrazia and Roger K. Newman, *Banned Films* (New York: R. R. Bowker, 1982).

6. In particular, Randall usefully sets forth the overall legal context, bureaucracy, and procedures of state and city censorship, while DeGrazia and Newman provide a synoptic reference book of major local censorship cases. But Randall, while containing an historical survey and an overview of distributors' options for negotiating with censors (112–22), provides primarily a synchronic look at the workings of local censorship in the specific period of the mid- and late 1960s. DeGrazia and Newman focus on what they term "representative" censorship cases that came to trial (providing an informative survey of the legal arguments different distributors and exhibitors made); their work necessarily neglects that entire dimension of informal negotiations that ensued between distributors and local censors.

Carmen, who is concerned with the impact of Supreme Court rulings on local censors, was the most useful of the three volumes for this study. Pp. 212–14 describe the history of the Atlanta censor, pp. 141–53 describe that of New York State, and pp. 266–75 and 315–24 contain responses of New York and Atlanta censors, respectively, to a questionnaire about their background, procedures, and criteria for judging films. Carmen's is the only book to discuss the Atlanta *Scarlet Street* controversy (214), but his account is limited to a one-page synopsis of Universal and the city's suits and countersuits.

7. Michael Budd, "The Moments of *Caligari*," in his *The Cabinet of Dr. Caligari: Texts, Contexts, Histories* (New Brunswick: Rutgers University Press, 1990), 56–120. See also Ellen Draper, "'Controversy Has Probably Destroyed Forever the Context': *The Miracle* and Movie Censorship in America in the Fifties," in this volume, for a discussion of the absence of legal or social consensus in 1950s America about the nature of movies and movie censorship.

Francis G. Couvares, in his "Introduction: Hollywood, Censorship, and American Culture," *American Quarterly* 44, no. 4 (1992): 511–17, reprinted and expanded in his *Movie Censorship and American Culture* (Washington, D.C.: Smithsonian Institute Press, 1996), 1–15, discusses new trends in American Studies and the writing of censorship history. Couvares's own "Hollywood, Main Street, and the Church: Trying to Censor the Movies Before the Production Code" in the same issue discusses disagreements within Protestant groups and the changing alliances that led the MPPDA to adapt the Production Code, 585–87; rpt. in *Movie Censorship*, 129–58.

8. A 1939 play adaptation *Yes, My Darling Daughter* (Warner Bros.) had been temporarily banned in new York until deletions were made. The New York board had not barred

the exhibition of a film since the notorious United Artists 1943 release *The Outlaw.* "Film Censors Ban 'Scarlet Street'"; "Atlanta Bans 'Scarlet.'"

9. See Garth Jowett's essay, "'A Capacity for Evil': The 1915 Supreme Court *Mutual Decision*" in this volume for a thorough discussion of this decision.

10. Randall, *Censorship,* 117.

11. See Matthew Bernstein, "Fritz Lang, Incorporated," *The Velvet Light Trap,* no. 22 (1986): 41; and *Walter Wanger, Hollywood Independent* (Berkeley: University of California Press, 1994), 297–308, for discussions of the making of *Scarlet Street.*

12. Budd Rogers, letter to Walter F. Wanger, January 7, 1946, Box 90, File 33, Walter F. Wanger Collection (hereafter WFW).

13. Maurice Bergman, telegram to John Joseph, March 14, 1946, Box 90, File 33, WFW.

14. Budd Rogers, letter to Walter F. Wanger, January 7, 1946, WFW.

15. Ibid.

16. Ted Bonnet, memo to Walter F. Wanger, February 15, 1946, Box 90, File 33, WFW.

17. Henry B. Troutman (Atlanta), letter to Walter F. Wanger, February 14, 1946, Box 90, File 33, WFW.

18. See Paul Boyer, *By the Bomb's Early Light* (New York: Pantheon, 1985); George Lipsitz, *Class and Culture in Cold War America* (South Hadley: Praeger, 1981); Elaine Tyler May, *Homeward Bound: American Families in the Cold War Era* (New York: Basic Books, 1988); and Lary May, ed., *Recasting America: Culture and Politics in the Age of Cold War* (Chicago: University of Chicago Press, 1989) for insightful examinations of postwar American society and culture.

19. Richard Maltby, "*Film Noir:* Politics of the Maladjusted Text," *Journal of American Studies* 18, no. 1 (1984): 49–71.

20. Hedda Hopper, "Looking at Hollywood," *Chicago Tribune,* January 26, 1946, 13.

By something of a coincidence, footage shot in an earlier Fritz Lang film, *You Only Live Once,* was sold by the film's distributor (United Artists) to Monogram for use in *Dillinger.*

21. The Breen Office had rejected several previous attempts to adapt *La Chienne,* the basis for *Scarlet Street,* in Hollywood, particularly a version entitled "The Poor Sap" that Ernst Lubitsch sponsored in the mid- and late 1930s. See the first *Scarlet Street* file in the Production Code Administration Collection, Margaret Herrick Library, Academy of Motion Picture Arts and Sciences, Beverly Hills, California.

22. "Red Light for 'Immoral' Films," *Variety,* January 16, 1946: 1; "'Forever Amber' Script-Title Fracas Points Up Industry's Firm Code Stand," *Variety,* January 23, 1946, 1.

23. "Red Light for 'Immoral' Films," *Variety,* January 16, 1946, 1; "Protestant Legion to Sift Pix," *Hollywood Reporter,* March 15, 1946, 1; "Political Censoring Sweeps Nation; Put Up to Johnston," *Hollywood Reporter,* March 15, 1946, 11, 17.

24. "Catholic Group Gives Banned Film B Rating," *New York Times,* January 7, 1946, 17; "Legion of Decency in New Steps to Force 'Cleanup' of H'wood Pix," *Variety,* April 3, 1946, 1.

25. "Political Censoring Sweeps Nation . . ."; "MPAA May Join Civil Liberties Group to Challenge Film Censorship," *Variety,* March 27, 1946, 7; Fred D. Moon, "No Censorship Trend Despite Atlanta Act," *Atlanta Journal,* March 3, 1946, 15-C, cites a *Boxoffice* article, which apparently makes no reference to state censorship boards, which were a much greater threat to distributors. See Ruth Vasey, *The World According to Hollywood, 1918–1939* (Madison: University of Wisconsin Press, 1997), for a description of the formation of the MPPDA.

26. Randall describes the remedies available to distributors (*Censorship,* 81–86).

27. Budd Rogers, letter to Walter F. Wanger, January 7, 1946, WFW.

28. See Bernstein, *Walter Wanger,* 134–42, for background on Wanger's censorship battles of the late 1930s. See also Greg M. Smith, "Blocking *Blockade:* Partisan Protest, Popular Debate, and Encapsulated Texts," *Cinema Journal* 36, no. 1 (1996): 18–38.

29. "Statements About the Cuts Demanded by the NY Censorship for 'Scarlet Street,'" n.d., Box 90, File 33, WFW.

30. My analogy between James Wingate's and local censors' approach to deleting of-

fending scenes is premised on Lea Jacobs's enlightening analysis of Wingate's working methods. Wingate's cuts often left the transgressions of the fallen woman offscreen, while film endings ensured some kind of punishment or reform of her (she meets an unhappy end, falls in love and gives up her material gains, or is roundly denounced by other characters). From a moral point of view, this still left filmmakers with many ways of suggesting immoral behavior. From an aesthetic or entertainment perspective, these deletions could leave a film at best inconsistent, at worst incoherent. See Jacobs, *Wages of Sin*, 27–105, for a discussion of the Wingate approach.

31. As Jacobs describes him, in *Wages of Sin*, 106–49, Joseph Breen, learning from the Studio Relations Committee's oversights, took a more comprehensive approach to regulating film content from January 1934 on. Besides proving more attentive to visual representations of the rewards of immorality, mere deletions of sex scenes were no longer enough: they had to be contradicted by subsequent scenes to create a studied ambiguity for the audience of where, how, and whether the character engaged in immoral activity. Where the Studio Relations Committee might use a single scene to condemn immoral characters, the Breen Office worked to reshape entire narratives in a coherent fashion to denounce and punish characters.

32. "'Scarlet St.' to Open in N.Y. Feb. 20 After Getting Censor Okay," *Variety*, January 30, 1946, 8.

33. Bosley Crowther, "The Censors Again," *New York Times*, January 13, 1946, sec. 2:1.

34. Archer Winsten, "Censors' Face Saving Cuts to Lift Ban on 'Scarlet St.,'" *New York Post*, January 29, 1946.

35. John T. McManus, "Speaking of Movies: Scarlet Street and Censorship," *PM*, January 7, 1946 (on microfiche at the Film Study Center, Museum of Modern Art, New York).

36. Maxine Garrison, "Director Fritz Lang Defends His Movie, 'Scarlet Street,'" *Pittsburgh Press*, March 10, 1946.

37. H. Phillips, "The Sun Dial," *New York Sun*, January 30, 1946. Phillips's poem ran for six stanzas. It is worth noting that Martin Quigley, editor of the trade journal *Motion Picture Herald* and a major contributor to the writing of Hollywood's Production Code, also saw through Conroe's maneuver of face-saving cuts; and as for Conroe's reference to the film dealing with important sociological problems, Quigley wrote, "he is not sure of what he is talking about." See "Censorship Again," *Motion Picture Herald*, February 2, 1946, 7.

38. Evidence of concern with juvenile delinquency in Milwaukee includes: "Links Crimes, Broken Homes; Plea for Family Life," *Milwaukee Journal*, January 24, 1946, 15; and "Crime Decline Is Noted Here; Talk by Police Chief," *Milwaukee Journal*, January 31, 1946, 22. Police made explicit the role of movies in encouraging delinquency in "Urges Tighter Movie Control," *Milwaukee Journal*, January 30, 1946, 15.

There is some discrepancy in reports of the vote in Milwaukee. Wanger's advertising representative Ted Bonnet wrote Wanger in a memo dated February 15, 1946, Box 90, File 33, WFW, that on the ten-person board, four members (including a police inspector) had voted to ban the film, two members had voted against banning, and four members were undecided. Wanger fed this information to *Daily Variety*, "Hollywood Inside," February 27, 1946. By contrast, the *Milwaukee Journal* reported that the ban was agreed on by a vote of 11 to 4; "Censors' Ban Put on 'Scarlet Street.'" The important point remains that the censorship board was not unanimous in its vote.

39. John J. O'Connor, Charles D. Purtzman, Adolph Schimel, Maurice Bergman, and Budd Rogers, telegram to Walter Wanger, Nate Blumberg, and John Joseph, February 27, 1946, Box 90, File 33, WFW.

40. Milwaukee represented a larger population (by roughly one hundred thousand) than Atlanta. But it represented a less important market to Universal, in terms of its influence on the region, than Atlanta did in the Southeast. For a discussion of the film industry's estimate of the Southern box office from 1920 to 1940, see Thomas R. Cripps, "The Myth of the Southern Box Office," in James C. and Louis L. Gould, eds., *The Black Experience in America: Selected Essays* (Austin: University of Texas Press, 1973), 116–43.

Significantly, the *Scarlet Street* ban aroused little discussion in the *Milwaukee Journal* in January or February 1946, or in the *Milwaukee Sentinel,* which published few letters to the editor in general. But Buck Herzog, the *Sentinel*'s entertainment reporter and critic, took swipes at the city's film commission for the banning, noting the film's acceptance elsewhere, speculating on commission leader Lester J. Bradshaw's mayoral ambitions, reporting the film's fate in the Atlanta bannings, and relating the paradox that one of Milwaukee's censors was "laughing himself silly over the ribald dialogue and lascivious situations emanating from the play 'School for Brides.'" Herzog's comments appear in Buck Herzog, "Along Amusement Row," *Milwaukee Sentinel,* January 15, 1946, 5; March 20, 1946, 12; March 26, 1946, Part 2, 4 (quoted above); April 10, 1946, 6; and April 19, 1946, Part 2, 11. One letter in the *Journal* commented on the hypocrisy of banning the film while allowing a local stage production of the teen romance *The Voice of the Turtle:* "Zola and Maupassant might be sordid according to some people, but yet I prefer them to glamorous promiscuity on the stage or murder in settings a la Lubitsch. Truth seldom hurts an intelligent adult." Jeanne Mercier, "'Scarlet Street' and 'Turtle,'" *Milwaukee Journal,* January 29, 1946, 12.

41. Nate Blumberg, telegram to Walter F. Wanger, February 27, 1946, Box 90, File 33, WFW.

For the aftermath of the resolution of the *Scarlet Street* banning, see "Council Balks at Censor Law," *Milwaukee Sentinel,* October 29, 1946, 4; John L. Bohn, "Letters to the Editor," *Milwaukee Sentinel,* October 31, 1946, 14. Interestingly, the city film commission chairman Lester J. Bradshaw was forced to retire at this time when the Tower Theater's new manager (a GI) claimed that Bradshaw had, in the paper's words, "solicited him for the Tower's insurance business after mentioning three deletions which might have made the picture [*The Outlaw,* recently banned by the commission] acceptable."

42. Where New York State maintained a censorship board under a supervisor appointed by the state Board of Education, Atlanta had a city censor who was subject to the review of board appointed by the (central Atlanta) Fulton County public library.

43. Concern with juvenile delinquents early in the year is evident in William T. Ellis and Earl L. Douglass, "Undisciplined Youth Seen Gravest Problem of Day," *Atlanta Journal,* February 9, 1946, 4; and Morgan Blake, "One Way to Combat Seeds of Delinquency," *Atlanta Journal,* April 15, 1946, 11. In her responses to Ira Carmen's interview, conducted in the early 1960s, Smith affirmed that her primary concern was to protect "the immature." See Carmen, *Movies,* 321.

44. Harold H. Martin, *Atlanta and Environs: A Chronicle of Its People and Events,* Vol. III: *Years of Change and Challenge, 1940–1976* (Atlanta Historical Society, Athens: University of George Press, 1987), 123, quotes from newspaper accounts of the juvenile delinquents' activities; novelist Anne River Siddons fictionalized these events in her *Peachtree Road* (Philadelphia: Harper & Row, 1988), 113–18. I am grateful to Dr. Dana White, an Atlanta historian in the Graduate Institute of Liberal Arts at Emory University, for these references and for his insights into Atlanta politics in the mid-1940s.

45. "First Divorce Granted Under No-Jury Law," *Atlanta Constitution,* February 1, 1946, 1; "DeKalb to Hear 164 Divorce Cases," *Atlanta Journal,* March 8, 1946, 6.

46. Fred Moon, "Fate of 'Scarlet Street' in Lap of City Attorney," *Atlanta Journal,* February 14, 1946, 22.

47. "Dr. Louie Newton Opposed to Wanger Film," *Atlanta Constitution,* February 14, 1946, 10; see also the letter from the Atlanta Gospel Ministers' Association to the *Atlanta Journal,* April 9, 1946, 10: "It is tragic that many people look to Hollywood for their commandments. The result has been a wholesale violation of God's laws and the resulting breaking of many lives."

48. Paul Jones, "'Scarlet Street' Filmers Pledge Finish Fight on Ban," *Atlanta Constitution,* February 4, 1946, 2.

49. Ibid.; "Universal Maps 'Finish Fight' to Lift Ban on 'Scarlet Street,'" *Atlanta Journal,* February 4, 1946, 4.

50. "Milland Loses Week-End; Wins an Oscar With Joan," *Atlanta Journal,* March 8, 1946, 1. The article was accompanied by a large photo of Joan Crawford receiving her stat-

uette in bed from director Michael Curtiz. See also "Did Lana Concealing? She Should Was Spanked [sic]," *Atlanta Journal*, March 17, 1946, 1.

On the "Atlanta Spirit," see Dana F. White, "Foreword: The Dogwood and the Dollar," *AIA Guide to the Architecture of Atlanta* (Athens: University of Georgia Press, 1992), xix; on the Lamar Trotti promotion, see the *Atlanta Constitution*, February 3, 1946, 8. For accounts of the Atlanta premiere of *Gone With the Wind*, see Matthew Bernstein, "Selznick's March: Hollywood Comes to White Atlanta for *Gone With the Wind*," *Atlanta History* 43, no. 2 (1999); Gary M. Pomerantz, *Where Peachtree Meets Sweet Auburn* (New York: Scribner's 1996), 129–39; David Thomson, *Showman: The Life of David O. Selznick* (New York: Knopf, 1992), 120–24; Darlene R. Roth and Andy Ambrose, *Metropolitan Frontiers: A Short History of Atlanta* (Atlanta: Longstreet, 1996), 108–10; and Herb Bridges and Terry L. C. Boodman, *Gone With the Wind: The Definitive Illustrated History of the Book, The Movie, and the Legend* (New York: Simon & Schuster/Fireside, 1989), 205–29.

51. Ralph McGill, "Let's Not Become Another Boston," *Atlanta Constitution*, February 5, 1946, 8.

52. Ralph T. Jones, "A Few Short Items About This and That," *Atlanta Constitution*, February 6, 1946, 6.

53. Fred D. Moon, "Wanger to Fly Here in Fight for 'Scarlet Street,'" *Atlanta Journal*, February 8, 1946, 1, 12.

54. Wanger sounded these notes in a letter to *Life* magazine as well. Walter Wanger, letter to the editor, *Life*, February 11, 1946: "Certainly my wife, Joan Bennett, and I would not be party to any picture or program which anyone could construe as obscene or inciting crime. All of us feel that *Scarlet Street* is a fine achievement."

55. *Atlanta Constitution*, February 10, 1946, 10B.

56. Morgan Blake, "Thinks Atlanta Should Uphold Movie Censor," *Atlanta Constitution*, February 11, 1946, 13.

57. "Wanger Arrives to Fight Ban by City on 'Scarlet Street,'" *Atlanta Constitution*, February 12, 1946, 20.

58. "Report of Censor for February 1946," Fulton County Library, Atlanta, Georgia.

59. "Wanger Arrives to Fight Ban by City on 'Scarlet Street.'"

60. Fred Moon, "Wanger, Here, Deplores 'Scarlet Street' Row," *Atlanta Journal*, February 13, 1946, 9.

61. Wanger expressed these sentiments to the industry as well as to Atlanta; see "Wanger Raps Ostrich Act," *Variety*, February 6, 1946, 9; and "'More Serious Pix or Lose Foreign Market'—Wanger," *Variety*, November 13, 1946, 3, 20. Wanger repeated his comments to the Atlanta censor board when Universal brought suit against it: Affidavit of Walter F. Wanger on Behalf of Petitioners, Universal Film Exchange, Inc. and Diana Productions, Inc. to Superior Court of Fulton County, No. 137063, March 26, 1946, Box 90, File 32, WFW.

62. "Fate of "Scarlet Street' in Lap of City Attorney," *Atlanta Journal*, February 14, 1946, 22; Paul Jones, "City Attorney Sustains Ban on 'Scarlet Street,'" *Atlanta Constitution*, February 15, 1946, 14.

63. Maurice Bergman, telegram to John Joseph, February 19, 1946, Box 90, File 33, WFW.

64. Fidler's remarks included the following:

> I can understand why Wanger would try to protect his investment.
> What I cannot understand is why he ever made *Scarlet Street*. . . .
> If he can't edit his film to meet with the approval of the Atlanta
> censors then he should pocket his pride and his financial setback.

Wanger later initiated on unsuccessful libel suit against Fidler. Fidler's comments were transcribed for Wanger's suit; Box 91, File 4, WFW.

65. In her February 1946 report, Smith reported having received letters "from all over the country," telephone calls, and telegrams of which only very few were critical of Atlanta's banning; various local groups such as the Atlanta chapter of the United Daughters of the Confederacy, the Baptist and Methodist Ministers Associations, local Better Films Committees,

and various Civic Clubs had also approved Smith's action. In her March 1946 report, Smith complained that the newspapers "have not published letters received in support of our position and they have not correctly stated my objections to the picture." Atlanta Fulton County Library. She would subsequently let Howard Hughes's controversial *The Outlaw* play Atlanta in a cut version, she explained, because she "hesitated to risk another controversy" so soon after the *Scarlet Street* mess.

66. Henry Graham is quoted in Paul Jones, "'Scarlet Street' Filmers Pledge Finish Fight on Ban," and in "Showdown Fight Looms Over Ban on 'Scarlet,'" *Boxoffice*, February 4, 1946.

67. The Methodist minister's letter appeared in the *Atlanta Constitution*, March 6, 1946, 6. Other letters regarding the censorship action appeared in the *Atlanta Journal* on February 8, 1946, 16; February 11, 1946, 12; February 14, 1946, 14; February 27, 1946, 10; March 5, 1946, 8; March 8, 1946, 16; March 15, 1946, 18; March 19, 1946, 10; and March 22, 1946, 16. Letters appeared in the *Atlanta Constitution* on February 20, 1946, 6; February 28, 1946, 8; and April 12, 1946, 10.

68. "A Statement about the Motion Picture 'Scarlet Street,'" *Atlanta Constitution*, February 24, 1946, 15A.

69. Ralph McGill, "If the Censor Can Stand It, So Can We," *Atlanta Constitution*, March 21, 1946, 8.

70. Wright Bryan, "Censorship Is a Matter of Personal Opinion," *Atlanta Journal*, March 3, 1946, 14A.

71. Petition of Universal Film Exchange, Inc. and Diana Productions, Inc. to Superior Court of Fulton County, February 16, 1946, Box 90, File 32, WFW; Breen's affidavit is in the second "Scarlet Street" File, Production Code Administration Collection, Margaret Herrick Library, Academy of Motion Picture Arts and Sciences, Beverly Hills, California. I am grateful to Professor Mark Williams of Dartmouth College for making available to me his notes on Breen's statement. An account of the city's case appears in Ted Bonnet, letter to David Hanna, April 25, 1946, Box 90, File 33, WFW.

72. "Almand Rules Against City's 'Scarlet' Bans," *Atlanta Journal*, April 14, 1946, 1; "'Scarlet Street' Ban 'No Action,' Says Courts," *Atlanta Constitution*, April 14, 1946, 1; "'Scarlet Street' Held Neither Lewd Nor Immoral," *Daily Variety*, April 25, 1946, 4; "Atlanta 'Scarlet' Censors Reversed," *Hollywood Reporter*, April 15, 1946.

73. Fred Moon, "'Scarlet Street' Fails to Shock First Patrons," *Atlanta Journal*, May 1, 1946, 10.

74. Robert Sams, letter to Walter F. Wanger, October 12, 1946, Box 90, File 33, WFW. For an account of the demise of Atlanta's city censorship, see Pat Murdock's essay in *Atlanta History* 43, no. 2 (1999).

75. Harriet Pilpel, "Is It Legal?" (letter to the editor), *New York Times*, January 20, 1946, sec. II:3.

76. Elmer Rice, telegram to Walter F. Wanger, January 7, 1946, Box 90, File 33, WFW; and Fritz Lang, memo to Walter F. Wanger, April 22, 1946, Box 47, File 18; WFW.

77. Randall, *Censorship*, 116.

78. Cf. Couvares, "Hollywood," 610: "In efforts to defend itself, Hollywood might assemble and rearrange its alliances, finding advantage where it could, but never either clearly comprehending the field of play or controlling the outcome." Couvares's own study shows that censorship studies reveal social dynamics broader than hegemony theory can account for (acquiescence, accommodation, resistance, evasion).

79. There was even debate within the Hollywood community about what kinds of films the industry should be making in the early postwar years. Wanger's sentiments in favor of frank realism was echoed by those Hollywood filmmakers who envied the freedom of foreign filmmakers, such as producer Mark Hellinger, who told journalist Ezra Goodman, "*Open City*, about which many people are shouting, could never have been made here under any circumstances"; quoted in Leff and Simmons, *Dame*, 421–22. *Scarlet Street* screenwriter Dudley Nichols agreed: "A few people in Hollywood are trying to make films grow up and give real sustenance to the public." He wrote Wanger:

> If they surmount ignorance and timidity in Hollywood, are they
> then to be stopped by restrictions based on false morality and mis-
> taken conceptions in every other city in the United States? If so
> we had better sit back, stop making films, and wait for good for-
> eign films to take over the domestic market. For honest films will
> be made in Europe and they will be shown here, for the public in
> their good judgment will find a way to see them.

Dudley Nichols, letter to Walter F. Wanger, n.d., Box 91, File 2, WFW.

On the other hand, producers such as Arthur Hornblow Jr. denounced (without naming names) "lurid realism" movies like *Scarlet Street*, even if "they underscore a story point that is morally correct," for "regardless of the grosses they run up . . . the flareback from exhibition singes not only the individual producer but all producers and all exhibitors." See William R. Weaver, "Hornblow Cites Producer Responsibility to Decency," *Motion Picture Herald*, May 4, 1946, 39.

80. *Atlanta Journal*, February 27, 1946, 10.

81. Dudley Nichols, letter to Walter F. Wanger, n.d., Box 91, File 2, WFW.

82. E. Ann Kaplan, "Ideology and Cinematic Practice in Lang's *Scarlet Street* and Renoir's *La Chienne*," *Wide Angle* 5, no. 3 (1983): 42.

83. "Censor Explains Objections to 'Scarlet Street,'" *Atlanta Journal*, May 1, 1946, 26.

84. Maxine Garrison, "Director Fritz Lang Defends His Movie, 'Scarlet Street.'"

85. The *New York Times* ads used the image of Kitty under the lamppost immediately before and after *Scarlet Street*'s premiere, with the question, "Why is everyone talking about Scarlet Street?" and "The year's most discussed picture." The *Times* ads otherwise emphasized the film's similarities to *The Woman in the Window*, and relied on a street sign logo for the film's title, with shots of Bennett's and Robinson's faces (sometimes with Duryea) at opposite ends of the ad.

On occasion the ads featured purple prose copy: "As violent as their first embrace and as dangerous as their last kiss" or "The things she does to men can only end in murder." The streetwalker motif was a highly provocative one; see Darryl F. Zanuck's complaints about it to Joseph Breen in his letter of April 2, 1946, reprinted in Rudy Behlmer, ed., *Memo from Darryl F. Zanuck* (New York: Grove, 1993), 107–8. For sample ads, see the *New York Times*, February 14, 1946, 33; February 22, 1946, 21; and February 24, 1946, sec. 3:20.

86. Wanger made these comments in his letter to Abraham Bienstock, April 23, 1948, Box 5, File 8, WFW.

As reported in *Motion Picture Herald*'s "What the Picture Did for Me" column from March through early September 1946, *Scarlet Street* did poorly in rural and small-town theaters. Managers voice objections to everything from the film's immorality to its lack of action scenes, traits some managers associated with foreign films. See *Motion Picture Herald*, March 9, 1946, 44; April 6, 1946, 54; April 27, 1946, 50; May 11, 1946, 56; June 1, 1946, 38; June 22, 1946, 43; August 17, 1946, 52; September 7, 1946, 52. The one exception was Gray, Georgia: "Publicity of a censored picture is great for this small town. Thanks to the Atlanta censor, but I can't understand why a picture of this type was censored, and neither can my patrons." *Motion Picture Herald*, April 20, 1946, 59.

87. Breen is quoted in Leff and Simmons, *Dame*, 145.

88. See Draper, "Controversy," 202: "Whether or not a sordid theme could be the basis of art was the subject of the public discussion of [*Baby Doll*] and not the means and validity with which the movie could be censored."

89. *Motion Picture Daily* wrote of *Scarlet Street*, "It is not pretty. It is certainly for adults only." "'Scarlet Street,'" *Motion Picture Daily*, December 21, 1945. Obviously, *Scarlet Street* would not have been censored if Universal had marketed it as an adults only film. See Justin Wyatt's essay in this volume for a discussion of the segmented market appeals of American films of the late 1960s and early 1970s.

*Ellen Draper*

# "Controversy Has Probably Destroyed Forever the Context": *The Miracle* and Movie Censorship in America in the 1950s

On December 12, 1950, a trilogy of foreign movies entitled *Ways of Love* opened at the Paris Theatre in New York City. The trilogy contained Jean Renoir's *A Day in the Country*, Roberto Rossellini's *The Miracle*, and Marcel Pagnol's *Jofroi*. The movies had been duly approved by the licensing board of the New York State Department of Education; and yet twelve days after *Ways of Love* opened, New York City Commissioner of Licenses Edward McCaffery, a former Commander of the Catholic War Veterans and an associate of the Democratic political machine in Bronx County,[1] threatened to revoke the license of the Paris Theatre if *The Miracle* was not removed from the screen. Commissioner McCaffery stated that he found *The Miracle* "officially and personally blasphemous" and mentioned that he "felt there were hundreds of thousands of citizens whose religious beliefs were assailed by the picture."[2]

When McCaffery attributed his personal objections to *The Miracle* to hundreds of thousands of fellow "citizens" and banned the film, he in effect issued a call to arms. It was answered. Although within two weeks Joseph Burstyn, the distributor of the *Ways of Love* trilogy, had obtained an injunction against McCaffery's ban from New York City and state Supreme Court justices and had resumed showing the movie, the New York Board of Regents responded to mounting public furor by reconsidering its license of the picture. In an unprecedented action the Board of Regents revoked the license of *The Miracle* in February 1951. When the New York State Court of Appeals upheld the Regents' ban, Burstyn appealed the case to the U.S. Supreme Court. In *Joseph Burstyn, Inc. v. Wilson, Com-*

From *The Velvet Light Trap*, no. 25 (1990): 69–79. Reprinted by permission of the author and the University of Texas Press. All rights retained by the University of Texas Press.

*misoner of Education of New York* in 1952, the Supreme Court ruled in favor of Joseph Burstyn and for the first time extended the protection of free speech under the First Amendment to movies.[3]

Like all censorship controversies, the *Miracle* case offers us a unique opportunity to study the public reception of a film: because of the controversy surrounding *The Miracle*, the reception of the film could not be taken for granted—even by those viewers and critics who found the film itself uninteresting. A wide variety of responses to the film were documented in print, though as the debate progressed the reception of the film became important as an issue in and of itself, so that the record cannot be said to represent simply the unselfconscious reception of a film in the early 1950s. The reception of *The Miracle* that we can document consists of statements that lie somewhere between heartfelt private responses to the film and proclamations made with an eye toward the historical occasion that the *Miracle* case had become.

This essay will consider the debate surrounding *The Miracle* case as it made its way through the courts. I am particularly interested in the relation—or the lack of relation—between the legal rulings and the public debate on the subject of movie censorship. Neither the legal rulings nor the public debate were conclusive in the early 1950s, as the courts and the public struggled with the question of whether a single cinematic moral code could be mandated, and by whom. By 1957 the Supreme Court would distinguish free speech from obscenity on the basis of community standards in *Roth v. United States* and *Alberts v. California*,[4] and thus recognize a diversity of communities and standards. By 1957 the American public would demonstrate, in debating the merits of *Baby Doll*, an ability to discuss a controversial film without becoming completely diverted by tangential arguments about censorship. In 1951, however, the legal concept of differing community standards was not yet on the horizon and the public debate about *The Miracle* had little to do with film criticism. The inconclusiveness of the legal and the public consideration of movie censorship in the early 1950s was the result of a basic confusion about the nature of the film medium as much as a confusion about the aims of censorship.

Unlike the public discussion of movie censorship in the United States. in the 1930s, which prompted the formation of the Production Code Administration to enforce the Code of the Motion Picture Producers and Directors of America, the discussion of movie censorship in the 1950s was marked by a bitter factionalism, a deep disagreement about the proper role of film in society, and a lack of unified response to the public's concerns from within the film industry. Except for Hortense Powdermaker's anthropologically based study of the movies, *Hollywood, the Dream Factory* (1951),[5] and John Howard Lawson's Marxist tract, *Film in the Battle of Ideas* (1953),[6] I can find no American books considering the nature of film, let alone film censorship, from this period.

This contrasts markedly with the spate of books published in the 1930s as a part of the public discussion of movie censorship. The eager, if scientifically inconclusive, study of the movies undertaken by the Committee on Educational Research of The Payne Fund produced no less than eight books,[7] which were then interpreted in a "popular summary," *Our Movie Made Children,* by Henry Forman in 1933.[8] This in turn evoked books such as *Are We Movie-Made?* by Raymond Moley,[9] who went on to question Hollywood's self-regulation in *The Hays Office* in 1945.[10] The 1936 collection of views on movie censorship edited by William J. Perlman, *The Movies on Trial,* was introduced as "an attempt . . . to present, between the covers of this volume, the issues involved in the recent controversy" over movie censorship.[11] Perlman's symposium includes articles by William Allen White, The Most Reverend John J. Cantwell, Edward G. Robinson, and the Spanish poetess Gabriela Mistral.

The wide-ranging discussion of movie censorship begun in the 1930s extended into the 1940s: in 1947, the Commission on Freedom of the Press, operating under a grant made by Time, Inc. and Encyclopedia Britannica to the University of Chicago, published Ruth Inglis's extremely broad study of movie censorship, *Freedom of the Movies.*[12] In 1950, Martha Wolfenstein and Nathan Leites's *Movies: A Psychological Study* examined American movies as the common day-dreams of a culture with a "scientific" distance and focus.[13] During the 1950s, however, the public discussion of movie censorship took place almost exclusively in periodicals and newspapers: the very arena of the discussion indicates the factionalism, uncertainty, and inconclusiveness of the debate about movie censorship. The broader and more abstract considerations presented in the books of the previous decades gave way in the 1950s to outbursts by individuals who made no pretence of having scientific expertise and who expressed no expectation that a consensus on censorship would be reached. *The Miracle* became the center of this debate for reasons as complex and difficult to isolate as the changing understanding of the nature of the cinema.

## Discussion of *The Miracle* in the Courts

Four years prior to *Burstyn v. Wilson,* Justice Douglas addressed the issue of First Amendment protection for movies in *United States v. Paramount Pictures.* As Ira Carmen notes:

> Though freedoms guaranteed under the Bill of Rights had no bearing on the facts of the controversy, as Douglas freely admitted, he felt it necessary to assert that if such were the case then the Court's focus upon the issues would be regulated by the basic principle that "we have no doubt

that moving pictures, like newspapers and radio, are included in the press whose freedom is guaranteed by the First Amendment."[14]

Despite this pronouncement by Douglas, the Court denied certiorari to two other cases involving film censorship before it decided to hear *Burstyn v. Wilson*.

The first of these two earlier cases, *United Artists Corp. v. Board of Censors of Memphis*, involved the movie *Curley*, a comedy-drama set in an integrated classroom. The Memphis Board of Censors banned the film; Lloyd T. Binford, Chairman, notified the movie's distributors that "The Memphis Board of Censors . . . is unable to approve your "Curley" picture with the little negroes as the south does not permit negroes in white schools nor recognize social equality among the races even in children."[15] This ban was upheld by the Tennessee Supreme Court, which ruled that the legal issue on which the case turned was the distributor's standing to sue rather than the issue of censorship.[16] The U.S. Supreme Court thus was not able to use *United Artists v. Memphis* as the basis for a censorship ruling, as they would later use *Burstyn v. Wilson*.

The second of these cases, *RD-DR Corp. and Film Classics v. Smith*, involved the Atlanta censor's ban on *Lost Boundaries*,[17] a movie about a black doctor's family passing for white in New Hampshire. This case might seem to have offered the Supreme Court almost the same issues that the *Miracle* case did the following year. It is not possible to ascertain why the Court denied certiorari to the *Lost Boundaries* case; but one speculation is that the Court was not ready to address too directly the problems of racial discrimination. In an article in the *Cornell Law Quarterly*, Kupferman and O'Brien reported that "The rumor was that the Supreme Court did not feel it wanted to pass on another discrimination case at this time and used the excuse of the challenge to the legal status of the RD-DR Corporation to deny review."[18] In this light the Atlanta case posed a complicated problem regarding the legal issues of movie censorship. Since Mrs. Smith, the Atlanta censor, claimed that showing *Lost Boundaries* would "adversely affect the peace, morals, and good order" of that city,[19] the Supreme Court would have had to confront the movie's potential effect upon its audiences, and impose a legal definition of the nature of film upon the city of Atlanta. In the *Miracle* case the Court could proceed more cautiously in affirming only that "motion pictures are a significant medium for the communication of ideas"[20] and should be "included within the free speech and free press guaranty of the First and Fourteenth Amendments,"[21] without further defining the medium of film.

In the closing paragraph of the opinion of the Court in *Burstyn v. Wilson* the Court's caution in restricting film censorship is made clear in Justice Clark's statement that

> Since the term "sacrilegious" is the sole standard under attack here, it is not necessary for us to decide, for example, whether a state may censor

motion pictures under a clearly drawn statute designed and applied to prevent the showing of obscene films. That is a very different question from the one now before us. We hold only that under the First and Fourteenth Amendments a state may not ban a film on the basis of a censor's conclusion that it is "sacrilegious."[22]

In rejecting "sacrilege" as a homogeneous standard the Court did not deny the possibility of censorship; in fact, the Court explicitly recognized such a possibility. Justice Reed, concurring in a single paragraph, stated:

> Assuming that a state may establish a system for the licensing of motion pictures, an issue not foreclosed by the Court's opinion, our duty requires us to examine the facts of the refusal of a license in each case to determine whether the principles of the First Amendment have been honored. This film does not seem to me to be of a character that the First Amendment permits a state to exclude from public view.[23]

Despite its recognition of the states' power to censor films, a series of Supreme Court decisions in the 1950s gradually eroded the authority of the local censor. Richard Randall explains that

> In one line of cases that followed [the *Miracle* decision], various other statutory censorial criteria, such as "harmful," "immoral," and "indecent," used freely by censors, were held unconstitutional. By a process of elimination, these decisions made it clear that obscenity would be the only permissible criterion for governmental prior restraint of movies.[24]

It was only in *Roth v. U.S.* in 1957 that the Court accepted as the test for obscenity a book's "impact upon the average person in the community" on the assumption that the "present-day standards of the community" could be objectively known, and could differ from community to community.[25]

Between its extension of First Amendment protection to movies in *Burstyn v. Wilson* and its definition of obscenity in *Roth v. U.S.*, the Supreme Court heard six cases involving movie censorship, specifically involving the licensing of movies. In five of these cases the Court reversed lower courts' bans on movies per curiam;[26] in the sixth, *Kingsley International Pictures v. Board of Regents*, the Court held that a ban on the film adaptation of *Lady Chatterley's Lover* was a bar to the discussion of ideas.[27] None of these cases clarified the Court's position on prior censorship of movies, or moved toward articulating a standard for evaluating censorship based on differing responses to a film from different communities. Richard Randall points out that

> Though the *Kingsley Pictures* case and the five rather cryptic *per curiam* decisions failed to provide clear guidelines, the Supreme Court may actually have done all that it was capable of doing under the circumstances. It seems clear now that use of the *per curiam* method [in which the court issues a single opinion not attributed to any justice] was forced by the lack

of essential agreement among the Justices on the constitutional issue, particularly since oral argument was heard on the cases. The extent of this disunity was later obvious in *Kingsley Pictures,* where six opinions were filed in a unanimous decision. And still later, when the constitutional issue was finally drawn in *Times Films v. Chicago* [in which the Court applied the *Roth* standard to a film censorship case], the Court was divided five to four. In the ten years following the *Miracle* case, it was much easier for nine Justices to repair an abuse of prior censorship than to agree upon a theory for doing so.[28]

The theory that was lacking was an understanding of film as a medium of fiction. It was not merely a judicial confusion; in fact, the Supreme Court's rulings on movie censorship in the 1950s reflect the public's confusion directly.

## Public Discussion of *The Miracle*

The public's interest in the *Miracle* controversy did not remain focused on the nature of film and the cinema's right to First Amendment protection. In a modest editorial on January 2, 1951, while McCaffery's suppression of *The Miracle* was in effect, the *New York Times* remarked that

> There is no doubt that the film in question deeply offends the religious sensibilities of a sizable body of the population. On the other hand, it has been widely praised, the New York film critics choosing the three-film group of which it is a part as the best foreign-language cinema offering of the year. Neither of these conflicting views, held by sincere people of unquestioned good faith, can be lightly dismissed. But when there is doubt, it seems to us essential to lean away from censorship.[29]

This rationality disappeared in a wild array of charges and countercharges five days later when Cardinal Spellman took up the issue from within the Catholic Church. Although the attempt of McCaffery to ban *The Miracle* had been legally enjoined, the Cardinal's attack on the film could not be enjoined; and the debate on the censorship of the film moved beyond the courts' provenance.

Spellman had a statement condemning *The Miracle* read at all masses in St. Patrick's Cathedral on January 7, 1951. The statement announced, misleadingly, that the movie had been condemned in Rome by the Pontifical Film Commission, when the papacy had in fact approved the showing of *The Miracle* in Italy. Spellman's statement attacked the New York State Supreme Court for enjoining McCaffery from closing the Paris Theatre; and it accused *The Miracle* of being "a despicable affront to every Christian," "a mockery of our faith," a Satanic perversion, "a

*Figure 30. Anna Magnani in* The Miracle. Courtesy of the Museum of Modern Art/Film Stills Archive.

vicious insult to Italian womanhood," and a communist plot.[30] Spellman described the theme of *The Miracle* as "the seduction of an idiotic Italian woman," claimed the movie presented the Italian woman as "moronic and neurotic and, in matters of religion, fanatical," and went on to demonstrate something like his own religious fanaticism, if not neuroticism, by proclaiming

> We are a religious nation. The perpetrators of *The Miracle* unjustly cast their poisonous darts of ridicule at Christian faith and at Italian womanhood, thereby dividing religion against religion and race against race. This divisive act upsets domestic tranquility and makes enemies of people who should be friends and brothers.
>
> Divide and conquer is the technique of the greatest enemy of civilization, atheistic communism. God forbid that the producers of racial and religious mockeries should divide and demoralize Americans so that the minions of Moscow might enslave this land of liberty.[31]

In the wake of Cardinal Spellman's attack, the public debate over *The Miracle* was understandably somewhat unfocused. In particular, Spellman's assertion that the Catholics were "the guardians of the moral law"[32] drew a great deal of criticism. Joseph Burstyn responded the following day, January 8, in an interview with the press, to Spellman's charges:

There seems to me to be a motive behind this big ado. . . . The Legion of Decency has been quite harsh—quite tough—on films coming in from Europe. It is my impression that the Legion is trying to establish itself as the official censor of the City of New York.[33]

On January 14 a Protestant clergyman in Brooklyn, the Unitarian Reverend Karl Chworowsky, complained from his pulpit that he had seen the picture and that at no time did he find "the slightest urge to think unkindly of Italian womanhood or the Catholic religion."[34] Chworowsky went on to say that

As a Protestant and as a religious liberal of the Christian persuasion I resent a public statement calling the Catholics of the nation "the guardians of the moral law" and I further and deeply resent the insinuation of the Cardinal that everyone refusing to share his opinions regarding *The Miracle* is thereby classified as an "indecent" person.[35]

Like Chworowsky's response to Cardinal Spellman's attack on *The Miracle,* the public debate that ensued centered on the role of the Catholic Church in movie censorship rather than on the medium of film as an organ of free expression.

As the Catholics picketed the Paris Theatre with signs reading "This Picture Is an Insult to Every Decent Woman and Her Mother" and "This Picture Is Blasphemous," signs which later included "This is the kind of picture the Communists want" and "Don't be a Communist—all the Communists are inside," pressure mounted on the New York Department of Education, headed by the Board of Regents, to revoke the license it had granted *The Miracle.* Pressure from anticensorship groups also mounted. Prominent Protestant clergymen, the ACLU, the Authors' League, the American Book Publishers Council, the Society of Authors Representatives, The Theatre Library Association, and various individuals urged the Board of Regents not to revoke the license. Clergymen from Columbia's Department of Religion, Princeton's Theological Seminary, and Tufts School of Religion defended *The Miracle* before the Board's subcommittee.

Meanwhile, the Paris Theatre played the movie to standing-room audiences at every showing. The crowd awaiting admission to the movie often outnumbered the pickets outside the theater, and two bomb threats which emptied the theater did not deter the ticket-purchasers. The New York film critics, who had selected the *Ways of Love* trilogy as the best foreign-language picture of 1950, moved their awards ceremony from the Radio City Music Hall to the Rainbow Room in Rockefeller Center after Martin J. Quigley advised the Radio City Music Hall that if the ceremony were held there the theater might be subject to a Catholic boycott. The box office and critical success of *The Miracle* were inseparable from the movie's notoriety: it is difficult to tell how much the public appreciated the movie that was first legally protected under the Bill of Rights.

In a letter to the *New York Times* Alan Tate forwarded his personal analysis of the movie—he argued that

> The picture seems to me to be superior in acting and photography but inferior dramatically. Passive suffering is not a subject of first-rate art in any medium, and I cannot believe that an imbecile, as the main character, can sustain a plot of dramatic significance[36]

—and then went on to discuss the Catholics' attempt to suppress *The Miracle. Harper's Magazine* called the movie's opening scene "a memorable piece of filmmaking, though it now seems unlikely ever to be judged for itself."[37] In the press, at least, the movie was not judged for itself. The letter writers and editorialists who carried on the debate in print took the means the Catholic Church used to censor *The Miracle* as their subject, rather than the movie and its alleged sacrilegiousness. Otto Spaeth was correct when he observed in *The Magazine of Art* in February 1951, that

> Here, again, the quality of an admittedly controversial film and the motives of its producers were not the issue. . . . Controversy has probably destroyed forever the context in which the film originally appeared. The chasm between its condemnation by the Legion of Decency and the acclaim of other critics will not be resolved by any court. . . . The most regrettable side of this controversy is that *The Miracle* now lends itself to the kind of exploitation that attended displays of manicured versions of salacious baubles like *The Outlaw.*[38]

## Public Discussion of the Nature of Film

The debate over movie censorship in the United States between 1951 and 1957 was not a concerted discussion of the relative merits of the films involved, but a series of outbursts by organized groups and individuals, outbursts that were often only tangentially related. After decades of viable national consensus on the representations of moral issues in movies, Americans were faced in the 1950s with changes in the movie industry, movie audiences, and the medium itself that defied the established system of industry-regulated movie censorship.[39]

The effectiveness of the Motion Picture Production Code between 1934 and whatever point in the 1950s one wants to isolate as the end of its authority resulted from the Code's success as a definition of the medium of film, manifest in American movies.[40] When the Code began to fail as a definition of film, when there was no longer a viable consensus on what movies were, or could be, or should be, there was also no longer a focus for the debate on the means and aims of censorship.

To isolate opposing positions within the debate surrounding *The*

*Miracle* ignores the complexity of the debate by suggesting falsely that a focus for the discussion existed, when it did not. The Protestants' objection to the Catholic influence in movie censorship was not a unified attack on the Catholic Church, but a series of individual protests. For that matter, Cardinal Spellman's outspoken criticism of *The Miracle* and other movies was not representative of all Catholics in the country, and drew criticism from others within the Church.[41] However, the Protestant-Catholic fight over *The Miracle* proffered some terms in which the nature of film and film censorship could be discerned.

In his account of "The Strange Case of *'The Miracle'*" Bosley Crowther intimated disapproval of the Catholics' role in movie censorship:

> the authority of the Legion is so broadly and firmly applied that American producers and exhibitors generally accede to it, rather than run the risk of strife and boycotts.
>
> There is one area, however, in which the Legion has not yet imposed its will. That is the marginal area of foreign-language films.[42]

Readers of *The Atlantic Monthly* interpreted this article as an insult to their religion, much as Spellman interpreted *The Miracle* as an insult to Catholicism. Letters angrily proclaimed

> As a Catholic I am proud of the fine job the Legion has done to discourage movie producers from parading across the American screen immoral, filthy stories, from the shadows of life. The Legion's strength is truth and it fights for morality and clean entertainment.[43]

and

> Yes, the Catholic Church is a power; it is demonstrating its great power each day. It must do so. Today the Church stands as the only unified body strong enough to combat the pseudo-philosophies of the modern world.[44]

Other readers commended *The Atlantic Monthly*, but in more restrained terms. It may be that the Catholics' insistence on their Church as "the only unified body strong enough to combat the pseudo-philosophies of the modern world" was the basis of the eventual failure of Catholic censorship of movies in the United States, for in regard to the films themselves the Catholic Church's understanding of the nature of film was not that different from the understanding of other Americans in the 1950s.

An article by Andrew Ruszkowski in *America* in January 1952 conveniently summarized the Catholic Church's understanding of film:

> While we are the first to defend the right of the cinema to the noble title of Art, we do not fail to realize that it is before all else a language, and is therefore used to express ideas which have no artistic qualities. On the other hand, the impact of this language is so direct, it touches human sense and sensibility so deeply, that its impression produces considerable

modifications on behavior. The Church's role obliges it, therefore, to intervene lest danger overtake the souls entrusted to its care.[45]

This is something like the understanding of other groups who initiated boycotts of movies in the 1950s. The Jewish groups who held up U.S. distribution of the British film *Oliver Twist* until *The Miracle* case made religious censorship such a pointed issue, the American Legion posts who boycotted Chaplin's *Limelight* because Chaplin had been an alleged Communist, and the NAACP in its objections to the rerelease of *The Birth of a Nation* all assumed that the cinema was capable of portraying "ideas which have no artistic qualities" with enough power to corrupt viewers. This was essentially the understanding of film upon which censors like Lloyd Binford of Memphis and Christine Smith of Atlanta acted, also. Binford explained that *Lost Boundaries* "couldn't play in the South" because

> It deals with social equality between whites and Negroes in a way we do not have in the South. We banned it for that reason. On the other hand, *Home of the Brave* deals with a Negro associating with white soldiers. It's a military picture and that could happen.[46]

This assumption that good films must be literally true was defended by the Catholics in print through the 1950s, and enforced by state and local officials as a result of the series of Supreme Court per curiam decisions in the period.

As early as 1909, some form of censorship board was established within the American film industry to regulate the content of motion pictures, and some form of production code was supposed to be in effect, by the industry at least, from that time on. If American audiences did not unite to pressure the movie industry to adhere strictly to the standards it professed to embody until 1934, there nevertheless existed, for over two decades prior to the public's concerted action, an implicit agreement between audiences and producers about what censoring movies would mean. This agreement about the nature of censorship could only be based on an agreement about the nature of film. This consensus that brought about the suppression of violence, obscenity, and profanity in Hollywood movies created the "language" that Ruszkowski described in his article of 1952. It was by no means a limited one, if it was limiting. In 1937 Olga Martin observed with more than adequate authority that

> True realism in a [motion picture] story limns the conduct of its principals against the ethical background of the society in which those fictionized beings live. The reflection of the legal, social, and ethical dictates of the society are necessarily closely related to the lives of its members.[47]

Within fifteen years it was no longer possible to assert that film realism depended upon the accurate reflection of "the legal, social, and ethical dictates of the society" in the United States.

The dissent to the understanding of film and film censorship that underlay the Production Code was made publicly by Morris Ernst and Pare Lorentz in 1930 in a book called *Censored: the Private Life of the Movie.* Bemoaning the work of censors as an adulteration of art, Ernst and Lorentz contended that

> Not the producer, not the public, nor even a small part of the public is responsible for the sterility of the American movie. Nor can the producer alone be blamed for the gross, vapid illusions of life contained in the ordinary movie. The censor, the forces giving him power, are responsible.[48]

They compared the seduction and debauchery permitted in movies like *The Ten Commandments* (1930) and *The Prodigal* (1930), in which the sinners are briefly punished after reels of well-detailed sin, to the extreme censorship of foreign movies such as *Variety;* they deplored the changes made in American movies in anticipation of state and local censorship. Ernst and Lorentz sound like prophets of liberal movie critics in the 1950s, who would repeat these charges almost verbatim.

Perhaps as an overreaction to attempts to suppress foreign films in the early 1950s, liberal critics writing for national publications hailed the foreign films that appeared in the United States as revealed truths about the nature of the film medium. This critical reasoning led to a denunciation of Hollywood movies as mere commercial products consumed by ignorant viewers. Gilbert Seldes made the broadest objections of this kind in *The Great Audience* in 1950, in which he maintained that American movies were creating a "mass man" who accepted passively what was put before him on the screen.[49] Seldes's opening paragraph compared Hollywood movies to pablum explicitly:

> Except for the makers of baby foods, no industry in the United States has been so indifferent to the steady falling away of its customers as the movies have been . . . in one generation the movies have lost two-thirds of their customers and have survived only because a satisfactory birth rate provides new patrons for the seats left empty when people arrive at the years of discretion and stop going to the movies. This information has been received with a nonchalance that ought to make a banker's blood run cold; it has had virtually no effect on the quality of the product, which, like baby food, comes in cans. The parallel with strained foods breaks down in one detail: the foods would be worthless if the consumer didn't outgrow them, and the manufacturer virtually guarantees that they will become unnecessary in time and give way to other, more varied nourishment; the makers of movies pretend that what they offer is a balanced ration for adults also. But the reason the customers stop buying the product is the same: in each case the formula no longer satisfies.[50]

Seldes accused the Production Code of being a "fixed rule that actuality must be distorted"[51] and intimated that foreign movies were exempt from this distortion.

During the public discussion of the *Miracle* case, these accusations were repeated in a wide variety of periodicals. In the diocesan newspaper of Davenport, Iowa, the *Catholic Messenger,* Frank Getlein asserted that the Paris Theatre in New York City consistently showed better and more overtly Catholic films than "the gaudy palaces specializing in wholesome and harmless, odorless, colorless, tasteless, lifeless native American fare."[52] *The Nation* charged that Hollywood producers "long ago submitted abjectly to prior censorship in the Production Code and have never challenged the manifest unfairness of denying films the protection of the First Amendment."[53] *The New Republic* speculated that

> Perhaps a sense of high purpose coupled with a practical desire to earn revenues from neglected specialized audiences now that television strikes at the lowest common denominator will bring movie executives to guard their freedom of expression as jealously as have some newspaper publishers.[54]

Hollis Alpert remarked in *The Saturday Review* in an interview with New York State censor Dr. Hugh Flick that "Hollywood . . . had done little to promote its own interests" in abolishing censorship and had let "a small independent distributor" do the fighting for it.[55]

This last charge prompted a reply by Philip J. O'Brien Jr. in a letter to *The Saturday Review.* Mr. O'Brien pointed to the cases involving *Curley* and *Lost Boundaries* denied certiorari by the Supreme Court (*United Artists Corp. v. Board of Censors of Memphis* and *RD-DR Corp. and Film Classics v. Smith,* respectively), and claimed that

> But for the fact that the Texas Court of Criminal Appeals failed to render a decision between May 1951 (when the case was submitted), and January 30, 1952, the *Pinky* case [*Gelling v. Texas*] might have preceded or accompanied *The Miracle* in the Supreme Court of the United States.[56]

His point was "that 'Hollywood' did more than a little to assist in the fight to overturn censorship."

It is a point we must keep in mind. Although foreign films were the focus of many of the censorship controversies in the early 1950s—films such as *The Bicycle Thief* (1946), *The Miracle, La Ronde* (1950), and *M* (1931)—the liberal critics' claims that these films were de facto superior to American product were not supported by the economic reception of foreign films in the United States in the early 1950s. Hence it would be a mistake to assume that foreign films represented some broad, new understanding of the nature of film among the American public. One must rather assume the obvious: that these films were controversial because they were aesthetically and morally foreign to many of the people who saw them.

*"Controversy Has Probably Destroyed Forever the Context"*

## Foreign Films on American Screens

The presence of foreign films on American screens in the early 1950s was not simply the result of box office demand. The *Paramount* decision, in which the Supreme Court dissolved vertically integrated film companies in 1950, broke the production-distribution-exhibition chain which had prevailed in the United States for decades. Exhibitors who had fought for the chance to book pictures independently discovered that as production costs rose and an assured market was lost with the breakup of vertical integration, American studios produced fewer movies; and there were not as many pictures available as the exhibitors could use.

At the same time, economic factors favored the importation of foreign films. In postwar trade agreements with Britain and France the Motion Picture Export Association of America limited the profits the American film companies could withdraw from those countries. Under the Franco-American Film Agreement of September 1948, for example, American film companies agreed to withdraw only $3,625,000 annually, leaving about $10 million blocked each year.[57] These blocked funds could be invested in filmmaking in the foreign country, and be used to acquire distribution rights to foreign films.

In Italy the American subsidization of a national film industry was even more direct. In 1951 the MPEA agreed to pay 12.5 percent of all American film earnings in Italy to an organization called Italian Film Exports, established to promote and distribute Italian films in the United States. By the end of 1952, IFE Releasing Corporation had also been established. American exhibitors complained that IFE was acquiring the good Italian films for the U.S. market on terms that the independent distributors could not meet. In 1953 the subsidy to IFE from American film companies was reduced to 10 percent and in 1954, as the American exhibitors brought their complaint before the Federal Trade Commission, it was stopped altogether. Eric Johnston, president of the Motion Picture Association of America, estimated that IFE received between $4 million and $4.5 million from American film companies.[58] If this did not establish an Italian distribution company that could penetrate the American market, it inspired the formal complaint with the FTC by American exhibitors of Italian films, and a 1952 visit by Catholic priests with advice on how to avoid infringements of the American moral code.[59]

When foreign films did appear in America, they tended to be shown in "art" theaters, where they attracted a specialized audience. It is not clear how profitable foreign films shown in the United States in the early 1950s were. *Variety* reported in 1956 that "foreign grosses in the U.S. have never been published until now," and estimated the total foreign film box office receipts of 1956 at only $10,132,000, with French and Italian totals in 1956 just over $2 million each.[60] Cobbett Steinberg estimates that

American box office receipts in 1956 were $1,394,000,000.[61] The American public was not casting its box office ballots for foreign movies in any appreciable amount in the early 1950s.

## Conclusion

To what degree did the "foreignness" of *The Miracle* make it the subject of the public and legal debate about movie censorship in the early 1950s? *The Miracle* did not represent mainstream American cinema, and some of the public hostility toward the film was doubtless due to the fact that *The Miracle*'s subject matter and style were foreign. Certainly the critics who championed the film held that its difference warranted its protection from censorship. When the Supreme Court extended First Amendment protection to *The Miracle*, the Court was able to propose that films were guaranteed freedom of expression without having to address the complicated issue of whether or not, and how, Hollywood's censorship of its own product represented the standards of the moviegoing public. That issue would not be broached until 1961, when the Court upheld the right of the city of Chicago to censor the film *Don Juan* in *Times Film Corp. v. Chicago*;[62] and even then the Court split 5–4 and, as Richard Randall points out, there was such a divergence between the majority and minority opinions that "a dialogue between them is not easily joined."[63]

What *The Miracle* case exposed for the first time were the enormous differences in Americans' understandings of film, and the unwillingness of large segments of the public to recognize these differences. The 1950s have been stereotyped as a decade in which differences in opinion and understanding were rather ruthlessly suppressed. Studying the public and legal debate on movies in the period in which *The Miracle* case was adjudicated, I sense confusion, more than repression, fueling the controversy. The Supreme Court's hesitancy to define the role of local and state censors during this period is remarkable. It seems to me less striking that the Catholic Church organized to ban movies such as *The Miracle*, as it had been doing for decades, than that the Church was denounced for its attempts and accused of trying to influence non-Catholics in their beliefs via the Production Code. The fervor with which liberal critics hailed foreign films and scorned Hollywood's movies merely avoided the problem.

The role of movies as representations of moral beliefs in the 1950s could not be addressed legally or publicly as a problem until it was felt as one. *The Miracle* controversy seems to have felt like a problem of national importance for the first time. Hollywood could not simply wait until the problem of adjusting the movies to a newly diverse audience was settled in the public and legal arenas, but neither could it suddenly produce "foreign" movies.

*Figure 31. Caroll Baker as the infantile title character in the controversial* Baby Doll *(1956), with husband Karl Malden and interloper Eli Wallach.* Courtesy of the Museum of Modern Art/Film Stills Archive.

I posit 1957 as the end of the process of identifying the problem of movies as representations of moral beliefs. In 1957 the Supreme Court accepted community standards as a definition of obscenity, thus recognizing that standards differed from community to community. The Production Code, amended in 1951 to allow movie treatment of suicide but also to forbid completely abortion and drug addiction as subjects,[64] and amended again in 1954 amid some public uproar in its sections on miscegenation, liquor, and profanity,[65] was overhauled in 1956. Outright bans on depicting illegal drug traffic, abortion, white slavery, and kidnapping were lifted, and the only two subjects remaining completely forbidden were sexual perversions and venereal disease, with depiction of crimes still limited.[66] The Code attempted a more general ruling prohibiting any film that tended "to incite bigotry or hatred among people of different races, religions, or national origins."[67] This last attempt to modify the Code extensively as a definition of morals in movies relaxed many previous bans and recognized diverse audiences.[68]

In December 1956 Elia Kazan's *Baby Doll* was released. That film sparked a controversy in the press almost as heated as *The Miracle* controversy, but by 1957 the debate could focus on the nature of film. Whether or not a sordid theme could be the basis of art was the subject of the public discussion of the movie, and not the means and validity with which the movie could be censored.[69] The role of the movies in America's moral life, and the nature of film as a representational medium, were at last the focus of the discussion of movie censorship.

## NOTES

1. Bosley Crowther, "The Strange Case of 'The Miracle,'" *The Atlantic Monthly* 187 (1951): 35–39. This article gives a detailed and fairly objective summary of the initial controversy over *The Miracle*.

2. Ibid., 37.

3. *Joseph Burstyn, Inc. v. Wilson, Commissioner of Education of New York, et al.,* 343 U.S. 495 (1952).

4. *Roth v. United States,* 354 U.S. 476 (1957) and *Alberts v. California,* 354 U.S. 476 (1957). The cases were considered together by the Supreme Court.

5. Hortense Powdermaker, *Hollywood, the Dream Factory* (Boston: Little, Brown, 1950).

6. John Howard Lawson, *Film in the Battle of Ideas* (New York: Masses and Mainstream, 1953).

7. They were: W. W. Charters, *Motion Pictures and Youth,* combined with R. W. Holaday and George D. Stoddard, *Getting Ideas from the Movies;* Ruth Peterson and L. L. Thurstone, *Motion Pictures and the Social Attitudes of Children,* combined with Frank Shuttleworth and Mark May, *The Social Conduct and Attitudes of Movie Fans;* W. S. Dysinger and Christian Ruckmick, *The Emotional Responses of Children to the Motion Picture Situation,* combined with Charles C. Peters, *Motion Pictures and Standards of Morality;* Samuel Renshaw, Vernon Miller, and Dorothy Marquis, *Children's Sleep;* Herbert Blumer, *Movies and Conduct;* Edgar Dale, *The Content of Motion Pictures* combined with Dale's *Children's Attendance at Motion Pictures;* Herbert Blumer and Philip Hauser, *Movies, Delinquency and Crime;* Paul Cressey and Frederick Thrasher, *Boys, Movies and City Streets;* and Edgar Dale, *How to Appreciate Motion Pictures.* The Macmillan Company of New York published all of these in 1933; they have since been reprinted by the Arno Press.

8. Henry James Forman, *Our Movie Made Children* (New York: Macmillan, 1934).

9. Raymond Moley, *Are We Movie-Made?* (New York: Macy-Masius, 1938). See also Milton Anderson, *The Modern Goliath* (Los Angeles: David Press, 1935), which advocated extreme censorship and proposed incredible uses of nontheatrical motion pictures.

10. Raymond Moley, *The Hays Office* (New York: Bobbs-Merrill, 1945).

11. William J. Perlman, ed., *The Movies on Trial* (New York: Macmillan, 1936).

12. Ruth A. Inglis, *Freedom of the Movies* (Chicago: University of Chicago Press, 1947).

13. Martha Wolfenstein and Nathan Leites, *Movies: A Psychological Study* (Glencoe, Ill.: The Free Press, 1950).

14. Ira H. Carmen, *Movies, Censorship and the Law* (Ann Arbor: University of Michigan Press, 1966), 45.

15. Theodore Kupferman and Philip O'Brien Jr., "Motion Picture Censorship—The Memphis Blues," *Cornell Law Quarterly* 36 (1951): 276.

16. Ibid. "Motion Picture Censorship—The Memphis Blues" has an extensive analysis of this ruling by the Tennessee Supreme Court as an avoidance of the constitutional issue of movie censorship.

17. Like Lloyd Binford, the Memphis censor who, when asked what yardsticks he applied in censoring movies, replied "Yardsticks? It's just our own opinion," the Atlanta censor, Mrs. Christine Smith, took censorship to be a personal matter and had her opinions of

movies taken seriously, that is, legally, by movie distributors and exhibitors. For an interview with Mr. Lloyd Binford, see "You Can't See That Movie: Censorship in Action," *Colliers*, May 6, 1950. For pronouncements of Mrs. Smith, see the *New York Times*, February 5, 1950, sec. 2:5, and *Motion Picture Daily*, April 26, 1950.

18. "Motion Picture Censorship," 286, n. 87.

19. *New York Times*, February 5, 1950.

20. *Burstyn v. Wilson*, 501.

21. Ibid., 502.

22. Ibid., 505–6.

23. Ibid., 506–7.

24. Richard Randall, "Censorship: From The Miracle to Deep Throat," in Tino Balio, ed., *The American Film Industry* (Madison: University of Wisconsin Press, 1976), 433.

25. *Roth v. U.S.*, 490.

26. The five cases the Court heard and decided per curiam were: *Gelling v. Texas*, 343 U.S. 960 (1952), involving a Marshall, Texas ban on *Pinky; Commercial Pictures v. Board of Regents*, 346 U.S. 587 (1954), involving a New York ban on *La Ronde; Superior Films, Inc. v. Department of Education of Ohio*, 346 U.S. 587 (1954), involving an Ohio ban on *M; Holmby Productions v. Vaughn*, 350 U.S. 870 (1955), involving a Kansas ban on *The Moon Is Blue;* and *Times Film Corp. v. Chicago*, 355 U.S. 35 (1957), involving a Chicago ban on *Game of Love.* Justices Douglas and Frankfurter wrote concurring opinions in *Gelling v. Texas*, which was decided just one week after *Burstyn v. Wilson.* No other opinions were written in these cases. *Times Film Corp. v. Chicago* was decided after *Roth v. U.S.*, which comprises *Alberts v. California. Alberts v. California* was cited in the per curiam decision. This is why Richard Randall speaks of the "constitutional issue" being "finally drawn" in this case.

27. *Kingsley International Pictures v. Board of Regents*, 360 U.S. 684 (1959).

28. Richard S. Randall, *Censorship of the Movies* (Madison: University of Wisconsin Press, 1968). Chapter 2, "From 'Business' to 'Speech,'" provides a useful history and analysis of the legal issues in film censorship from the beginning of the century through the 1960s.

29. *New York Times*, January 2, 1951, 22.

30. *New York Times*, January 8, 1951, 14.

31. Ibid.

32. Ibid.

33. *New York Times*, January 9, 1951, 31.

34. *New York Times*, January 15, 1951, 23.

35. Ibid.

36. *New York Times*, February 1, 1951, 24.

37. "Miracle on 58th Street," an editorial signed by Mr. Harper, *Harper's Magazine* 202 (1951): 108.

38. Otto Spaeth, "Fogged Screen," *The Magazine of Art* 44, no. 2 (1951): 44.

39. Tom Doherty provides a succinct account of the changes in the American film industry and the demise of the Code on pp. 29–34 of *Teenagers and Teenpics: The Juvenilization of American Movies in the 1950s* (Boston: Unwin Hyman, 1988).

40. Michael Conant argues in "The Impact of the *Paramount* Decrees" in *The American Film Industry* that in the wake of the anti-trust rulings in 1948 the industry lost the strength to regulate its product:

> The Production Code Administration, the industry's agency of self-censorship which had been a barrier to the entry of independent producers, found its power of enforcement markedly reduced by the divorcement [of production-distribution companies from theater chains]. The majors had used the PCA to bar the entry of novel pictures of many types. Following divorcement, the control which the major distributors had exercised through ownership of

first-run theaters was lost. Pictures such as *The Moon Is Blue, Man With the Golden Arm,* and *I Am a Camera* were successfully produced and distributed although they were denied PCA approval. As a result, in order to preserve at least part of its former powers, the Code was revised in 1956 more nearly to fit its original purported purpose of barring obscenity rather than its monopoly purpose of barring novelty.

Conant, writing in 1960, charts the growth in independent film production during the 1950s and concludes that although prices were up, product was better. See "The Impact of the *Paramount* Decrees," in *The American Film Industry,* 346–70.

41. For example, in the *Catholic Messenger,* a diocesan newspaper published by Bishop R. L. Hayes in Davenport, Iowa, film critic Frank Getlein deplored the kind of censorship imposed by the Catholic Legion of Decency, and concluded that

> The worst point about this whole affair—the bitter personal attacks on Rossellini, the violence and threats of bombing, the madness in Queens—is that once again the Church has been viciously misrepresented, and, as so often, by the spokesmen of the Church themselves.

The report of this response to Spellman's attack on *The Miracle,* and of other responses from Catholics, was made by Alfred H. Barr Jr. in a letter to the editor of *The Magazine of Art* 44, no. 5 (1951): 194.

42. Bosley Crowther, "The Strange Case of 'The Miracle,'" *The Atlantic Monthly* 187 (1951): 35.

43. Vincent J. Argondezzi, of Morristown, Pennsylvania, in a letter to *The Atlantic Monthly* 188 (1951): 15–16.

44. Joan B. Whiting, of Albany, New York, in a letter to *The Atlantic Monthly* 188 (1951): 15–16.

45. Andrew Ruszkowski, "Catholics Look at the Movies," *America* 86 (1952): 421. This description is not to be taken as Catholic dogma, but as a useful summary of a surprisingly consistent Catholic perception of film. The first indication of a more sophisticated understanding of film on the part of a devout Catholic that I can find was Malcolm Boyd, *Christ and Celebrity Gods* (Greenwich, Conn.: Seabury, 1958). Boyd's book compared the "celebrity cult" of the mass media to Christian witness, and concluded that a contemporary Christian "must know how to interpret, in terms of his Christian faith, what he sees, hears, and reads." To do this he must recognize that the view of life presented by a movie, say, is not that of the Christian faith. Boyd's argument, that movies needed to be understood on their own terms, which might then be compared to the terms of the individual's faith, was a significant break with the assumption that the cinema was a language with the unmitigated power to present ungodliness and corrupt those who viewed it.

46. *The Film Daily,* August 23, 1949, 7; cited in "Motion Picture Censorship—The Memphis Blues," 276–77, no. 28.

47. Olga J. Martin, *Hollywood's Movie Commandments: A Handbook for Motion Picture Writers Reviewers* (New York: H. W. Wilson, 1937), 77–78.

48. Morris L. Ernest and Pare Lorentz, *Censored: The Private Life of the Movie* (New York: Jonathan Cape and Harrison Smith [1930]), 5.

49. Gilbert Seldes, *The Great Audience* (New York: Viking, 1950), 6.

50. Ibid., 9–10.

51. Ibid., 69.

52. Getlein is quoted by Alfred H. Barr in his letter to *The Magazine of Art,* 194.

53. Margaret Marshall, "Notes by the Way," *The Nation* 173, no. 21 (1951): 452.

54. "The Miracle Decision," *The New Republic,* June 23, 1952, 8.

55. Hollis Alpert, "Talk with a Movie Censor," *The Saturday Review*, November 22, 1952, 50.

56. "Hollywood Did More," a letter to the editor of *The Saturday Review*, December 27, 1952, 23.

57. See Thomas H. Guback, *The International Film Industry* (Bloomington: Indiana University Press, 1969), 16–19.

58. Ibid., 76–80.

59. For an account of this visit in an editorial protesting Catholic censorship of the movies, see Henry Brill, "Will We Gag Italian Films?," *The Nation* 175, no. 7 (1952): 132–33.

60. Guback, *International Film Industry*, 84.

61. Cobbett Steinberg, *Reel Facts: The Movie Book of Records* (New York: Vintage Books, 1978).

62. *Times Film Corporation v. Chicago*, 365 U.S. 43 (1961).

63. Randall, *Censorship*, 37.

64. See Garth Jowett's discussion of changes in the Production Code in *Film, The Democratic Art* (Boston: Little Brown, 1976), particularly pp. 413–27, for this amendment.

65. See "Movie Producers Stand by the Code," *American* 89 (1953): 587; "Movie Censorship Gets Shakier," *Business Week*, January 9, 1954, 33; "Shall Movies Exploit Filth for Profit?," *The Christian Century* 71 (1954): 37; "'Modernize' the Movie Production Code?," *America, America*, 90 (1954): 551; "A Free Screen?," *Life*, February 8, 1954, 28; and Walter Goodman, "Who Censors Your Movies?," *The New Republic* 130 (1954): 12–14. Garth Jowett mentions the amendment briefly in *Film*, 415. See also articles in the *New York Times* in 1954: January 10, sec. II:1; February 7, sec. II:5; February 15, 19; February 21, sec. II:1; September 14, 24.

66. See Jowett, *Film*, 417.

67. Ibid. Jowett is citing *Variety*, December 12, 1956, 1.

68. These changes were not greeted with optimism. See, for example, Raymond Moley, "The Code and the Church," *Newsweek*, January 7, 1957, 72.

69. To follow this debate, see "Some Notes on *Baby Doll*," *America*, 96 (1956): 320; "Blunt and Banned," *Newsweek*, December 17, 1956, 106; "The Production Code and *Baby Doll*," *America*, 96 (1956): 367; "Should It Be Suppressed?," *Newsweek*, December 31, 1956, 59; "Reflections on a Condemned Film, *America* 96 (1957): 386; "The Bitter Dispute over 'Baby Doll,'" *Life*, January 7, 1957, 60–65; "Baby Doll," *The Commonweal* 65 (1957): 371; "The 'Baby Doll' Controversy," *The Commonweal* 65 (1957): 381; "The Trouble with *Baby Doll*," *Time*, January 14, 1957, 100; Janet Winn, "The Crass Menagerie," *The New Republic* 136 (1957): 21; "The *Baby Doll* Furor," *The Christian Century* 74 (1957): 110–12; and "More on *Baby Doll*," *The Commonweal* 65 (1957): 465. *See also* the New York Times in 1956: November 28, 32; December 9, sec. II:5; December 17, 28; December 19, 40; December 23, 17; sec. IV:2, 8; December 24, 14; December 30, 24; sec. II:5; in 1957: January 4, 19; February 4, 22; May 25, 25.

*Jeff Smith*

# "A Good Business Proposition": Dalton Trumbo, *Spartacus,* and the End of the Blacklist

On August 8, 1960, Murray Schumach of the the *New York Times* reported that Universal-International (U-I) had decided to give Hollywood black-listee Dalton Trumbo screen credit for authoring the script for *Spartacus* (1960). With the subsequent release of *Spartacus,* U-I became the first of the major studios to break the Waldorf agreement of 1947, which initiated the blacklist. Although the studio's announcement was a clear signal to the public that the blacklist was ending, it followed a series of attempts by Dalton Trumbo to secure screen credit while writing under various pseudonyms on the black market. These efforts included the Robert Rich-Academy Award controversy of 1957, in which Trumbo won an Oscar for a black market script; the 1959 Academy decision to rescind the by-law that prohibited blacklisted writers from award eligibility; and Otto Preminger's public announcement on January 20, 1960, that Trumbo was the screenwriter for *Exodus* (1960). Trumbo's screen credit for *Spartacus,* which premiered some two months before *Exodus,* was his first since the blacklist began and the culmination of his efforts to end this ignoble institution.

Yet Trumbo's efforts alone could not have succeeded in ending the blacklist. Numerous economic and political factors influenced U-I's decision regarding Trumbo. This institutional context for the end of the blacklist has never been sketched in since most writers and historians focus their attention on the initiation of the blacklist and the 1947 and 1951 hearings of the House Un-American Activities Committee (HUAC). As Larry Ceplair and Steven Englund note in their introduction to *The Inquisition in Hollywood,* too many writers concentrate on the HUAC hearings themselves, and thus overlook the professional and political contexts out of which the blacklist arose.[1] Ironically, however, the very same

From *The Velvet Light Trap,* no. 23 (1989): 75–100. Reprinted (revised) by permission of the author and the University of Texas Press. All rights retained by the University of Texas Press.

criticism might be leveled at Ceplair and Englund with regard to the black-list's end. While the authors do commendable work tracing the events lead-ing up to the blacklist, they show very little interest in the blacklist period after 1953 and they devote only a page and a half to the actual dissolution of the blacklist.[2]

The minimal attention to the blacklist's demise logically derives from the "drama" metaphor that informs most writing on the subject. The "theatre" of the HUAC hearings has affected many accounts of the polit-ical and ethical issues raised by the blacklist's initiation. Thus, writers like Victor Navasky cast historical figures in a "surrealistic morality play."[3] The pages of these accounts are populated by inquisitors (J. Parnell Thomas, chairman of HUAC), informers (Larry Parks, the hearings' most famous cooperative witness), and victims (the Hollywood Ten). In several works, such as *Scoundrel Time, A Journal of the Plague Years, Naming Names*, and *The Inquisition in Hollywood*, the titles themselves reflect this tendency to treat historical agents as Manichean symbols of good and evil.[4] Since the end of the blacklist does not provide a properly dramatic climax to his "morality play," Navasky simply ignores it; *Naming Names* contains only a single page on the end of the blacklist.[5]

More important perhaps, the "morality play" metaphor charac-terizes the relationship between blacklistees and the institution of the Hollywood blacklist as one of heroes and villains, protagonists and an-tagonists. As a result, Trumbo's efforts to end the blacklist are described in such valiant and noble terms that they would make a Hollywood screen-writer blush with embarrassment. In his biography of Trumbo, Bruce Cook writes, "Cracks were appearing in the rampart with routine regularity. But Trumbo kept pounding away at it, determined to breach it at any price."[6] Similarly, Helen Manfull, who edited a collection of Trumbo's letters from 1942 to 1962, writes that Trumbo was "going to fight for the destruction of the detested blacklist," and speaks elsewhere of "moves to crush the blacklist."[7] Like these passages, the phrase "breaking the blacklist" itself suggests the opposition and struggle usually ascribed to the relationship between blacklistees and Hollywood.

However, Trumbo's relationship with Hollywood was far too complex to be so easily viewed as an individual struggle. The blacklist and the Hollywood black market had become major public relations problems for Hollywood after 1957, and they could significantly impact a film's performance at the box office. Such problems were due not only to the overall change of the political atmosphere from 1947 to 1960, but more specifically, to Hollywood's relationship with outside institutions such as the government and political pressure groups. Realizing that he would receive screen credit only after these public relations problems were solved, Trumbo worked with, instead of against, Hollywood. His primary strat-egy for gaining employment was to provide producers with economic in-centives, such as cheap labor and product differentiation. Viewed in this light, Trumbo's screen credit for *Spartacus* was the product of a whole series of conciliatory attempts to work in his own best interests as well as those of the industry. In doing so, Trumbo sought to end the blacklist by gradually improving the public image of the blacklisted screenwriter.

## The Black Market

In the years following World War II, political rhetoric in the United States gradually shifted from "Win the War"sentiments to predominantly anticommunist feelings.[8] After Roosevelt's death in 1945 and the election of a Republican Congress in 1946, President Harry Truman responded to increased attacks from the right by adopting a much stronger position against domestic communism. The anticommunist movement derived further grass roots support from private organizations such as the American Legion, the Catholic War Veterans, the Daughters of the American Revolution, the Knights of Columbus, and the Veterans of Foreign Wars.

HUAC rode this wave of anticommunism, and on October 27, 1947, the Committee began its investigation of communist influence in Hollywood. During the investigation, ten "unfriendly" witnesses, a group of writers and directors who became known as the Hollywood Ten, refused to answer the Committee's questions, claiming that HUAC was violating their constitutional guarantee of freedom of speech. Despite their protests, the Ten were nonetheless cited for contempt of Congress. After the hearings, the major motion picture studios were faced with the threat of further outside interference from the government, and a number of public relations problems caused by the negative publicity connected with the investigation. Thus, the studio heads met at the Waldorf Astoria Hotel in New York on November 24–25, 1947, to determine a course of action.

According to Ceplair and Englund, among the public relations problems that resulted from the HUAC hearings were a number of anti-Hollywood newspaper editorials, protests in Kansas and California aimed at films associated with the Ten, and, most troubling of all, a possible nationwide boycott by the American Legion.[9] Having just endured the Catholic War Veterans' campaign against Charlie Chaplin, the studios were well aware of the effects of such a boycott and knew that it would translate into significantly lower box office revenues.[10] They also faced the possibility of an even wider campaign if the Legion convinced any other anticommunist organization to join its protest. With the prospect of future government interference, a deluge of negative publicity, and fewer box office dollars, the major studios responded by stating that they had collectively suspended each member of the Hollywood Ten and that they would not knowingly employ a Communist in the future. Through this declaration—the so-called Waldorf agreement of 1947—the studios formally instituted the Hollywood blacklist.

Although the studios had hoped their actions would forestall further investigations by HUAC, a series of national and international events after 1947, including the Alger Hiss trial, the Soviets' development of atomic weaponry, and the beginning of the Korean War, served to problematize their position. As a result, in 1951 HUAC began an even more vigorous and extensive investigation of political subversion in Hollywood that resulted in the blacklisting of over two hundred writers, directors, and actors.

Dalton Trumbo had been a key figure in the 1947 HUAC hearings as a member of the Hollywood Ten. Prior to the hearings, Trumbo was a top screenwriter whose work in the early 1940s included *Kitty Foyle* (1940), *Thirty Seconds Over Tokyo* (1944), and *Our Vines Have Tender Grapes* (1945). Trumbo was under contract to MGM and earned $75,000 per script when he was subpoenaed to appear before HUAC. Like the other members of the Hollywood Ten, Trumbo was suspended without pay by his employer as part of the Waldorf agreement. According to Cook, the day Trumbo returned from the HUAC hearings, he was contacted by the independent production team, the King Brothers, to write the script for *Gun Crazy* (1949). Though the $3,750 offered by the Kings was considerably less than the terms of his MGM contract, Trumbo quickly realized he was considered "unemployable" by the major studios and accepted their offer.[11] However, since Trumbo knew he would be suing MGM for breach of contract, he did not want to appear in violation of the same contract.[12] Thus, starting with *Gun Crazy*, Trumbo began writing scripts using either fronts or pseudonyms, a practice that he continued throughout the 1950s.

After Trumbo's citation for contempt of Congress during the HUAC hearings, he was subsequently tried and convicted. When his judicial appeals failed, Trumbo entered the Federal Correctional Institute in Ashland, Kentucky, on June 21, 1950. After serving nine and a half months, Trumbo returned to his work on the black market. During the 1950s, he surreptitiously worked on several films, among them *The Prowler* (1951), *Roman Holiday* (1953), *Carnival Story* (1954), *Heaven Knows Mr. Allison* (1957), and *The Young Philadelphians* (1959).

Initially, Trumbo sold original stories for the screen with a front, a person who put his or her name on work written by a blacklisted writer. In exchange for the use of his or her name, the front was paid either a percentage or a flat fee once the property was sold. With this type of arrangement, a blacklisted screenwriter could still earn money for his talents while appearing to have no connection with the motion picture industry. Fronts were not always trustworthy, though, and could prove to be a liability for the blacklisted screenwriter. If the front violated the confidence needed to maintain such a working situation, the damage to the blacklisted

*Figure 32. Dalton Trumbo, one of the top screenwriters of the 1940s, was forced to write under a variety of pseudonyms following his blacklisting in 1947.* Courtesy of the Wisconsin Center for Film and Theater Research.

screenwriter's career would be extensive. In addition, if the front began to take an inflated view of his or her role in the relationship, and demanded a larger cut of the sale of a script, the business relationship would quickly become unprofitable for the screenwriter.

In order to ensure that such problems never occurred, Trumbo typically used fellow screenwriters as fronts, a situation that afforded him a certain number of advantages. First, since these screenwriters already had reputations within the film industry, they could command higher fees for Trumbo's black market projects. Second, the use of fellow screenwriters as fronts alleviated certain communication problems between the producer and blacklisted writer.[13] Depending on who was involved and the extent of studio participation in the project, the secrecy of the black market often precluded meetings among the producer, director, and blacklisted writer. As such, the producer's input regarding script revisions would have to be filtered through the front to the writer, which further complicated an already complicated process. However, these communication problems were eliminated if the front did all the rewrites. For *Roman Holiday*, Trumbo wrote the original story and screenplay while Trumbo's front, Ian McLellan Hunter, did most of the rewrites. Ironically, Hunter later won a Best Original Screenplay Oscar for *Roman Holiday*.[14]

As more and more names were added to the blacklist, however, friends who had once fronted for Trumbo, such as Hunter and Hugo Butler, suddenly found themselves among the "unemployable." As a result, Trumbo increasingly used pseudonyms when writing on the black market. In doing so, he also contracted more frequently with independent producers, who not only knew the blacklisted screenwriter's identity, but also often had face-to-face meetings with him.

Of course, it was largely independent production that allowed the black market to thrive in the first place. Because independent producers typically had much greater latitude in choosing screenwriters, they sometimes purchased black market scripts as a means of cutting costs. Say Ceplair and Englund, "The black market was a buyer's paradise; some of the finest screenwriting talent in the world was available at bargain rates to small independent producers who turned out 'C' films on shoestring budgets."[15] Likewise, in describing the King Brothers' decision to hire Trumbo for *Gun Crazy*, Frank King noted, "We just had a short budget to make a picture and saw this as an opportunity to get a fine writer to work for us who we could not otherwise afford."[16]

For those independent producers who used black market talent, however, economic risks came along with economic advantages. In a letter to Frank King dated May 4, 1962, Trumbo implies that public knowledge of his involvement with the King Brothers would have resulted in the loss of production financing and distribution for their films.[17] If Trumbo's statement is accurate, then it reveals the extent to which independent producers were caught in a double bind. Because they depended on banks and studios for their films' financing and distribution, independent producers were especially vulnerable to any outside political pressures exerted during the blacklist. Yet it was precisely this control over financing and distribution, and the often unfavorable financial terms resulting from this, that motivated independent producers to use the cheap labor of the black market in the first place.[18]

As one might expect, the lower costs of black market scripts derived both from their economic risks and from the diminished exchange value of a screenwriter's pseudonym. As Janet Staiger notes, screen credit was the only means for writers to establish their exchange value within the industry.[19] As is true of other segments of the industry, a screenwriter's asking price is largely determined by his or her previous credits. Of course, an invented pseudonym has no previous credits and therefore no perceived exchange value. For this reason, Trumbo's black market fees depended almost entirely on his ability to deliver a script without its origin being discovered. In Trumbo's case, the problem of exchange value was exacerbated by the use of different pseudonyms on different projects in order to maintain secrecy for each individual client. Noting his ability to survive such conditions, Trumbo wrote:

> I cannot tell producer B that the excellent picture currently released by producer A is an example of my work. I must prove myself to each producer as if he were the only producer. . . . I make all changes that are requested without additional charge, and, in addition, I am often called by telephone from the studio or even from cities in foreign countries, for dialogue changes that are needed in the course of shooting. Operating in this way I have not got rich, but neither have I been lacking employment.[20]

Trumbo's desire to satisfy each producer established a conciliatory, yet pragmatic, stance toward his employers that was to continue in all of his relationships with independent producers throughout the decade. In addition, Trumbo's desire to please helped to slowly but surely raise his exchange value. After a producer had been satisfied with Trumbo's work on a first project, he often returned for a second and a third. With each second or third project for a given producer, Trumbo's price rose.[21] Accordingly, Trumbo's salary gradually rose from $18,000 in 1953 to $40,000 in 1956.[22]

Because the relationship between the independent producer and blacklisted screenwriter depended on secrecy, Trumbo took a number of precautions to assure that the producer's risk in employing black market talent was minimized. First, Trumbo insisted that his clients meet him in his own study. Trumbo sarcastically described these meetings in a letter to Murray Kempton of the *New York Post:*

> By emphasizing the hellish peril of having me in their houses, I compel them to drive thirty miles to my back door. I invent assumed names which, spoken to their secretaries, bring them leaping to the telephone like startled hares. I permit them one conference at the beginning of a script and bid them come well prepared. A second conference is granted upon completion, but between conferences not a word or a page. For the good of their souls I surround myself with legally phony bank accounts, mysterious rituals, and awesome oaths. . . . Once they emerge from it, clutching a script as good or as bad as their taste, I crown them with the accolade Great and Dauntless Enemy of the Blacklist. They stagger off in a glow of moral grandeur, better, sounder-sleeping men for my ministrations.[23]

The "phony bank account" to which Trumbo refers was a second account he kept as a clearinghouse for all checks made out to his pseudonyms.[24] This was done so that money transactions between the producer and Trumbo could not be traced. Moreover, to avoid the necessity of keeping corporate records, Trumbo often relied on verbal agreements and cash transactions between himself and his clients. Finally, according to his signed agreements for *The Brave One, Carnival Story,* and *The Syndicate* (unproduced), Trumbo waived his right to screen credit and allowed the King Brothers to give credit to whomever they pleased.[25] All of these precautions fit the pattern of complicity and conciliation more generally evident in Trumbo's actions throughout the blacklist.

However, some of the steps taken by black market writers left them vulnerable to producer dishonesty. Without a written contract, a black market writer had little recourse if a producer violated their verbal agreement. For example, in his work on *The Brave One,* Trumbo had a number of problems with the King Brothers. Trumbo was supposed to receive $10,000 for the original story with the understanding that the King Brothers would not show it to other producers, and that they would return the story to Trumbo, at his request, if they had done nothing further with the property. The King Brothers, in turn, violated every part of this agreement, paying him just $1,500 initially, showing the story to other producers, and refusing to return the story when Trumbo set up a new deal. Trumbo eventually received the money the King Brothers owed him, but calculated that he had lost more than $11,000 as a result of their shenanigans.[26]

Although the black market had its problems, Trumbo made the best of them because he believed it was the key to ending the blacklist. In a 1954 letter to Hugo Butler, Trumbo wrote:

> I think right now the black market is beginning to grow, and that eventually—barring a Korean War or some such disaster—it will break wide open, and that viewed from the long haul, now is an excellent time to get into it and build. I think that the time will come when names again appear on the screen. When, I don't know; or what group will be first; or how it may come about: but it *is* now within the realm of possibility.[27]

From Trumbo's observations on the black market, we can draw some conclusions about the blacklist's consequences. First, economic determinants proved to be far more important to the black market's development than the political or social factors that had created the blacklist. Although writers had been blacklisted ostensibly because of their politics, their politics did not prevent them from securing work nor did it deter independent producers from surreptitiously hiring them. For the producer, the black market offered top talent at low costs, but also entailed the risk of losing financing and distribution agreements if the producer's clandestine contacts with black market writers became publicly known. For the writer, the black market allowed an opportunity to slowly reestablish his exchange value, but it also ensured that the writer was underpaid for his services. Second, far from being antagonistic, the secrecy of the black market forced blacklisted writers and independent producers into complicit and conciliatory relationships. Trumbo not only catered to every whim of his clients, but he also took a number of steps to protect producers in his associations with them. These economic factors and Trumbo's conciliatory stance toward the industry made black market work a good business proposition, one that under the circumstances fulfilled the best interests of both himself and Hollywood.

### *Friendly Persuasion*, *The Brave One*, and the 1957 Oscars

By 1957, the country's political atmosphere had changed. The Korean War was over, the Cold War was beginning to thaw, and Senator Joseph McCarthy had been censured by Congress. With the black market thriving, blacklisted writer Michael Wilson gave Hollywood the first in a series of public relations problems associated with the Academy Awards. Wilson had written a first-draft screenplay for *Friendly Persuasion* in 1946, but no film was made from the script until 1956. During the production, producer/director William Wyler brought in two writers to rewrite Wilson's first draft. One writer was Wyler's brother, Robert; the other was Jessamyn West, the author of the stories on which Wilson's screenplay was based. Working together, West and Wyler polished the screenplay before the film went into production and provided daily rewrites on the set, often as the scenes themselves were being filmed. When the time came to determine credits, William Wyler persuaded Allied Artists, the film's distributor, to give the screenwriting credit to West and his brother, Robert, as a reward for their diligent work during shooting. When Michael Wilson learned of Wyler's plans, however, he ledged a formal protest with the Screen Writers Guild and forced credit arbitration. The Guild ruled in Wilson's favor, a decision that angered Wyler for several reasons, not the least of which was their failure to consider the finished film, which itself differed markedly from both the shooting script and Wilson's first-draft screenplay. Although Wyler suggested a compromise solution that awarded credit to all three writers, Allied Artists feared that Wilson's name would provoke pickets by the American Legion. When *Friendly Persuasion* was released in 1956, it was without any screenwriting credit whatsoever.[28]

On February 6, 1957, sensing that *Friendly Persuasion* was likely to win an Oscar nomination for screenwriting, the Academy enacted a bylaw that made any blacklisted person ineligible for the Academy Awards. However, the Academy stipulated that the enactment of this bylaw would only be made public in the event that *Friendly Persuasion* was nominated.[29]

When *Friendly Persuasion*'s nomination was followed by a statement that the writer was ineligible under Academy bylaws, the Writers Guild was not pleased, and on February 20, 1957, it lodged a formal protest of the Academy's action. A joint statement issued by Edmund Hartman, president of the Writers Guild of America, and Edmund North, president of the Screen Writers Branch, stated:

> It should be understood that the screen writers in Hollywood nominated Mr. Wilson's work only as writers judging his art and only by sufferance of the Academy with which neither the Writers Guild of America, West, nor the Screen Writers Branch of the Guild has any official status whatsoever. In the event, however, that Mr. Wilson should win in our awards, for which his screenplay is nominated and which will be decided on March 7, he will receive his due. We will not cavil.[30]

On March 7, Wilson, ineligible for an Oscar, won the Writers Guild award for Best American Drama for *Friendly Persuasion.*

This incident suggested the extent to which blacklisting polarized the industry. The Guild's protest on behalf of Wilson suggests that they saw *Friendly Persuasion*'s credit arbitration and award nominations as opportunities to force the issue of blacklisting into the public arena. William Wyler recalled years later in his authorized biography, "I think it was kind of a backlash against the whole McCarthy trauma, with the Guild leaning over backwards so it couldn't be accused of refusing Wilson on political grounds."[31] Though the change in political atmosphere enabled the Guild's challenge, the conservative forces in Hollywood were determined not to give up the blacklist so easily.

On Oscar night, *Friendly Persuasion* lost the Academy Award for Best Screenplay Adaptation to *Around the World in 80 Days* (1956). However, despite the Academy's best efforts to keep a blacklistee from winning an award, Dalton Trumbo won the Oscar for the Best Original Story for *The Brave One*, a black market script he had written under the alias "Robert Rich." Trumbo took the name as an inside joke, because the film's producers, the King Brothers, employed a nephew named Robert Rich as a messenger. At the ceremony, when Rich was announced as the winner, no one approached the stage. In the midst of the confusion, Jesse Lasky Jr., vice president of the Screen Writers Guild, rushed to the stage to accept the award on behalf of Rich, who he claimed was at the hospital for the birth of his first child. Adding to the confusion was the fact that the King Brothers' nephew had called the Academy earlier that day hoping to scam some free tickets to the ceremony.[32]

Reporters quickly seized on the question of Rich's true identity. On April 1, 1957, the *New York Times* suggested that "Robert Rich" was in fact a pseudonym for a blacklisted writer. Two days later, Trumbo was on the front page of *Variety* refusing to either confirm or deny that he was Rich.[33] Meanwhile, producer Frank King insisted that Robert Rich did

*Figure 33. "Who is Robert Rich?": Photograph taken off the air during the broadcast of Bill Stout's interview with Dalton Trumbo.* Courtesy of the Wisconsin Center for Film and Theater Research.

exist, but was unable to attend the Oscars because he was performing military service in Europe.[34]

Far from clarifying the situation, the press's speculation only deepened its mystery. Unable to identify the true author, the King Brothers faced plagiarism suits from some five different people claiming Rich had stolen the idea for the story. According to the King Brothers, these suits had no basis, but unless they were willing to have Trumbo testify that he was Rich, they could not fight them. Although they considered such suits a form of blackmail, the King Brothers settled the first of them for $750,000 just thirteen days after the Oscars.[35]

In order to quell further speculation, the King Brothers asked Trumbo to be interviewed by Los Angeles newsman Bill Stout on April 10, 1957. During the interview, Trumbo admitted that he had been working on the black market for years, and claimed that he had received Oscar nominations, but refused to specify which films had been nominated. When asked about allegations that he was Rich, Trumbo once again refused to either confirm or deny.[36] This refusal was a publicity strategy worked out by the King Brothers and Trumbo that fulfilled each of their interests. For the King Brothers, Trumbo's refusal to deny his involvement with *The*

*Brave One* left enough lingering doubts that it ended further plagiarism suits until the summer of 1958. Furthermore, Trumbo's refusal to confirm he was Rich did nothing to contradict prior statements that Rich was actually in Europe, and consequently allowed the King Brothers to appear as though they had not broken the blacklist. The interview also helped Trumbo by allowing him to dissociate himself from bad films that he had written while, at the same time, linking himself to excellent films with which he actually had no connection.

In addition to the Stout interview, Trumbo also publicized the existence of the black market through an article he had written for *The Nation*. The article, which was entitled "Blacklist = Black Market," portrayed the Hollywood black market as a thriving underground enterprise.[37] Yet the very existence of a black market proved that the blacklist had not stopped members of the Hollywood Ten from working in the industry. By demonstrating its impracticality, Trumbo believed he could diminish public support for the blacklist.

Similarly, one might view the Academy Award for *The Brave One* as still another attempt to force the issue of blacklisting into the public eye. In fact, there is the remote possibility that Academy members voted for *The Brave One* because they actually knew that Trumbo was "Robert Rich." Because *The Brave One* failed to gross even $1 million at the box office by the end of 1957, it seems unlikely that Academy screenwriters could have voted for a film that no one had seen, written by a person no one knew.[38] In addition, the front-page *Variety* story on Trumbo just a week after the Oscars proves that reporters went right to Trumbo when the mystery developed, indicating that rumors of his connection with Rich might have been circulating. Whether or not the Academy was secretly aware of Rich's true identity is uncertain.[39] Regardless, the Rich incident provided Trumbo with a valuable opportunity to publicize his black market activities and focus attention on the blacklist.

By the end of 1957, the incident achieved enough notoriety that CBS planned a comedy loosely based on Robert Rich for early in the week of the 1958 Academy Awards. In developing the project however, CBS attempted to downplay the political nature of the incident by suggesting that its fictional screenwriter was blacklisted for slugging a producer.[40] Recognizing the public interest in Robert Rich, Trumbo devised a plan to use the controversy as a means of receiving screen credit for *Mr. Adam*, a script he wrote for the King Brothers under the pseudonym of "Beth Fincher." If the King Brothers agreed, Trumbo's plan called for them to keep the pseudonym throughout the film's cutting, advance publicity, and press screening. "However," Trumbo wrote, "on the night the picture opens, there will be a switch. The credit will read: screenplay by Robert Rich."[41] Trumbo even envisioned advertising (designed by Saul Bass) that would highlight the Rich mystery.[42] Trumbo hoped that the resulting publicity furor would culminate with the revelation that he was Robert Rich, but *Mr. Adam* had so many problems with the Production Code Administration that it was never produced.

The plan to expose Rich provides more evidence of Trumbo's conciliatory stance toward the industry. Trumbo's idea assumed that Robert Rich's name would not only generate a lot of publicity, but would also bring audiences into theaters. Much as a star's name does, Robert Rich's name would thus serve as a somewhat unusual form of product differentiation. And by stressing the potential profits the King Brothers would receive from the plan, Trumbo once again attempted to fulfill the best interests of both his employers and himself.

## Dalton Trumbo and Bryna Productions

By December 1957, nine months after the Academy Awards, the secrecy of the black market had diminished to the point that Trumbo's lawyer, Aubrey Finn, requested contracts for all the verbal agreements that the screenwriter currently had with producers. While Trumbo normally signed such contracts with whatever pseudonym he was utilizing at the time, he used his own name on a contract with George Bilson, producer of *Story of an Illegitimate Baby* (later called *Cry of the Unborn*), an indication that Hollywood's political atmosphere had changed to the extent that Trumbo's name could now circulate among potential financial backers and distributors.[43]

Meanwhile, Kirk Douglas's production company, Bryna Productions, was putting out feelers for black market writers. Bryna was formed in 1955 with rather ambitious plans for producing a number of films. According to Trumbo, the scope of Bryna's production schedule prompted their lawyer to recommend hiring black market writers for the reasons outlined earlier. Said Trumbo, "He represented it as a good business proposition simply because the labor to be acquired in the black market was a bargain."[44]

A Bryna report from March 1959 indicates that the company heeded their lawyer's suggestion. Bryna employed five blacklisted writers at that time—Dalton Trumbo, Paul Jarrico, Mitch Lindemann, John Howard Lawson, and Ring Lardner Jr.—who were the sole suppliers of screenplays for Bryna's motion picture and television projects.[45] More important, Bryna not only employed blacklisted writers, but they also proposed a plan to give one of them screenwriting credit. Trumbo detailed the plan in a letter to Aubrey Finn:

> someone has come up with the idea of suggesting to Douglas he use one of the black market people openly. He has declared himself willing to do this. The idea would be that whoever broke way as the first writer would

work practically for expenses—that is to say $5,000 to $7,500—for the concession that his name would appear on the screen. If, when the release date arrived, bankers or distributors caused too much trouble, the producing company would have the right to take the name off, but would compensate the author handsomely for the lost credit.[46]

Trumbo told Bryna that he was interested in their plan, and within twenty-four hours, they offered to show Trumbo every property they owned. In January 1958, Trumbo signed an agreement with Bryna that was very close to the plan outlined in his letter to Finn. The contract called for Trumbo to adapt Edward Abbey's novel *The Brave Cowboy* under the name "Sam Jackson." Trumbo was to receive $5,000 for the completed screenplay. The contract also stipulated that if the producer did not offer screen credit to "Jackson," the screenwriter would receive an additional $10,000 upon completion of the principal photography, and 5 percent of the producer's share of the net profits. If offered screen credit, "Jackson" would not receive the additional monies, but could designate any name he wished to receive the credit.[47] Thus, plans were in place for Trumbo to finally receive screen credit for *The Brave Cowboy,* and by March 30, 1958, Bryna hired a special publicity man to assess public reaction to the possibility of screen credit for Dalton Trumbo.[48]

Also among Bryna's properties was the Howard Fast novel *Spartacus.* When Trumbo was negotiating with Bryna, they already had a first-draft screenplay for *Spartacus* written by Fast, but were extremely unsatisfied with it. When Bryna contacted Trumbo about *Spartacus,* they initially planned to have another writer do the bulk of the rewriting, with Trumbo doing the final draft.[49] When negotiations with other writers fell through, Bryna settled on Trumbo to do all of the *Spartacus* revisions, once again using the pseudonym "Sam Jackson." In contrast to plans for *The Brave Cowboy,* however, Bryna had no intention of giving Trumbo screen credit for it. Because the film was to be released before *The Brave Cowboy,* and since it was budgeted at $5 million, it was simply too risky financially to make *Spartacus* a test case for ending the blacklist. Instead, Bryna planned to give the screenwriting credit to Fast.[50]

Bryna's finalized agreement with Trumbo for *Spartacus* was typical of all their agreements with blacklisted writers. The film's producer, Eddie Lewis, would front for the writer for all press releases, for the Screen Writers Guild, and for Universal-International management. Bryna wrote checks out to Lewis for Trumbo's services, and then Lewis would pay the writer either in cash or with checks written on his personal checking account.[51] Unlike the low salaries usually paid to other black market writers, Trumbo's fee for *Spartacus* would be between $50,000 and $75,000 with a percentage of the producer's share of the net profits.[52] Trumbo further cemented his relationship with Bryna by negotiating separate deals to write two more scripts (later produced as *The Last Train from Gun Hill*

[1959] and *The Last Sunset* [1961]).[53] These projects not only provided Trumbo with more work and more money, but they also proved to be important bargaining chips later on when Trumbo when would negotiate for screen credit.

## The Academy Bylaw Rescinded and the Real "Robert Rich" Unveiled

In early June 1958, an important meeting took place between Bryna executive Kirk Douglas and Vice President Richard Nixon. Douglas met with Nixon with the hope of receiving a statement against the blacklist. Douglas apparently assumed that a statement from Nixon would facilitate the public hiring of blacklisted writers like Trumbo.[54] Trumbo sent a letter to Douglas through Eddie Lewis that he hoped Douglas would show to Nixon. The letter detailed the activities of blacklisted writers in foreign countries, made reference to the Robert Rich affair, and explained the public relations problems that resulted from the Academy bylaw barring blacklistees from award eligibility.[55] Nixon refused to make a statement against the blacklist, but emphasized that the blacklist was an industry problem and should be handled as such.[56] This statement of neutrality from Nixon, who had been a member of HUAC in the late 1940s and was the prosecutor in the Alger Hiss case, implied that the government would not interfere in Hollywood's handling of the blacklist. With the threat of government interference gone, a major obstacle to ending the blacklist was removed.

In this new political atmosphere, the industry's knowledge of Nedrick Young's involvement with *The Defiant Ones* (1958) began to filter out to the public.[57] Young, a blacklisted screenwriter hired by producer Stanley Kramer, had coauthored the script with Harold Smith and submitted it under his pseudonym, "Nathan E. Douglas." In fact, the hire had been so open, it became something of an inside joke in Hollywood. The credit sequence of *The Defiant Ones* featured Young in a bit part as the driver of a truck of chain gang prisoners. As the credits rolled over this scene, the name of Young's pseudonym flashed onscreen at the same time that Young himself appeared. Two weeks before Christmas of 1958, individual Academy members approached Young and Smith about helping to rescind the bylaw prohibiting blacklistees from eligibility for awards. The Academy realized that *The Defiant Ones* was a likely nominee for a screenwriting award, and they wanted to avoid any further public embarrassment from the problems that resulted from the bylaw.

After the *Friendly Persuasion* and Robert Rich fiascos at the 1957 Oscars, the Academy bylaw had become an annual problem. The 1958 Oscar ceremony was plagued by scuttlebutt surrounding *The Bridge on the River Kwai* (1957). A *Newsweek* article prior to the awards linked blacklisted

*Figure 34. Harold Smith and Nedrick Young ("Nathan E. Douglas") receiving Oscars for* The Defiant Ones *in the 1959 Academy Awards ceremony, another embarrassment for the industry.* Courtesy of the Wisconsin Center for Film and Theater Research.

screenwriters Carl Foreman and Michael Wilson with the film even though the screenwriting credit had gone to the novel's author, Pierre Boulle.[58] When Boulle failed to appear on Oscar night to accept his award for Best Screenplay Adaptation, rumors swirled regarding the reason for his absence. As it turns out, an acceptance speech by Boulle would have exposed the whole farce on national television because the author barely spoke English.

    With the possibility of a third annual public relations disaster with *The Defiant Ones*, the Academy hoped to join Young and Smith in a united public relations front in lieu of the elimination of the bylaw. Young and Smith, unsure of what to do, turned to Trumbo, who suggested that they wait until they had won some awards before breaking the story in the national press. However, after Young and Smith won the New York Drama Critics Award on December 31, 1958, the *New York Times* threatened to break the story with or without Young and Smith's cooperation. Thus, they went ahead and broke the story to *Times* reporter Thomas Pryor.

Trumbo also arranged for them to be interviewed by Bill Stout on local Los Angeles television that same evening. Soon after, the Academy began debating whether or not to rescind the bylaw.[59]

Meanwhile, in January 1959, the King Brothers asked Trumbo to come forward as Robert Rich in order to thwart yet another lawsuit on *The Brave One*.[60] This posed certain problems for Trumbo since such a disclosure could create a backlash within the Academy regarding the revocation of the Academy bylaw. Thus, on January 11, 1959, Trumbo sent a letter to former president George Seaton stressing that the imminent disclosure was not an attempt to discredit the Academy.[61] After rescheduling the Rich announcement in the hope that the bylaw situation could be quickly resolved, Trumbo drafted a letter clarifying his position on the Academy's pending decision. He wrote, "We do not wish to attack or embarrass the Academy, and it is our assumption the Academy does not wish to embarrass us. Forbearance, tact, and mutual assistance toward a desireable (sic) end seem to us far the better tactic."[62] In addition, Trumbo suggested an alternative to the potentially volatile outright rescission of the bylaw. He recommended that the Academy revise the rule so that it only disallowed persons convicted of treason, conspiracy, or the incitement of racial, religious, or political violence.[63] This revision would effectively make blacklisted writers eligible for awards, but would not appear as an outright revocation to the public.

Trumbo's suggestion proved unnecessary because on January 15, 1959, the Academy officially rescinded the bylaw prohibiting blacklisted writers from eligibility for awards.[64] With no need to wait any longer, Trumbo publicly announced that he was the real "Robert Rich" only two days later.[65] In the aftermath of the Rich revelation, Academy President George Stevens made some unflattering remarks about Trumbo and other black market writers. Trumbo immediately wrote George Seaton a letter, which he hoped Seaton would show to Stevens, saying that the Academy was no longer in a position to bully blacklisted writers. He added that as long as he was not insulted, Trumbo would maintain a conciliatory public relations position:

> The blacklist is being swept away so fast that some spectacular open hirings are at hand, and the victory over the blacklist simply *must* not appear to the public as victory over the Academy. . . . I am solely interested in breaking the blacklist, that it *will* be broken—and that even there I can see no possible conflict between his interests and mine.[66]

The Academy decision and Trumbo's "Rich" announcement confirmed what had been implied by the publicity surrounding the black market: the blacklist simply had not worked. After each public relations embarrassment, the general public was forced to ask itself the question that John Cogley posed in *Commonwealth:* what was so subversive about these writers if they were winning major awards? As the impending nomination of Nedrick Young and *The Defiant Ones* drew near, it became clear that it was in the Academy's best interests to revoke the bylaw and risk the possibility that the blacklist appeared a failure, rather than affirm the blacklist and risk further public relations problems.

The circumstances around this decision once again raise the issue of how previous writers have treated the blacklist period as a whole. The focus on political and moral issues that were raised by the blacklist have obscured that fact that by early 1959 the blacklist was becoming more and more impractical. As is obvious, the rescission of the bylaw was not the product of struggle between blacklisted writers and Hollywood. However, it would be equally wrong to attribute this progress solely to the efforts of blacklistees. It is highly unlikely that blacklisted writers would have achieved such a decision without support from inside the Academy. As I have stated throughout, progress toward ending the blacklist came only when it first suited the interests of Hollywood.

A month after the Rich revelation, Trumbo wrote to Michael Wilson regarding the question of how, and who would be first, to get screen credit. Trumbo emphasized that a conciliatory stance must be kept to allay fears that blacklisters or informers would face reprisals from those returning to the industry. Trumbo added that the blacklist would not end until the public judged the work rather than the writer. Said Trumbo, "The blacklist will not be broken by the triumph of morality over immorality. It will not be broken by the triumph of one organization over another organization. It will be broken by the sheer excellence of the work of two or three blacklisted writers."[67]

In this quote, Trumbo implies that a meritocracy had developed within the black market. Only Albert Maltz, Michael Wilson, and Trumbo himself had established high enough exchange values for a producer to be willing to negotiate screen credit for them. Thus, Trumbo believed that Maltz, Wilson, or himself would be the first to receive screen credit. Though it was obvious at this point that Wilson could receive screen credit in Europe, Trumbo argued that "the real breakthrough has to come in Hollywood, through Hollywood, and with a picture designed to capture an American audience."[68] Until such credit was available, Trumbo suggested that each of the three writers—Maltz, Wilson, and himself—use one pseudonym for all his future projects until that pseudonym became synonymous with the respective writer's real name.

Trumbo believed that such a tactic would work because rumors had already spread that he was working on *Spartacus*. By this time, the entire cast and crew of *Spartacus* knew that Trumbo was writing the script, everyone in Bryna knew, and MCA head Lew Wasserman knew. Trumbo joked that the only two people in Hollywood that did not know of his involvement with *Spartacus* were the two chief executives at U-I.[69] Moreover, rumors of Trumbo's involvement also circulated in the general press. During the week of March 21, 1959, both Walter Winchell and the *Hollywood Reporter* acknowledged Trumbo was writing *Spartacus* for a $50,000 fee.[70]

Though such rumors circulated, Bryna remained tight-lipped on the subject. Neither Trumbo's name nor the name of any screenwriter was mentioned in any of Bryna's press releases for *Spartacus*. In an attempt to further protect itself, Bryna hoped to receive a letter from Trumbo as "Sam Jackson," in which Jackson would legally give producer Eddie Lewis the right not to use Jackson's name in the credits.[71] By June 9, 1959, the problem became acute enough for Bryna comptroller Jeff Asher to suggest a meeting with attorney Leon Kaplan and Lew Wasserman, president of MCA. Asher was to suggest at the meeting that the names of "Sam Jackson" or even "Dalton Trumbo" be filed with the Screen Writers Guild.[72] With Bryna and U-I executives discussing the possibility of screen credit for Trumbo on *Spartacus*, the likelihood that his name would appear onscreen became even greater. Only one potential problem remained: the American Legion.

## From the American Legion to *Exodus*

The change in the political atmosphere from 1947 to 1959 was remarkable. Many of the politicians who had taken part in the anticommunist crusades of the 1940s and 1950s adopted quite different private and public political stances by 1959. As president, Harry Truman had ordered that loyalty oaths be taken by all federal employees; by 1959, Truman was publicly speaking out against the Hollywood blacklist.[73] Following the Academy bylaw rescission, however, the American Legion renewed its pressure on the major studios to maintain the blacklist. The Legion remained a force to be reckoned with for some of the same reasons as when the blacklist had first been initiated. The Legion could generate a lot of negative publicity regarding the major studios and a Legion boycott could do significant damage to a film's potential box office revenues.

In response to this situation, Trumbo wrote to his lawyer, "For some reason the American Legion has been able to convince Hollywood— and Hollywood alone—that it is the largest and most powerful organization in the country. It simply is not."[74] Trumbo went on:

> As for the information conveyed to me that I am personally the principal target of the Legion campaign, I am not at all disturbed. The Legion is as powerless against me as it is against the producers. The difference lies in the fact that I know it, and the producers are only becoming dimly aware of it. . . .
>
> When he (Mendel Silberberg, Columbia Pictures' lawyer) states that

in the present situation my personal interests and the interests of his clients entirely coincide, I agree with this exception: the two interests have *always* coincided. The now blacklisted artists of Hollywood spelled out the coincidence of interests in great detail twelve years ago, while the producers have become aware of it only lately. . . .

I suggest . . . that the interests of the Hollywood blacklistees and the producers always *will* coincide, and that when this fact is fully understood on the producers' side we shall be able to meet together and put a civilized end to a situation which presently is far more embarassing [sic] (as distinguished from painful) to producers than blacklistees.[75]

At first, the majors put up some resistance to the Legion's renewed attack, but in August 1959, Academy President and Columbia Pictures Vice President B. B. Kahane kowtowed to the American Legion at their national convention in Minneapolis. Murray Schumach of the *New York Times* reported on Kahane's appearance by asking, "Did the major studios, in return for limited absolution from the Legion, offer the independents as scapegoats and at the same time promise to behave in the future?"[76] In addition to feeling sold out, independent producers claimed that the majors had abandoned both their own and the independent producers' right to hire and fire without outside guidance.[77] More troubling for Trumbo was the fact that the *Minneapolis Morning Tribune* and *Variety* both reported that Kahane had called Trumbo a "hard core Communist."[78] Trumbo said nothing about this publicly, but privately threatened to sue Kahane. Although Trumbo hoped to obtain a retraction from Kahane that he could circulate within the industry,[79] the matter was dropped when he was called away to work on *Exodus*. Soon after, Kahane died.

Trumbo was not director Otto Preminger's first choice for the screen adaptation of *Exodus*, however. In a November 11, 1959, letter, Albert Maltz informed Trumbo that he was working on the film adaptation of *Exodus* and that Preminger was "very eager to have my name on it."[80] Shortly thereafter, Preminger became dissatisfied with Maltz's work on the film, and about six weeks later, replaced Maltz with Trumbo. The fact that Preminger was eager to use Maltz's name, but not Maltz, strongly suggests that he wanted to be the first to break the blacklist, and almost any blacklisted writer would do.

Why had independent producers such as Kirk Douglas and Otto Preminger expressed such interest in putting the names of blacklisted writers on the screen? Clearly there was no longer any financial savings in using black market writers. By the time of completion, Trumbo's salary on *Spartacus* rose to $100,000 plus 4 percent of the net producer profits.[81] Although Kirk Douglas has asserted his personal opposition to the blacklist as one reason for hiring Trumbo, it is important to note that a blacklisted writer's name had become a rather unusual form of product differentiation.[82] As Trumbo's exploitation of "Robert Rich" had demonstrated, the controversy surrounding blacklisted writers piqued public curiosity. In 1960, U-I commissioned a report on Dalton Trumbo from Sindlinger and Co., a market research firm that analyzed demographics and box office trends for the industry. Their report estimated that over four million people recognized Trumbo's name. Next, the Sindlinger report asked those respondents if screen credit for Trumbo would affect their attendance. Fifty percent of those interviewed said that Trumbo's name on the film would not make any difference either way. Twelve and one-half percent said that screen credit for Trumbo would keep them from attending the film. The remaining 37.5 percent said that Trumbo's name on the picture alone would be reason enough to see the film.[83]

Thus, when Otto Preminger publicly announced on January 20, 1960, that Dalton Trumbo was writing *Exodus*, many were unsurprised. While Preminger insisted he was merely asserting his right as an employer to hire and fire as he pleased, *Variety* noted that many people saw it merely as another one of Preminger's publicity stunts.[84] Previous publicity gimmicks included Preminger's nationwide talent search for a girl to star in *Saint Joan* (1957), his battles with the Legion of Decency on *The Moon Is Blue* (1953), his struggle with the Production Code Administration on *The Man with the Golden Arm* (1955), and the casting of Army–McCarthy hearings lawyer Joseph Welch in *Anatomy of a Murder* (1959).[85] The attention that *Exodus* received as a result of the announcement suggests that it was a very successful means of publicizing the film. At the very least, Trumbo's connection with *Exodus* did not hurt the film's box office potential. The film was distributed by United Artists on a roadshow basis and set an all-time record with more than a million dollars' worth of advance ticket sales.[86] Perhaps prompted by Preminger's announcement, Stanley Kramer announced shortly afterward that he had hired Nedrick Young to write *Inherit the Wind* (1960), and Frank Sinatra announced that Albert Maltz would write *The Execution of Private Slovik* (not produced by Sinatra, but later made in 1974 as a TV movie starring Martin Sheen). Both industry and public response was generally favorable. Harry Brandt of the Independent Theater Owners Association wrote in the *Independent Film Journal* on February 17, 1960, "As an exhibitor, I am confident that an informed public will make proper decisions at the box office based on the content of a motion picture and not by reason of a suspected political inclination of a person associated with its production."[87] Bosley Crowther, the *New York Times* film critic, pointed out that Kramer and Preminger were offering the public an honest choice not to go see a film because of the writer, something the major studios had not done when they released films using the pseudonym of a black market writer.[88] This is not to say that there were no dissenting voices. Hedda Hopper, for instance, said, "Sure all leftists will go to see his (Kramer's) pictures, also 'Exodus' and 'Spartacus' and others written by Dalton Trumbo, but they'll find real Americans are not so gullible."[89]

Figure 35. *Publicity for* Spartacus *depicted the film as a celebration of "man's eternal struggle for freedom," emphasizing the slaves' revolt.* Courtesy of the Wisconsin Center for Film and Theater Research.

## *Spartacus* and the End of the Blacklist

The premiere of *Spartacus* marked the first time since the blacklist that a blacklisted writer's name actually appeared in the credits of a film. Because the blacklist dissolved so gradually, it is impossible to claim that *Spartacus* marked the definitive "end of the blacklist." Yet *Spartacus* proved once and for all that a blacklisted writer's name was not box office poison, so its premiere nonetheless signified the beginning of the end. *Exodus* may have had high advance ticket sales, but that is not the same as facing boycotts and protests at theaters, which *Spartacus* did a few months before *Exodus*.

Kirk Douglas claims that he personally decided to give Trumbo credit for *Spartacus* after a meeting with director Stanley Kubrick and Eddie Lewis, in which Kubrick offered to accept the screenplay credit himself.[90] Although Douglas does not date this meeting, it likely took place in late 1959, at least a month before Preminger's January 1960 announcement. Yet it would be seven months before Trumbo's credit was officially confirmed at Universal-International and in Bryna Productions correspondence. As subsequent events showed, the intention of putting a blacklisted writer's name onscreen and actually doing so are clearly two different things. Shortly after Preminger's announcement, blacklistees Ned Young and Albert Maltz were announced as the writers of *Inherit the Wind* and *The Execution of Private Slovik*, respectively. Yet, when *Inherit the Wind* was released, it used Young's pseudonym, and *Private Slovik* was killed because of Maltz's connection with the film.[91]

Similarly, even after the generally favorable response to Preminger's announcement regarding Trumbo, Bryna remained cautious. Preminger made his announcement during preproduction on *Exodus* while *Spartacus* was already in postproduction. As such, the executives at U-I realized that their $12 million investment on *Spartacus* would be jeopardized long before *Exodus* reached theaters. Preminger's announcement, however, enabled them to carefully gauge public response before making a final decision. Certainly the Sindlinger Report and the response to *Exodus* favored putting Trumbo's name on *Spartacus* rather than waiting for *The Brave Cowboy* to be produced.

Despite the optimistic outlook, Bryna and U-I's actions suggest that they held their cards rather close to the vest. Five days after Preminger's announcement, Fred Banker of U-I stated in a letter that the only writing credits available on *Spartacus* were that the screenplay was by Howard Fast and Eddie Lewis based on the best-selling novel, *Spartacus*, by Howard Fast.[92] In addition, a tour by Banker on behalf of *Spartacus* was postponed due to the unresolved Trumbo issue.[93] Lastly, Stan Marguilies, Bryna's publicity director, carefully monitored American Legion activities to determine what action, if any, would be taken against *Spartacus*. In March 1960, Trumbo was reinstated in the Screen Writers Guild after paying the back dues owed for the period that he was blacklisted.[94] With his name linked with *Spartacus* in the press and now a member in good standing with the Guild, everything seemed ready for Trumbo to receive screen credit. Yet, as late as July 14, 1960, no decisive action had been taken as Bryna awaited a Guild decision on five writers' claims for credit on *Spartacus*.[95] On August 2, 1960, Bryna finally made it official. The screenwriting credit for *Spartacus* would read:

Screenplay by Dalton Trumbo
Based on the Novel by Howard Fast[96]

When *Spartacus* premiered, the American Legion protests occurred, but they were largely ineffective. Bryna's Stan Marguilies, who had been following the Legion's activities, obtained a copy of a letter about *Spartacus* being circulated nationally to Legion posts. Attached to the Legion letter was a letter written by Marguilies to Bryna management on June 24, 1960, that stated:

It (the Legion letter) is an interesting document both in what it says and the action it implies. I think it provides us plenty of room to defend the picture—if a defense should be needed—on the grounds of its content rather than on contributing personnel.[97]

This is precisely what Bryna did. *Spartacus* was the story of a slave revolt in Ancient Rome, and as such, Bryna's publicity stressed that it was a film about freedom. Months before *Spartacus* was released, Kirk Douglas replied to angry letters regarding Trumbo's employment by stressing this theme of freedom. A letter from Douglas to J. David Johnson was typical: "The movie speaks not only for itself, but for all of us here at Bryna who had a hand in making it. I hope you will see it and then I know you will agree with me that it is a courageous and positive statement about mankind's most cherished goal—freedom."[98] Likewise, a *Spartacus* study guide, published for circulation in schools with U-I's participation, said, "The struggle for freedom, both physical and spiritual, has long interested writers in many lands, and among the fighters for freedom Spartacus for more than two thousand years has remained one of its greatest symbols."[99]

The popular press piggybacked on Bryna's publicity discourse and continued to emphasize the film's theme of freedom. The *Hollywood Reporter* said, "there is nothing more subversive in 'Spartacus' than contained in the Bill of Rights and the Fourteenth Amendment."[100] *Time* said specifically of Trumbo that he had "imparted to *Spartacus* a passion for freedom and the men who live and die for it—a passion that transcends all politics."[101] Perhaps the most important gesture of public support came from President Kennedy, who crossed American Legion picket lines in Washington, D.C., to attend *Spartacus*.[102] By the end of the year, *Exodus* and *Spartacus* occupied the number one and number two spots on *Variety*'s weekly box office chart, positions that the two films would exchange throughout the early months of 1961.

The irony of emphasizing *Spartacus*'s theme of freedom was that the novel was considered by some right-wing factions to be a Marxist parable, was a popular work in the Soviet Union, and was written by Howard Fast prior to his renunciation of communism before HUAC. When blacklisting began in 1947, it was to keep such subversive material from reaching American movie screens. In some quarters, *Spartacus* was precisely the type of story from which HUAC was trying to protect America.[103] However, because the American Legion focused on the politics of *Spartacus*'s personnel rather than its subject matter, Bryna used the film's depiction of the struggle for freedom to deflect criticism of Trumbo's involvement.

The press's linkage of Trumbo with the notion of freedom had a curious side effect. Dalton Trumbo, who had been considered "un-American" in 1947, emerged as an American hero in 1960. The *Hollywood Reporter* said of *Exodus*'s New York premiere: "The biggest surprise of the evening came during the credits when spontaneous applause went to script writer Dalton Trumbo."[104] Moreover, on April 9, 1961, the Teacher's Union

*Figure 36. Dalton Trumbo is honored at a Teacher's Union Awards dinner held at the Waldorf Astoria, April 9, 1961.* Courtesy of the Wisconsin Center for Film and Theater Research.

honored Trumbo with its Teachers Union Award, saying his "creative gifts as a writer and stalwart stand against the Un-American blacklist have enriched our culture."[105] Ironically, the ceremony took place at the Waldorf Astoria Hotel where thirteen and one half years earlier, the major studios declared Trumbo "unemployable."

Even after *Exodus*'s premiere, Trumbo maintained a conciliatory stance toward his employers. In a letter to Robert Jennings on December 21, 1960, Trumbo said, "With two major studios, simultaneously and for the first time, using my name on the screen, I feel a deep responsibility to do and say nothing that can upset the present delicate balance."[106] Trumbo added:

> I do therefore hope there will be no implication of contempt, hostility, or flippancy on my part toward UA, U-I, or (Otto) Preminger and (Kirk) Douglas. The officials of U-I, in their multi-million dollar *Spartacus* gamble, have behaved extraordinarily well toward me throughout what has, for them, been a difficult public relations period. I never asked that my name be used on *Spartacus*, and they, by contract, had the right to use any other name they chose to none at all. It was their decision to put my name up, and I think it a decision that honors them.[107]

Despite Trumbo's success with *Spartacus* and *Exodus*, this did not mean the blacklist was suddenly over. Rather, it dissolved much more gradually. Michael Wilson, for example, wrote the final draft of the screenplay for *Lawrence of Arabia* (1962), but playwright Robert Bolt got the film's sole screenwriting credit. Wilson would not get his own name back on screen until *The Sandpiper* (1965), which he co-wrote with Dalton Trumbo. Albert Maltz, whose association with *The Execution of Private Slovik* ended that project during preproduction, waited until *Two Mules for Sister Sara* (1970) to get screen credit. The reasons for such a gradual dissolution of the blacklist have not yet been fully explored. Further case studies of writers such as Ned Young, Albert Maltz, and Michael Wilson need to be done to both understand the end of the blacklist more clearly, and understand why it took so long after *Spartacus* for these writers to get their names back onscreen.

## Conclusion

Trumbo's transition from being "un-American" in 1947 to emerging from the blacklist in 1960 as a "super-American" is doubly paradoxical, because, at least privately, Trumbo's politics never changed. This suggests that the politics of the Hollywood Ten were never particularly important to the studios in the first place. Ceplair and Englund themselves wrote in *The Inquisition in Hollywood:* "In the broadest sense, of course the decision not to hire certain artists—that is, to capitulate to political reaction at the highest level of government—was highly political. Reduced to its essence, however, the decision to blacklist was economic—fear of adverse box office required their dismissal."[108] Despite the sensitivity to economic factors displayed within this quote, Ceplair and Englund, like many other historians, generally subordinate such considerations to the overall political context out of which the blacklist grew.

As the blacklist wore on, the general political shift away from anticommunism encouraged moves toward ending the blacklist, but Hollywood only took those steps in response to specific economic incentives. Independent producers, who were subject to economic pressures placed on them by financing and distribution agreements made with the majors, sought out black market talent because those writers offered high-quality scripts at low prices. Later in the 1950s, the controversy surrounding black market writers made them a valuable means of differentiating product for independent producers. Furthermore, the risks taken by independents in using black market writers were economic risks, including the loss of financing and distribution agreements and later the threat of box office boycotts.

In addition, the emphasis that previous historians have given to political and moral issues has given rise to a "drama" metaphor that permeates most writing on blacklisting. The use of this "drama" metaphor has encouraged historians to characterize the relationship between blacklistees and Hollywood as one of antagonism and conflict. While the independent production wing of the industry influenced the terms by which the black market operated, it would be wrong to suggest that the black market situation was one in which blacklistees struggled to overcome the oppression of the institutions of Hollywood. Rather, the nature of the relationship between blacklistees and Hollywood was one of negotiation and conciliation. The blacklisted writer mediated several competing interests, among them were Hollywood studios, independent producers, the Motion Picture Academy, gossip columnists, and the moviegoing public. Given the publicity problems created by the awareness of the black market, it was in the best interests of the studios and the Academy to find an uncontroversial means of ending the blacklist. In doing so, they actively sought out black market writers as spokespeople in order to present a united public relations front. Blacklistees, in turn, found progress toward ending the blacklist would come only when that progress fit the larger needs of Hollywood.

Within this set of interwoven interests, blacklistees actively worked toward ending the blacklist and, as Dalton Trumbo was well aware, the effectiveness of their actions would be diminished if they operated outside the interests of Hollywood. For Trumbo, this meant subordinating political concerns to professional ones and eliminating politics as an element of his public image. Only in this way could the publicity surrounding *Spartacus* and *Exodus* emphasize story content over the political past of their authors. In the 1947 hearings, for a brief moment, Dalton Trumbo had the world as a forum in which he unsuccessfully championed the civil rights he believed were given to each American. Yet the public saw him only as a political subversive. Ironically, after years of deemphasizing his politics, Trumbo became a symbol of civil rights, albeit in a way that was seemingly packaged for public consumption by Hollywood studios. Perhaps this is the paradox which best characterizes the blacklist; an ostensibly political action in which politics played only a minor part.

## NOTES

I thank the editors of *The Velvet Light Trap* for their valuable suggestions for this essay.

1. Larry Ceplair and Steven Englund, *The Inquisition in Hollywood: Politics in the Film Community, 1930–1960* (Garden City: Anchor/Doubleday, 1980), xiii.

2. Ibid., 418–19.

3. Victor Navasky, *Naming Names* (New York: Viking, 1980), viii.

4. Lillian Hellman, *Scoundrel Time* (Boston: Little, Brown, 1976), Stefan Kanfer, *A Journal of the Plague Years* (New York: Atheneum, 1973), Navasky, and Ceplair and Englund all carry this dramatic bias to varying degrees.

5. Navasky, *Naming Names*, 326–27.

6. Bruce Cook, *Dalton Trumbo* (New York: Scribner, 1977), 263. Cook also wrote in an earlier article on Trumbo, "Cracks were appearing in the wall that Hollywood had thrown up to protect the American public against the subversion of the motion picture industry" (Cook, "The Black Years of Dalton Trumbo," *American Film* 1, no. 1 [1975]: 32).

7. Dalton Trumbo, *Additional Dialogue: The Letters of Dalton Trumbo, 1942–1962,* ed. Helen Manfull (New York: M. Evans, 1970), 469, 413.

8. For more on the years leading up to the blacklist, see Ceplair and Englund's *Inquisition in Hollywood*, which does an excellent job of tracing the development of left-wing political movements in Hollywood, from the Popular Front groups of the 1930s to the postwar crackdown on political subversion; and of describing the effect of World War II on U.S.–Soviet relations and the consequences of this on American left-wing politics. See also Nancy Lynn Schwartz, *The Hollywood Writers' Wars* (New York: Alfred A. Knopf, 1982).

9. Ceplair and Englund, *Inquisition*, 329.

10. At the April 11, 1947, premiere of *Monsieur Verdoux*, representatives of the Catholic War Veterans publicly challenged Chaplin about his political affiliations and his reluctance to become a U.S. citizen. The incident resulted in some negative publicity about the film and was a contributing factor to the film's poor box office performance. David Robinson, *Chaplin: His Life and Art* (New York: McGraw-Hill, 1985), 539–43.

11. Cook, *Dalton Trumbo*, 191. Trumbo's meeting with Frank King raises the issue of whether or not the studios decided to blacklist the Hollywood Ten prior to the Waldorf conference of November 24–25, 1947, traditionally considered the start of the blacklist. Both Bruce Cook and Helen Manfull discuss a meeting on Thanksgiving Day in 1947 between Trumbo and Sam Zimbalist, at which Zimbalist delivered the news that the Ten would be blacklisted. (See Cook, *Dalton Trumbo*, 189–90, and Trumbo, *Additional Dialogue*, 58.) This indicates that at least one member of the Ten knew of the decision to blacklist prior to the Waldorf Statement of December 3, 1947. Manfull implies and Cook states quite bluntly that Trumbo's meeting with Zimbalist was the first time the screenwriter became aware of the decision. Cook's account of the *Gun Crazy* deal, however, appears to run counter to that. King's call to Trumbo the day of his return from the HUAC hearings was based on the assumption that Trumbo was no longer an employee of MGM, and would not be hired by any of the other majors. That Trumbo would accept such a low salary, and violate a very lucrative MGM contract, suggests that the screenwriter expected to be blacklisted well before the Waldorf conference. Cook does not give the precise date that King contacted Trumbo, but presumably it was weeks ahead of the Waldorf conference. Further research needs to be done to determine if the studios did, in fact, decide to blacklist prior to the Waldorf meeting.

12. It was believed by Hollywood Ten lawyers that Trumbo's suit against MGM, among all the personal and collective suits filed by Hollywood Ten members, had the best chance of winning. This was due to the fact that Trumbo alone did not have a "morals" clause in his contract with MGM. The lawyers also felt, however, that if Trumbo won his suit based on the absence of this clause, then certain defeat would come to all other Hollywood Ten lawsuits. Thus, the lawyers persuaded Trumbo to drop his personal lawsuit against MGM, and join the other nine in a collective suit against all the major studios. The suit was settled out of court for $259,000, of which Trumbo received $75,000. Cook, *Dalton Trumbo*, 192–93, 212–13.

13. On the black market, communication problems between producers and writers were inevitable. Yet some situations were better than others. The worst situation was a front who was not a writer. In such a situation, the front could not answer the producer's questions about characterization, story construction, or dialogue, and if the script's origins were to remain a secret from the producer, the front's inability to answer such questions might lead the producer to suspect that the script was from the black market. At the very least, the front's ignorance of the screenwriting process meant that requests for script revisions had to be filtered through someone who did not necessarily understand what was meant by them.

14. See Cook, *Dalton Trumbo*, 295–96; and Trumbo, *Additional Dialogue*, 85.

15. Ceplair and Englund, *Inquisition*, 404.

16. Cook, "Black Years," 32.

17. Letter from Trumbo to Frank King, 4 May 1962, Box 9, *The Brave One* file, Dalton Trumbo Collection, U.S. Mss 24AN, Wisconsin Center for Film and Theater Research, State Historical Society, Madison, Wisconsin. All letters and contracts are from this collection, unless otherwise noted.

18. For more on the majors' control over financing and distribution, see Tino Balio,

"When Is an Independent Producer Independent? The Case of United Artists after 1948," *The Velvet Light Trap* 22 (1986): 53–64.

19. See David Bordwell, Janet Staiger, and Kristin Thompson, *The Classical Hollywood Cinema: Film Style and Mode of Production to 1960* (New York: Columbia University Press, 1985), 312–13.

20. Letter from Trumbo to John Wexley, April 3, 1958, Box 6, File 3.

21. Two letters from Trumbo to Hugo Butler, ca. 1954, Box 5, File 2. Also, see letter from Trumbo to John Wexley, April 3, 1958, Box 6, File 3, and letter from Trumbo to Murray Kempton, March 5, 1957, Box 6, File 2. The latter is reprinted in Trumbo, *Additional Dialogue*, 390–94.

22. Letter from Trumbo to Hugo Butler, ca. 1954, Box 5, File 2. Letter from Trumbo to Alvah Bessie, June 18, 1957, Box 6, File 2. Both letters are reprinted in Trumbo, *Additional Dialogue*, 313–21 and 395–97, respectively.

23. Letter from Trumbo to Murray Kempton, March 5, 1957, Box 6, File 2. Reprinted in Trumbo, *Additional Dialogue*, 390–94.

24. Letter from Trumbo to Eddie Lewis, June 3, 1958, Box 7, File 1.

25. Written agreements between Trumbo and the King Brothers, September 22, 1952; ca. May 1954; August 13, 1954; Box 9, *The Brave One* file.

26. Letter from Trumbo to the King Brothers, December 29, 1955, Box 9, *The Brave One* file.

27. Letter from Trumbo to Hugo Butler, ca. 1954, Box 5, File 2. Reprinted in Trumbo, *Additional Dialogue*, 313–21.

28. See Navasky, *Naming Names*, 185; Jan Herman, *A Talent for Trouble: The Life of Hollywood's Most Acclaimed Director, William Wyler* (New York: G. P. Putnam's Sons, 1995), 376–78; and Don Mankiewicz, "Sojourn in an Alien Land," *New York Times*, February 10, 1957, sec. VII:6. Jessamyn West must have been quite confident of her contribution, because she wrote a book, *To See a Dream*, about her experiences in Hollywood rewriting the script for *Friendly Persuasion*.

29. Academy press release announcing the enactment of bylaw, Box 10, Notes for "Blacklist = Black Market." See also Emanuel Levy, *And the Winner Is . . .* (New York: Ungar, 1987), 316; and Mason Wiley and Damien Bona, *Inside Oscar*, ed. Gail McColl (New York: Ballantine, 1986), 273.

30. Thomas Pryor, "Writers Protest 'Oscar' Omission," *New York Times*, February 20, 1957, 36.

31. Axel Madsen, *William Wyler* (New York: Thomas Crowell, 1973), 326.

32. See Cook, *Dalton Trumbo*, 259–60; and "'Author' of Movie Deepens Mystery," *New York Times*, April 1, 1957, 18.

33. See *Variety*, April 3, 1957, 1.

34. See "'Author,'" *New York Times*: 18; and "Case of the Missing Scripter," *Time*, April 15, 1957, 116.

35. See the memo written by Trumbo for the collection, Box 9, *The Brave One* file; "'Oscar' Mystery Takes New Turn," *New York Times*, April 4, 1957: 40; and Thomas Pryor, "Studios Settle Suit Over Story," *New York Times*, April 9, 1957, 40.

36. Letter from Trumbo to Lewis Metzer for transmission to the Writers Guild Board, ca. January 1959, Box 7, File 2; and Thomas Pryor, "Trumbo Evaded Film Ban," *New York Times*, April 11, 1957, 39. See also Cook, *Dalton Trumbo*, 260.

37. Dalton Trumbo, "Blacklist = Black Market," *The Nation*, May 4, 1957, 383–87.

38. *The Brave One* was not on *Variety*'s yearend box office report for 1956 or 1957. Each report listed for approximately one hundred films, the lowest of which made $1 million. See "Top Film Grossers of 1956," *Variety*, January 2, 1957, 1, 4; and "Top Grossers of 1957," *Variety*, January 8, 1958, 30.

39. Two years after the incident, however, Trumbo insisted that the Oscar for Robert Rich was simply a coincidence. In a letter to Lewis Metzer, Trumbo said, "The first Robert Rich incident two or three years ago resulted from (a) a producer's blunder and (b) an even greater

blunder by the Academy." Yet since Trumbo had written the letter to placate angry Writers Guild members, it was clearly in his best interests to make it appear that the award was merely the result of a "producer's blunder." Since Trumbo never specifies what the error was, it is difficult to understand what was meant by the statement. Letter from Trumbo to Lewis Metzer for transmission to the Writers Guild Board, ca. January 1959, Box 7, File 2.

40. See letter from Trumbo to Aubrey Finn, November 19, 1957, Box 6, File 2; and Patrick, McGilligan and Paul Buhle, eds., *Tender Comrades: A Backstory of the Hollywood Blacklist* (New York: St. Martin's, 1997), 466. Trumbo later noted that CBS Studio One did a bit on "Robert Rich" two days before the 1958 Academy Awards ceremony. Letter from Trumbo to Michael Wilson, March 30, 1958, Box 6, File 3. Reprinted in Trumbo, *Additional Dialogue*, 414–17.

41. Letter from Trumbo to Aubrey Finn, December 8, 1957, Box 6, File 2. Reprinted in Trumbo, *Additional Dialogue*, 406–8. The story of *Mr. Adam* was about the only man left on Earth capable of fathering a child. All of the other men in the world were infertile. All of the women in the world, on the other hand, wanted to have babies. Despite its apocalyptic premise, *Mr. Adam* was a comedy.

42. Ibid.

43. Letter from George Bilson to Aubrey Finn, December 8, 1957, Box 6, File 2. Attached to the letter was the contract between Trumbo and George for *Story of an Illegitimate Baby*.

44. Letter to Aubrey Finn, December 8, 1957, Box 6, File 2. Reprinted in Trumbo, *Additional Dialogue*, 406–8.

45. Bryna Productions file on Screenwriters Employment, ca. March 1959, Box 11, File 24, Kirk Douglas Collection, U.S. Mss 102AN, Wisconsin Center for Film and Theater Research (hereafter KD).

46. Letter from Trumbo to Aubrey Finn, December 8, 1957, Box 6, Folder 2.

47. Written agreement between Trumbo and Bryna Productions regarding *The Brave Cowboy*, January 14, 1958, Box 6, File 3. The film was later produced under the title *Lonely Are the Brave* (1962).

48. Letter from Trumbo to Michael Wilson, March 30, 1958, Box 6, File 3. Reprinted in *Additional Dialogue*, 414–17.

49. Letter from Trumbo to Eddie Lewis, April 29, 1958, Box 6, File 3. See also memo from Stan Margulies to Eddie Lewis, March 11, 1958, KD.

50. Bryna file on Screenwriter Employment, ca. March 1959, Box 11, File 24, KD.

51. Having Eddie Lewis front for Bryna's black market stable of writers would become particularly important later during a Writers Guild strike. Since writer-producers were exempted from the strike, Bryna was able to keep production going without any questions asked.

52. Of the $75,000, Eugene Frenke's Springfield Productions received $37,500. They received this because technically Trumbo was contracted to them as an employee. Actually though, this was probably Trumbo's way of paying back Frenke for his services as an agent and for keeping Trumbo on the payroll as an employee of Springfield Productions during periods of unemployment. Cook, *Dalton Trumbo*, 169–270. See also Bryna Productions file on Screenwriters, ca. March 1959, Box 11, File 24, KD.

53. Bryna file on Screenwriter Employment, ca. March 1959, Box 11, File 124, KD. See also letter from Trumbo to Aubrey Finn, August 30, 1958, Box 7, File 1.

54. Trumbo, *Additional Dialogue*, 425.

55. Letter from Trumbo to Eddie Lewis, May 1, 1958, Box 6, File 3. Reprinted in Trumbo, *Additional Dialogue*, 424–29.

56. Trumbo, *Additional Dialogue*, 425.

57. Letter from Trumbo to Albert Maltz, January 9, 1959, Box 7, File 2. Reprinted in Trumbo, *Additional Dialogue*, 470–74.

58. "Whose 'River Kwai'?," *Newsweek*, March 24, 1958, 104. See also Wiley and Bona, *Inside Oscar*, 289.

59. Letter from Trumbo to Albert Maltz, January 9, 1959, Box 7, File 2. Reprinted in Trumbo, *Additional Dialogue*, 470–74.

60. "Film Suit on 'Brave One,'" *New York Times*, July 25, 1958, 11. See also the letters from Trumbo to Frank King, April 28, 1962, and May 4, 1962, Box 9, *The Brave One* file; letter from Trumbo to Lewis Metzer for transmission to the Writers Guild Board, ca. January 1959, Box 7, File 2; and the memo written by Trumbo for the collection, Box 9, *The Brave One* file.

61. Letter from Trumbo to George Seaton, January 11, 1959, Box 6, File 3.

62. Letter from Trumbo to George Stevens, Valentine Davies, George Seaton, and Perry Leiber, ca. early January 1959, Box 7, File 1.

63. Ibid.

64. Thomas Pryor, "Academy Repeals Ruling on 'Oscars,'" *New York Times*, January 16, 1959, Box 81, Miscellaneous Blacklist Clippings.

65. "Robert Rich Identified," *New York Times*, January 17, 1959, 10.

66. Letter from Trumbo to George Seaton, January 20, 1959, Box 5, File 3. Reprinted in Trumbo, *Additional Dialogue*, 477–80.

67. Letter from Trumbo to Michael Wilson, February 24, 1959, Box 7, File 2. Reprinted in Trumbo *Additional Dialogue*, 480–86.

68. Ibid.

69. Ibid.

70. Walter Winchell, *New York Daily Mirror*, March 21, 1959, Box 81, Miscellaneous Blacklist Clippings; and *Hollywood Reporter*, March 24, 1959, Box 81, Miscellaneous Blacklist Clippings.

71. Letter from Jefferson Asher to Leon Kaplan, June 5, 1959, Box 11, File 24, KD.

72. Memo from Jefferson Asher, June 9, 1959, Box 11, File 24, KD.

73. "Harry Truman Blasts Hollywood Blacklist," *Variety*, April 9, 1959, 1. "Truman Again Rips House Committee," *Los Angeles Times*, May 1, 1959, 28.

74. Letter from Trumbo to Aubrey Finn, August 4, 1959, Box 7, File 2. Reprinted in Trumbo, *Additional Dialogue*, 493–507.

75. Ibid.

76. Murray Schumach, "Attack by Legion Confuses Film Men," *New York Times*, September 3, 1959, 30.

77. Murray Schumach, "Hollywood Blues," *New York Times*, September 6, 1959, sec. II:7.

78. Letter from Trumbo to B. B. Kahane, October 2, 1959, Box 7, File 2. Reprinted in Trumbo, *Additional Dialogue*, 490–93. The file contains a number of other drafts of this letter.

79. Letter from Trumbo to B. B. Kahane (never sent), October 2, 1959, Box 7, File 2. This is a different draft of the letter footnoted in note 78; letter from Trumbo to B. B. Kahane (never sent), October 9, 1959, Box 7, File 2. This is yet another draft of the letter footnoted in note 78.

80. Letter from Albert Maltz to Trumbo, November 21, 1959, Box 7, File 2.

81. Letter from Trumbo to Ingo Preminger, January 14, 1960, Box 7, File 3.

82. For an account of Kirk Douglas's opposition to the blacklist, see his autobiography, *The Ragman's Son* (New York: Simon and Schuster, 1988), 205, 308, 323.

83. Trumbo, *Additional Dialogue*, 494.

84. Hy Hollinger, "Preminger's Private Hornet: Trumbo," *Variety*, January 27, 1960, 5. See also A. H. Weiler, "Movie Maker Hires Blacklisted Writer," *New York Times*, January 20, 1960, 1.

85. For more on Preminger's approach to publicity and exploitation, see Tino Balio, *United Artists: The Company That Changed the Film Industry* (Madison: University of Wisconsin Press, 1987), 200–201.

86. "'Exodus' Advance Sale Setting an All-Time Record," *Hollywood Reporter*, April 7, 1960, 1, Box 80, Blacklist Clippings on *Exodus*.

87. Harry Brandt, "A Member's Lament," *Independent Film Journal*, February 27, 1960, Box 80, Blacklist Clippings on *Exodus*.

88. Bosley Crowther, "Hitting the Blacklist," *New York Times*, February 14, 1960, sec. II:1.

89. Hedda Hopper, "Widmark Film to Have Post-War Theme," *Chicago Tribune*, February 11, 1960, Box 81, Miscellaneous Blacklist Clippings.

90. Douglas, *Ragman's Son*, 323.

91. Cook, *Dalton Trumbo*, 280. See also Murray Schumach, "Sinatra Dismisses Blacklisted Writer," *New York Times*, April 9, 1960, Box 59, Clippings on the Sinatra–Maltz Affair. The firing may not have been a result of Legion pressure; it is possible that the Kennedy family asked for Maltz's dismissal because of Sinatra's involvement in John F. Kennedy's presidential campaign.

92. Letter from Fred Banker to Al Baer, January 25, 1960, Box 33, File 12, KD.

93. Letter from Phil Gerard to Jeff Livingston, February 24, 1960, Box 33, File 13, KD.

94. "Trumbo Is Reinstated," *New York Times*, March 31, 1960, 30.

95. Letter from Stan Marguilies to Mischa Kallis, July 14, 1960, Box 33, File 20, KD.

96. Letter from Stan Marguilies to Kathryn McTaggert, August 2, 1960, Box 33, File 21, KD.

97. Letter from Stan Marguilies to Kirk Douglas, June 24, 1960, Box 33, File 19, KD.

98. Letter from Kirk Douglas to J. David Johnson, May 6, 1960, Box 33, File 16, KD. See also letter from Kirk Douglas to K. L. Kerins, May 6, 1960, Box 33, File 16, KD.

99. *Spartacus* Study Guide, *Photoplay Studies.* Prepared by Joseph Mersand, General Editor, William Lewin, Ph.D., distributed by the National Council of Teachers of English, 25, 4 (August 1960), Box 37, File 14, KD.

100. James Powers, "'Spartacus' Magnificent Picture, Should Be Smash Attraction," *Hollywood Reporter*, October 7, 1960, Box 79, *Spartacus* Reviews and Press.

101. *Time*, October 24, 1960, Box 79, *Spartacus* Reviews and Press. Reviews of *Exodus* continued in the same vein. For example, the *San Diego Union* wrote, "It (*Exodus*) is a picture illustrative of the longing, the internal bickering, the selfless heroism, and sacrifices that men have paid to breathe the air of freedom." The *Cleveland Press and News* added, "Suffice it to say that this (*Exodus*) is a chapter in the history of man's yearning for and acquisition of freedom." See James Meade, "'Exodus' Is Big Exciting Picture," *San Diego Union*, May 24, 1961; Stan Anderson, "Stirring *Exodus* Opens Tonight," *Cleveland Press and News*, March 14, 1961, Box 80, *Exodus* Reviews and Press.

102. See Cook, *Dalton Trumbo*, 277; Navasky, *Naming Names*, 327; "Kennedy Attends Movie in Capital," *New York Times*, February 5, 1961, Box 80, *Spartacus* Clippings.

103. See, for example, the national Catholic magazine, *The Sign*, which says of the film, "It glamorizes the slave Spartacus, who has risen high in Marxist hagiography" (*The Sign*, December 1960, 51, Box 37, File 14, KD). Attached to the magazine is a note from Jeff Livingston to Stan Marguilies that says, "An ominous 'Sign.'"

104. Radie Harris, "Broadway Ballyhoo," *Hollywood Reporter*, December 20, 1960, 4, Box 80, Miscellaneous Blacklist Clippings.

105. *New York Teachers News*, Box 80, Blacklist Clippings on *Exodus*.

106. Letter from Trumbo to Robert Jennings, December 21, 1960, Box 7, File 3. Reprinted in Trumbo, *Additional Dialogue*, 538–39.

107. Ibid.

108. Ceplair and Englund, *Inquisition*, 330.

Justin Wyatt

# The Stigma of X: Adult Cinema and the Institution of the MPAA Ratings System

Two years after the official shutdown of Hollywood's Production Code Administration, the Motion Picture Association of America instituted a nationwide system of voluntary ratings in 1968. Backed by theater owners and motion picture producers and distributors, the system was designed to limit the possibility of governmental intervention in production or censorship, even after the Supreme Court granted movies the right to First Amendment protection. Whereas the PCA worked behind the scenes to limit offensive material for all audiences, the ratings classified films in terms of their suitability for various audience segments. In particular, one of the primary functions of the ratings system was stated as offering advice to parents on the appropriateness of movie content for viewing by their children. This objective illuminates a crucial distinction between the PCA and the MPAA ratings. While the PCA aimed to produce harmless entertainment for all ages, the ratings board placed films into different categories according to their potential audience, in some ways segmenting and expanding the potential audience and age groups for different films.

The possibility of exploiting particular audiences through the ratings was demonstrated most clearly by the X, one extreme of the spectrum. During a period when increasingly explicit content became more prevalent in response to shifts in the country's demographics and its culture, the category of X served, in part, to configure a market segment of adult viewers ignored by the major studios. Thus, the MPAA, at times inadvertently and at times by design, substantially contributed to the trend in which the adult film—ranging from serious examinations of sexuality and human nature (*I Am Curious [Yellow]* [1967]) to erotica designed to titillate (*Deep Throat* [1972])—became an important force within the American film marketplace. Indeed, the market proved to be so lucrative that the major studios eventually elected to distribute adult films themselves. This essay will explore how the X category allowed filmmakers to exploit particular audiences and gain box office revenue through the ratings.


## The Formation of the Adult Market Segment: Demographics, Sexuality, and the MPAA


The movement toward the adult film market was driven by a combination of determinants, most broadly by the larger sociological and demographic shift within the film marketplace that also aided the constitution of adult films. With the oldest part of the baby boom generation reaching their early twenties by the late 1960s, Hollywood began to recognize the commercial significance of this segment. A widely reported market research study in 1968 conducted by Daniel Yankelovich and Associates illustrated that the youth market, aged 16 to 24, accounted for 48 percent of box office admissions.[1] As one producer of the era commented on the implications of this statistic, "each one of the majors should have at least one bright young guy under 30 on its board, just to help in setting up films for today's youth market."[2] On the basis of the Yankelovich report, Jack Valenti, industrious president of the Motion Picture Association of America and former special assistant to President Johnson, predicted that the potent youth audience segment would boost overall revenues in a sizable manner for the industry. Valenti estimated that motion picture theater audiences would be 40 percent larger in 1975 than in 1967.[3]

Institutionally, the youth revolution occurred at the same time as the 1969 recession in the film industry. As Tino Balio notes, the majors suffered more than $200 million in losses that year, added to the steadily declining theatrical attendance (average weekly attendance was down to 17.5 million from the 1946 high of 90 million, and declining revenues had been compensated only slightly by almost tripled admission prices).[4] This recession led Hollywood to believe that the youth picture—low cost, targeting the 15–28 age group specifically—held the key to rejuvenation. In the last two years of the 1960s, *The Graduate, Goodbye, Columbus, Easy Rider, Alice's Restaurant,* and *Midnight Cowboy* all demonstrated, as *Variety* recounts, "the story of low capital investment versus boffo box office."[5] The youth 'revolution' served to feed the increasing freedom in terms of subject matter, further enhancing the marketability of the adult/porno feature.

Within the 1968 release schedule for the majors, the youth pictures attained some visibility amid a range of product still targeted at other demographics: thrillers such as *The Thomas Crown Affair*, science-fiction films such as *Planet of the Apes*, mainstream comedies such as *The Odd Couple* and *With Six You Get Eggroll*, musicals (*Star!, Finian's Rainbow,*

*Chitty Chitty Bang Bang*), and war films (*The Green Berets*). Successes of the era suggested to the trade paper *Variety* that the youth demographic were attracted by "a conjunction of original sights and sounds" rather than "straightforward storytelling."[6] The novel sensory experiences—echoing the self-conscious narrational devices of the art cinema—were to be augmented by a focus on experiences common to the young: rock music, drugs, dance, motorcycles, and sex.[7]

The anxiety with which the mainstream industry viewed youth is evident throughout the industry trades, with articles stressing that the 'older' audiences must not be forgotten by producers, that the youth film audiences are fickle and unpredictable in terms of attendance, and that youth culture is merely a passing phase.[8] In terms of the youth segment, the most visible component, the hippies, was a particular target for the industry, with communication from the trades offering contradictory advice. While one *Variety* piece expounded on the "way-out attire and hippie haircuts" of the European film producers, another from the same year reported on an exhibitor in Toronto who forced an employee to carry a sign in front of the theater proclaiming "No Admittance to Hippies."[9]

Sexuality and the revision of restrictive sexual conventions were often posited within the media as major aspects of the youth counterculture. As William Masters (*The Human Sexual Response*) claimed in 1969, "The '60s will be called the decade of orgasmic preoccupation."[10] Following Masters's lead, pop sociologist Vance Packard, after demystifying the powers of advertising in *The Hidden Persuaders*, reported on the sexual revolution in his book, *The Sexual Wilderness*. Packard's major claim centered on the increased sexual experience of unmarried females in North America, claiming an increase in sexual intercourse of nearly 60 percent in that group from 1948 to 1968.[11] In reporting Packard's findings, *Time* magazine chose to juxtapose a picture of the author with a still from *Blow Up* (1966), supported by the wording "Aggressive girls in 'Blow Up.' The roles are being reversed." The match illustrates the equation between the arts and freer sexual expression made by the mass media of the era—from Philip Roth's book *Portnoy's Complaint* to the theatrical production *Oh, Calcutta* and a large number of independent and imported films (*Coming Apart* [1969], *Therese and Isabelle* [1968], *I, a Woman*, and *Inga*).

Several court battles aided the infiltration of adult-themed films from the mid- to late 1960s. First, in 1965, the Supreme Court unanimously ruled in *Freedman v. Maryland* that precensorship of motion pictures was unconstitutional.[12] The state censorship board had to prove why a certain film under contention could not be shown; the burden was shifted away from the distributor and toward the local board.[13] This change responded to the often lengthy and costly litigation forced upon the independent distributor under the previous system. This litigation acted as a violation of freedom of expression according to the Court. The move served to highlight the contradictions between definitions of 'prurient' and 'obscene' material from city to city, state to state.[14] In working through these differences, many adult-oriented films were allowed to play large-scale 'art house' releases; censor bans focused on a small number of films, such as Audobon's *Therese and Isabelle* and Grove's *I Am Curious (Yellow)*, which already had received great publicity and box office in their run.[15]

Perhaps most consequential were two Supreme Court cases from 1968 opening the door for a model of nationwide classification. *Ginsberg v. New York* offered a distinction between material that could be considered obscene for children rather than for adults. *Interstate v. Dallas* ruled against that city's classification system due to its vagueness, but suggested that classification was permissible as long as it was "constitutionally drawn."[16]

The climate for adult filmmaking was also fostered by the abolishment of the Production Code and by the establishment of the MPAA in 1966.[17] With the introduction of the MPAA, certain films were tagged as 'Suggested for Mature Audiences,' although no admission restrictions were enacted. *Who's Afraid of Virginia Woolf?* and *Alfie*, both released in 1966, received such a disclaimer.[18] With the Supreme Court cases opening the door for nationwide ratings, the end of the Production Code, and the tentative step of labeling certain films as 'mature,' the move to a classification system truly developed along several fronts. MPAA president Valenti argued vehemently that in the current environment the film industry would be subject to censorship and urged filmmakers to be restrained in their depiction of possibly offensive material. "If the depiction of violence or permissive sex should offend the sensibilities of the public, then censorship, which sticks its no's (sic) into everyone's business, will be on the scene," he remarked in April 1968 as part of an article for the Directors Guild of America.[19]

Also under fire from the National Catholic Office for Motion Pictures, known as the Legion of Decency until 1965, to institute a nationwide ratings system, the Motion Picture Association established the voluntary ratings system (G/M[GP/PG]/R/X) for all films released after November 1, 1968, with the X rating barring those under 16 without qualification.[20] Under the MPAA system, nonmember distributors were welcome to self-apply X ratings, but not the less restrictive categories.[21] The possibility of a self-imposed rating grew from the MPAA not copyrighting the X rating (although all other ratings categories received copyrights). Valenti explained that this decision was made to ensure that the new ratings system would not limit potential releases, a concern since the studios were making fewer and fewer films: "We didn't copyright the X rating from a legal standpoint. It had to be open-ended so that if somebody doesn't want to submit a picture, they can use the X. Otherwise, we could be challenged on First Amendment grounds."[22]

Even before the new system was instituted, independent distributors lobbied against exhibitors playing only films with MPAA ratings. Since the majority of the independent films were directed at 'adult' audiences (and would therefore be the recipients of X ratings), the independents felt that their films would have little to gain by having an MPAA rating.[23] Many of these distributors also balked at the cost of submitting the film to the board for a rating that would have no bearing on their potential adult audience.

In addition to classifying films into one of four ratings categories, the MPAA also enacted certain guidelines that aided the Board in deciding on ratings. Despite the supposed movement away from moral judgments, the MPAA explicitly listed values and vices that influenced ratings decisions. For instance, "the basic dignity and value of human life shall be respected and upheld," while restraint was requested for portraying, among others, "evil, sin, crime, wrongdoing," "sex aberrations," "excessive cruelty," and "illicit sex relationships."[24] The impact of these transgressions on the rating was unspecified, leaving wide room for interpretation on the part of the administration. As well as film classification, a system of regulating all advertising and titles for motion pictures was developed. The MPAA warned against "indecent or undue exposure of the human body" in trailers, print, and television advertising and "salacious, obscene, or profane" titles.[25]

At the time of its inception, some producers were optimistic that the MPAA ratings system would actually expand the audience for film. Conservatives would admire the censorship aspects and the self-regulation of the industry, and liberals might appreciate the anticipated freer themes and content in light of restrictions on admittance to certain films.[26] Yet problems within the structure of the ratings system became evident even before the official starting date of November 1. Perhaps fearing that the age restriction would limit the potential audiences, the majors desperately avoided the X rating. Of the initial thirty-nine pictures submitted for ratings, only one (Warners' *Girl on a Motorcycle*) received an X.[27] Following the classification system in Britain, X became associated with a certain breed of 'adult' motion pictures, mainly sexually explicit films. In Britain, the X rating had gained a reputation as a no-cost marketing tool, advertising to a specific adult demographic; ad lines such as "the sex-x-x-x-iest film ever" were used in British promotional campaigns.[28]

Within six months of the ratings system introduction, several filmmakers and distributors objected to the X rating assigned to their adult-oriented, but not sexually explicit, films. Under the new regime, they protested before the autonomous Code and Ratings Appeals Board, which included members from the MPAA, NATO (National Association of Theater Owners), and IFIDA (independent distributors).[29] A screening of the film under appeal was followed by presentations from both the Code and Rating Administration and the company appealing the original rating. Soon after the inception of the process, Brian De Palma's antiwar comedy *Greetings* (1968) received an X for frontal nudity, as did Lindsay

Anderson's *If* (1968). Tiny *Greetings* distributor Sigma III eventually acquiesced to the rating by withdrawing the appeal, but Paramount fought the rating of *If* on the basis of strong reviews that had made no mention of the nudity or supposed 'exploitation.'[30] The rating was upheld, with reediting eventually securing an R for the picture. Robert Aldrich's *The Killing of Sister George* (1968) also received an X based on the lesbian-centered plot and some relatively mild nudity and largely offscreen simulated sex. Aldrich complained to the trades regarding the rating, fearing that the film would be marginalized by it. As industry analyst Stuart Byron commented at the time, "Despite the MPAA's allegations that the fourply classification system has nothing to do with moral or aesthetic quality, an assumption has grown that films rated X are those which are 'artistically' unworthy of 'higher' tags."[31] Art house exhibitor Walter Reade also complained about the functioning of the X rating a year after the institution of the system, focusing his arguments on the self-application of the X by independents. Reade suggested that "the code for all practical purposes was basically connected with dirty pictures for a large number of the film-going US public."[32]

Confusion over the meaning of the X rating within the film industry furthered the separation of the X movie from mainstream studio production. In June 1968, a *Variety* article centered on the widespread bewilderment over the X rating on the part of both exhibitors and distributors: one report claimed that any film which was not submitted to the MPAA would automatically receive an X, with no admittance to those under 17, regardless of the film's content.[33] Another industry spokesman commented that "It is not expected that any film submitted for a classification would be placed in the fourth category."[34] Even Code and Rating Administration board member Jacqueline Bouhoutsos commented that X implied "garbage, pictures that shouldn't have been made for anybody, films without any kind of artistic merit, poor taste, disgusting, repulsive."[35]

The difficulty of judging an X rating was evident only three weeks after the system commenced with the cases of *The Fox*, an adaptation of the D. H. Lawrence novella, and *Birds in Peru*, an erotic drama starring Jean Seberg and directed by Romain Gary. *The Fox*, featuring female masturbation and above-the-waist nudity, received an R, while, *Birds in Peru*, featuring a sex scene without any nudity whatsoever, received an X rating.[36] As *Variety* commented on the discrepancy, "Many in N.Y. trade simply cannot understand the criteria employed for these two pix."[37] Some considered that the ratings indicated an aesthetic judgment on the part of the MPAA, with *The Fox* garnering a less restrictive rating for its overall 'sensitive' treatment of a delicate theme and for being the adaptation of a classic D. H. Lawrence novella.

With the institution of the system, exhibitors' confusions transformed into a concern that would plague the MPAA for the next two decades: a 1969 exhibitor survey on the MPAA concluded that there was a pressing need to distinguish between exploitation X pictures and those with "serious artistic intent," with *Midnight Cowboy* and *Medium Cool* mentioned as examples of the latter category.[38] Barry B. Yellen, president of the Cinecom Corporation, suggested that a new category, AO (adults only), be substituted for R and X. The move would aid all films that could conceivably run afoul of obscenity and pornography statutes. Further, the new classification would not have the branded quality of X—as Yellen commented, "we have the 'X' category, we have created a monster."[39]

The pressure to obtain an R over an X rating by the majors correlates with an increase in the number of R-rated films over the first decade of the ratings system: this shift was most dramatic in the early years, with R ratings accounting for 23 percent in 1968–69, but 37 percent in 1969–70. The figure increased through the early 1970s, reaching a plateau of 48 percent in 1974–75.[40] The increase in the R rating category is explained by a fall in the number of G/family films. This redistribution aided the separation of the market for X films—in effect, a major studio viewed the X rating as inconsistent with the potential for a mass audience. For the majors, the R rating became the tag that signified adult, yet which did not limit attendance since underage patrons still could attend with parent or adult guardian.

Despite the suspicions of some independents and confusion in the industry, the MPAA ratings system in fact acted as an economic benefit, effectively segmenting the marketplace for film—the X rating became synonymous with stronger adult (later pornographic) content. The consequences of the X for the majors were dire: approximately 50 percent of theaters across the country refused to play X films, and as many as thirty large city newspapers, along with many television and radio stations, refused to advertise them.[41] Desperate to maintain their presence in circuit theaters, the studios routinely submitted scripts to the MPAA for a reading on the projected rating on the completed film; for instance, *The French Connection* (1971), the western *Wild Rovers* (1971), and the crime drama *Dealing* (1972) were altered at the script level during preproduction to avoid an X rating.[42] According to Stephen Farber, the Board tended to be harsher in their assessment of script content than for material in its final cinematic form. Often on the basis of a line of dialogue or a brief description of a character, the Board suggested that a script veered toward the X rating. As a result, in October 1970, for example, six of nine scripts from the majors received an X in their 'script letters.'[43] The studios' fear of producing X films essentially allowed the independents to exploit this market segment. Within six months of the institution of the MPAA ratings system, companies such as American International, Cinerama, Cinemation, Times Films, and Trans-Lux were self-applying X to their films.[44] In *Variety*, the phrase 'self-imposed X' became a common part of the credits in the beginning of film reviews.

## Characterizing Adult Cinema: The View from the Center

The MPAA ratings system, the use of X as a marketing tool, and the confusions around the meaning of the ratings all served to nurture the adult film as a marketplace phenomenon. While exploitation films had mined the adult market for several decades, the 1960s offered a marked difference from previous eras through the degree of assimilation of adult features into the overall marketplace and through the shifting social attitudes that helped to validate adult film as a legitimate form of entertainment.[45]

Growing from the tradition of art films stretching the boundaries of free expression (*And God Created Woman* [1957], *Room at the Top* [1959], *La Dolce Vita* [1960]), the adult features of the period were supplied by European producers. The influx of product from Sweden and Denmark played with subtitles in art houses, thus giving an aura of class and sophistication to the films. The economic power of the adult film became stronger and stronger toward the close of the 1960s—from the foreign imports, such as *I Am Curious (Yellow)*, breaking capacity records in 1969 New York and placing #1 on *Variety*'s weekly Top Grossing Films Chart (November 26, 1969), to the sexploitation films, such as *The Stewardesses, I, A Woman*, and *Therese and Isabelle*. Of course, today the possibility of any soft-core, independent film, foreign or domestic, reaching the top of the *Variety* chart is ludicrous. This is not due to any current lack of public interest in pornography and erotica, rather the contemporary market for this product is now primarily dominated by video and cable.

The increased visibility of the adult feature toward the end of the decade was accompanied by more freedom in content: in 1968, for example, a case before the Maryland State Censor Board demonstrated that exploitation features had progressed from upper torso nudity to full frontal nudity in features such as *Walls of Flesh* (1968) and *Savage Blonde* (1968). As a trade paper reported on this transformation, "Time was when a nudie made exclusively for the exploitation house had the male retain some dress, usually a pair of shorts, and the female her panties."[46]

The issue was extended even further with the U.S. distribution of the Swedish film *I Am Curious (Yellow)*. Featuring simulated sexual intercourse in medium and long shot, the film offered a rather unsettling mix of political, sexual, and social satire with a story centering on the 'radical' lifestyle choices of Lena, a young Swede unbound by sexual and social conventions. Banned outright in Norway, Vilgot Sjoman's film was censored heavily in Britain, France, and Germany.[47] Grove Press picked up the American distribution rights, only to have the film impounded by the U.S. Customs Service. Until the circuit court of appeals ruled that the film could be shown uncut, Grove Press continued to maximize publicity around the film through releasing a paperback copy of the script, with over 250 stills for those who preferred looking at the pictures.[48] When the film

*Figure 37. American distributor Grove Press capitalized on the controversy surrounding* I am Curious (Yellow) *(1967), exploiting "the national dialogue over sexual freedom and expression."* Courtesy of the Museum of Modern Art/Film Stills Archive.

finally was cleared for release with an X rating, Grove Press was able to extract strong terms from exhibitors due to the media controversy surrounding the film: the distributor asked for $50,000 in advance and 90 percent/ 10 percent split favoring the distributor after recoupment of the advance.[49] The New York opening in March 1969 was phenomenally successful, with an opening week of $91,785 at two small theaters, the Cinema 57 Rendezvous and the Evergreen.[50] Within six months of release, the film grossed $4 million in less than twenty-five theaters.

*I Am Curious (Yellow)*'s performance illustrates the power of publicity and the ability of one film to exploit the national dialogue over sexual freedom and expression. The foreign origin and the film's treatment of sexuality as a social issue certainly helped qualify the film as within the art, not exploitation, category and therefore worthy of consideration. Reporting on the controversy, *Look* European editor Leonard Gross foregrounded the dramatic and moral qualities of *I Am Curious (Yellow)*: "It is a serious film with a noble theme, and, in dramatic terms, it is original. . . . And [director] Sjoman, whom friends describe as both moral and concerned, uses sex artistically to make a political point: lack of commitment in affairs of state is as disastrous as in affairs of heart."[51] While the box office performance was impressive, the figure is extraordinary given the dry, didactic film, distinguished only by the more sexually frank material. As the reviewer for *Time* described the film, "If it were not for the sex scenes, *Yellow* would probably never have been imported. It is simply too interminably boring, too determinedly insular and, like the sex scenes themselves, finally and fatally passionless."[52]

In terms of the marketplace, *I Am Curious (Yellow)*, like many of the breakthrough adult films, primarily developed in urban centers: opening first in New York, followed by Washington, Chicago, and Philadelphia.[53] Despite the lengthy legal battle ending with the U.S. Court of Appeals (second only in authority to the Supreme Court), exhibitors feared local raids by police. Costly litigation against Audobon's *Therese and Isabelle*, for instance, dampened exhibitor interest in booking *I Am Curious (Yellow)* in Pittsburgh.[54] To alleviate some of these concerns, Grove agreed to cover the legal costs of any theaters charged. Grove's lawyer, Edward De Grazia, also was placed as legal representative for these theaters.[55] The rural resistance against adult film became formalized through organizations such as the North Central Association of Theatre Owners (a regional division of NATO). President Ray Vonderhaar appealed for a relief from screen "oversexiness," warning the majors that they would lose the small town market through organized boycotts by the "rebellious" public.[56] The threat was supported by the vigorous attempts by local law enforcement in small towns and the South to curtail the showing of adult cinema: Grove faced huge legal fees defending the rights of the Kimo South Theatre in Overland Park, Kansas, to show their film, and Grove fought the stringent obscenity laws in Atlanta before even attempting to secure a playdate for *I Am Curious (Yellow)*.[57] Of course, the X rating, used to signify adult material, did not prevent the film from receiving these legal challenges.

While the adult film was becoming a serious economic factor in the marketplace, the awareness and visibility of the adult feature within this market was negotiated by the industry trade papers, *Boxoffice, Motion Picture Herald,* and *Weekly Variety.* Especially for exhibitors, distributors, and producers outside the large urban centers, these trades represented, and to some extent still represent, a significant 'lifeline' to the changing marketplace. Mirroring the larger battles played out in the arena of the sexual revolution, the trade papers offered a (sometimes warped) characterization of the adult cinema as an economic force. This social aspect was matched by a contradictory agenda within the trades. Being a bastion for studio moviemaking, the trades frequently deplored the adult film that could not become the major focus for studio production. Nevertheless, the commercial opportunities of the adult film and its partial integration into more mainstream studio fare were continually discussed throughout articles in the trades during the late 1960s.

Focusing in the period 1969 through 1971, initially the adult feature was viewed in terms of contagion. The front-page headline from *Variety* (May 7, 1969) proclaimed, "Italy's New 'Lust Horizon': 25 Films with Lesbo Angles."[58] Suggesting that the foreign art film was "to blame" for the frank sexual content in contemporary films, the writer stressed the lack of support, financial and artistic, which these pictures received in their home countries. Not surprisingly, less than two months later, the same writer proclaimed, "Italy's Porno Pix Crackdown" from government leaders, political parties, and, of course, the Vatican.[59] The Italian scenario was replicated with *Variety*'s continuing reports on the degradation of New York's 42nd Street in the late 1960s. Clearly invoked as a metaphor for the rising wave of sexploitation across large cities in North America, the articles foregrounded, to use the trades' terms, 'pornos-winos-homos' and their unrestrained dominance of the formerly grand theater district.[60] Evidencing a simultaneous repulsion for and fascination with the trend, *Variety* writers balanced pleas for greater police crackdowns on 'winos' and 'homos' with descriptions on how to spot prostitutes and the most popular street corners for both prostitutes and porno theaters.

While this thread of Puritanism runs throughout, the trades were also interested in the commercial exploitation of sex in cinema, such as an article describing a barbershop that ran soft-core porn for its customers.[61] Marketing sexploitation also became a focus for the trades since many of the features could not be sold through images in mainstream publications. The most obvious method of selling was through the inclusion of the X rating in the print ad campaign: along with the film's title and 'tamed' visual ad images, the classification tag became a key element for advertising the sexploitation film. At times, understatement became a very effective means of selling. Describing the most inflammatory of advertising campaigns, *Variety* (April 16, 1969) reported that the Presidio Theater in San Francisco refused even to print the title of their midnight show in the local newspapers. Ads were constituted by a strong disclaimer, reading, in part, "Our underground show tonight at midnight is not recommended for those offended at the grotesque and atrocious sexual behavior characteristic of a sick segment of our society."

The trades also attempted to demystify the new sexual freedom of the adult film for those unfamiliar with the boundaries of the sexual revolution. Amazingly, *Variety* even attempted to define the 'genre' of the porno film, suggesting that every porno film contain "1. simulated heterosexual congress, a minimum of two scenes; 2. one lesbian segment; 3. at least one orgy; 4. a violence scene; 5. fellatio and/or cunnilingus" (August 13, 1969). This checklist was followed the next month with a front-page article heralding, "New Sex Aberration Discovered for Pic." Describing the practice, *Variety*'s resident psychoanalyst defined tokenism as "what occurs when a person gets a sexual fixation on an object associated with the human body and thus differs from fetishism which refers to items that are human-oriented" (September 10, 1969).

Trade papers more specifically concerned with exhibition—*Motion Picture Herald, Boxoffice*—offered a more conservative view on the long-term possibilities for adult film. *Motion Picture Herald* editor-in-chief Martin Quigley Jr.'s editorials on the matter traced an increasing distrust of the system. As Quigley's father, a devout Catholic, was instrumental in authoring the original Production Code, Quigley Jr. was perhaps predisposed to replicate the desire for a 'production ethic' for film production through the ratings system.[62] Quigley started by urging all exhibitors to follow the guidelines of the new system: "every exhibitor playing post-November 1 releases should make sure that he conforms to the practices of the rating plan including in the trailer, in advertising, and by posting information at the box office."[63] Quigley implied that the ratings system would help to divide motion picture product by audience segments in a meaningful way for exhibitors. This hope was short-lived. Not long after the plea for compliance, Quigley adopted a dour, moralistic tone in describing the ways in which freedom from censorship and court restraint implicitly offered by the new ratings system has permitted a "headlong race in indecency, obscenity, and pornography." Ending his impassioned plea against adult cinema, Quigley cited nothing less than the fall of American culture and social standards as a consequence of the MPAA ratings system: "the history of ancient Athens and Rome, as well as that of Restoration England, shows that the acceptance of obscenity and pornography in public entertainment has heralded or contributed to a breakup of society."[64] Nevertheless, even in the *Motion Picture Herald*, the possibilities for exhibitors exploiting X-rated product became a point of discussion. The trade paper, for example, covered the 1970 New York opening of X-rated *Female Animal* ('she's woman enough, are you man enough?'), complete with photos of an illuminated float for the film in Times Square and the on-site appearances by the film's models and actresses.[65]

The hesitation and hostility evidenced within the exhibition trades reflects the division of exhibition along urban and rural lines: the small town exhibitors were particularly reluctant to play adult-oriented pictures, citing the lack of support from their patrons. Even an R-rated film such as *M\*A\*S\*H* (1970) fell prey to these concerns. In the monthly column "The Exhibitor Has His Say about Pictures" in *Boxoffice* magazine, A. E. Jarbol, manager of the Ritz theater in Cameron, Missouri, dismissed Altman's film in the following manner: "Another R Picture on which the gross was small. Clean Pictures do better."[66] The studios certainly realized this distinction and targeted the adult-oriented (R/X) material to urban sites as much as possible. Warner Bros., for instance, advertised their summer 1970 product through the rural/urban division and through ratings categories for families (G/GP) versus adults (R/X) with the tag line, "This summer Warner Bros. has the next best thing to a month in the country for the whole family" matched with a bucolic setting and print ads for Jerry Lewis in *Which Way to the Front?* (G), John Wayne in *Chisum* (G), and *Start the Revolution Without Me* (GP). On the adjoining page, the ad continued "And for you city slickers . . ." atop skyscrapers advertising *Performance* (X) and *Woodstock* (R).[67] Significantly, much of the publicity from the annual National Association of Theater Owners convention that same year was centered around the desire for many exhibitors to see the end of "smut, sex, and profanity."[68] In sum, the discourse within the industry presented a mixed reaction to the opportunity of adult film: while local exhibitors expressed hesitation about the onslaught of adult pictures, many articles and some advertisements attempted to position the adult film as a viable economic possibility for exhibitors, particularly for those in urban areas.

## Dividing the Market: Adult, Soft, and Hard

By the end of the 1960s, the market for adult film had branched into three distinct areas: adult dramas, which incorporated increasingly explicit sex scenes and subject matter; soft-core pornography often utilizing X as a ratings attraction; and hard-core pornography limited to large cities and linked to hard-core bookstores and strip clubs. Both soft and hard employed the X in their selling, with the rating unable to signal the difference between the two. Soft-core was distinguished from hard-core by the degree of 'realism': soft involved simulated sex, while hard included insertion and orgasm shots. Reflecting the growing competition from mainstream cinemas, the Presidential Commission on Obscenity and Pornography estimated that adult film receipts dropped 10 to 20 percent from 1969 to 1970 due, in large part, "to increased competition from sexually oriented motion pictures playing outside the exploitation market."[69]

The majors responded to the more liberal climate by aligning themselves with more explicit subjects often made 'palatable' by their association with adjoining art forms. Adaptations of Philip Roth's *Goodbye, Columbus* (1969) and *Portnoy's Complaint* (1972) and John Updike's *Rabbit, Run* (1970) all classified as 'serious' fiction, arrived on screen with the trades describing their appearance as an attempt by the major studios 'to broaden sexploitation.'[70] Distributors Cinema V and Continental continued to buttress their release schedules with adult-oriented dramas—*Ulysses* (1967), *Putney Swope* (1969), *Trash* (1970), *W.R.—Mysteries of the Organism* (1971)—containing explicit material, yet firmly within the realm of the art cinema. The combined distribution and exhibition arms of both companies aided these films, which were alternately too strong, esoteric, and foreign for the majors, and too arty and serious for the porn market.

By 1970, porno films also split into soft-core and hard-core markets. The shift was precipitated by the emergence of 16mm automated hard-core theaters showing 'real' or unsimulated sexual intercourse. The porn market seized on the cheaper alternative of 16mm for production and exhibition, with shorts progressing from silent female striptease to sexual intercourse.[71] The hard-core market developed initially in New York, San Francisco, and Los Angeles, and, with a typical admission price of $5, the market proved even more profitable than the soft-core business. To differentiate their product even further from the soft-core market, hard-core theaters began to integrate live entertainment: live sex shows as special attractions in the evenings.[72] New York's Mini-Cinema instituted the policy in 1970, offering eleven live shows daily in between the hard-core shorts. Soon after, the 47th and 49th St. Playhouses, the Doll and Paree theaters shifted to include live entertainment.[73] On a smaller scale, yet still incredibly lucrative, hardcore homosexual films also became a market presence in New York and Los Angeles with the same combination of cinema and live entertainment.

In terms of market structure and organization, the separation of the adult market into three regions—adult, soft, and hard—was enhanced by definite institutional differences among the segments. Whereas adult-oriented material was primarily the domain of the studios, soft- and hard-core were marked for independents through several factors: exhibition (with theaters playing X-rated films solely), pricing (with the higher ticket price for porno theaters), and, despite the intentions of the MPAA, the X rating. Without copyright and appearing in a vast array of styles and print types in ads, the rating became a crucial method for indicating the soft- and hard-core markets. With the split of the sexploitation market in 1970, the exhibition house, technology, and additional live entertainment effectively divided hard-core from soft-core through institutional and industrial forces, apart from the differences in explicit sexual content. Consequently, the separation of the market into adult-soft-hard must be understood not just in terms of cinematic sexual freedom, but also as aided by crucial structural factors within the overall marketplace, subdividing the market into three distinct segments.

The hard-core market did erode the soft-core audience as evidenced by the demise of several of the largest soft-core distributors by the early 1970s. Jerry Gross's Cinemation Industries illustrates the difficulty experienced by soft-core distributors after the rise of hard-core film. Formed in 1965, Cinemation relied on a mixture of in-house products and negative pickups for their distribution schedule. While Cinemation handled distribution for the art house company Rizzoli (reissues of *Red Desert* [1964], *Juliet of the Spirits* [1965], and *Baby Doll* [1956], among others), the majority of the release schedule was comprised of soft-core product emphasizing sex and exploitable sensationalistic subjects: *Fanny Hill* (new . . . and from Sweden), *Teenage Mother* (She did her homework in parked cars!), *God's Little Acre* (See how they live! Their kind of kinship means anything goes!), and *Mondo Cane* Nos. 1 and 2 (The 'With-It' Sex Highs! Naked Witchcraft Murders! See Priests on Fire!). By 1970, with Gross commenting that "the sexploitation film is definitely on the decline," the company shifted toward other forms of marginalized cinema.[74] With this

*Figure 38.* Deep Throat *(1972) was "one of the most significant commercial successes of hard–core," but it also faced suppression battles around the country on the grounds that it was obscene.* Courtesy of the Museum of Modern Art/Film Stills Archive.

strategy, Cinemation realized its greatest success in 1971 with Melvin Van Peebles's *Sweet Sweetback's Baadasssss Song*, a classic of black cinema.[75] By the mid-1970s though, Cinemation's release schedule diversified with little long-term success: ranging from X-rated cartoons (*Fritz the Cat*) to horror (*I Drink Your Blood*), true-life melodramas (*Abduction*, the Patty Hearst story), and a shift to a more heavily art house leaden schedule (*Stavisky, Turkish Delight,* and *La Trompe d'Oeil*). In 1975, Cinemation filed for bankruptcy, and a year later its assets were auctioned.[76]

One of the most significant commercial successes of hard-core, *Deep Throat* (1972), also illustrates the limits of the hard-core market shifting into a more mainstream commercial context. With a capsule review from *Variety* stating "Hardcore hetero sex feature with humor a plus. Tops in the current market," the film initially benefited commercially from a rave review in *Screw* magazine.[77] The opening week at the New Mature World Theatre in Manhattan broke box office records for an adult feature: $30,033 for the single house.[78] Within nine months, *Deep Throat* had grossed $1.2 million at its initial engagement.[79] While this success was replicated in many markets across the country, obscenity cases against the film furthered box office in some areas and scared potential exhibitors in others.

In New York, Mayor John V. Lindsay's antismut campaign took hold, with the film seized late in its run at the World Theatre. New York Criminal Court Judge Joel Tyler found the exhibitors guilty on charges of promoting obscenity. Tyler's twenty-nine-page decision discussed in detail the graphic depictions in the film, often almost in lurid tones: "The camera angle, emphasis and closeup zooms were directed toward a maximum exposure of the genitalia during the gymnastics, gyrations, bobbing, trundling, surging, ebb and flowing, eddying, moaning, groaning and sighing, all with ebullience and gusto. There were so many and varied forms of sexual activity one would tend to lose count of them. However, the news reporters counted seven separate acts of fellatio and four of cunnilingus."[80] With the print seized from the theater and the financial records of the exhibitor impounded, the World Theater changed their marquee to read "Judge Cuts Throat, World Mourns."[81]

Legal injunctions also interrupted, or in some cases eliminated, runs in Baltimore, Beverly Hills, Memphis, Atlanta, San Antonio, St. Paul, Ft. Worth, Boston, and Houston. Defendants claimed protection of the First Amendment right to freedom of expression, while prosecutors, following two different interpretations of obscenity, argued either that the film had 'no redeeming social value' or that it was obscene under 'local community standards.' The latter charge proved most thorny for both sides, with much debate over what constituted 'the community' for legal purposes. As Justice John Paul Stevens claimed regarding the trial in eastern Kentucky: "What is the purpose of defining the community? Should it be the economic market of a film's distribution area or a frame of reference for the jurors?"[82] In this specific instance, the community might have been formed by eastern Kentucky, the greater Cincinnati area, or some other geographic region made up of the two. The community standard question led to some curious situations in the *Deep Throat* case; for example, while the film was restricted from Manhattan, simultaneously, a jury in the New York suburb of Binghamton found the film not to be obscene.[83] One exhibitor suggested bus trips from the "more conservative" Times Square to Binghamton for frustrated Manhattan moviegoers.

As *Deep Throat* was the first hard-core feature to attract nationwide attention, the film also garnered a large share of interest from authorities. Consequently, despite its reputation, *Deep Throat* actually grossed less than Gerard Damiano's follow-up, *The Devil in Miss Jones:* amazingly, *Miss Jones* ($7.7 million) ranked as the seventh largest grosser of 1973, sandwiched between the James Bond film *Live & Let Die* and Peter Bogdanovich's *Paper Moon.* In comparison, *Deep Throat* ($4.6 million) was ranked slightly lower, in eleventh position, between *Deliverance* and *Sleuth.* Following the litigation over *Deep Throat,* though, the attraction of hard-core became more limited in the industry. Particularly noteworthy in terms of a deterrent was Judge Tyler's move to fine the defendants twice the actual gross of *Deep Throat* at the World Theater, a figure slightly greater than $2 million.[84] In terms of prosecution, authorities shifted from theater employees (cashiers, doormen, projectionists, salaried theater managers) to actually prosecuting the owners of the hard-core theaters. This move was sufficient to convince some to shift their focus from hard-core to soft-core, and to limit the encroachment of hard-core material into the suburbs.

The hard-core market was further undermined by the U.S. Supreme Court's June 21, 1973 decision in *Miller v. California* for 'local option' of pornography; in effect, the Supreme Court relinquished power over deciding on obscene media to the individual states and localities.[85] Free-speech proponents feared that this move would lead to broader censorship, far beyond hard-core, which had already come under fire. As an example, industry analysts pointed to the *Miller v. California* case in which Justice Burger described an acceptable formulation of state obscenity law: "patently offensive representations or descriptions of sexual acts, normal or perverted, actual or simulated."[86] Including the word *simulated*, this definition opened the possibility for prosecution of soft-core material in which sex acts appear without shots of actual penetration and orgasm. The implications for the porno market were far-reaching—suddenly producers and distributors of both hard- and soft-core feared that their market faced erosion through possible prosecution on a market-by-market basis across the country. As producer Max Stein pleaded to a Supreme Court spokesman, "At least at the onset of Prohibition, one knew that in six months you couldn't sell liquor. But with this nobody knows what you will or won't be able to portray on screen. Can I show a bikini? a navel? What words can I use?"[87] This confusion over 'acceptable' content echoed the ambiguities inherent in the ratings for adult films from the recent past.

While litigation dampened interest in hard-core, the presence of more upscale 'quality' fare, such as *Deep Throat*, actually polarized the hard-core market further. Indeed, while *Deep Throat* earned box office success, smaller hard-core theaters suffered through a lack of product and, partly due to *Deep Throat*, a suddenly more discerning hard-core audience. As *Variety* reported in an article entitled "N.Y. Porno Finds Own Level: Selective Buffs Seek 'Quality,'" a 1972 product shortage of feature-length hard-core features forced New York theaters to program hard-core shorts, often on a "sub-sub-run basis."[88] The situation resulted from several factors, including exhibitor disdain for patronage ("they'll sit through anything, even if they've seen it before") and distributors repackaging an old film with a new title. Some hard-core distributors were charged with selling a film as "a New York first run" to several theaters in Manhattan under different titles. Gay porno theaters replicated the straight market—a product shortage, few high quality items—with even the most famous gay hard-core theater, the Park-Miller, reduced to playing a double-bill revival (of *The Right Boy for Peter* and *The Case of the Hooded Man*).[89]

*Figure 39. Protesters at a Manhattan theater showing Bernardo Bertolucci's art house, X-rated success,* Last Tango in Paris *(1972). Courtesy of the Museum of Modern Art/Film Stills Archive.*

As with most potential threats to the mainstream industry, pornography also was assimilated by the majors. Although content was limited to the arena of soft-core, major studios began to integrate increasingly explicit material. Several films were significant in this regard. United Artists released *Midnight Cowboy* with the X rating in 1969. The film's strong commercial performance and, even more dramatically, a Best Picture Academy Award helped to legitimate X as a rating for the majors. After their success with *Midnight Cowboy*, United Artists released Bernardo Bertolucci's *Last Tango in Paris*. The film was also rated X, and it generated much press not only through its rating but also through the concentration on sexuality and the match of subject matter with an icon from the 1950s. The art house/foreign origins were made more accessible given Brando's status as American star—the mix of the domestic and the imported framed *Last Tango* as a different breed of adult film.[90] This difference was maximized by United Artists in their advertising: most notoriously through a two-page ad in the *New York Times* (December 24, 1972) which reprinted, in full, Pauline Kael's ecstatic review of the film.[91] Claiming that the showing of *Last Tango* at the New York Film Festival represented "a

*Figure 40. Columbia Pictures' release of the soft-core porn film* Emmanuelle *in 1974 demonstrated "how comfortable the majors had become with softcore."* Courtesy of the Museum of Modern Art/Film Stills Archive.

landmark in movie history," Kael's rapturous comments must be viewed as an attempt by United Artists to broaden the dialogue around the film to artistic triumph rather than solely around its sex scenes. The accumulation of this evidence, that is, the American star, the talented young foreign director (making his first film since *The Conformist*), an uncompromising vision of sexuality, and the critical acclaim, suggested that perhaps an X rating could signify more than explicit sex scenes. Regardless, the film faced obscenity charges in different areas, although the critical accolades and studio legal powers mitigated the charges. Court battles ensued in many markets (Radford, Winnipeg, Lubbock, Shreveport, Atlanta, Toledo, Montgomery, Cincinnati), but UA attorney Gerald Phillips countered all allegations with positive results: "Everywhere we were threatened, we brought an action and were successful."[92]

While Bertolucci's film retained a vestige of prestige and serious purpose, Just Jaeckin's *Emmanuelle*, released in North America by Columbia Pictures, could only be described as soft-core porn, pure and simple. Indeed, *Emmanuelle*'s entry into the market, sponsored by a large studio, indicated how comfortable the majors had become with soft-core by 1974. The case of *Emmanuelle* illustrates how the majors' involvement with soft-core was mediated by an attempt to differentiate their product from other forms of pornography. Columbia president David Begelman was attracted to *Emmanuelle* by its audience composition in Paris: as he recounted, "The line outside the theater was made up of about 75 to 80% women. We would have had no interest in the film if its appeal was totally to men. Then it could be taken as pornographic."[93] Begelman and former Young & Rubicam president Steve Frankfurt devised an ad campaign for the North American release centered upon the catch phrase "X was never like this." In effect, through the line and the film's European origin, Columbia was able to separate their film from other adult product while still reaping all the commercial benefits of the X rating. In addition, the campaign also operated by ambiguity: if X was never like this, Columbia merely implied that *Emmanuelle* was different somehow . . . but how? That was left to the individual moviegoer: to some the phrase could have indicated that *Emmanuelle* was even more graphic in its content than previous X pictures; to others the phrase could have implied that *Emmanuelle* was more artistic or sophisticated than other X pictures.

In large markets, the full text of Columbia's ad campaign helped to demonstrate just how committed the company was to this reorientation of the X rating: the complete ad copy began with "X has never been known for its elegance. Or for its beautiful people. Or for its intelligent story line. X has been known for other things. At Columbia Pictures we're proud to bring you a movie that will change the meaning of X. A movie that begins with the sensual and takes it places X has never been before." The ad continued to position the film as erotica and as a lifestyle alternative to hard-core pornography, suggesting that this X caused no guilt and stimulated the mind, "the most sensual part of your body." Matched to the omnipresent ad line and the film's logo of the title leading to an apple with a woman's head, *Emmanuelle*'s slick ad campaign and graphically bold logo seem most in line with the high concept films—*Jaws, Grease, The Omen, Saturday Night Fever*—of the same decade. Suddenly, softcore porn was being sold through a saturation ad campaign and simple, graphically distinctive designs that established a visual presence for the film on a repeated basis. In terms of the marketplace, this move also polarized the adult market into just two segments: on the one hand, hardcore and, on the other, mainstream studio movies integrating soft-core material. The strategy of redefining the X rating was integral to Columbia's and the other majors' attempts to mine the adult audience while simultaneously separating themselves from the hard-core market.

As the case of *Emmanuelle* demonstrates, the ratings system facilitated the efforts of the major studios to co-opt the soft-core movie market. While the ratings at first seemed to be a blessing for independent producers and distributors who could utilize X for soft-core and hard-core product untouched by the majors, eventually the major studios were able

# X was never like this.

Emmanuelle is sensual, but she's elegant.
Emmanuelle is fantasy, but she's fun.
But most important, she leaves you with a singular lack of guilt.
And that's the clue to its overwhelming popularity.

"Sex done with taste and beauty."
— *Cosmopolitan*, Liz Smith

"...aphrodisiac in effect, not embarrassing for mixed company."
— *New York Post*, Archer Winsten

"Deluxe lechery."
— *After Dark*

"Gorgeous sexual couplings."
— *Village Voice*

English Sub-Titles

*Emmanuelle*

Lets you feel good without feeling bad.

Alain Cuny • Sylvia Kristel • Marika Green in Emmanuelle
(in the role of Bee) from the book D'Emmanuelle
A film by Just Jaeckin with Daniel Sarky • Jeanne Colletin • Christine Boisson music Pierre Bachelet
A Co production of TRINACRA FILM • ORPHEE PRODUCTIONS • Distributed by COLUMBIA PICTURES

THE *Paris*

5th Avenue & 58th Street • MU 8-2013
12, 1:35, 3:15, 4:55, 6:40, 8:20, 10:08

*Figure 41. An example of Columbia Pictures and the Paris Theater's unusual advertising campaign for* Emmanuelle *in the* New York Times, *with the catchphrase "X was never like this" (January 2, 1975).*

to benefit from the audience identified and separated by the X rating. In this manner, ultimately the classification system could be exploited by the majors, who were funding the system anyway by paying for the board to rate their pictures.

In the broadest sense, then, the ratings system benefited the majors economically in the late 1960s and early 1970s, albeit not in the fundamental ways that the PCA did during the studio era. At that time, when industry critics complained that the majors' dominance meant theaters were forced to show 'poor quality and immoral' pictures through the practice of block booking, the MPPDA answered them by alluding to the PCA's skill at keeping offensive elements in studio films to a minimum; thus no further dismantling of the studio oligopoly was necessary.[94] After the Paramount case divorcement decrees and with the threat of local censorship greatly reduced, the MPAA ratings system still functioned as a public relations strategy while movie content grew increasingly explicit. But the MPAA was no longer fighting to preserve vertical integration and major studio dominance of the market from the threat of federal anti-trust action

Yet the particular example of the X rating, and the integration of X-rated films into the majors' distribution slate in the early 1970s, illustrates how the studios ultimately benefited economically from the classification system and provides another instance of the resilient, hegemonic power of the studios even in a period of extreme upheaval socially and industrially. With hard-core diminished by litigation and the fear of litigation, and soft-core integrated into the mainstream through the label of erotica rather than porn, the adult feature ceased to be a major presence in theatrical release for the independents. As an indication of this integration, the MPAA and Jack Valenti had begun to focus on other issues than the problem of X (e.g., the shift from GP to PG, for example, garnered much press in 1972, the year of *Last Tango in Paris*).[95] Nevertheless, with each shift or adjustment in the ratings system, the major studios were able to arrange for a way to benefit commercially: by integrating more adult material in PG-13 films, the category introduced to mediate between PG and R in 1984, and by attempting to exploit audiences for the 'art house' X rating, NC-17, in 1990 with Universal's *Henry and June*, for example.[96]

The period from the late 1960s through mid-1970s occupies a unique position in film history: an era in which institutional/regulatory and economic forces acting within a larger social context configured a market that was not immediately served by the major studios and thus became a focus for independent production. As the market developed, its fragmentation into adult, soft, and hard diminished the impact of independent companies and increased the majors' presence in the adult marketplace. The MPAA ratings were instrumental in the identification, separation, and co-optation of this marketplace and they have continued to help the industry effectively negotiate 'new' audience segments since this turbulent period.

## NOTES

My thanks to Matthew Bernstein, Hilary Radner, Eric Schaefer, and Tom Schatz for comments on an earlier version of this essay. Thanks also for research materials made available by Rick Worland and the former Southwest Film and Video Archives.

1. "Pix Must 'Broaden Market,'" *Variety*, March 20, 1968, 1.

2. Lee Beaupre, "Pic Biz Booby-Trap: 'Youth,'" *Variety*, July 31, 1968, 62.

3. "Valenti Predicts Increased Attendance Based on Research by MPAA," *Motion Picture Herald*, January 29, 1968, 8.

4. Robert J. Landry, "To Be 'Youthful' Not Enuf," *Variety*, November 19, 1969, 5; Tino Balio, *Hollywood in the Age of Television* (Boston: Unwin Hyman, 1990), 259–62; Harold L. Vogel, *Entertainment Industry Economics* (New York: Cambridge University Press, 1990), 359.

5. Abel Green, "B.O. Dictatorship by Youth," *Variety*, January 7, 1970, 38.

6. Beaupre, "Pic Biz," 62.

7. The issues addressed by Beaupre are also considered by Robert J. Landry, "Generation-Bridging Pics," *Variety*, July 17, 1968, 8.

8. See, for instance, Addison Verrill, "Youth Angles Can Drop Dead," *Variety*, July 21, 1971, 5; and Abel Green, "Over-25 Audience Dormant, Not Dead," *Variety*, December 24, 1969, 1.

9. Stuart Byron, "Way-Out Attire and Hippie Haircuts Common With European Film Folk," *Variety*, September 4, 1968, 2; and "Hippies Admittable If They Don't Reek," *Variety*, May 1, 1968, 19.

10. "Sex as a Spectator Sport," *Time*, July 11, 1969, 61.

11. "Ah, Wilderness," *Time*, August 16, 1968, 52.

12. Malcolm Dean, *Censored! Only in Canada* (Toronto: Virgo, 1981), 247.

13. "Burden on the Censor," *Newsweek*, March 29, 1965, 88.

14. For a discussion of the impact of these rulings, see Vincent Canby, "Ratings to Bar Some Films to Children," *New York Times*, October 8, 1968, 1.

15. "Power of Local Condemning," *Variety*, November 20, 1968, 7.

16. "'Vagueness' No Fatal Flaw," *Variety*, May 1, 1968, 7. For more on the Dallas classification system, see Brian O'Leary, "Local Government Regulation of the Movies: 1966–93," *Journal of Film and Video* 48, no. 3 (1996): 46–56.

17. For a capsule history of film censorship during the PCA era and before, see Bruce A. Austin, *Immediate Seating: A Look at Movie Audiences* (Belmont: Wadsworth, 1989), 106–8; and Erik Lunde, "The Story of Censorship and the American Film Industry," in Barry R. Litman, ed., *The Motion Picture Mega-Industry* (Needham Heights: Allyn & Bacon, 1998), 198–210.

18. For a discussion of the *Alfie* and *Who's Afraid of Virginia Woolf?* cases, consult Jack Vizzard, *See No Evil: Life Inside a Hollywood Censor* (New York: Pocket Books, 1971), 266–75.

19. "Valenti's Warning: Films Go Too Far," *Variety*, April 10, 1968, 19.

20. "MPAA Code Wants Catholic Support," *Variety*, August 17, 1966, 3.

21. "X Marks the Spot (Self-Interest)," *Variety*, April 28, 1969, 3.

22. Glenn Collins, "Film Ratings: Guidance or Censorship?," *New York Times*, April 9, 1990, C11.

23. "'Classification' by Indies?," *Variety*, August 31, 1966, 7.

24. "MPAA's New Code & Rating Rules," *Variety*, October 9, 1968, 4.

25. Ibid.

26. "'Ratings' An All-Things Thing," *Variety*, September 18, 1968, 5.

27. "39 Pix 'Rated,'" *Variety*, October 23, 1968, 1.

28. Dean, *Censored!*, 231.

29. For a description of the appeals procedures and discussion of several early cases, consult Stephen Farber, *The Movie Rating Game* (Washington, D.C.: Public Affairs Press, 1972), 73–82.

30. "Critics Are Useful Sometimes; Paramount Cites Its Reviews On *If*; Hope to Erase That X," *Variety*, March 26, 1969, 3.

31. Stuart Byron, "Though Unintended, 'X' Still is Taken as 'Dirty' or 'Shoddy'; This Condition a Poser for Valenti," *Variety*, February 26, 1969, 7.

32. "Reade Sez Self-Applied X Ratings Dangerous; Brands Code a 'Failure,'" *Variety*, November 12, 1969, 6.

33. "By Default," *Variety*, June 26, 1968, 16.

34. Ibid.

35. Quoted in Farber, *Movie Rating Game*, 47.

36. "MPAA Ratings to Now: G(43), M(29), R(22); Puzzle: X for 'Birds' But R for 'The Fox,'" *Variety*, December 4, 1968, 18.

37. Ibid.

38. Robert B. Frederick, "'Young NATO' Group Advises MPAA's 'G' Rating Be Purified in Sex, Gab," *Variety*, November 19, 1969, 22.

39. Martin Quigley Jr., "Rating Simplification Plan," *Motion Picture Herald*, February 25, 1970, 5.

40. "MPAA Film Ratings: 1968–81," *Variety*, November 11, 1981, 36.

41. Stephen Farber and Estelle Changas, "Putting the Hex on 'R' and 'X,'" *New York Times*, April 9, 1972, D1.

42. Ibid., D15. As the 1970s progressed, the MPAA continued to consult with the studios about ways to dodge the X rating. For William Friedkin's thriller *Cruising* (1980), set in the gay S&M world, Dr. Aaron Stern, former head of the Board, advised Friedkin and producer Jerry Weintraub on cuts necessary to secure an R rating for the United Artists release. The production team followed the suggestions fully. Friedkin describes the process in the following way:

> Eventually [CARA chief] Heffner breaks down and tells Jerry to take the picture to Aaron Stern, his predecessor at the board and the guy who got *The Exorcist* through. Stern was now working as a psychiatrist in New York, and Heffner had an agreement with him that if there were any really difficult pictures, Stern would look at them. So we took the picture to him, and at a cost of $1,000 a day he worked for about 40 days suggesting cuts, sending it back to the board, having them go through the roof again, taking it back and looking at it again, until finally we arrived at a version they would approve.

Quoted in Mark Kermode, "Cruise Control," *Sight and Sound* 8, no. 11 (1998): 23.

43. Farber, *Movie Rating Game*, 55.

44. "X Marks the Spot (Self-Interest)," 3.

45. For a history of the exploitation film in the 1930s and the various institutional and industrial factors bolstering these films, see Eric Schaefer, "Resisting Refinement: The Exploitation Film and Self-Censorship," *Film History* 6, no. 4 (1994): 293–313.

46. "From Nearly to Total Nude Pix," *Variety*, October 2, 1968, 1.

47. "'Curious': Sexy-Dull Shocker," *Variety*, March 19, 1969, 7.

48. Michael F. Mayer, "A Not So Curious Result," *Motion Picture Herald*, January 29, 1969, 13–14. The Grove Press book includes not only the screenplay and stills, but also an appendix of pertinent testimony about the film by key witnesses in the U.S. district court case (Vilgot Sjoman, *I Am Curious [Yellow]* [New York: Grove, 1968]).

49. Kent E. Carroll, "Some Fear to Be 'Curious,'" *Variety*, April 9, 1969, 5.

50. "Sex Dominates B'way First-Runs," *Variety*, March 19, 1969, 9.

51. Leonard Gross, "After Nudity, What, Indeed?," *Look*, April 29, 1969, 80–81.

52. "Dubious Yellow," *Time*, March 14, 1969, 98.

53. Carroll, "'Curious,'" 5.

54. "Pittsburgh's Yellow," *Variety*, April 9, 1969, 5.

55. Edward DeGrazia is the co-author, with Roger K. Newman, of a major book of film censorship, *Banned Films* (New York: R. R. Bowker, 1982). See also "Grove's Rosset: All Censors Wrong, Valenti Is Encouraging Vigilantes," *Variety*, September 17, 1969, 25.

56. "Fed Up With Sex Complaint," *Variety*, April 5, 1967, 13.

57. "'Grove Press Running the Show'; Convoluted Legalistics in Kansas," *Variety*, September 3, 1969, 20. Grove's concerns about Atlanta were fueled by the experience of Sherpix distributing Andy Warhol's *Lonesome Cowboys* in which the Atlanta print was seized, the manager/projectionist was arrested, and photographs were taken of audience members. See Margia Kramer, "The Warhol File," in Michael O'Pray, ed., *Andy Warhol Film Factory* (London: BFI, 1989), 178–81.

58. Hank Werba, "Italy's New 'Lust Horizon,'" *Variety*, May 7, 1969, 1.

59. Hank Werba, "Italy's Porno Pix Crackdown," *Variety*, June 25, 1969, 7.

60. See, for example, Jo Cohen, "Hookers, Homos, Pornos Unchecked Under Civil Rights, in 'Slime Square,'" *Variety*, November 6, 1968, 1; and Abel Green, "Porno-Wino-Homo Gulch (42nd Street) May Be Renewed to Match Times Square," *Variety*, August 13, 1969, 1.

61. For instance, Aubrey Tarbox, "High Brow Novels to Screen: Broaden 'Sexploitation,'" *Variety*, March 12, 1969, 5.

62. For Martin Quigley's role in the formulation of the Production Code, see Richard Maltby, "The Genesis of the Production Code," *Quarterly Review of Film and Video* 15, no. 4 (1995): 5–6.

63. Martin Quigley Jr., "The Rating Age," *Motion Picture Herald*, November 6, 1968, 5.

64. Martin Quigley Jr., "Out of Control!," *Motion Picture Herald*, March 12, 1969, 4.

65. "Manager's Round Table," *Motion Picture Herald*, February 25, 1970, 13.

66. "The Exhibitor Has His Say about Pictures," *Boxoffice*, December 21, 1970, 191.

67. Summer 1970 Warner Bros. ad, *Motion Picture Herald*, June 17, 1970, 16–17.

68. "Give Us More 'G' Film Is Plea at NATO Meeting," *Motion Picture Herald*, November 18, 1970, 2.

69. "Porno Study; 600 US Film Sites Comprise Playoff for Sexploitation," *Variety*, October 7, 1970, 7.

70. Aubrey Tarbox, "High Brow Novels to Screen," *Variety*, March 12, 1969, 8.

71. Addison Verrill, "Skinpix Face 'New Dilemma,'" *Variety*, October 21, 1970, 5.

72. Addison Verrill, "Porno Vaudfilm Strippers," *Variety*, June 23, 1971, 1.

73. Ibid.

74. "Cinemation to Release 30 to May 1971," *Boxoffice*, September 7, 1970, 4.

75. "Black-Slanted Pic Looms Next at Cinemation," *Variety*, March 27, 1974, 4.

76. Jim Robbins, "Jerry Gross Org's Blueprint for Tighter Yet Broader Future," *Variety*, January 6, 1982, 4.

77. Review, *Deep Throat*, *Variety*, June 28, 1972, 26.

78. *Deep Throat* ad, *Variety*, June 28, 1972, 25.

79. Vincent Canby, "What Are We to Make of Deep Throat?," *New York Times*, January 21, 1973, 1, 33.

80. "In 'Greatest Money Notice' Ruling, Judge Tyler Cuts 'Deep Throat' Film," *Variety*, March 7, 1973, 6.

81. Addison Verrill, "No-Jury, 10 Day Throat Trial; 'Obscene' Ruling by Judge Tyler Foreshadows Fine of $2,000,000," *Variety*, March 7, 1973, 6.

82. "Bjork 'Confesses' Error in Kentucky 'Deep Throat' Case," *Variety*, November 3, 1976, 30.

83. Addison Verrill, "No-Jury, 10 Day 'Throat' Trial," *Variety*, March 7, 1973, 6.

84. Ibid.

85. Addison Verrill, "Porno Thicket Now Jungle?," *Variety*, June 27, 1973, 5.

86. Ibid. For a discussion of the long-term impact of *Miller v. California* on the adult film industry, consult Robert J. Stoller and I. S. Levine, *Coming Attractions: The Making of an X-Rated Video* (New Haven: Yale University Press, 1993), 227–28.

87. "Hello, Supreme Court? Listen . . . ," *Variety*, July 4, 1973, 5.

88. Addison Verrill, "N.Y. Porno Finds Own Level," *Variety*, October 18, 1972, 5.

89. "'Quality' Hardcore Is Lacking," *Variety*, July 10, 1974, 22.

90. For an account of the film's reception in domestic and international markets, consult Tino Balio, *United Artists: The Company That Changed the Film Industry* (Madison: University of Wisconsin Press, 1987), 293–300.

91. *New York Times*, December 24, 1972, D5–D6.

92. Harlan Jacobson, "Climaxing Many Legal Wins, Tango Returns to Cincy," *Variety*, March 19, 1975, 17.

93. "Analyzing Emmanuelle's B.O. Impact on the U.S. Market," *Variety*, May 7, 1975, 56.

94. Ruth Vasey, *The World According to Hollywood, 1918–1939* (Madison: University of Wisconsin Press, 1996), 48.

95. Jack Valenti, "Massive Effort to Inform Nation on PG Change in Film Ratings," *NATO News*, February 1972, 1.

96. In 1998, *Henry and June* director Philip Kaufman commented that the long-term impact of NC-17 had been negligible. Whereas the hope was the NC-17 would allow adult films to be distributed without the stigma of the X rating, as Kaufman explains the development of the rating's utilization, "Everyone backed away from the issue and allowed NC-17 to become the new X" (Christopher Stern, "Cheers, Jeers on Ratings Code Birthday," *Variety*, November 28, 1998, 7).

# Annotated Bibliography

The library of scholarly writing on movie censorship is enormous. What follows is not comprehensive, but a listing of (mostly scholarly) essays and books from recent decades that present crucial research or influential perspectives on the phenomena of censorship, regulation, and self-regulation of Hollywood movies. The notes to each essay offer additional readings as well.

Armour, Robert A. "Effects of Censorship Pressure on the New York Nickelodeon Market, 1907–1909." *Film History* 4 (1990): 113–21.

> An examination of the December 1908 citywide closing of New York's nickelodeons and its impact on that city's film business, on the rise of the National Board of Censorship/Review (hereafter NBC/R), and on D. W. Griffith's turn to literary adaptations.

Ayer, Douglas, Roy E. Bates, and Peter J. Herman. "Self-Censorship in the Movie Industry: A Historical Perspective on Law and Social Change." *Wisconsin Law Review* 3 (1970): 791–838. Reprinted in Gorham Kindem, ed. *The American Movie Industry: The Business of the Movies.* Carbondale: Southern Illinois University Press, 1982, 215–53.

> A valuable survey of self-regulation in the film industry through 1970, noting relevant court cases, influential national groups, the development of obscenity laws, and the formation and workings of the ratings system.

Black, Gregory D. "Hollywood Censored: The Production Code Administration and the Hollywood Film Industry 1930–1940." *Film History* 3 (1989): 167–89.

> A concise and informative account of the creation and operation of the PCA, with particular attention to Catholic influence over the Code and the PCA's operation, using Mae West in *Belle of the Nineties* and Ernst Lubitsch's *The Merry Widow* as examples of Code enforcement, and *The President Vanishes* and *Black Fury* as instances of "industry policy" considerations.

———. "Movies, Politics, and Censorship: The Production Code Administration and Political Censorship of Film Content." *Journal of Policy History* 3 (1991): 95–129.

> A fact-filled survey of the formation of the MPPDA and the creation of the Production Code. It also examines several politically controversial films (*Hells Highway, I Am a Fugitive from a Chain Gang, Gabriel Over the White House,* and *Idiot's Delight* among them) from the 1930s and how the PCA handled them.

————. *Hollywood Censored: Morality Codes, Catholics, and the Movies.* Cambridge: Cambridge University Press, 1994.

Drawing on numerous Hollywood and Catholic group and personnel archives, this compelling volume examines the creation of the Production Code Administration and its operations through the 1930s, emphasizing the impact of the Catholic Church and the Legion of Decency on Hollywood filmmaking by examining particularly "troublesome" films.

————. *The Catholic Crusade Against the Movies, 1940–1970.* Cambridge: Cambridge University Press, 1997.

Like *Hollywood Censored,* to which it is something of a sequel, this informative, entertaining, and well-researched volume examines Catholic involvement in film censorship from 1940 to 1970. Case studies of particular films (from *The Outlaw* to *Last Tango in Paris* and after) detail how the Legion of Decency and the Production Code Administration responded to changing movie mores.

Budd, Michael. "The National Board of Review and the Early Art Cinema: *The Cabinet of Dr. Caligari* as Affirmative Culture." *Cinema Journal* 26, no. 1 (1985): 3–18.

An important discussion of the "dance of interlegitimation" between the American film industry in the teens and the NBC/R, with particular emphasis on the Board's assessment of a ground-breaking, German Expressionist work.

Carmen, Ira. *Movies, Censorship and the Law.* Ann Arbor: University of Michigan Press, 1966.

A major study of landmark court cases, most notably Supreme Court rulings, and their impact on the existence and workings of various state and city censor boards. Includes detailed descriptions of how then-existing censoring bodies work, their legal provenance, and the impact of court cases, as well as interviews with censors, and a plea for a classification system of movies.

Couvares, Francis G., ed. *Movie Censorship and American Culture.* Washington, D.C.: Smithsonian Institution Press, 1996.

A superb collection of recent essays, most by prominent scholars, covering the history of film censorship from before cinema's beginnings through protests against films of the 1980s. Topics examined include connections between theater and film censorship, the role of women's groups in film regulation, the censoring of race films, the relation of foreign distribution to Hollywood's depictions of ethnicity, the Hollywood Ten, and the *Miracle* decision.

————. "Hollywood, Main Street, and the Church," *American Quarterly* 44, no. 4 (1992): 584–616. Reprinted in Couvares, *Movie Censorship and American Culture,* 129–58.

An insightful and informative account of disagreements within Protestant groups and the changing alliances among religious organizations during the 1920s that led the MPPDA to adapt Catholic suggestions and drafts of the Production Code in 1930. Also important for suggesting that censorship studies reveal social dynamics broader than cultural studies and hegemony theory can account for (acquiescence, accommodation, resistance, evasion).

Curry, Ramona. "Mae West as Censored Commodity: The Case of *Klondike Annie." Cinema Journal* 31, no. 1 (1991): 57–84.

One of the few essays to discuss censorship in relation to a particular star, this article explores how Paramount toned down West's transgressive sexuality in *Klondike Annie* in response to PCA suggestions during a period of widespread criticism of industry oligopoly. It clarifies that West did not inaugurate censorship controversies of the early 1930s but appeared amidst them.

Czitrom, Daniel. "The Redemption of Leisure: The National Board of Censorship and the Rise of Motion Pictures in New York City, 1900–1920." *Studies in Visual Communication* 10, no. 4 (1984): 2–6.

A concise discussion of the relationship between Progressives' goals for making leisure morally worthwhile and the economic imperatives of the growing film industry.

———. "The Politics of Performance: Theater Licensing and the Origins of Movie Censorship in New York." *American Quarterly* 44, no. 4 (1992): 525–53. Reprinted in Couvares, *Movie Censorship and American Culture,* 16–42.

An examination of theater licensing practices in New York at the turn of the century as a means of social control of the patronage of vaudeville, the legitimate stage, and the movies. This essay stresses the links between these performance venues and city politics, particularly in relation to the infamous closing of all New York city nickelodeons in December 1908 and the formation of the NBC/R.

deCordova, Richard. "Ethnography and Exhibition: The Child Audience, The Hays Office and Saturday Matinees." *Camera Obscura* 23 (1990): 91–108.

An intriguing examination of the movement to generate child matinees during the teens and mid-1920s as an effort by the MPPDA and supportive groups to regulate movies and their impact on vulnerable young viewers.

———. "Child-Rearing Advice and the Moral Regulation of Children's Movie-Going." *Quarterly Review of Film and Video* 15, no. 4 (1995): 99–109.

A tentative but suggestive discussion of the discourses of parenting in the 1920s and 1930s in relation to reformers' efforts to influence children's movie-watching, as part of the Film Education Movement and the Young Reviewers Clubs, which encouraged children to develop critical views of the movies as a form of self-discipline.

DeGrazia, Edward, and Roger K. Newman. *Banned Films.* New York: R. R. Bowker, 1982.

An invaluable resource that provides a detailed overview of movie censorship and individualized accounts of 122 major court cases, from 1908 to 1981. DeGrazia is a celebrated defender of First Ammendment rights who represented the film industry in several cases.

Farber, Stephen. *The Movie Ratings Game.* Washington, D.C.: Public Affairs Press, 1972.

Farber provides an insider account of the workings of the ratings system in its early years. His work is valuable as a description of the evaluation process and as a public condemnation of the hypocrisy he found where the board severely rated depictions of sexuality while ignoring screen violence.

Feldman, Charles Matthew. *The National Board of Censorship (Review) of Motion Pictures, 1909–1922*. New York: Arno, 1977.

This dissertation remains the only book-length study of this important agency of film regulation and self-regulation. A major resource for scholars interested in the NBC/R.

Fisher, Robert. "Film Censorship and Progressive Reform: The National Board of Censorship of Motion Pictures, 1909–1922." *Journal of Popular Film* 4 (1975): 143–56.

A concise overview of the troubled career of the NBC/R.

Gardner, Gerald. *The Censorship Papers: Movie Censorship Letters from the Hays Office, 1934–1968*. New York: Dodd, Mead, 1987.

A selection of correspondence from the MPPDA case files.

Goldstein, Cynthia. "Early Film Censorship: Margaret Sanger, *Birth Control* and the Law." In Bruce Austin, ed. *Current Research in Film: Audience, Economics, and Law*. Vol. 4. New York: Ablex, 1988, 188–200.

An interesting account of court cases involved in banning birth control films in the mid-teens. The essay is notable for situating birth control films in relation to obscenity laws and for recounting the Progressive views of one judge about movies' First Ammendment protection during the era of the *Mutual* decision.

Hamilton, Marybeth. "Goodness Had Nothing to Do With It: Censoring Mae West." In Couvares, *Movie Censorship and American Culture*, 187–211.

An intelligent and engaging analysis of Mae West's 1930s films that argues that all of them were produced with major input from the MPPDA, that West presented a particular challenge because of her "urban realism," and that MPPDA attempts to restrain her controversial scripts wound up re-creating that realism through comic devices.

Haralovich, Mary Beth. "The Mandates of Good Taste: The Self-Regulation of Film Advertising in the Thirties." *Wide Angle* 6 (1984): 50–57.

An account of the operations of the Advertising Advisory Council of the MPPDA during the 1930s, with particular attention to the drafting of the 1933 Advertising Code and its erosion by "candid camera" photography in photojournalism by World War II.

———. "Film Advertising, the Film Industry, and the Pin-up: The Industry's Accommodations to Social Forces in the 1940s." In Bruce Austin, ed. *Current Research in Film: Audience, Economics, and Law*. Vol. 1. Norwood, N.J.: Ablex, 1985, 127–64.

An informative, thoughtful discussion of how film advertising shifted from demure women of the late 1930s to the pin-ups of the war years and after, stressing industry self-regulation, candid camera photography, and Howard Hughes's *The Outlaw*. It includes a careful consideration of research methodologies.

————. "The Proletarian Woman's Film of the 1930s: Contending with Censorship and Entertainment." *Screen*, 31, no. 2 (1990): 172–87.

An insightful study of a subgenre of the woman's film, which places greater emphasis on the economic constraints affecting "woman's daily existence." The essay argues that "censorship works in concert with other conditions of Hollywood film production, notably the star system and merchandising, to displace concerns about any morally difficult meanings circulating through the film" (187).

Jacobs, Lea. "The Censorship of *Blonde Venus:* Textual Analysis and Historical Method." *Cinema Journal* 27, no. 3 (1988): 21–31.

Examines the production history of a major studio film with particular attention to debates within the MPPDA's SRC about the representation of female sexuality, exploring "the *mechanisms* by which social conflicts impinged on a given text" through negotiations and disputes among studio, director, and censors.

————. "Reformers and Spectators: The Film Education Movement in the Thirties." *Camera Obscura*, no. 22 (1990): 29–50.

An examination of the "theoretical account of film viewing" adopted by educators (as well as that of the Payne Fund Studies) in the 'film education movement' as they argued for modifying the conditions in which children viewed films during the decade.

————. *The Wages of Sin.* Berkeley: University of California Press, 1995 (University of Wisconsin Press, 1991).

A seminal study of the workings of the MPPDA from the 1920s through the 1930s, with particular focus on the Studio Relations Committee and the Production Code Administration's work on the genre of the "fallen woman" film in the areas of script development, star performance, and set design. A major rethinking of Hollywood's self-regulation of movies.

————. "*An American Tragedy:* A Comparison of Film and Literary Censorship." *Quarterly Review of Film and Video* 15, no. 4 (1995): 87–98.

A revealing examination of the MPPDA's negotiations with Paramount over the adaptation of the famous Theodore Dreiser novel, comparing book censorship and much more strict film self-regulation of the late 1920s and early 1930s. It also considers the MPPDA's general approach to naturalism as a literary movement.

Jacobs, Lea, and Richard Maltby, eds. "Rethinking the Production Code." *Quarterly Review of Film and Video* 15, no. 4 (1995).

This special issue of *Quarterly Review of Film and Video* includes significant essays by Jacobs, Maltby, Ruth Vasey (reprinted in this volume), and Richard deCordova, as well as an important "Documents" section that reproduces heretofore neglected, various drafts and versions of the Production Code itself, as it underwent various negotiations within the industry and with interested groups.

Jowett, Garth S. *Film: The Democratic Art.* Boston: Little, Brown, 1976.

A landmark social history of American movies with particular attention to audience responses to films and the film industry through the mid-1970s. Several sections focus directly on censorship and self-regulation, and the entire volume is an invaluable resource.

———. "Moral Responsibility and Commercial Entertainment: Social Control in the United States Film Industry 1907–1968." *Historical Journal of Film, Radio and Television* 10 (1990): 3–31.

A concise, synoptic history of attempts to regulate or censor movies from the 1907 Chicago censorship ordinance to the ratings system through the 1980s.

———. "'A Significant Medium for the Communication of Ideas': The *Miracle* Decision and the Decline of Motion Picture Censorship, 1952–1968." In Couvares, *Movie Censorship and American Culture*, 258–76.

A close and illuminating analysis of the *Miracle* case which granted First Amendment free speech to the movies, of the controversy surrounding *The Miracle*, and of the ruling's impact on movie censorship and self-regulation through the advent of the ratings system.

———, Ian Jarvie, and Kathryn Fuller. *Children and the Movies: Media Influence and the Payne Fund Controversy.* Boston: Cambridge University Press, 1996.

A thorough, scholarly examination of the well-known Payne Fund Studies of the late 1920s and early 1930s, which galvanized protests against movie content. This volume examines the history of the studies and includes unpublished portions.

Kanfer, Stefan. *A Journal of the Plague Years.* New York: Atheneum, 1973.

A highly readable account of blacklisting in the entertainment industries.

Koppes, Clayton R., and Gregory D. Black. "What to Show the World: The Office of War Information and Hollywood, 1942–1945." *Journal of American History* 64 (1977): 87–105. Reprinted in Janet Staiger, ed. *The Studio System.* New Brunswick: Rutgers University Press, 1995, 279–97.

A concise overview of the Office of War Information's development, rationale, and gradual involvement in Hollywood production during World War II, with brief reference to specific films affected.

———. *Hollywood Goes to War: How Politics, Profits, and Propaganda Shaped World War II Movies.* Berkeley: University of California Press, 1990 (The Free Press, 1987).

Drawing on studio, Hollywood, and government archives as well as periodicals, this is a definitive chronicle of the work of the Office of War Information's motion picture division during World War II. The OWI had as much impact on Hollywood movies during the period as the PCA; its activities were "the most comprehensive and sustained government attempt to change the content of a mass medium in American history."

Kuhn, Annette. *Cinema, Censorship and Sexuality.* New York: Routledge, 1988.

Although this volume focuses primarily on case studies in British censorship from 1909 to 1925, it recasts censorship in Michel Foucault's terms, focusing on the meanings within both films and the discourses surrounding them, rethinking censorship as part of an apparatus for the play of power, and conceiving of censorship as not only prohibitive, but productive of a film's meaning. A seminal work.

Leff, Leonard J., and Jerrald Simmons. *The Dame in the Kimono: Hollywood, Censorship, and the Production Code from the 1920s to the 1960s*. New York: Grove Weidenfeld, 1990.

An extremely entertaining and informative account of the workings of the MPPDA's SRC and PCA, singling out films from *Dead End* to *Who's Afraid of Virginia Woolf*, which represented a major challenge to those agencies.

Lyons, Charles. "The Paradox of Protest: American Film, 1980–1992." In Couvares, *Movie Censorship and American Culture*, pp. 277–318.

An efficient summary of Lyons's *The New Censors*, surveying various protests of Hollywood films of the 1980s, and noting the necessity of coexisting rights to protest with their potential to censor.

———. *The New Censors: Movies and the Culture Wars*. New York: Columbia University Press, 1997.

An informative and well-conceived look mostly at protest groups in the 1980s and how they have affected American film culture and sometimes Hollywood companies. Specific films include *Dressed to Kill*, *The Year of the Dragon*, *Basic Instinct*, and *The Last Temptation of Christ*.

Maltby, Richard. "'Baby Face,' or How Joe Breen Made Barbara Stanwyck Atone for Causing the Wall Street Crash." *Screen* 27, no. 2 (1986): 22–45. Reprinted in Janet Staiger, ed. *The Studio System*. New Brunswick: Rutgers University Press, 1995, 251–78.

A case study of how the representation of the 1920s in an early 1930s Warner Bros. "fallen woman" film was shaped by the PCA. Worthwhile in particular for outlining the cultural milieu of the 1920s and how post–Depression culture viewed it.

———. "The Genesis of the Production Code." *Quarterly Review of Film and Video* 15, no. 4 (1995): 5–32.

A detailed examination of the historical context surrounding the writing of the Production Code in 1930 and the process by which it was drafted. The essay stresses the economic rationale for Hollywood self-regulation (distracting the government from anti-trust action by controlling movie content), and argues that the drafting and acceptance of the Code in late 1929 was precipitated by various social, institutional, and business factors rather than by protest against movie content.

———. "'To Prevent the Prevalent Type of Book': Censorship and Adaptation in Hollywood, 1924–1934." *American Quarterly* 44, no. 4 (1992): 554–83. Reprinted in Couvares, *Movie Censorship and American Culture*, 97–128.

Centering on Paramount's commercially and critically unsuccessful adaptation of Theodore Dreiser's *An American Tragedy*, this essay argues that Hollywood's often sanitized adaptations of modernist, popular, or artistic novels and plays of the 1920s were an essential part of its defensive, public responses to reformers and critics of the industry, even as those plays and novels participated in the 1920s culture of consumption that embraced artistic novelty.

———. "'Grief in the Limelight': Al Capone, Howard Hughes, the Hays Code and the Politics of the Unstable Text." In James Combs, ed. *Movies and Politics: The Dynamic Relationship.* New York: Garland, 1993, 133–82.

An informative account of the immediate historical context surrounding the "classic" cycle of gangster films in the early 1930s, which coincided with the demise of major "public enemies" like Al Capone. The essay discusses the negotiations between the MPPDA and the makers of *Scarface* within this context.

McCarthy, Kathleen D. "Nickel Vice and Virtue: Movie Censorship in Chicago, 1907–1915." *Journal of Popular Film* 5, no. 1 (1976): 37–55.

A consideration of the politics and discussions of moviegoing in Chicago that led to the city's censorship practices.

McGilligan, Patrick, and Paul Buhle. *Tender Comrades: A Backstory of the Hollywood Blacklist.* New York: St. Martin's, 1997.

A volume of revealing and fascinating interviews with thirty-six artists who endured the Hollywood blacklist, ranging from star directors, screenwriters, and actors to less well-known talents. A remarkable and invaluable resource.

Miller, Frank. *Censored Hollywood: Sex, Sin and Violence on Screen.* Atlanta: Turner, 1994.

An entertaining and well-written (if not always accurate) popular history of movie censorship and industry self-regulation, which also discusses exploitation films, and devotes two chapters to more recent ratings controversies of the 1980s and 1990s.

Murdock, Pat. "The Lone 'Lady Censor': Christine Smith Gillian and the Demise of Film Censorship in Atlanta." *Atlanta History* 43, no. 2 (1999).

An insightful discussion of the end of city censorship in Atlanta, Georgia, with particular reference to controversies surrounding *Room at the Top* and *Never on Sunday* in the early 1960s.

Musser, Charles. "Passions and the Passion Play: Theater, Film and Religion in America, 1880–1900." *Film History* 5 (1993): 419–56. Reprinted in Couvares, *Movie Censorship and American Culture,* 43–72.

Discusses a peculiar wrinkle in the regulation of visual representations whereby slides and cinematic, narrated versions of the Passion Play were less controversial to diverse religious groups in New York City than theatrical versions. The author relates this brief episode of tolerance of the movies to Walter Benjamin's notions of photography's destruction of the aura of traditional art.

Naremore, James. "From Dark Films to Black Lists." In *More Than Night: Film Noir in Its Contexts.* Berkeley: University of California Press, 1998.

This illuminating chapter considers, among other things, the Production Code Administration's general handling of film noir (where corrupt police and politicians, sexual perversity, and less than ideal heroes abound), with extended accounts of the shaping of *The Blue Dahlia* and *Crossfire* and the intimate connections among 1930s liberalism, postwar noir films, and paranoid films like *The Manchurian Candidate*. Bristling with insights and brilliant observations.

Navasky, Victor. *Naming Names.* New York: Viking, 1980.

A landmark study of blacklisting in the entertainment industry, based primarily on interviews with participants in the two rounds of House Committee on Un-American Activities (HUAC) investigations.

Parker, Alison M. "Mothering the Movies: Women Reformers and Popular Culture." In Couvares, *Movie Censorship and American Culture,* 73–96.

A straightforward and enlightening survey of the neglected but important subject of women's reform groups, particularly the Women's Christian Temperance Union, and their activities to regulate films through the 1930s, their stands on subject matter, their skepticism of the Hays Office, and their insistent lobbying for national censorship until 1934, all in the name of protecting impressionable, neglected youths.

Patton, Cindy. "White Racism/Black Signs: Censorship and Images of Race Relations." *Journal of Communication Studies* 45, no. 2 (Spring 1995): 67–77.

A thought-provoking discussion of the censorship case surrounding the banning of *Pinky* in 1949 and the representation of race relations at that time.

Randall, Richard. *The Censorship of the Movies.* Madison: University of Wisconsin Press, 1968.

An indispensable and detailed discussion of the overall legal context, bureaucracy, and procedures of state and city prior restraint censorship and informal censorship mechanisms in the 1960s. It includes a valuable history of censorship and self-regulation.

———. "Censorship: From *The Miracle* to *Deep Throat.* In Tino Balio, ed. *The American Film Industry.* 2nd ed. Madison: University of Wisconsin Press, 1985, 510–36.

An excellent summary of pre-*Miracle* local censorship, the impact of that Supreme Court case, the development of obscenity criteria in the Court, and the workings and controversies of the ratings system.

Regester, Charlene. "Black Films, White Censors: Oscar Micheaux Confronts Censorship in New York, Virginia and Chicago." In Couvares, *Movie Censorship and American Culture,* 159–86.

A unique survey of how state censors in New York, Virginia, and Chicago responded to some of the controversial films of the most prominent race filmmaker of the 1920s.

Rosenbloom, Nancy J. "Between Reform and Regulation: The Struggle over Film Censorship in Progressive America, 1909–1922." *Film History* 1 (1987): 307–25.

A thorough, superlative overview of the NBC/R's formation, operations, and demise, stressing its changing fortunes and relations with a film industry itself undergoing major shifts, with political leaders, and with the censorship battles of the teens.

———. "In Defense of Moving Pictures: The People's Institute, the National Board of Censorship and the Problems of Leisure in Urban America." *American Studies* 33, no. 2 (1992): 41–61.

An intelligent, close look at the rationales behind the People's Institute's support of motion pictures as leisure activity during the first two decades of the twentieth century, as well as the relationship of the NBC/R to American Progressivism and the Board's efforts to fight censorship.

Schaefer, Eric. "Of Hygiene and Hollywood: Origins of the Exploitation Film." *The Velvet Light Trap*, no. 30 (1992): 34–47.

A fascinating discussion of how the suppression of formerly supported venereal disease films after World War I gave rise to the enduring exploitation film.

Schumach, Murray. *The Face on the Cutting Room Floor: The Story of Movie and Television Censorship.* New York: De Capo, 1975.

Although not scholarly and lacking documentation, this journalistic chronicle of movie censorship (political censorship, self-regulation, pressure groups, the black-list, ratings) is informative and suggestive.

Simmons, Jerrald. "The Production Code Under New Management: Geoffrey Shur-lock, *The Bad Seed* and *Tea and Sympathy.*" *Journal of Popular Film and Television* 22, no. 1 (1994): 2–11.

An informative look at two film projects and the challenges they represented to Joseph Breen's more liberal and literate successor. The approval of these projects persuaded film producers that they could plan to produce controversial material under Shurlock's regime.

Sklar, Robert. *Movie-Made America: A Cultural History of American Movies.* New York: Vintage, 1975 (rev. 1994).

A seminal and highly influential social history of the American film, stressing the function of movies as an arena for struggles over social power and prestige.

Smith, Greg M. "Blocking *Blockade:* Partisan Protest, Popular Debate, and En-capsulated Texts." *Cinema Journal* 36, no. 1 (1996): 18–38.

A thoughtful case study of the promotion, advertising, reviews, and protest and general reception of an extremely controversial message movie of the 1930s, emphasizing the importance of these contexts and arguing that films are "en-capsulated" (in capsule form) to make them more manageable in popular dis-courses.

Staiger, Janet. *Bad Women: Regulating Sexuality in Early American Cinema.* Min-neapolis: University of Minnesota Press, 1995.

A well-researched, carefully argued study of historical conditions and discursive formations as they relate to the representation of women and sexuality in films between 1907 and 1915. Chapter 4 examines specifically the political background to the December 1908 closing of nickelodeons in New York City and the forma-tion and operation of the NBC/R.

Streible, Dan. "A History of the Boxing Film, 1894–1915: Social Control and Social Reform in the Progressive Era." *Film History* 3, no. 3 (1989): 235–57.

A fascinating account of the controversial history of early prize fight films, which were subject to constant criticism and were eventually suppressed by Progressive era reformers and politicians, who were motivated by a mix of humane and (in the case of Jack Johnson films) racist concerns. In exploring this topic, the author finds many contradictions within the reform movement itself.

Vasey, Ruth. "Foreign Parts: Hollywood's Global Distribution and the Representation of Ethnicity." *American Quarterly* 44, no. 4 (1992): 617–42. Reprinted in Couvares, *Movie Censorship and American Culture*, 212–36.

Provides a valuable economic basis for discussion of Hollywood's representation of ethnicity. It discusses the primary role foreign distribution of American films, and the sensibilities and policies of foreign markets, played in Hollywood's representation of foreign and exotic nationalities (including colonials).

———. *The World According to Hollywood, 1918–1939.* Madison: University of Wisconsin Press, 1997.

A highly intelligent, thoroughly researched, and thought-provoking account of the MPPDA's operations, with particular focus on Hollywood's worldwide distribution networks and the impact of box office concerns, particularly of foreign nations, on PCA activities and policies.

Vaughn, Stephen. "Financiers, Movie Producers and the Church: Economic Origins of the Production Code." *Current Research in Film*. Vol. 4. New York: Ablex, 1988, 201–18.

Reviewing the history of investment business's involvement in the studios' conversion to sound and early Depression finances, this essay argues that investment bankers (particularly Stuart Halsey) were heavily involved in Hollywood's embrace of the Production Code.

———. "Political Censorship During the Cold War: The Hollywood Ten." In Couvares, *Movie Censorship and American Culture*, 237–57.

A concise survey of the 1947 HUAC hearings into "Hollywood Communism," which profiles the ten defendants blacklisted and jailed for contempt of Congress.

Vizzard, Jack. *See No Evil: Life Inside a Hollywood Censor.* New York: Pocket Books, 1971.

A lively, informative, and insightful account of work in the Production Code Administration, from the 1940s to the start of the ratings system, that draws on the fate of specific films to illustrate how the PCA thought about its work.

Waldman, Diane. "The Justice Department versus the National Film Board of Canada: An Update and Analysis." In Bruce Austin, ed. *Current Research in Film*. Vol. 4. New York: Ablex, 1988, 170–87.

A close look at the 1983 Justice Department's labeling of three Canadian documentaries (*If You Love This Planet* and two exposés about acid rain) as political propaganda under an obscure federal rule and the films' producers and distributors' attempt to challenge it.

Waller, Gregory. *Main Street Amusements: Movies and Commercial Entertainment in a Southern City, 1896–1930*. Washington, D.C.: Smithsonian Institution Press, 1995.

A thoroughly researched and fascinating study of movie and entertainment culture in Lexington, Kentucky, which includes accounts of local and national censorship movements.

Walsh, Frank R. "*The Callahans and the Murphys* (MGM, 1927): A Case Study of Irish-American and Catholic Church Censorship." *Journal of Film, Radio and Television* 10, no. 1 (1990): 33–45.

A straightforward and informative look at an otherwise overlooked episode of successful religious and ethnic efforts to have a (lost) vulgar comedy recut and ultimately withdrawn from distribution, which the author casts as a preview of the Legion of Decency's 1934 boycott campaign.

———. *Sin and Censorship*. New Haven: Yale University Press, 1996.

An intelligent, well-researched, and highly readable history of Catholic efforts to influence Hollywood filmmaking from the 1920s and the Legion of Decency through the demise of the National Catholic Office for Motion Pictures and *The Last Temptation of Christ*.

# Contributors

MATTHEW BERNSTEIN is the author of *Walter Wanger, Hollywood Independent* and editor (with Gaylyn Studlar) of *Visions of the East: Orientalism in Film*. His essays and reviews have appeared in *Film History, Film Quarterly, Griffithiana,* and *The Velvet Light Trap*. He teaches Film Studies at Emory University in Atlanta, Georgia.

GREGORY D. BLACK is Professor of Communication Studies and Director of American Studies at the University of Missouri–Kansas City. He is the author of *Hollywood Censored* and *The Catholic Crusade Against the Movies* and co-author, with Clayton R. Koppes, of *Hollywood Goes to War*.

ELLEN DRAPER is currently working on "The Virtual Screening Room," an interactive Film Studies project at MIT. She has taught Film Studies and writing at many colleges in the Boston area, most recently at Simmons. Her articles on film have appeared in many journals and in *Feminist Literary Theory: A Dictionary; Godard's "Je Vous Salue, Marie";* and *Inventing Vietnam*.

LEA JACOBS is the author of *The Wages of Sin: Censorship and the Fallen Woman Film,* and co-author, with Ben Brewster, of *Theater to Cinema: Stage Pictorialism and the Early Feature*. She teaches film at the University of Wisconsin–Madison.

GARTH S. JOWETT is a professor at the School of Communication, University of Houston. His previous books include *Film: The Democratic Art; Movies as Mass Communication* (with James L. Linton); *Propaganda and Persuasion* (with Victoria O'Donnell); and *Children and the Movies: Media Influence and the Payne Fund Controversy* (with Ian Jarvie and Kathryn Fuller). He is currently completing a book on "Hollywood in the Fifties" as well as beginning the first draft of "A Social History of American Television."

CLAYTON R. KOPPES is Dean of the College of Arts and Sciences at Oberlin College, Oberlin, Ohio. An historian of the twentieth-century United States, he is the author (with Gregory Black) of *Hollywood Goes to War: How Politics, Profits, and Propaganda Shaped World War II Movies*. He is writing a history of movie censorship since the days of the nickelodeon.

RICHARD MALTBY is Head of Screen Studies at the Flinders University of South Australia. Among his publications are *Harmless Entertainment: Hollywood and the Ideology of Consensus; The Passing Parade: Popular Culture in the 20th Century;* and *Hollywood Cinema: An Introduction,* as well as numerous essays on the history of the American cinema. He is currently completing *Reforming the Movies: Politics, Censorship, and the Institutions of the American Cinema, 1908–1939*.

*Contributors*

JEFF SMITH holds a Ph.D. in film studies from the University of Wisconsin–Madison. He teaches Film Studies in the Performing Arts Department at Washington University. He is the author of *The Sounds of Commerce: Marketing Popular Film Music* from Columbia University Press.

SHELLEY STAMP is author of *Movie-Struck Girls: Women and Motion Picture Culture After the Nickelodeon.* She is Assistant Professor of Film and Video at the University of California–Santa Cruz, where she recently won the Excellence in Teaching Award.

RUTH VASEY is Lecturer in Screen Studies at the Flinders University of South Australia. Her book, *The World According to Hollywood, 1918–1939,* won the Kraszna-Krausz Moving Image Book Award in 1998.

JUSTIN WYATT is an Associate Professor of Media Arts at the University of Arizona, and author of *High Concept: Movies and Marketing in Hollywood* and *Poison.* His major areas of research interest include media economics and film marketing, with a particular emphasis on contemporary industries. Wyatt is the series editor for Commerce and Mass Culture at the University of Minnesota Press.

# Index

*Note*: Page numbers in italics refer to Figures.

Abbey, Edward, 219
*Abduction*, 252.
Academy Awards, and the blacklist, 206, 214–15, 217, 220–24
Academy of Motion Picture Arts and Sciences, 163
African Americans, 130–52. *See* Office of War Information, propaganda campaign of; racism
Agee, James, 144, 149
*Alberts v. California* (1957), 187, 203n
Aldrich, Maude M., 40n
Aldrich, Robert, 243
Alexander, Will, 153n
*Alfie* (1966), 241
*Alice's Restaurant* (1969), 239
Alkow, J. M., 80
Allied Artists, 214
Almand, Judge, 172–73
Alpert, Hollis, 198
*America* (1924), 76
American Association for the Advancement of Atheism, 125n
American Association of Social Workers, 106
American Book Publishers Council, 193
American Civil Liberties Union (ACLU), 174, 193
American Federation of Labor, 36, 103
American International, 244
American Legion, 196, 208, 224–25, 228–29
*Anatomy of a Murder* (1959), 226
*And God Created Woman* (1957), 245
Anderson, Eddie (Rochester), *143*, 144
Anderson, Lindsay, 243
Andrews, George Reid, 60, 74, 77, 78, 79, 82, 83

Anti-Defamation League, 81
anti-Semitism, 39n
Arbuckle, Fatty, 162
*Are We Movie-Made?* (1938), 188
Armstrong, Louie, 144
Arnold, Henry H. "Hap," 151
*Around the World in 80 Days* (1956), 215
*Arrowsmith* (1931), 138
Asher, Jeff, 224
Associated Advertising Clubs of the World, 103
Association of Exhibitors (New York), 24
Atlanta: and the "Atlanta Spirit," 167; city censor, 182n; and *Scarlet Street*, 10, 159, *157*, *159*, 160, 165–70, 172–73, *173*, 181n
*Atlanta Constitution*, 167–68, 168–69, *171*
*Atlanta Journal*, 167, 168
*Atlanta Monthly, The*, 195
Atlantic Charter, 133
*Atlantic Flight*, 126n
*Auction in Souls* (1933), 126n
Authors' League, 193

Babson, Roger W., 67
*Baby Doll* (1956), 187, 201–2, *201*, 251
*Baby Face* (1933), 8, 96
*Back in Circulation*, 126n
*Bad Man, The* (1937), 120–21
Baker, Caroll, *201*
Balderston, John L., 139, 155n
Balio, Tino, 239
Banker, Fred, 228
*Banned Films* (1982), 3, 157
Barnes, George A., 135, 145
Barranca, 121

Barrymore, Lionel, *140*, 142
Barton, Bruce, 63–64, 68, 69–70, 71–74
*Basic Instinct* (1991), 13
Bass, Saul, 217
*Bataan* (1943), 9, 147–48, *147*
Beatty, Jerome, 114
*Beau Geste* (1926), 116–17
*Beau Sabreur* (1928), 117
Beaver, Louise, 138
Begelman, David, 257
*Behind the Headlines*, 126n
Bell, Ulrich, 145
*Bells of St. Mary, The* (1946), 162
*Ben Hur* (1926), 62, 78
Benedit, Ruth, 152n
Bennett, Joan, 157, *158*, *166*, 167, 168
Berlin, Irving, 148, 156n
Bertolucci, Bernardo, 255
*Between Friends* (1924), 103
*Bicycle Thief, The* (1946), 198
Bills to Establish a Federal Motion Pic-
    ture Commission (1914, 1916), 31–35
Bilson, George, 218
Binford, Lloyd T., 189, 196, 202–3n
Birchard, Robert S., 60, 79, 83n
*Birds in Peru* (1968), 243
*Birth of a Nation, The* (1915), 5, 196
Black, Gregory D., 9
*Black Fury* (1934), 3, 105, 141
"Black List = Black Market," 217
black market, 11, 208–14
*Black Reconstruction in America*
    (1935), 140
blacklist, 11, 206–14; "drama"
    metaphor and, 206–7, 231–32; end
    of, 227–31; and fronts, 209–11, 233n;
    and pseudonyms, 211–12
Blake, Morgan, 169
block booking, 259
*Block v. Chicago* (1909), 22–23, 25
*Blockade* (1938), 2, 163
Bloodworth, J. M. B., 170
*Blow Up* (1966), 240
Blun, John Morton, 154n
B'Nai B'Rith, 80, 81
Bode, Dick, 152n
Bogart, Humphrey, 146, *146*
Bogdanovich, Peter, 253
Bolt, Robert, 230

*Bombadier* (1943), 151
Bond, James, 253
Bordwell, David, 99–100n
Bouhoutsos, Jacqueline, 243
Boulle, Pierre, 221
Bow, Clara, *89*
*Boxoffice*, 162, 247, 249–50
Boy Scouts, 103
Boyd, Malcolm, 204n
Bradley, John D., 35
Bradshaw, Lester J., 182nn
Brady, Cyrus Townsend, 34
Brandt, Harry, 226
*Brave Cowboy, The*, 219, 228
*Brave One, The* (1956), 213, 215–17,
    222
Breen, Joseph I., 7, 8, 90, *93*, 94, 97, 98,
    100n, 108, 161–62, 176, 181n
Breen Office, 180n, 181n
*Bridge on the River Kwai, The* (1957),
    220–22
British Chamber of Shipping, 105–6
Broadway Temple, 68
Browne, Porter, 120
Bryan, Wright, 172
Bryna Productions, 218–20
Buck, Pearl S., 151, 153n
Budd, Michael, 42
Bureau of Social Hygiene, 46
Burger, Justice, 254
burlesque, 18
Burstyn, Joseph, 186–87, 192–93
"Business Bible Class," 67
*Business Man of Syria, The* (1923),
    70–71
Butler, Hugo, 211, 213
Byron, Stuart, 243

*Cabin in the Sky* (1943), 9, *143*,
    144–45
Cadman, S. Parkes, 79
*Call Her Savage* (1932), *89*, 96
*Call to Arms*, 105
*Callahans and the Murphys, The*
    (1927), 119
*Camille* (1937), 8, 98, *99*
Cantwell, John J., 188
Canty, George R., 128n
*Captain Marvel*, 164

Carmen, Ira, 3, 29, 157, 179n, 188–89

*Carnival Story* (1954), 209, 213

Cartwright, James H., 23

*Casablanca* (1943), 9, 145–47, *146*

*Case of the Hooded Man, The*, 254

Castle, William, 119

Catholic Church, 17, 37, 195–96. *See also* Legion of Decency

*Catholic Messenger*, 198, 204n

Catholic War Veterans, 208, 233n

Cayton, Horace, 130, 133

*Censored* (1930), 197

censorship, function of, 13

*Censorship of the Movies* (1976), 3, 157

"Century of the Common Man," 136

Ceplair, Larry, 206–7, 208, 211, 231

Chang, T. W., 151

Chaplin, Charlie, 114, 196, 208, 233n

Chase, William Sheafe, 23, 32, 34, 35, 36, 76

Chatterton, Ruth, 95

Chicago City Council movie censorship ordinance (1907), 21–22, 42

Chinese Theatre (Los Angeles), 79

*Chisum* (1970), 249

*Chitty Chitty Bang Bang* (1968), 240

*Christian Century*, 82

Church and Drama Association, 78, 82, 83

*Churchman, The*, 82

Chworowsky, Karl, 193

Cinema V, 250

Cinema 57 Rendezvous (New York), 246

Cinemation Industries, 244, 251–52

Cinerama, 244

Citizens League of Maryland for Better Motion Pictures, 36

Clark, Justice, 189–90

*Claws of the Hun, The* (1918), 113

Clift, Denison, 114

Clinton, Bill, 15n

Clurman, Harold, 143

Cochrane, Robert, 118

Cocks, Orrin G., 55–56, 56–57

Code and Ratings Appeals Board, 242

Coffin, Henry Sloane, 68

Cogley, John, 222–23

Cohen, Sammy, 116

Collier, John, 23–24, 29–31, 58n

Collins, C. L., 63

*Colonel Effingham's Raid* (1946), 167

Columbia Broadcasting System (CBS), 131

Columbia Pictures, 257

Columbia University: Department of Religion, 193; study of World War II films, 149–50

Columbine High School, 15n

*Coming Apart* (1969), 240

*Command to Love, The* (1930), 121

*Commercial Pictures v. Board of Regents* (1954), 203n

*Commercialized Prostitution in New York City* (1913), 46

Commission on Freedom of the Press, 188

Committee to Defend America by Aiding the Allies, 131

communism, 208

Conant, Michael, 203–4n

*Conformist, The* (1972), 256

Connelly, Marc, 144

Conroe, Irwin, 160, 162, 163–65, 174–75

Continental, 250

Cook, Bruce, 207, 232n, 233n

*Cornell Law Quarterly*, 189

Couvares, Francis G., 4, 14n, 14–15n, 44, 179n

*Covered Wagon, The* (1923), 76

Cowles, Gardner, Jr., 131, 136

Crafts, Wilbur F., 31–33, 76

Cranston, Alan, 152n

*Crash Dive* (1943), 147

Craven, Avery, 141

Crawford, Joan, 182–83n

Creel Committee, 131

Cripps, Thomas, 139

Criterion Theater, 165

Cronin, A. J., 151

Crowther, Bosley, 164, 195, 226

*Cruising* (1980), 261n

*Cry of the Unborn. See Story of an Illegitimate Baby*

cultural studies, 4, 158–59

*Curley*, 189, 198

*Daily Worker*, 139, 141

Dairymen's League Cooperative Association, 103

Damiano, Gerard, 253

Daughters of the American Revolution, 103, 208

Davis, Bette, 172

Davis, Elmer, 130–31, 136, 137

*Dawn* (1928), 119

*Day in the Country, A* (1936), 186. *See also Ways of Love*

*Dealing* (1972), 244

*Deep Throat* (1972), 238, 252–54, *252*

*Defiant Ones, The* (1958), 220

DeGrazia, Edward, 3, 157, 179n, 247

*Deliverance* (1972), 253

Dellahanty, T. S., 123

DeMille, Cecil B., 6–7, 61, 72, *72*, 73, 79, 80

De Palma, Brian, 242

Department of Moral Welfare of the Presbyterian Church of the United States of America, 36

*Devil in Miss Jones, The* (1973), 253

Diana Productions, 162, 163, 173

*Diary of a Chambermaid* (1946), 162

*Dictator, The* (1922), 123

*Dillinger* (1945), 161, 165, 180n

Disney, 13–14, 15n

*Doctor Maniac*, 164

*Don Juan* (1961), 200

Double V campaign, 133–34, 153n

Douglas, Kirk, 218, 220, 225, 227, 229

"Douglas, Nathan E.," 220

Douglas, William O., 174, 188–89

*Dracula* (1932), 121, 123

*Dragon Seed* (1942), 151

*Dressed to Kill* (1980), 13

Du Bois, W. E. B., 132, 140

Dunning, William, 141

Duryea, Dan, *166*

Dyer, Frank L., 32

*Easiest Way, The* (1931), 95

*East is West* (1930), 123

*Easy Rider* (1969), 239

educational theory, 19

Eighteenth Amendment, 21

Eisenhower, Milton S., 131

*Ellen*, 13

*Emmanuelle* (1974), 256–57, *256;* advertising for, *258*

Englund, Steven, 206–7, 208, 211, 231

Ernst, Morris, 197

*Eternal City, The* (1923), 113

Evergreen (New York), 246

*Exclusive* (1937), 126n

*Execution of Private Slovik, The* (1974), 226, 228, 231

*Exodus* (1960), 206, 225–26, 228, 229–30

*Exorcist, The* (1973), 261n

Fair Employment Practices Commission, 134, 135

Fairbank, John K., 152n

*Faithless* (1932), 96

fallen woman cycle, 94–98

Famous Players, 77

*Fanny Hill* (1968), 251

Farber, Manny, 144, 145

Farber, Stephen, 244

Fast, Howard, 219, 228, 229

Faulkner, William, 97

Federal Council of Churches of Christ in America (FCCCA), 76–79

Federal Trade Commission (FTC), 199

*Female* (1933), *95*, 96

*Female Animal* (1970), 249

Fidler, Jimmy, 170, 183n

*Fight, The*, 43, 58n

*Fight for Life, The*, 164

*Film Daily Yearbook* (1933), 88

film genre, 3, 94

*Film in the Battle of Ideas* (1953), 187

"Fincher, Beth," 217

*Finian's Rainbow* (1968), 239

Finn, Aubrey, 218

First Amendment protection, 2, 5, 10, 16, 21, 25, 28–29, 174, 188–89, 200. *See also Miracle* decision; *Mutual* decision

First National, 77

Fisher, James, 121, 123, 123–24, 126n

*Five Star Final* (1931), 107

Flick, Hugh, 198

Flinn, John C., 61, 81
Ford, John, 138, 162
*Ford Products and their Sales* (1923),
   71
*Foreign Correspondent* (1940), 162
*Foreign Legion, The* (1928), 117–18,
   117
Foreman, Carl, 221
Forman, Henry, 188
Fosdick, Harry Emerson, 66–67, 69, 70
*Four Horsemen of the Apocalypse,
   The* (1926 rerelease), 113–14
Four Square Gospel, 65
Fourteenth Amendment protection,
   190; due process clause, 22
*Fox, The* (1968), 243
Foy, Bryan, 108
Franco-American Film Agreement
   (1948), 199
Frankfurt, Steve, 257
Frazier, E. Franklin, 143–44
*Freedman v. Maryland* (1965), 240–41
*Freedom of the Movies* (1947), 188
Freeman, Y. Frank, 160
*French Connection, The* (1971), 244
Frenke, Eugene, 235n
Friedkin, William, 261n
*Friendly Persuasion* (1956), 214–18
*Fritz the Cat* (1972), 252
*From the Manger to the Cross* (1912),
   62
*Front Page, The* (1931), 107
*Furnace Troubles* (1929), 104

*Gabriel Over the White House* (1933),
   163
Gaiety Theatre (New York), 78
*Gallant Gringo, The* (1928), 119–20
*Game of Love* (1950), 203n
Gandhi, 133
Garbo, Greta, 99
Garver, Frank M., 141
Gary, Elbert H., 67
Gary, Romain, 243
Gaynor, Justice, 23
*Gelling v. Texas* (1952), 198
General Federation of Women's Clubs,
   103

Getlein, Frank, 198, 204n
*Ginsberg v. New York* (1968), 241
*Girl on a Motorcycle* (1968), 242
Gish, Dorothy, 143
*Gitlow v. New York* (1925), 29
*Give 'Em Hell, Harry* (1975), 155n
*God and the Groceryman* (1927), 71
*Godless Girl, The* (1929), 106, 125n
*God's Little Acre*, 251
Goebbels, Josef, 137
Goldwyn, Samuel, 107, 113, 137, 150
Gomery, Douglas, 87
*Gone With the Wind* (1939), 3, 167
*Good Earth, The* (1937), 152
*Goodbye, Columbus* (1969), 239, 250
"Government Information Manual for
   the Motion Picture Industry," 138
*Graduate, The* (1967), 239
Graham, Henry, 170, 172
*Grapes of Wrath, The* (1940), 142
Graumann, Sid, 79
*Grease* (1978), 257
*Grease Paint* (1928), 118
*Great Audience, The* (1950), 197–98
*Green Berets, The* (1968), 240
*Greetings* (1968), 242
Grieveson, Lee, 39–40n
Griffith, D. W., 5, 60, 76, 77, 81
Gross, Jerry, 251
Gross, Leonard, 246
Grove Press, 245–46, 247, 262n
*Gun Crazy* (1949), 209
Gunning, Tom, 42

*Hannegan v. Esquire* (1946), 29
*Harper's Magazine*, 194
Hartman, Edmund, 215
Hartsfield, William B., 160, 169, 170
Hastie, William H., 155n
Hays, Will H., 6, 35, 57, 74–76, 75, 77,
   83, 92, 100n, 113, 116, 119, 120; as
   "Czar," 85n
Hays Office, 35–36, 137, 138; "Open
   Door Policy," 35
*Hays Office, The* (1945), 7, 89–91, 188
Hearst, William Randolph, 107
*Heaven Knows Mr. Allison* (1957), 209
Hecht, Ben, 143

Hellinger, Mark, 184n

*Henry: Portrait of a Serial Killer* (1990), 176

*Henry and June* (1990), 12, 176

*Her Man* (1930), 121, *122*, 123, 123–24, 129n

Herron, Frederick ("Ted"), 8, 116, 117–18, 119, 121, 123

Herzog, Buck, 182n

*Hidden Persuaders, The*, 240

Higham, Charles, 61, 79

Hilton, Arthur, 163–65

*His Girl Friday* (1940), 108

Hiss, Alger, 209, 220

Hitchcock, Alfred, 105, 148, 162

*Hollywood, the Dream Factory* (1951), 187

*Hollywood Goes to War* (1990), 9

*Hollywood Reporter*, 162, 224, 229

Hollywood Jury, 89–90

Hollywood Ten, 207, 208, 233nn

*Holmby Productions v. Vaughn* (1955), 203n

Holmes, Oliver Wendell, Jr., 26

*Home of the Brave* (1949), 196

Hopper, Hedda, 161, 226

Hornblow, Arthur, Jr., 185n

Horne, Lena, 138, *143*, 144, 145, 155n

Horwits, Al, 168–69

Houghton, Arthur, 105–6

*House of Bondage, The* (1910), 43, 57

House Un-American Activities Committee (HUAC), 206, 208–9, 229

Houseman, John, 152n

Howe, Frederic C., 6, 42, 52, 55–56, 56–57, 58n

Hoyt, E. Palmer, 131

Hughes, Charles Evan, 26

Hughes, Dudley M., 31

Hughes, Howard, 173, 184n

*Human Sexual Response, The*, 240

*Hun Within, The* (1918), 113

Hunter, Ian McLellan, 211

*I, a Woman*, 240, 245

*I Am a Camera*, 204n

*I Am Curious (Yellow)* (1969), 238, 241, 245–47,*246*

*I Am a Fugitive from a Chain Gang* (1932), 111, 138

*I Drink Your Blood*, 252

*I Take This Woman* (1928), 119, 120

*Idiot's Delight* (1939), 141

*If* (1968), 243

*Imitation of Life* (1935), 105

*Indiana Jones and the Temple of Doom* (1984), 12

"industry policy," 8; domestic concerns, 8, 102–12; international concerns, 8, 113–24

*Inga*, 240

Inglis, Ruth, 188

*Inherit the Wind* (1960), 226, 228

*Inquisition in Hollywood, The* (1980), 206–7, 233n

*Inside of the White Slave Traffic, The* (1913), 6, 50–55

International Federation of Catholic Alumnae, 36

*Interstate v. Dallas* (1968), 241

*Intolerance* (1916), 81

*Is Any Girl Safe?* (1916), 57

Italian Film Exports (IFE), 199

"Jackson, Sam," 219, 224

Jacobs, Lea, 181nn

Jaeckin, Just, 256

*James Boys, The* (1909), 22

Jarbol, A. E., 249

Jarrico, Paul, 218

*Jaws* (1975), 257

Jennings, Robert, 230

*JFK* (1991), 13

*Jofroi* (1934), 186. *See also Ways of Love*

Johnson, Andrew, 9, 139, 141, 142

Johnson, J. David, 229

Johnson, Jack, 39n

Johnston, Eric, 162, 199

Jones, Dorothy, 141

Jordan, Robert, 153n

*Joseph Burstyn, Inc. v. Wilson, Commissioner of Education of New York* (1952). *See Miracle* decision

*Journal of the Plague Years*, 207

Jowett, Garth S., 3, 88, 92

Joy, Jason, 90, 100–101n, 103, 106–7, 107–8, 111, 116, 118, 119, 120, 123, 124

*Juliet of the Spirits* (1965), 251

juvenile delinquency, 161, 165, 166, 182nn

Kael, Pauline, 255–56

Kahane, B. B., 225

Kaplan, E. Ann, 175

Kaplan, Leon, 224

Kaufman, Philip, 12, 263n

Kazan, Elia, 11, 201

Kempton, Murray, 212

Kennedy, John F., 229, 237n

Kent, Arnold, *115*

*Keys of the Kingdom* (1941), 151

Kiesling, Barrett, 61

*Killing of Sister George, The* (1968), 243

*Kim*, 150

Kimo South Theatre (Overland Park, Kans.), 247

King, Frank, 211, 215–16

King Brothers, 209, 211, 213, 215–17, 222

*King of Kings, The* (1927), 6–7, 60–86, *61*

*Kingsley International Pictures v. Board of Regents* (1959), 190

*Kitty Foyle* (1940), 209

Knights of Columbus, 208

Kontingent, 113–14

Koppes, Clayton R., 9, 15n

Kramer, Stanley, 220, 226

Kubrick, Stanley, 227

*La Chienne* (1931), 180n

*La Dolce Vita* (1960), 245

*La Ronde* (1950), 198, 203n

*La Trompe d'Oeil*, 252

*Lady Chatterley's Lover* (1955), 190

Lang, Fritz, 162–63, 163, 165, 174, 176, 180n

"Lantern Bearers, The," 30

Lardner, Ring, Jr., 218

Lasky, Jesse, Jr., 215

*Last Days of Pompeii, The* (1935), 79

*Last Sunset, The* (1961), 220

*Last Tango in Paris* (1972), 12, 255–56; protesters and, *255*

*Last Temptation of Christ, The* (1988), 13

*Last Train from Gun Hill, The* (1959), 219–20

Lattimore, Owen, 152n

Lawrence, D. H., 243

*Lawrence of Arabia* (1962), 230

Lawson, John Howard, 187, 218

Leah, Daniel, 148

Lears, T. J. Jackson, 66, 67, 73, 84

Lee, Canada, 143, 148

Lee, Roland V., 127n

Legion of Decency, 1, 7, 37, 87–88, 90, 92–93, 101nn, 137, 141, 142, 160, 162, 193, 195, 226. *See also* National Catholic Office for Motion Pictures

Leites, Nathan, 188

Lenin, 137

LeRoy, Mervyn, 138

Lewis, Eddie, 219, 224, 227, 228, 235n

*Lifeboat* (1944), 148

*Limelight* (1952), 196

Lindemann, Mitch, 218

Lindsay, John V., 253

*Little Colonel, The* (1935), 138

*Little Girl Next Door, The* (1916), 57

*Live & Let Die* (1973), 253

local/political censorship, 1–2, 158

Locke, Alain, 132

*Lolita* (1997), 13

London, Samuel H., 46, 50, 51, 52, 53

*Lonesome Cowboys* (1968), 262

*Long Voyage Home, The* (1940), 162

Lord, Daniel, 60, 73, 74

Lord, Robert, 105

Lorentz, Pare, 197

*Lost Boundaries* (1949), 1, 189, 196, 198

*Love is Free* (1937), 126n

Lowry, Edward G., 128n

Lubitsch, Ernst, 180n

*Lure, The* (1915), 43, 57

Lynd, Helen Merrell, 67

Lynd, Robert S., 67

Lyne, Adrian, 13
Lyons, Alexander, 80
Lyons, Charles, 13

*M* (1931), 198, 203n
MacLeish, Archibald, 131
MacManus, John T., 164
*Madame Sans-Gene* (1924), 113
Magnani, Anna, *192*
*Maid of Salem* (1933), 138
Malden, Karl, *201*
Maltby, Richard, 4, 161
Maltz, Albert, 223, 225, 226, 228, 231,
  237n
*Man Nobody Knows, The* (1925), 63,
  66, 69–70
*Man with the Golden Arm, The*
  (1955), 204n, 226
Manfull, Helen, 207, 233n
*Manhattan* (1924), 103
Manheim, N. L., 117–18
March on Washington Movement, 134
Marguilies, Stan, 228
Marshall, Thurgood, 131
Martin, Olga, 196
Marx Brothers, 121
*M\*A\*S\*H* (1970), 249
Masters, William, 240
McCaffery, Edward, 186
McCarthy, Joseph, 214
McClafferty, Monsignor, 160
McClellan, George B., 23, 39n
McDaniel, Hattie, 138, 149, *150*
McGill, Ralph, 167–68, 172, 175
McGoldrick, Rita, 103
McGuire, William D., Jr., 43
McKenna, Justice, 26–28
McKenzie, Maurice, 105, 126n
McMahon, Charles A., 36, 103
McManus, John T., 142
McPherson, Aimee Semple, 64–65
McQueen, Butterfly, 138
McWilliams, Carey, 65
*Medium Cool* (1969), 244
Mellett, Lowell, 131, 139, 140–41, 143,
  150
*Merry Widow, The* (1932), 121
Merton, Robert, 135–36
MGM, 90, 120, 139, 140–41, 142

Middletown (Conn.), 67
*Midnight Cowboy* (1969), 12, 239, 244,
  255
Milam, Aubrey, 167, 170
Milestone, Lewis, 107
Millbank, Jeremiah, 79
*Miller v. California* (1973), 254
Milliken, Carl, 81, 82
*Mills of the Gods* (1934), 105
Milwaukee, and *Scarlet Street*, 10,
  159–60, 157, 165, 173, 181n,
  181–82n, 182n
Mini-Cinema (New York), 251
*Minneapolis Morning Tribune*, 225
*Miracle, The* (1950), 2, 174, 186, *192.*
  *See also Miracle* decision
*Miracle* decision (1952), 2, 10–11, 158,
  186–94, 200–202
Mistral, Gabriela, 188
Moley, Raymond, 7, 89–91, 188
*Mondo Cane* Nos. 1 and 2, 251
*Monsieur Verdoux* (1947), 233n
*Moon Is Blue, The* (1953), 203n, 204n,
  226
"moral coercion," 6, 23, 42
*Morocco* (1930), 111
Morris, Sam, 128n
Morro Castle, 123
Mostel, Zero, 143
Motion Picture Alliance for the Preser-
  vation of American Ideals, 161
Motion Picture Association of Amer-
  ica (MPAA); Code and Rating Ad-
  ministration (CARA), 11; ratings
  system, 2, 12, 238–63, 263n. *See
  also* Breen Office's Motion Picture
  Producers and Distributors of Amer-
  ica
Motion Picture Council, 162
Motion Picture Export Association
  (MPEA), 199
*Motion Picture Herald*, 139, 247,
  248–49
*Motion Picture News*, 50
Motion Picture Patents Company, 24
Motion Picture Producers and Distributors of America (MPPDA), 2, 4–5,
  6, 7, 8, 57; Better Films Committees,
  36, 63; Committee on Public Rela-

tions, 102–3, 124–25n; Committee on Religious Pictures, 76–77; and *The King of Kings*, 62–63, 74–83; Production Code Administration (PCA), 2, 57, 90–91, 97, 98, 104, 106, 124, 203–4n, 226, 238; Studio Relations Committee, 2, 89–91, 97, 103. *See also* "industry policy"; Motion Picture Association of America; Production Code; self-regulation, and textual determination
Motion Picture Research Bureau, 127n
*Motion Picture Story Magazine*, 32
*Motography*, 50
*Movie-Made America* (1975), 3–4
*Movies* (1950), 188
*Movies, The* (1976), 3–4
*Movies, Censorship and the Law* (1966), 3, 157
*Movies on Trial, The* (1936), 188
*Moving Picture World*, 30, 49–50
*Mr. Adam*, 217–18, 235n
*Mr. Smith Goes to Washington* (1939), 108
Murphy, George, 148
Muse, Clarence, 138
*Mutual* decision, 3, 5–6, 10, 16–40, 159, 174
Mutual Film Corporation, 25–26
*Mutual Film Corporation v. Industrial Commission of Ohio* (1915). *See Mutual* decision
"Mutual Weekly," 26

*Naming Names* (1980), 207
Nash, Philleo, 135, 136
Nash, Roderick, 65
*Nation, The*, 198
National Association for the Advancement of Colored People (NAACP), 196
National Association of Theater Owners (NATO), 250
National Billiard Association, 103
National Board of Censorship (NBC), 2, 6, 23–24, 30, 31, 41–59. *See also* National Board of Review
National Board of Review, 6, 24. *See also* National Board of Censorship

National Catholic Office for Motion Pictures, 241. *See also* Legion of Decency
National Catholic Welfare Council, 36, 76, 82, 103, 119
National Congress of Mother and Parent-Teachers Associations, 103
National Endowment for the Arts, 13
Navasky, Victor, 207
*Negroes and the War* (1936), 136
New Mature World Theatre (New York), 252–53
*New Republic, The*, 198
New York City Council motion picture theater law, 38n
New York State: censorship board, 182n; and *Scarlet Street*, 10, 159, 157, 162–65, 173
*New York Times*, 159, 176, 177, 185n, 221–22, 255
Newman, Alfred, 144
Newman, Roger K., 3, 157, 179n
Newton, Louis, 166–67, 169, 170
Nichols, Dudley, 175, 184–85n
nickelodeons, 18, 20
Nietszche, Friedrich Wilhelm, 84n
*Night Riders* (1909), 22
Nixon, Richard, 220
*Noah's Ark* (1928), 79
North, Edmund, 215
North Central Association of Theatre Owners, 247
*Nothing Sacred* (1937), 126n

O'Brien, Philip J., 198
O'Connor, John J., 160
*Odd Couple, The* (1968), 239
*Of Human Bondage* (1932), 172
Office of Facts and Figures, 132
Office of War Information (OWI), 9; agencies comprising, 152n; Bureau of Motion Pictures, 137; and portrayal of African Americans, 137–52; and portrayal of Asians, 150–51; propaganda campaign of, 130–56
*Oh, Calcutta*, 240
*Oil for the Lamps of China* (1935), 105
*Old Ironsides* (1926), 76
*Oliver Twist* (1948), 196

*Omen, The* (1976), 257

O'Neill, J. J., 125n

*Only Angels Have Wings* (1939), 121

*Open City* (1945), 184n

Opie, Thomas F., 68–69

Oscars, 1957, 214–18

*Our Country* (1885), 17

*Our Movie Made Children* (1933), 188

*Our Vines Have Tender Grapes* (1945), 209

*Outlaw, The* (1942, 1946), 1, 173, 180n, 184n

Owen, Chandler, 136

*Ox-Bow Incident, The* (1943), 9, 145, 147

Packard, Vance, 240

Pagnol, Marcel, 186

*Paper Moon* (1973), 253

Papini, Giovanni, 77

Paramount, 90, 138, 243

*Paramount* decision (1948), 174, 188–89, 199, 259

Paramount Theater, 173

Paris Theatre (New York), 186, 193, 198

Park-Miller Theater, 254

Parks, Larry, 207

Pathé, 79, 121

Patterson, Joseph Medill, 16

Payne Fund, The: Committee on Educational Research, 188; Studies, 127n

*People v. Doris* (1897), 21

People's Institute, 23, 41–42, 58n

*Performance* (1970), 249

Perlman, William J., 188

Phillips, Gerald, 256

*Pick Up* (1933), 96

*Pink Chemise, The* (1932), 123

*Pinky* (1949), 198, 203n

*Pittsburgh Courier*, 133

Pius XI, 137

*Planet of the Apes* (1969), 239

*Plastered in Paris* (1928), 116

Pontifical Film Commission, 191

pornography: adult drama, 250, 251, 259; hard-core, 250–51, 259; soft-core, 250, 251, 257–58, 259

*Portnoy's Complaint* (1972), 240, 250

Powdermaker, Hortense, 187

Powell, Adam Clayton, Jr., 132

Poynter, Nelson, 131, 138, 141, 142, 145

Preminger, Otto, 206, 225, 226, 228

*President Vanishes, The* (1934), 163

Presidential Commission on Obscenity and Pornography, 250

Presidio Theater (San Francisco), 248

Price, Vincent, 143

*Priest* (1994), 13

Princeton Theological Seminary, 193

Pringle, Henry, 152n

prior-restraint, 2, 5, 21, 24–25, 26, 27, 29

*Private Number* (1936), 98

*Prodigal, The* (1930), 197

Production Code (1930), 2, 5, 7, 8, 10, 37, 89, 94, 101n, 102, 104, 111–12, 123, 161–62, 194, 198, 201; and the "Don'ts and Be Carefuls," 104

Progressivism, 18–21

prohibition, 19–20, 21

Protestantism, 16–21, 37; typified in *King of Kings. See King of Kings, The*

*Prowler, The* (1951), 209

Pryor, Thomas, 221

*Putney Swope* (1969), 250

Quigley, Martin J., 181n, 193, 248–49

Rabbinical Assembly of America, 81

*Rabbit, Run* (1970), 250

racism, 8, 9. *See also* Office of War Information, propaganda campaign of

Radio City Music Hall, 193

Randall, James, 141

Randall, Richard, 3, 157, 179n, 190, 190–91, 200

Randolph, A. Philip, 133

*RD-DR Corp. and Film Classics v. Smith* (1949), 189, 198

Reade, Walter, 243

Reagan, Ronald, 148

*Real Glory, The* (1942), 150

*Red Desert* (1964), 251

Reed, Justice, 190

Reimers, David, 17

Reisner, Christian F., 68

Religious Motion Picture Foundation, 77

Renoir, Jean, 186

Rice, Elmer, 107, 174

"Rich, Robert," 206, 215–18, 234–35n; unveiling of, 220–24

*Right Boy for Peter, The*, 254

Riskin, Robert, 146, 152n

Riverside Church (New York), 66

Rizzoli, 251

RKO, 90

*Road to Yesterday, The* (1925), 71

Robeson, Paul, 138

Robinson, Bill, 138

Robinson, Edward G., 157, *158*, 188

Robinson, Fredrick, 52

Rockefeller, John D., Jr., 46–49, 66

Rockefeller, Nelson A., 152n

*Roman Holiday* (1953), 209, 211

*Room at the Top* (1959), 245

Roosevelt, Franklin D., 9, 130, 152n, 154n

Rossellini, Roberto, 174, 186

Rosten, Leo, 152n

Roth, Philip, 240, 250

*Roth v. United States* (1957), 187, 190

Ruszkowski, Andrew, 195–96

*Sahara* (1943), 147

*Saint Joan* (1957), 226

*Sanctuary*, 97

*Sandpiper, The* (1965), 231

*Saratoga Trunk* (1946), 162

*Saturday Night Fever* (1977), 257

*Savage Blonde* (1968), 245

*Scarface* (1932), 123

*Scarlet Street* (1945), 10, 157–85, *158*, *166*; advertisement for, *178*; Chris Cross in, 175; and rural/small-town audiences, 185n

Schaefer, Eric, 59n

Schenck, Joe, 114

Schlesinger, Arthur, Jr., 152n

Schumach, Murray, 206, 225

*Scoundrel Time* (1976), 207

Screen Writers Guild, 214, 215

*Screw* magazine, 252

Seabury, William Marston, 33

Seaton, George, 222

Seberg, Jean, 243

*See No Evil* (1971), 90

Seldes, Gilbert, 197–98

self-regulation, 2, 7–8, 13; stages, 92; and textual determination, 87–101. *See also* blacklist

Selznick, David O., 3, 105–6, 149

*Sexual Wilderness, The*, 240

*She Done Him Wrong* (1933), 159

Sheen, Martin, 226

Sherwood, Robert, 131

*Shoulder Arms* (1927 rerelease), 114

Shurlock, Geoffrey, 90, *93*, 100n

*Siege* (1998), 13

Siegfried, Andre, 17

Sigma III, 243

Silberberg, Mendel, 224–25

Sinatra, Frank, 226, 237n

*Since You Went Away* (1944), 149, *150*

Sindlinger and Co., 226

Sjoman, Vilgot, 245

Sklar, Robert, 3, 20–21, 92

*Sleuth* (1973), 253

Smith, Christina, 157, 160, 165–67, 169–70, 173, 174–75, 176, 183–84n, 196, 202–3n. *See also* Atlanta, and *Scarlet Street*

Smith, Harold, 220, 221, *221*

*So Proudly We Hail* (1943), 151

social gospel movement, 19

Society of Authors Representatives, 193

Sodality movement, 64

Sojourner Truth housing project, 135

*Soldier of Fortune* (1936 script), 123

*Song of the South, The* (1946), 3

Southern Baptist Convention (SBC), 13–14

Spaeth, Otto, 194

*Spartacus* (1960), 11, 219, 227–31, *227*

"Special Bulletin on Social Evil" (1914), 55, 56

*Spellbound* (1946), 162

Spellman, Cardinal, 10, 191–92, 195

Spencer, Kenneth, 147–48, *147*

Spielberg, Steven, 12

Springfield Productions, 235n

*Stagecoach* (1939), 162
Staiger, Janet, 48–49, 87, 211–12
*Star!* (1968), 239
*Start the Revolution Without Me*
  (1970), 249
state censorship, 25, 42, 88, 100n
*Stavisky* (1974), 252
Stein, Max, 254
Steinbeck, John, 142
Steinberg, Cobbett, 199–200
Stern, Aaron, 261n
Stevens, George, 222
Stevens, John Paul, 253
Stevens, Thaddeus, 139, 141, 142
*Stewardesses, The*, 245
Still, William Grant, 144
Stockton, Charles F., 70–71
Stone, Oliver, 13
*Stormy Weather* (1943), 9, 144–45
*Story of Christ, The* (1921), 77
*Story of G.I. Joe, The* (1946), 162
*Story of an Illegitimate Baby*, 218
*Story of Temple Drake, The* (1933),
  96–97, *96*
Stout, Bill, 216, 222
*Strange Love of Molly Louvain, The*
  (1932), 108
Strasberg, Lee, 143
*Street Scene* (1931), 106–7
Strong, Josiah, 17
Sunday, Billy, 69
*Superior Films, Inc. v. Department of
  Education of Ohio* (1954), 203n
*Survey, The*, 30
*Sweet Sweetback's Baadasssss Song*
  (1971), 252
*Syndicate, The*, 213

Talmadge, Norma, *115*
*Tampico* (1933), 120
Tate, Alan, 194
Taylor, Robert, *99*
Teacher's Union Award, 229–30
*Teenage Mother*, 251
Temple, Shirley, *150*
*Ten Commandments, The* (1923), 62
*Tennessee Johnson* (1942), 9, 139–44,
  *140*, 150, 155n

Thalberg, Irving, 152
Theatre Library Association, The, 193
*There Goes My Girl* (1937), 126n
*Therese and Isabelle* (1968), 240, 241,
  245, 247
*Thirty Seconds Over Tokyo* (1944),
  209
*This Is the Army* (1944), 148–49, 156n
Thomas, J. Parnell, 207
*Thomas Crown Affair, The* (1968), 239
*Time*, 229, 240
*Times Film Corp. v. Chicago* (1957),
  191, 200, 203n
Times Films, 244
Totheroh, William W., 70–71
*Traffic in Souls* (1913), 6, 42–50, *45*,
  53–54, 56, 168; Little Sister in, 44,
  46; London print of, 58–59n; Mary
  Barton in, 44, 46; William Trubus
  in, 46–49, *49*
Trans-Lux, 244
*Trash* (1970), 250
Travellers' Vigilance Society, 46
Trotti, Lamar, 126n, 167
Truman, Harry S., 154n, 155n, 208,
  224
Trumbo, Dalton, 11, 138, 206–37, *210*,
  *216*, *230. See also* "Fincher, Beth";
  "Jackson, Sam"; "Rich, Robert"
Tufts School of Religion, 193
*Turkish Delight*, 252
Turner, Lana, 167
Twentieth Century-Fox, 90
*Two Against the World* (1936), 108–11,
  *110*
*Two Mules for Sister Sara* (1970), 231
Tyler, Joel, 253

*Ulysses* (1967), 250
"Uncle Sam's Family," 136
United Artists, 255
*United Artists Corp. v. Board of Cen-
  sors of Memphis*, 189, 198
*United States v. Paramount Pictures.
  See Paramount* decision
Universal, 43, 159–60, 162, 165, 170,
  172–73, 173–74. *See also Scarlet
  Street*

Universal-International (U-I), 206
Updike, John, 250
Upshaw, Representative, 36
U.S. Chamber of Commerce, 103
U.S. Department of Commerce, 115, 118, 125n
U.S. Supreme Court, and movies, 25–29. *See also* specific Court cases

Vail, Theodore, 67
Valenti, Jack, 11, 239, 241, 259
Van Poobloo, Melvin, 252
*Variety*, 50–51, 197, 215, 217, 225, 239, 240, 243, 244, 247–48; Top Grossing Films Chart, 245
vaudeville, 18
Veterans of Foreign Wars, 208
vice films, 41–59; advertisements for, *4*/
villains: Americanized, 124; Germans portrayed as, 8, 113–14; Russians portrayed as, 8, 112–15, 118, 128n
violence, depiction of, 15n
Vizzard, Jack, 91, 92
Volstead Act (1919), 21, 36
Vonderhaar, Ray, 247

Waldorf agreement (1947), 206, 208–9, 233n
Wallace, Henry A., 136
Wallach, Eli, *201*
*Walls of Flesh* (1968), 245
Wanger, Walter, 162–65, 167–70, 176, 183nn
Warburg, James P., 152n
Warhol, Andy, 262n
Warner, H. B., *64*, 72
Warner, Jack, 108, 156n
Warner Bros., 90, 105, 120–21, 124, 148
Washington (D.C.) Secular League, 35
Wasserman, Lew, 223, 224
Wayne, John, 249
*Ways of Love* (1950), 186, 193
*Weber v. Freed* (1915), 40n
*Weekly Variety*, 247–48
Weintraub, Jerry, 261n
Welch, Joseph, 226
Welles, Sumner, 152n

Welsh, William, 46
West, Jessamyn, 214
West, Mae, 15n, 159
*West of Shanghai* (1937), 121
*Which Way to the Front?*, 249
Whipper, Leigh, 147
White, Walter, 130, 138, 139–40, 141, 144, 152, 153n, 155nn
White, William Allen, 131, 188
*White Cargo* (1929), 100n
white slavery trafficking films. *See* vice films
*Who's Afraid of Virginia Woolf?* (1966), 241
*Wild Rovers* (1971), 244
Willkie, Wendell, 131, 138
Williams, J. B., 100n
Wilson, Dooley, 146, *146*
Wilson, Michael, 214, 221, 223, 230, 231
Wilson, Woodrow, 132
Winchell, Walter, 224
Wingate, James, 97, 103, 163, 181n
Winsten, Archer, 164
Wise, Stephen, 81
*With Six You Get Eggroll* (1968), 239
Wolfenstein, Martha, 188
*Woman Disputed, The* (1928), 114, *115*
*Women Men Marry* (1937), 126n
Women's Army Corps (WAC), 154n
Women's Christian Temperance Union, 36, 40n
Women's Cooperative Alliance, 36
*Woodstock* (1970), 249
World War II. *See* Office of War Information
*W.R.—Mysteries of the Organism* (1971), 250
Wright, Harold Bell, 71
Writers Guild of America, 215. *See also* Screen Writers' Guild
Wyler, Robert, 214
Wyler, William, 214, 215

X rating. *See* Motion Picture Association of America, ratings system

*Yale Law Journal*, 29

Yankelovich report, 239
*Year of the Dragon* (1985), 13
Yellen, Barry B., 244
*Yes, My Darling Daughter* (1939), 164, 179–80n
*Yip, Yip, Yaphank*, 148
YMCA, 103
*You Only Live Once* (1937), 162–63, 180n

Young, Nedrick, 220, 221, *221*, 226, 228. *See also* "Douglas, Nathan E."
Young, Owen D., 68
*Young Philadelphians, The* (1959), 209

Zanuck, Darryl, 98, 108
Zimbalist, Sam, 233n
Zwick, Edward, 13